The mathematicians' apprenticeship

The mathematicians' apprenticeship

Science, universities and society in England, *1560–1640*

MORDECHAI FEINGOLD

Society of Fellows, Harvard University

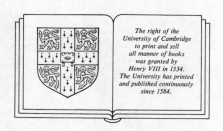

The right of the
University of Cambridge
to print and sell
all manner of books
was granted by
Henry VIII in 1534.
The University has printed
and published continuously
since 1584.

CAMBRIDGE UNIVERSITY PRESS

Cambridge
London   New York   New Rochelle
Melbourne   Sydney

Published by the Press Syndicate of the University of Cambridge
The Pitt Building, Trumpington Street, Cambridge CB2 IRP
32 East 57th Street, New York, NY 10022, USA
296 Beaconsfield Parade, Middle Park, Melbourne 3206, Australia

© Cambridge University Press 1984

First published 1984

Printed in Great Britain by
the University Press, Cambridge

Library of Congress catalogue card number: 83-1911

British Library cataloguing in publication data
Feingold, Mordechai
The mathematicians' apprenticeship
1. Science – History – England
I. Title
509'.42   Q127.G/
ISBN 0 521 25133 8

Contents

To Carol

Preface

This book grew out of my dissatisfaction with the traditional historiography of science which consistently debars the English universities from any share in the genesis of modern science. However different are the various orientations to scientific enterprise, these studies virtually always polarize 'reactionary' Oxford and Cambridge on the one hand, and 'progressive' London on the other. It has been my long-held belief that, despite differences in the direction of their scientific inquiry, the universities and London should not be discussed in isolation from each other, but instead should be viewed as components of the same intellectual framework, sharing many of the same features. To this end the following study – a revised version of a 1981 Oxford D.Phil. dissertation – is devoted. It is with a deep sense of obligation that I wish to acknowledge my gratitude to the many individuals who contributed to its various stages.

Yehuda Elkana was the first to introduce me to intellectual history of the sixteenth and seventeenth centuries and he has remained ever after an unfailing support. At Oxford I was fortunate to have Charles Webster as my supervisor. He not only commented on the various versions of my dissertation, but was supportive even about those issues which generated our own 'critical dialogue'. Hugh Trevor-Roper (Lord Dacre of Glanton), who took over my supervision for a term, continued to display unflagging interest in my research and I owe much to his great store of wisdom. My examiners Gerald Aylmer and Pio Rattansi made my oral examination a stimulating intellectual event and also provided me with invaluable comments and suggestions for revision. Finally, I wish to thank Julia and Robin Briggs who, always ready to contribute of their warmth and scholarship, were most helpful in making Oxford our home for three years.

Many other friends and colleagues shared with me their knowledge, either by reading the manuscript or by providing me with information, thus helping me to avoid more errors than I care to admit: Ian Adamson, Adam Apt, Alistair Crombie, Robert Evans, Rivka Feldchai, Robert Frank, Richard Garner, Owen Gingerich, Michael Hunter, Guy Lytle, Alec Marantz, John Roche, Charles Schmitt, John Shirley, Nicholas Steneck, Mayling Stubbs, Nicholas Tyacke and Robert Westman all are thanked.

vii

They do not always agree with everything I have said and I exonerate them from all errors that still remain.

Of the many librarians who assisted me in my research, special thanks are due to the staff of the Bodleian Library, Oxford, and the Cambridge University Library as well as the librarians of the following colleges: All Souls, Brasenose, Christ Church, Exeter, Queen's and Wadham at Oxford, and Gonville and Caius, and King's at Cambridge. All references to the Hartlib Papers at Sheffield University Library are quoted by the kind permission of their owner, Lord Delamere. I am also grateful to the Master and Fellows of Christ's College, Cambridge, for allowing me to consult Joseph Mede's notebooks.

My greatest debt, however, is to my wife, Carol, who shared with me all the delights and agonies of writing. It is to her patience, perseverance and devotion that this book is dedicated.

Introduction

Few historians have credited the early modern English universities with any positive contribution to the genesis of modern science. At best the universities of the period between 1560 and 1640 have been dismissed from serious consideration as repositories of traditional learning outside the mainstream of contemporary scientific–intellectual life; at worst they have been criticized as institutions inimical to scientific innovations of any sort. The bases for this judgement of an entire intellectual community are not difficult to find. An initial encounter with the official university and college statutes might easily justify such a bleak academic picture. These statutes were in effect for decades, quite often centuries, and whatever minor changes did occur in their corpus rarely affected the official curriculum; either science is not specified in the curriculum or it receives no more than cursory attention. The written testimony of some eminent alumni concerning the nature and quality of their early scientific instruction has done nothing to redeem the situation. There is hardly a book dealing with the history of the English universities that does not cite John Wallis's claim that he had not encountered the new philosophy before settling in London, some fourteen years after coming up to Cambridge. The unflattering revelations of Hobbes, Gascoigne and Ward on the limitations of their university education have also become standard reading for students of early modern England.

Since the curriculum of an institution and the accounts of its alumni are certainly among the most valuable documents available to the historian, such evidence is not to be dismissed lightly. And in this case such documents are doubly important, for only the scantiest evidence shedding light on the educational practices of the early English universities has survived. Unfortunately, however, these documents, first cited by nineteenth-century critics of the universities, rarely have been scrutinized since. For the most part historians of science have dealt with scientific instruction in the universities tangentially – only as a counterpoint to their detailed studies of scientific activity elsewhere – and consequently have been content to accept the well-known interpretation of such evidence without further investigation. Even historians of education who have begun to reevaluate the nature and quality of university instruction in our period have not bothered to reexamine the evidence that first prompted them to make their sweeping judgements. For all the above reasons a significant part of this book will be devoted to a scrutiny of the original documents in an attempt to ascertain whether they justify the interpretations long attributed to them.

Although the numerous scholars who have dealt with the universities of early modern England have moulded the material to different ends, they all have resolved the issue of scientific enterprise in a common manner; the failure of the universities to embrace the 'new science' and their lingering commitment to an Aristotelian framework have been considered proof enough of their members' ignorance of, and failure to teach, the more recent scientific modes of thought. Implicit or explicit in almost all these studies has been the abrogation of the universities' share in the genesis of modern science in early modern England. For the sake of simplicity, we might differentiate between four fundamental approaches to scientific enterprise in the seventeenth century. This classification clearly does injustice to the sophisticated nature of many of these studies, but if some licence is not made for simplification, it becomes impossible to discuss them briefly in a coherent manner.

First, there is the position taken by historians who trace the evolution of so-called rational and progressive scientific ideas throughout the centuries, demonstrating how each scientific discovery culminated in the next. Building on the premise that science develops linearly, regardless of the social context, and that scientific theories are propagated, developed and superseded like some self-perpetuating process, such historians assume that scientific enterprise may be interpreted with little reference to the environment in which it evolved. Such an 'internal' approach vindicates what time has clearly revealed as the correct road, while exposing the competing contemporary world-views as scientific dead-ends. Thus, their story has the Copernicuses, Keplers or Newtons as the protagonists with occasional references to certain minor figures who assisted the giants in their search for truth.

Implicit in their overall orientation is their dismissal of the universities for their alleged failure to serve as research centres and nurseries for future generations of scientists. As each generation of students was placed into the scholastic straitjacket, so the universities became increasingly isolated from the mainstream of progressive scientific ideas and moribund as centres of scientific activity. Westfall, for example, claims that: 'not only were the universities of Europe not the foci of scientific activity, not only did natural science have to develop its own centres of activity independent of the universities, but the universities were the principal centres of opposition to the new conception of nature which modern science constructed'. He continues, 'Nothing in the standard curriculum prepared the undergraduate for [Newton's] lectures; the tutorial system ... was directed toward wholly different ends'. In short, 'science did not seriously penetrate either the common rooms of the colleges or the curriculum of the universities'.[1]

At the other end of the spectrum are those historians who seek the rationale of scientific activity in the socio-religious and economic transformations of the age. Denying exclusivity to scientific enterprise, they build on the assumption that science – like art or religion – is rooted in time and place. Such an 'external' approach views the entire scientific enterprise, from choice of profession to choice of research topic, as a function of historically determined standards of judgement and interpretation. With regard to the seventeenth century, then, it was the need for applied research to solve specific problems in navigation, land-surveying and mining that spurred men to investigate the natural sciences and, ultimately, led to many advancements in the body of scientific knowledge. For the 'externalists' Aristotelianism and scholasticism were foreign to the ideals of the emergent middle classes, indifferent to the needs of society and hostile to applied science. Hence, the universities fostered the reactionary forces that obstructed the growth of modern science.

A case in point is the Puritan thesis which has been applied to the institutional history of Oxford and Cambridge. The bitter fight between the establishment and the Puritans was supposedly mirrored in the resistance of the universities to curricular changes, including those that would affect scientific instruction. Well known is the claim that it was only after the Puritans assumed power that the universities were somewhat purged of their scholastic frameworks and made even reasonably receptive to scientific inquiry. Indeed, whatever scientific curiosity infiltrated the universities was supposedly exhibited by Puritan students and instructors, and nurtured by Puritan colleges.[2] Somewhere between these two approaches lies a third approach taken by historians whose efforts are directed at achieving a due recognition of the occult in the genesis of modern progressive science. In contradistinction to the 'internalists' who

[1] R. S. Westfall, *The Construction of Modern Science: Mechanisms and Mechanics* (Cambridge, 1977), pp. 105, 107, 108. Among other historians such an attitude is evident by their exclusion of any discussion of the universities. See, for example, A. R. Hall, *The Scientific Revolution* (London, 1954); E. J. Dijksterhuis, *The Mechanization of the World Picture*, trans. C. Dikshoorn (Oxford, 1961). See also M. Boas, *The Scientific Renaissance 1450–1630* (London, 1962), pp. 239–41, and S. Drake, 'Early science and the printed book: the spread of science beyond the universities', *Renaissance and Reformation*, VI (1970), 43–52.

[2] R. K. Merton, *Science, Technology & Society in Seventeenth-Century England*, 2nd edn (New York, 1970); R. F. Jones, *Ancients and Moderns. A Study of the Rise of the Scientific Movement in Seventeenth-Century England*, 2nd edn (Berkeley and Los Angeles, 1965); C. Hill, *Intellectual Origins of the English Revolution* (Oxford, 1965).

limit their inquiry to the more rational aspects of science, these historians
address themselves to its irrational aspects. Seminal to their research is
the assumption that Hermetic and alchemical works encouraged experimentalism, while the Platonic–Pythagorean emphasis on numerology
contributed to the dissemination of modern cosmologies such as Copernicanism. Regardless of their shift in emphasis, however, these historians
also debar the universities from any share in scientific enterprise. The
Graeco-Roman contempt for the 'black arts', together with the exclusion
of magic from Aristotelian science, resulted in a heritage unsympathetic
to the scientific efforts of the Hermeticists, Rosicrucians and alchemists.
Yates was the first to claim that Oxford turned its back on the medieval
tradition of Roger Bacon and his contemporaries, an act 'which generated
and increased Aristotelian rigidity'. She regards Henry Savile and Richard
Hakluyt as 'individual exceptions to the predominantly grammarian and
unscientific character of Tudor Oxford ... [where] the general tone was
set by the contentious "Aristotelian Party" which despised the mathematical sciences'.[3]

Finally, mention should be made of historians of education who,
although not interested in science *per se*, have formulated opinions on the
nature and quality of scientific instruction in the universities. The
promulgation of the new university statutes in the mid-nineteenth century
first generated interest in the early university and college statutes and
occasioned the numerous collections of statutes published in the latter half
of the century. A by-product of this 'Victorian heritage' included implicit
– and sometimes explicit – criticism of the early modern English
universities as wayward institutions hostile to progressive reforms. The
Victorian educators often transposed their own contemporary educational
situation onto the sixteenth and seventeenth centuries, thereby assuming
that the prescribed statutes – which had remained virtually unchanged
for centuries – must have had an equally disastrous effect on the earlier
period as well. Isolated for criticism was the scholasticism they believed
dominated the early modern English universities and accounted for the
alleged lack of mathematical instruction in the sixteenth and seventeenth
centuries.

So far did they carry their reforming zeal that these educators contrasted
the conservative universities with the seemingly progressive schemes for
higher education put forward from the middle of the sixteenth century.

---

[3] F. A. Yates, 'Giordano Bruno's conflict with Oxford', *Journ. Warburg & Courtauld Insts.*,
II (1938–9), 230, 231, n. 1. The conclusions were carried over into her *Giordano Bruno
and the Hermetic Tradition* (London, 1964), pp. 167–8, 205–11. For a similar attitude,
see P. J. French, *John Dee: The World of an Elizabethan Magus* (London, 1972), pp. 22–7.
See also A. G. Debus (ed.), *Science and Education in the Seventeenth Century: The
Webster–Ward Debate* (London, 1970).

Such schemes included the various plans for academies, most of which never came to fruit, and the foundation of Gresham College in London in 1597 by one of the most prominent merchants of Elizabethan England, Sir Thomas Gresham. Not only was the college handsomely endowed: it was intended to provide practical instruction to the people of London on issues essential to their livelihood – such as navigation, commerce and medicine – free of charge and in English. Instruction was available in divinity, law, medicine, music, rhetoric and, most important of all, astronomy and geometry. These last two chairs were the first endowed scientific chairs in England and they attracted some of the most eminent men of science of the age.[4]

The continued authority of the Victorian heritage may be explained, at least in part, by the fact there is as yet no substitute for Mullinger's comprehensive history of Cambridge or Mallet's history of Oxford. In a similar manner, the numerous college histories written around the turn of the century rarely have been superseded, while the few later college histories continued to pay no more than cursory attention to the curriculum. Even the most recent university historians have done very little to modify this Victorian heritage. The only ones thus far to make any attempt to moderate this view have been Curtis and Frank. Curtis's work is an attempt to rehabilitate the universities as important intellectual centres, and for this reason he is only marginally concerned with scientific enterprise. Despite Curtis's reorientation to the universities, however, he mentions only a few university men interested in science and, in the final analysis, falls back on existing preconceptions as he cites the failure of the universities to serve as research communities capable of encouraging scientific enterprise.[5]

At the outset of his article Frank writes of his intention to correct the distorted view of early scientific instruction in the universities. Yet, as the evidence accumulates it becomes increasingly clear that Frank's ideas are not so very different from those of his predecessors. Building on the assumption that a student was exposed to scientific instruction with some

[4] J. Mullinger, *The University of Cambridge* (Cambridge, 1873–1911); W. W. Rouse Ball, *A History of the Study of Mathematics at Cambridge* (Cambridge, 1889); C. E. Mallet, *A History of the University of Oxford* (repr. New York, 1968); F. Watson, *The Beginning of the Teaching of Modern Subjects in England* (London, 1909); W. T. Costello, *The Scholastic Curriculum at Early Seventeenth-Century Cambridge* (Cambridge, Mass., 1958); R. L. Greaves, *The Puritan Revolution of Educational Thought: Background for Reform* (New Jersey, 1969); H. Kearney, *Scholars and Gentlemen: Universities and Society in Pre-Industrial Britain 1500–1700* (Ithaca, 1970).
[5] M. Curtis, *Oxford and Cambridge in Transition, 1558–1642* (Oxford, 1959), ch. 9, *passim*. An earlier historian upon whom Curtis relies is F. R. Johnson. The latter, however, also claimed that for the most part mathematics and astronomy were extra-curricular subjects, practised by only a few enthusiasts. See F. R. Johnson, *Astronomical Thought in Renaissance England* (Baltimore, 1937), pp. 10–13.

regularity only during the M.A. course of studies, Frank concludes that the majority who did not proceed beyond the B.A. 'had little idea of even an outdated system of natural knowledge, much less a modern one'. Moreover, whatever sporadic scientific instruction did take place was carried out by the newly created regent-masters, whose youth and inexperience would have handicapped them as instructors. This situation changed significantly only when the Savilian statutes were introduced at Oxford in 1619 and the Lucasian chair for mathematics was created at Cambridge in 1663.[6]

The rejoinders of Hill and Webster have done more to entrench the view of the universities as institutions incapable of stimulating scientific enterprise than ever Curtis's work has done to temper it. Hill's *Intellectual Origins* with its appendix on the universities remains one of the most influential textbooks in the subject.[7] Equally influential is Webster's charge that Curtis 'has seriously overestimated the degree to which the universities systematically exploited the humanist programme to develop an educational attitude conducive to widespread "teaching [of] the results of recent finds in mathematics and science"'. Elsewhere Webster builds upon the conclusions of Costello and Hill, emphasizing that whatever science did exist in the universities was the domain of the very few, the 'appearance [of mathematics] in the notebooks of Twyne being an exception'.[8] Virtually the only historian to reevaluate the state of science in the universities along the lines initiated by Curtis has been Tyacke. Although he deals only with Oxford and confines himself to the two decades before 1640, Tyacke provides strong evidence to suggest the flourishing state of science among Oxford scholars. However, the traditional view of Oxford and Cambridge is still very much alive, as is made evident by Morgan's recent survey of early modern universities. Morgan, who judges Hill's critique of Curtis most convincing, adds that Hill's 'judgment has tended to be confirmed in the most substantial recent contribution to this debate, by Dr. Webster, which suggests that in undergraduate teaching before 1640, Oxford and Cambridge were only marginally interested in mathematics and hardly at all in experimental science'.[9]

[6] R. G. Frank Jr, 'Science, medicine and the universities of early modern England: background and sources', *History of Science*, XI (1973), 201–2.
[7] Hill, *Intellectual Origins*, pp. 301–14.
[8] C. Webster, 'The curriculum of the grammar schools and universities, 1500–1660: a critical review of the literature', *History of Education*, IV (1975), 59; idem, *The Great Instauration* (London, 1975), pp. 115–29, *passim*. The quotation is on p. 119.
[9] V. Morgan, 'Approaches to the history of the English universities in the sixteenth and seventeenth centuries', *Bildung, Politik und Gesellschaft*, ed. G. Klingenstein, H. Lutz and G. Stourzh (Vienna, 1978), p. 155; N. Tyacke, 'Science and religion at Oxford before the Civil War', *Puritans and Revolutionaries. Essays in Seventeenth-Century History Presented to Christopher Hill*, ed. D. Pennington and K. Thomas (Oxford, 1978), pp. 73–93.

Owing to the position of Hill's argument as a cornerstone in many subsequent works treating scientific enterprise in the universities, I shall occasionally single him out as the source to be refuted, though quite clearly he is not alone in his views.

It is almost inevitable that in the process of constructing a framework capable of accounting for a period of exceptional scientific activity – as was the period between Copernicus and Newton – a historian will differentiate between those men who either generated or disseminated the epoch-making innovations and those who rejected or ignored their claims. What has occurred frequently, however, is that such a distinction has been magnified and stiffened out of all proportion. While the progressive scientific figures have been set into relief and isolated for intensive study, the allegedly inconsequential figures have been dismissed to the background and their scientific endeavours totally ignored. The more the so-called advocates of change have been cast as courageous visionaries combating the *status quo*, the more the allegedly reactionary men of science have been made to appear hostile to change of any sort. In the following few pages I should like to reverse the usual emphasis. Rather than concentrating upon the milestones in progressive science, I should like to investigate the nature of 'unenlightened' science in the period before 1640. I believe that such a shift in focus will not only reveal the rich texture of the background and redeem from oblivion those men who have been denied any recognition in the scientific enterprise; it will suggest that the major scientific figures were more firmly embedded in this background than is often believed. The gap between their positions and those of their contemporaries was not as great as is often assumed, and more often than not they shared certain, 'unenlightened', world-views. In this way I shall attempt to repudiate the adherence to the 'new science' – and especially the heliocentric theory – as a criterion of scientific worth for this early period as anachronistic and indicative of a failure to grasp the nature of scientific enterprise in pre-Civil War England.

With all due reservations, the period between 1560 and 1640 should be viewed as the prologue of modern science; the mathematical and physical sciences which were to evolve into highly specialized disciplines in the second half of the seventeenth century were just beginning to establish themselves in their new context. Although Copernicus published his *De Revolutionibus* in 1543, only in the last twenty years of our period did the heliocentric theory as a physical truth, or other components of what was later to be regarded as the new science, begin to generate widespread response. If the new science is interpreted as a product of the marriage between mathematics and astronomy, as it has sometimes been claimed, then it came into existence only when the works of Kepler and Galileo began to be widely studied and debated. If by the new science we mean the adoption of the new scientific modes of thought such as atomism, Cartesianism, mechanism and induction, then again it was only as our period drew to a close that they were put forward as capable of rivalling Aristotelianism as a comprehensive and adequate world-view. Bacon's major philosophical works were published from 1620 onward, those of Descartes only in the 1630s. Van Helmont's publications appeared after 1634, Galileo's impact was felt in the 1620s and 1630s, and Harvey did not publish his *De Motu Cordis* until 1628. Despite some early proponents of the mechanistic/atomistic theory such as Nicholas Hill – whose *Philosophia Epicurea* was published in 1601 – such a theory commanded a wide audience only in the third and fourth decades of the seventeenth century. Admittedly, magnetism stimulated some early ventures into the experimental method, but experimentalism as a research programme did not evolve until the 1610s and 1620s. As for the scientific societies, the organization of which heralded a more sophisticated form of scientific communication and the increasing professionalization of scientific enterprise, they, too, were a phenomenon of mid-century. Thus, to a great extent the publications of the twenty or so years before 1650 contributed to the ferment of that decade. The preceding years, however, should not be dismissed as years unresponsive to the seeds of change. Nor should the innovators be extrapolated out of the world-views that nurtured them. What I propose, therefore, is an examination of some of the most important scientific figures of the age together with some lesser-known men of science in order to demonstrate the fallacy of applying the new science as a criterion of scientific merit in the period under review.

The example capable of illustrating such claims is the Copernican theory which lies at the core of the scientific revolution. Formulated in the first half of the sixteenth century, its assumptions were studied and commented upon in various intellectual communities for the next century. During this time the superiority of the Copernican, over the older, astronomical theory in terms of alleged mathematical simplicity was becoming increasingly clear. For this reason Copernicanism provides one of the first substantial test cases for assessing man's willingness to abandon traditional views held for centuries in favour of new and tentative ones.

The current research of Westman into European Copernicanism demonstrates that by 1600 in all of Europe there could not be found 'more than ten thinkers who chose to adopt the main claims of the heliocentric theory'. Although 'to encounter an astronomer who rejected outright all features of Copernicus's version of the heliocentric theory is rare', what was adopted were 'those parts of the theory which did not depend upon the claim that the Earth moves'. This survey, it should be noted, included the various first-rate astronomers and philosophers who have been said to approve of the theory. Among the ten who committed themselves to the theory in full were two Englishmen, Thomas Digges and Thomas Harriot.[10]

The lack of early enthusiasm for the heliocentric theory is evidenced in the thinking of Francis Bacon, the 'father' of the Royal Society and indeed, it might be claimed, of modern English science. In spite of his endeavour to reformulate natural philosophy and his familiarity with the works of Copernicus and Galileo, Bacon remained anti-Copernican, claiming that it was 'the absurdity ... [of the astronomical hypotheses] that has driven men to the diurnal motion of the earth; which [he is] convinced is most false'.[11] The most he would ever concede towards the new cosmology was a suspension of judgement, at least until the theory could be better substantiated: 'As for the hypotheses of astronomers, it is useless to refute them, because they are not themselves asserted as true, and they may be various and contrary one to the other, yet so as equally to save and adjust the phenomena.'[12] Apart from being conservative in his cosmology, Bacon could also be accused of the 'crime' of regarding science only as part of a more comprehensive body of knowledge. In this attitude – as well as in certain others – Bacon was a practising Aristotelian.[13] And he was not alone. William Harvey, another figure whose ideas were seminal to seventeenth-century scientific thought, was essentially an Aristotelian, a fact, however, which did not prevent him from both criticizing and amending the Stagirite or developing his theory of the circulation of the blood. Nonetheless, Harvey was another of those flatly to reject the heliocentric theory.[14] The man who supposedly was the first to defend in print the new theory of the circulation of the blood, Robert Fludd, also shared Harvey's rejection of Copernicanism. Fludd's case is even more interesting. Although he was one of the most colourful of European Hermeticists, the alleged adoption of a heliocentric view of the universe by this group played no role in Fludd's choice of cosmology.[15]

[10] R. S. Westman, 'The astronomer's role in the sixteenth century: a preliminary study', *History of Science*, XVIII (1980), 106.

[11] *The Works of Francis Bacon*, ed. J. Spedding, R. L. Ellis and D. D. Heath (London, 1857–74), vol. 4, p. 348.

[12] Bacon, *Works*, vol. 5, p. 557.

[13] For Bacon's Aristotelianism, see R. E. Larsen, 'The Aristotelianism of Bacon's *Novum Organum*', *Journ. Hist. Ideas*, XXIII (1962), 435–50; L. A. Kosman, 'The Aristotelian Backgrounds of Bacon's *Novum Organum*' (Harvard Univ. Ph.D. thesis, 1964).

[14] W. Pagel, *William Harvey's Biological Ideas: Selected Aspects and Historical Background* (Basel/New York, 1967).

[15] For Fludd, see F. Yates, *Theatre of the World* (London, 1969); A. Debus, 'Harvey and Fludd: the irrational factor in the rational science of the seventeenth century', *Journ. Hist. Biology*, III (1970), 81–105; cf. R. S. Westman, 'Magical reform and astronomical reform: the Yates thesis reconsidered', in Westman and McGuire, *Hermeticism and the Scientific Revolution*, William Andrew Clark Memorial Library Seminar (Los Angeles, 1977), pp. 1–9.

Another interesting figure, Sir Thomas Browne, also joined the chorus of those refusing to accept the claim that the earth moves. As Johnson aptly puts it: 'Notwithstanding his zeal to detect old errors, he seems not very easy to admit new positions; for he never mentions the motions of the earth but with contempt and ridicule.' In the final analysis, Browne, like Bacon, withheld his firm support of the new cosmology despite his awareness of the growing corpus of astronomical thought of his day. As one of his biographers writes, 'though Copernicus, Galileo, Gilbert, and Descartes are mentioned with respect, they are not dignified to the level of authorities'.[16]

Scepticism bordering on censure also characterized the attitude of various mathematical and physical practitioners. William Barlow, an ardent astronomer as well as one of the earliest and most dedicated experimenters into magnetism, should be cited in this context. In 1616 his *Magneticall Advertisements*, which summed up forty years of research, was published. In both this work and his earlier *The Navigators Supply* (1597) Barlow made important contributions towards the knowledge of the compass and the compass needle. Notwithstanding his professed admiration for *De Magnete* and his indebtedness to Gilbert, Barlow strongly objected to Gilbert's insistence on the 'rotation of the earth' in book six of his work.[17]

Gilbert himself was a product of his time and like so many others he was moulded by the world-views in which he was educated. Steeped deeply in Aristotelianism, Gilbert did not carry over into all other spheres the openmindedness with which he approached magnetism. In fact, had it not been for the insistence of Edward Wright, it appears *De Magnete* would never have seen publication. One contemporary even went so far as to suggest that the same book six of *De Magnete* that was rejected by Barlow was written, not by Gilbert, but by Wright. Such a possibility was intimated by Mark Ridley – himself one of the fathers of English magnetism as well as a friend of both Gilbert and Wright – in his controversy with Barlow in which the latter was ridiculed for his anti-Copernican stance.[18]

[16] Dr Johnson's life of Sir Thomas Browne in *The Works of Sir Thomas Browne*, ed. S. Wilkin (London, 1852), vol. I, p. xvii; W. Dunn, *Sir Thomas Browne: A Study in Religious Philosophy* (Minneapolis, 1950), p. 8.

[17] W. Barlow, *Magneticall Advertisements: or Divers Pertinent Observations, and Approved Experiments concerning the Nature and Properties of the Load-Stone: very Pleasant for Knowledge, and most Needful for Practise of Travelling, or Framing of Instruments fit for Travellers both by Sea and Land* (London, 1616), sig. B3.

[18] M. Ridley, *Magneticall Animadversions. Made by Marke Ridley, Doctor in Physicke Upon Certaine Magneticall Advertisements, lately Published, From Maister William Barlow* (London, 1617), pp. 9–10; L. I. Abromitis, 'William Gilbert as Scientist: The Portrait of a Renaissance Amateur' (Brown Univ. Ph.D. thesis, 1977). Noteworthy is that Gilbert's disinclination to publish was not unique. The reluctance to commit one's work to print was shared by many Englishmen and was a more wide-ranging phenomenon in England than on the Continent. Harvey, Harriot, Bainbridge, Oughtred and Newton

While it may be argued that Bacon, Harvey and Barlow were still children of the Elizabethan Renaissance, Henry Gellibrand clearly belonged to the new generation. Gellibrand was educated under the newly instituted Savilian professors, John Bainbridge and Henry Briggs, and became acquainted with many of the leading Continental scientists of the day. He swiftly gained recognition as an extremely able mathematician and was installed as Gresham Professor of Astronomy in 1627. His *A Discourse Mathematicall* (1635) related the results of his observations of the variation of the magnetic needle and compared them with those made by William Borough in 1580. Such a comparison demonstrated for the first time the secular change of variation and by implication provided a most substantial piece of evidence to support the motion of the earth. Yet, in spite of his conclusions, Gellibrand remained a sceptic and refused to commit himself to the heliocentric theory. His conclusions deserve to be quoted in full:

I will not here enter into a dispute concerning the cause of this sensible diminution, whether it may be imputed to the Magnet, or the Earth, or both. It is not unknowne to the world, how the Greatest Masters of Astronomie, which this age hath afforded, for the more easy salving the apparent anomalar motions of the fixed and erratique caelestiall lights, and avoyding that supervacaneous furniture of the Ancients, do with all alacrity embrace that admirable *Copernicean Hypothesis* of the diurnal, Annual & Secular motions of the earth, in so much as conferring with that Great Astronomer D. *Phil. Lansberg* in *Zealand* about Astronomicall matters, did most seriously affirme unto me, he should never be disswaded from that Truth. This which he was pleased to stile a truth, I should readily receive as an *Hypothesis*, and so be easily led on to the consideration of the imbecillity of Mans apprehension, as not able rightly to conceive of this admirable opifice of God or frame of the world, without falling foule on so great an absurdity. Yet sure I am, it is a probable inducement to shake a wavering understanding. And which adds somewhat more, I understand by *Galilaeus* a *Florentine*, and a most acute and learned *Mathematician*, that an *Italian* Gentleman of the Family of the *Marsilij*, hath lately found the mutation of the Terrestriall *Meridians*, and penned a treatise thereof not yet published, which the said *Galilaeus* hath seene and read *con stupore*, not without amazement. His words are these ...

'Now there ariseth a fift noveltie, from which we may argue the mobility of the terrestriall Globe, by the meanes of that which most subtilie the most illustruous Gentleman *Sig; Caesar* of the most noble familie of the *Marsilij* of Bologna, a lyncean *Academicke* also, hath discovered, who in a most learned tract plainly sheweth how he hath observed a continuall mutation, although very slow, in the Meridian line; which discourse, which with wonder I lately saw, I hope he will impart to all those who are Studious of the wonders of nature'.

Surely if it be so, the due consideration of the premisses doth (as I conceive)

are just some who published their books only at the instigation of friends. Whether this was because of a deep-seated perfectionism or a fear of controversy is irrelevant; the fact remains that especially as regards lesser-known men of science, unless some manuscripts happened to survive their death, evidence of their scientific pursuits went unrecorded.

lay open a faire way for the salving of that Irregular Motion imputed to the Axis of the Earth. I meane the alterable obliquity of the Ecliptique, which to deny (as some yet doe, not without great violence offred to the Ancients) I shall hardly (without very strong argument) be perswaded. I pretermit likewise a supposition which might be made of the correspondent motion of the *Pole* of the magnet with those of some of the Planets, and divers other conceits, which must be all left to future times to discover, this Invention being but newly presented to the world in its infancy.[19]

Two facts emerge from this exposé of a commonly held attitude towards Copernicanism. First, with a significant number of scientific practitioners there is a negative correlation between world-view and scientific merit, with a so-called 'reactionary' world-view on the one hand and a positive scientific contribution on the other. Second, if men regarded and respected by their contemporaries as professional mathematicians and astronomers voiced such opinions on the Copernican theory, it should come as no surprise that other men for whom scientific research was not their sole vocation followed suit. This evidence should caution us against judging the various scientific practitioners by a double standard, thereby forgiving the Bacons, Harveys and Gilberts their partially conservative stances while condemning their lesser-known brothers for the same conservatism. In all cases what emerges is the reluctance of men, even the most progressive and 'modern' men of science, to abandon one system of thought before a sufficiently attractive alternative system had become available. Regardless of how aware of contradictions such men might have been, they shunned full commitment to a new cosmology, preferring instead to 'pick and choose', to concede certain issues while clinging to others. Bartholomew Keckermann, one of the most popular authors of natural philosophy textbooks in the early seventeenth century, expressed one of the chief underlying reasons for this evasive sidestepping of the issue in the following way:

Better to teach methodically ordered traditional positions, even if erroneous or questionable, rather than as-yet unmethodized new theories, even if true.[20]

Keckermann's insistence on the need for comprehensive, logical and methodically ordered arguments is not to be dismissed lightly, for the importance of a framework capable of organizing and transmitting knowledge was affirmed by all men of the age. And this brings us back

[19] H. Gellibrand, *A Discourse Mathematicall on the Variation of the Magneticall Needle, together with its admirable Diminution lately Discovered* (London, 1635), pp. 20–2.
[20] Quoted in P. Reif, 'The textbook tradition in natural philosophy, 1600–1650', *Journ. Hist. Ideas*, xxx (1969), 29. Similar is the pronouncement of the highly influential Italian Protestant Jerome Zanchi who prefers 'Aristotle to Plato because his writings are more comprehensive, orderly and teachable, as can be seen by comparing the *Physics* to the *Timaeus*'. See J. P. Donnelly, 'Italian influences on the development of Calvinist scholasticism', *Sixteenth Century Journal*, vii (1976), 94.

to the question of Aristotelianism, that long-despised, 'reactionary' world-view which has been the focal point of the attack upon the universities. Admittedly, this view has been on the retreat for the past few years as historians have begun to reevaluate the place of Aristotelianism *vis-à-vis* the new science. Nonetheless, for the most part this reevaluation has been carried out only as regards certain innovating individuals and has never been applied to the intellectual and scientific community as a whole.

Recent research suggests that by the end of the sixteenth century a new blend of Aristotelianism had emerged. Though broadly maintaining the familiar framework of previous centuries, it had become eclectic in nature as it incorporated concepts from neo-Platonism, Hermeticism and alchemy, as well as from the more 'positive' sciences.[21] Not only did Aristotelianism become more flexible; it was revitalized and made capable of generating new ideas. As Sister Reif has remarked: 'Nearly all the textbook writers refer[red] to the Copernican theory.' Many even accepted it as an astronomical hypothesis, although rejecting it as a reflection of the true nature of the world. Such men also referred to, or were at least aware of, the more recent discoveries of Kepler or Galileo. Even the specific commentaries of Aristotelian texts – such as the *Coimbra* commentaries – were very much up-to-date in knowledge.[22] As already suggested, despite criticism of the Stagirite, many so-called progressive thinkers nonetheless remained under the Aristotelian umbrella. Although Bacon, Harvey and Gilbert all carried specific issues beyond the Aristotelian framework, for the most part their scientific method or their perception of the aim of knowledge remained in accordance with this framework. A similar pattern has recently been detected in Galileo. To quote Crombie on the Italian astronomer:

I should argue that Galileo aimed in the end at total certainty, that it was Aristotle and no other who provided him with this ideal of truly scientific certain knowledge, and that he retained this ideal from his earliest to his latest writings, even as he rejected the methods and destroyed the content of Aristotle's physics, and even when he recognized that demonstration truly scientific by Aristotelian criteria eluded his grasp.[23]

[21] See, for example, C. B. Schmitt, 'Towards a reassessment of Renaissance Aristotelianism', *History of Science*, IX (1973), 159–93, and 'Philosophy and science in sixteenth-century universities: some preliminary comments', *The Cultural Context of Medieval Learning*, ed. J. E. Murdoch and E. D. Sylla (Dordrecht, Holland, 1975), pp. 485–537; J. McConica, 'Humanism and Aristotle in Tudor Oxford', *Eng. Hist. Rev.*, XCIV (1979), 291–317.
[22] P. Reif, 'The textbook tradition', pp. 24–5.
[23] A. Crombie, 'The sources of Galileo's early natural philosophy', *Reason, Experiment and Mysticism in the Scientific Revolution*, ed. M. L. Righini Bonelli and W. R. Shea (London, 1975), pp. 158–9; see also W. A. Wallace, *Galileo's Early Notebooks: The Physical Questions* (Notre Dame, 1977); idem, *Prelude to Galileo: Essays on Medieval and Sixteenth-Century Sources of Galileo's Thought* (Dordrecht–Boston, 1981).

Galileo is not the only man whose career demonstrates that a regard for Aristotle was not incompatible with either criticism of his ideas or scientific contributions of the highest order. In his account of the minimalist view, Schmitt echoes the claim of Keckermann as he demonstrates the importance of the English Aristotelian revival for scientific enterprise:

While I would not go so far as to claim that the new English interest in Aristotle produced a scientific revolution, it did provide a disciplined and structured framework for thought. In some ways – and more importantly, for some thinkers – a bad logic and a deficient natural philosophy are better than none at all. To go beyond Aristotle one had first to understand him or, at least, to understand some rudiments of his thought. Copernicus, Ramus, Telesio, Bruno, Patrizi, Galileo, Gassendi and Descartes all did. So too did Bacon, Harvey and Newton. For that reason, if for no other, the Aristotelian revival in England was important.[24]

Such evidence suggests that immersion in an Aristotelian framework implies neither ignorance of the alternative world-view or blind acceptance of scholasticism; conversely, advocacy of the new cosmology need not necessarily imply scorn of the Stagirite. It becomes increasingly manifest, therefore, that the intellectual and scientific frameworks of the period were in a continual process of modification, reformulation and integration of conflicting world-views. Rare indeed was an 'all or nothing' commitment to a world-view, and to ignore the degree of commitment and the nature of the reservations is to ignore the complexity of scientific enterprise in early modern England.

I have argued the reluctance of a large portion of the scientific and intellectual community to commit itself to the new cosmology before it became more capable of organizing both the observable physical phenomena and the philosophical implications of such phenomena, and of transmitting this knowledge to others. An obstacle faced by the Copernican theory – and one not to be dismissed lightly – was its failure to appeal to common sense. Until the heliocentric theory could demonstrate why objects were not left behind as the earth rotated or why a stone thrown upward should land in its initial starting point, many would be happier with the theory of a motionless earth. The existence of a plausible scientific alternative to Copernicanism – one capable of vindicating a geocentric theory in accordance with all available data – did much to reinforce the initial reluctance of many men to abandon an entrenched world-view. From his extensive astronomical observations Tycho Brahe was able to construct a theory which, while accepting the rotation of the planets around the sun, ascribed an additional rotation around the fixed earth. Although such a theory was more complicated than that posited by Copernicus and not free from inconsistencies, it nonetheless appealed to

[24] The quotation is taken from C. B. Schmitt's forthcoming book, *John Case*.

many men who preferred to suspend judgement until such time as the heliocentric theory could be corroborated both empirically and philosophically beyond any doubt.

What, then, we may well ask, occurred in the course of the first half of the seventeenth century to generate widespread favourable response to the heliocentric theory? Research into magnetism and the variation of the magnetic needle provided some of the answers; the invention of the telescope provided some others. But it was only in the 1620s and 1630s when such new modes of thought as mechanism and Baconianism were able to provide a structured experimental method – a framework capable of both containing the body of knowledge and expanding its frontiers in a more or less disciplined manner – that the heliocentric theory prevailed.

Further to complicate the situation, objections to the heliocentric theory were not always made on scientific grounds. Rejection sometimes followed an initial predisposition towards the theory, more often than not on religious grounds. The tenacity with which an entire intellectual community clung to features of the geocentric theory offers an excellent example of the way in which ideological factors may be brought to bear upon, and ultimately modify, the scientific body of knowledge. Scriptural fundamentalism was prevalent among Catholics and Protestants alike, the main difference being that the Protestants never placed an official religious ban upon Copernicus and Galileo. Owing mainly to the bold assertions of Giordano Bruno, which combined heliocentricity and the doctrine of a plurality of worlds – of more suns, more earths and more human beings elsewhere in the universe – philosophers and men of science alike were alarmed at what they regarded as the sinister implications of Copernicanism. A heliocentric interpretation of the universe, it was feared, might necessitate a total reevaluation of man's place in such a universe. The doctrine of a plurality of worlds proved equally shocking to Christians who had no wish to question the uniqueness of the crucifixion and to philosophers who preferred not to contemplate the insignificance of man. Milton allegedly avoided open advocacy of Copernicanism despite his description of it in 'a friendly fashion', precisely for this reason:

It appears reasonable to believe that because of the close association of the doctrine [plurality of worlds] and the true hypothesis [Copernicanism], Milton did not consider he was prepared to advocate openly the latter. His suspended judgement concerning the simple Copernican system is therefore apparently influenced by the similar attitude taken toward the doctrine of a plurality of worlds.[25]

[25] G. McColley, 'The theory of a plurality of worlds as a factor in Milton's attitude toward the Copernican hypothesis', *Modern Language Notes*, XLVII (1932), 325. See also C. Hill, *Milton and the English Revolution* (London, 1977), pp. 398–402, where Milton's 'defence of the Bible against astronomy' is elaborated upon at some length.

Such religious uneasiness was at the root of the rejection of the heliocentric theory by certain otherwise receptive thinkers, such as Mersenne in France and Christopher Wren Senior in England. As long as the scale did not seem to tip too heavily in favour of the heliocentric theory, the vast majority of men, prominent scientists included, preferred to cling to aspects of the older framework.

Before Galileo and Kepler forced the issue out into the open in both the scientific and religious spheres there also existed the comfortable solution of non-commitment. But as the seventeenth century progressed it became increasingly difficult to reserve judgement on the heliocentric theory. Once the issue of heliocentricity was forced upon the scientific community, however, the process of conversion was swift and by 1640 consensus had been reached; by then other issues had begun to excite the attention of the community and became the focus of controversy.

What does this study of the very gradual assimilation of the heliocentric theory to the existing corpus of knowledge reveal about the nature of scientific enterprise in the years between 1560 and 1640? It is my purpose to suggest that scientific knowledge in early modern England was not the result of a clear-cut victory over a reactionary position at some particular date. This is not to deny the scientific possibilities opened up by the Interregnum, but only to insist that to a considerable extent these possibilities owed their existence to a lengthy and complex process of scientific inquiry. Only as a result of the continuous exchange of world-views – both old and new – during the period 1560–1640 was the later scientific ferment of the mid-seventeenth century made possible. This early period should be viewed as an incubatory period during which rival theories, old and new cosmologies, rational and irrational elements of science not only coexisted, but were often enmeshed to form what today might appear as the most unlikely combinations. It was the very protean nature of this period that accounts for its ability to accommodate the most diverse world-views as well as to encompass the most heterogeneous forms of scientific activity, often within the same man.

Just as the scientific ideas were mercurial, so the scientific community was in a state of flux in the years between 1560 and 1640. Throughout this period the medieval concept of the unity of knowledge continued to animate the educational ideals of the scholarly community. Every educated man received instruction in the entire arts and science curriculum – which, it shall be argued, included mathematics as well as logic, rhetoric, music and philosophy – and was deemed capable of contributing to any one of its constituents. Similarly, the conviction that grounding in the various arts and sciences was a prerequisite for the study of theology continued to command respect, as did the belief in the inherent interdependence of all the arts and sciences. The product of such an ideal of education continued to be the 'general scholar' and for this reason scientific activity in the period under review was usually carried out as one component in a many-faceted intellectual enterprise. An examination of contemporaries interested in science suggests that, apart from the mathematical practitioners of London, most were practising divines, physicians, lawyers, antiquarians or orientalists. Even celebrated mathematicians and astronomers usually engaged in such studies as history, logic or chronology. This frequent channelling of energies into divergent studies must be borne in mind if the fragmentary evidence that has survived is to be interpreted correctly; to discount the contribution of a man known to be interested in science only because his one or two extant letters are not devoted to science is to misinterpret the nature of scientific enterprise in our period. For although certain men were far more talented and devoted mathematicians than others, many who never reached the frontiers of the field were still deemed respectable members of the scientific community by their colleagues and considered capable of participating in the process of dissemination of ideas.

The continued relevance of the ideal of the general scholar throughout our period, however, does not mean that competing ideals were lacking or that a tendency towards professionalization did not become increasingly apparent. As our period opens mathematics and astronomy were already what might be termed semi-liberated subjects in the university curriculum; although they were still treated as part of philosophy – as were chemistry and the life sciences – they were also autonomous subjects, albeit not on par with logic, rhetoric or philosophy. Moreover, even at this early date there were those from diverse walks of life who were convinced of the need for endowed mathematical lectureships and ready to devote themselves more fully to the mathematical sciences. Inappropriate and misleading as it is to treat mathematics as a professionally restricted discipline in the period between 1560 and 1640, one can nonetheless discern a trend that was to lead to its full professionalization by the close of the seventeenth century. By their very nature, the mathematical sciences required a relatively high degree of dedication as well as what may be termed a special aptitude or inclination, and for these reasons they were traditionally less appealing to general scholars than other disciplines. The inherent rigour and dedication demanded by the mathematical sciences advanced rapidly as the seventeenth century progressed until, as Ben-David has noted, 'the activities of the individual scientists and the academies were public only in the sense that there were no attempts at concealment and mystification'.[26] Indeed, it appears highly likely that this inevitable exclusion of most general scholars from active participation in

[26] J. Ben-David, 'Scientific growth: a sociological view', *Minerva*, II (1963–4), 464.

the mathematical and physical sciences by the time Newton published his *Principia* in 1687 was one of the contributing reasons for the opposition to the Royal Society.

Although many contemporaries in our period pursued a wide range of scientific disciplines, for the most part this book will treat only those committed to the mathematical sciences. This somewhat arbitrary restriction of subject is necessary for a few reasons. First, since the mathematical sciences constitute the core of the 'scientific revolution', it was by way of their examination that historians of science have come to dismiss the universities as institutions inconsequential to their rapid growth in the sixteenth and seventeenth centuries. Second, even in this early stage of the scientific revolution, mathematics and astronomy resembled their modern counterparts, and even historians who would protest against their so-called 'unprogressive' aspects would not refuse to recognize them as 'legitimate' sciences. Third, since the mathematical sciences were, by definition, demanding disciplines requiring a relatively high degree of aptitude and devotion, concentration on its devotees rather than on the devotees of botany and horticulture serves as a more reliable indicator of an individual's overall scientific orientation. Like heraldry, botany and horticulture were frequently pursued in a leisurely fashion by those of a certain class and were considered as basic as good manners.

If, however, we were to limit this study to what were eventually to become the professionalized mathematical disciplines, we would be contradicting the nature of scientific enterprise as it has been explored earlier in this Introduction. Astrology was a significant and constructive worldview of the period which, albeit with certain differences, was shared by most contemporaries; it was not until the second half of the seventeenth century that the mythical dimensions of certain celestial occurrences were purged from the consciousness of the educated classes.[27] It should also be borne in mind that more than an elementary knowledge of astrology necessitated some degree of mathematical and astronomical sophistication in order to carry out its complicated computations of the planetary system. In a similar manner, research into the vast area of chronology required more than a superficial grasp of astronomy – both ancient and modern – together with the ability to carry out what were often complex mathematical calculations. This does not mean, of course, that every divine contemplating the age of the world or every almanac-maker will be adjudged a man of science; only that the more sophisticated chronologers and astrologers do have a place in the scientific community.

[27] The recent studies of Thomas and Capp, however, make it possible to keep a discussion of astrology to a minimum. K. V. Thomas, *Religion and the Decline of Magic* (London, 1971); B. Capp, *Astrology and the Popular Press* (London and Boston, 1979). See also M. A. Bowden, 'The Scientific Revolution in Astrology: The English Reformers 1558–1686' (Yale Univ. Ph.D. thesis, 1974).

The choice of 1560 as the starting point of this study was motivated by the wish to avoid the religious, political and intellectual turmoil of the mid-sixteenth century. The accession of Elizabeth to the throne in 1558 initiated a period of stability and return to routine in all spheres of life. It also signalled a new era in the history of the universities. Oxford was granted the *Nova Statuta* in 1564, while Cambridge received its first set of Elizabethan statutes in 1558 followed by a second, more formal, set in 1570. My decision to confine this study to the period before 1640 – although this date should be considered more as a guideline than as a rigid limitation – stems from my conviction that this period played a critical role in the blossoming of scientific enterprise during the Puritan hegemony as well as from my dissatisfaction with the cursory attention it has received from historians of science. Since the 1620s and 1630s witnessed the dissemination of the ideas of Galileo, Bacon and Descartes, and ushered in modes of thought that previously had not existed, historians of science have focussed their studies on this fruitful period with little reference to its precedents in the previous century. In contrast, my aim is to concentrate on the early incubatory period, whose indispensability for the rapid scientific fermentation of the mid-seventeenth century characterizes it as the mathematicians' apprenticeship.

This Introduction began with an exposition of the most distinctive historical frameworks for viewing the genesis of science in early modern England. Each framework was upheld by a philosophical orientation to scientific enterprise in general and to the growth of knowledge in particular. Having explored the nature of scientific activity and the scientific community in the period between 1560 and 1640, I should like to return to the question of frameworks in order to formulate one that would best account for the complexity of scientific enterprise in this age and the multiplicity of factors bearing upon scientific activity.

Addressing himself to the problem of the growth of knowledge, Elkana has written:

In the early stages of development of a theory or of a new discipline, when only a few individuals share the context for understanding 'correctly' – in the new way – some of the theoretical or experimental findings, the approach to greater consensus is very important; it is conducive to the progress of knowledge. The scientists to whom the new ideas are addressed read and necessarily 'misinterpret' – according to their previous knowledge ... The innovators respond by correcting, perhaps attuning themselves to some of the old concepts or views which they had not thought of when they first presented their new ideas; the readers of the 'old school' read again and assimilate some of the new explanation; the result is a greater sharing of context. This goes on until at some point the belief spreads among the members of the given scientific community that a fruitful new theory has been established.

In his words it is the critical scrutiny of a theory on the part of a community as a whole – the 'struggle to establish consensus between the proponents of the different positions' – that generates scientific activity. But as consensus occurs on one level, a new conflict emerges, once again splitting the scientific community and thereby revitalizing the scientific dialogue. Complete consensus between competing world-views, or on a smaller scale, competing research programmes is only a theoretical possibility and the self-perpetuating nature of the critical dialogue is the impetus of scientific activity and its safeguard against stagnation.[28]

To such an intensive treatment of a scientific community in its entirety, Hesse has raised some objections. In the context of her discussion of Hermeticism, she has written:

Even the claim to get nearer the full picture by adding more factors should be treated with caution. Throwing more light on a picture may distort what has already been seen, and certainly judgements of relative significance are required if the picture is not to become flat and overcrowded. The historian's task is not to spell out in tedious detail every minor writing or trivial biography of forgotten figures, or every twist and turn of the social scene which had some bearing on the personnel and institutions of science.

Hesse ascribes to the historian the primary role of following up 'the loose ends of the received internal tradition' leaving the tangential aspects to later historical curiosity.[29] In this Introduction I have tried to suggest that close examination of the much larger scientific community will neither distort the picture nor undermine the achievements of the major scientific figures. Indeed, just the opposite is true. Only an intensive study of the milieu which nurtured the prominent scientists, shaped their intellectual development and fostered their conceptions of science will explain adequately in what manner they were both men of their time and precursors of a future time.

As regards the so-called unenlightened majority, it is wrong to assume that such men of science had neither access to up-to-date knowledge of the scientific transformations of the period nor the eclecticism that characterized their more eminent counterparts. As will become evident in the course of this study, the Copernican theory was taught in the universities in the period 1560–1640 and sometimes taught well by men, not all of whom professed belief in it. Even when the presentation of modern cosmologies was biased by the ideological commitments of the instructor, references to the sources were usually given and thereafter it

[28] Y. Elkana, 'A programmatic attempt at an anthropology of knowledge', *Sciences and Cultures: Anthropological and Historical Studies of the Sciences*, ed. E. Mendelsohn and Y. Elkana (Dordrecht, Holland, 1981), p. 37.
[29] M. Hesse, 'Hermeticism and historiography: an apology for the internal history of science', *Minnesota Studies in the Philosophy of Science*, ed. R. H. Stuewer, v (1970), 149.

was up to the student to follow up and to decide for himself. This is not to claim that all students did so, but only that the more gifted among them certainly took the initiative to seek further mathematical knowledge.

Most important, only a historical framework which takes into consideration the entire scientific community is capable of accounting for the complexity of scientific enterprise in this age. Although men and groups of men may have differed in their understanding and perception of the issues as well as in the nature of their scientific endeavours, together they comprised a single intellectual and scientific community. It is my contention that it was the critical scrutiny of a theory on the part of this community in its entirety rather than on the part of a few unique geniuses on the 'right' road that was largely responsible for the blossoming of science in the mid-seventeenth century. To a large extent the Puritan ascent to power merely coincided with these fruitful decades, and their seeds had been sown during the previous century by men, many of whom may be called unenlightened.

The aim of this book will be to demonstrate that the English universities contributed significantly to the critical dialogue that vitalized the scientific community in the period between 1560 and 1640. It will be argued that the stereotyped view of Oxford and Cambridge as institutions devoid of mathematical instruction and inimical to new scientific modes of thought is unfounded. To this end the first four chapters will be devoted to an assessment of the nature of scientific instruction and scientific associations in the universities. Chapter I will examine the university and college statutes of the period in order to determine whether, even as theoretical frameworks, they confirm the common view concerning the absence of mathematical studies in the curriculum. The second chapter will investigate evidence shedding light on the identity and possible qualifications of the various mathematical lecturers, college tutors and fellows as well as the probable content of their instruction. Evidence relevant to an evaluation of the extent to which mathematical instruction constituted part of the university course of studies and the degree of mathematical proficiency most likely attained by students will be examined in chapter III. At the risk of being tedious, both chapters II and III will present case study after case study, for it is only by way of a vast accumulation of data that it is possible to counter the popular claim that scientific enterprise in the universities was the exception, not the rule. Once a case has been made for the inclusion of the mathematical sciences in the curriculum of undergraduates and bachelors alike, evidence supporting the contribution of the allegedly inconsequential university men to scientific enterprise will be presented. Thus, chapter IV will focus upon the scientifically minded members of Oxford and Cambridge and their connections with scholars and men of science in England and abroad in order to assess the function of the universities as scientific centres. At this point two methodological notes are in order. First, since this study is confined to the period 1560–1640, such prominent university-trained men as John Dee and Thomas Digges will enter into our discussion only in so far as they link up with persons and events of this later period. Second, the underlying configuration of the university scientific community as it becomes increasingly manifest is, to some extent, a function of the evidence that has managed to survive. As I stress throughout, owing to the fragmentary state of our evidence chapter IV is intended to suggest only the contours of the scientific community, not to delineate in minute detail its every feature.

Against this picture of one intellectual–scientific community will be juxtaposed some of the scientific and educational possibilities of London. In contrast to the university men who have thus far been debarred from any positive contribution to science, the professors of Gresham College have been credited with bringing about important advancements in the body of scientific knowledge. In this effort they were assisted by London's mathematical practitioners, many of whom supposedly were the auditors of the Gresham lectures. Chapter V, therefore, will be devoted to an investigation of some features of 'London science' in an attempt to ascertain whether the existing evidence justifies the role Gresham College has been accorded as an important educational institution and, conversely, whether the multitude of London's practitioners developed as sophisticated a grasp of the recent scientific modes of thought as is often assumed. The last chapter will be devoted to a discussion of patronage, a social issue crucial to all aspects of scientific enterprise, both as it was carried on in the universities and in London. Patronage was frequently the decisive factor determining whether men of science left the universities, whether they pursued the purer or more applied aspects of science, and even whether they published their results. Although this chapter exposes only the tip of the iceberg of a subject – whose consequences extend to every aspect of intellectual life of our period – I believe it is impossible to discuss scientific enterprise without some explanation of perhaps the single most important external factor bearing upon the career patterns of most university-trained men of science.

I

The statutes

Much of the bleak portrayal of the state of science in the universities in the period between 1560 and 1640 derives from the failure of the university statutes effective for most of this period to make adequate mention of mathematics in the articles dealing specifically with the B.A. curriculum. On the basis of this omission historians have concluded that the universities failed to provide opportunities for undergraduates to obtain mathematical instruction. Although it is generally conceded that mathematical instruction was offered to graduate students, for the most part the M.A. curriculum has been neglected and its significance misunderstood.[1]

The first part of this chapter will be devoted to an examination of the university statutes of Oxford and Cambridge. My aim is to place the university statutes in their historical perspective so that their limitations as historical documents can be ascertained and their significance critically assessed. Once the utility of the statutes has been determined, it will then be argued that an examination of all the references to the curriculum contained in these statutes and not just the single article on 'method of study' suggests that as far as the university statutes touch upon the undergraduate curriculum, they fail to confirm the common historical prejudice concerning the absence of mathematical instruction. The second part of the chapter is a counterpart to the first and will deal with the various provisions for the mathematical instruction of undergraduates, both as set out in the statutes of the individual colleges and as suggested by other contemporary documents. Finally, if any valid conclusions concerning the opportunities for mathematical instruction as they are stipulated in the statutes are to be drawn, then neither the B.A. nor M.A. course of studies can be discussed in isolation from each other, but instead must be viewed as complementary forms of education.

[1] See, for example, Mullinger, *The University of Cambridge*, vol. 2, pp. 402–3; Watson, *The Beginning of the Teaching of Modern Subjects in England*; S. E. Morison, *The Founding of Harvard College* (Cambridge, Mass., 1935), pp. 76–7; Costello, *The Scholastic Curriculum*, pp. 102–6; Hill, *Intellectual Origins*; Mallet, *History of the University of Oxford*; Frank, 'Science, medicine and the universities of early modern England', 201; Westfall, *The Construction of Modern Science*, pp. 107–8.

It should be emphasized at the outset that in no way does this chapter purport to reconstruct or evaluate the actual practice of Oxford and Cambridge as regards mathematical instruction. Its sole purpose is to review the statutes and other documents in order to ascertain what they suggest about the official provisions for scientific instruction.

Theoretically speaking, the Elizabethan statutes promulgated in the early years of Queen Elizabeth's reign should be the sources for any information on the various curricular requirements of Oxford and Cambridge in the period between 1560 and 1640. But as no set of statutes should ever be examined in a historical void, it becomes necessary to trace briefly the complex history of the statutes of both universities.

During King Edward VI's reign almost identical sets of statutes were issued to both Oxford and Cambridge in 1549, but Edward's death in 1553 and the accession of his Catholic sister Mary brought into effect a new set of statutes in 1556. These statutes, in turn, were abolished two years later following Elizabeth's succession to the throne. Elizabeth granted Cambridge two sets of statutes, the first in 1558, and a second, more elaborate and formal, set in 1570. Oxford, on the other hand, did not receive a formal set of statutes before the seventeenth century. The *Nova Statuta* granted Oxford in 1564/65 were no more than a compilation of injunctions and articles, the corpus of which received numerous additions throughout the late sixteenth and early seventeenth centuries. Only in 1634 did Oxford receive a formal set of statutes when Archbishop Laud imposed his massive code upon the university, which remained in effect until the middle of the nineteenth century.

It is most instructive to compare the curricular provisions of the Elizabethan statutes with those of the Edwardian statutes. In the Edwardian statutes of 1549 the article outlining the 'method of study' for undergraduates stipulates the following: 'The Student freshly come from a grammar school, mathematics are first to receive. He is to study them a whole year, that is to say, arithmetic, geometry, and as much as he shall be able of astronomy and cosmography. The following year shall teach him dialectics. The third and fourth shall add philosophy.'[2] This article was drastically altered in the subsequent Cambridge statutes of 1558 and 1570 and in its place there appears a single cryptic sentence: 'The first year shall teach rhetoric, the second and third logic, the fourth shall add

---

[2] *Collection of Statutes for the University and Colleges of Cambridge*, trans. J. Heywood (London, 1840), p. 1, hereafter cited as Heywood, *Collection*; J. Lamb (ed.), *A Collection of Letters, Statutes, and other Documents from the MS Library of Corp. Christ. Coll. Illustrative of the History of the University of Cambridge during the period of the Reformation from 1500 to 1572* (London, 1838), p. 125 for the Latin text, hereafter cited as Lamb, *Documents*.

philosophy.'³ In the *Nova Statuta* of Oxford the exact curriculum for undergraduates is even more difficult to ascertain for there is no article outlining 'method of study'; all that the statutes specify is three terms of arithmetic, two of music, four of rhetoric, two of grammar and five of dialectics, without any reference to the year in which they were to be studied.⁴

From 1619 onward, all instruction in the mathematical sciences in Oxford was governed by the Savilian statutes, which were later incorporated *en bloc* into the Laudian statutes of 1634. The Savilian statutes stipulated that every student, having completed his second year of studies, was to attend lectures in geometry, which included arithmetic. The professor of geometry, for his part, was required to deliver two lectures a week as well as to

employ himself at his own lodgings, or in some place near, for the space of an hour in instructing young men (who choose to call on him for the purpose of learning) in practical logic or arithmetic of all kinds, which is best communicated without any formality, and in the vulgar tongue if he thinks fit. And also, that at convenient seasons, when it is agreeable to him, he shall show the practice of geometry to his auditors (who choose to attend him) in the fields or spots adjacent to the University.⁵

When determining the extent of scientific activity in the universities, historians tend to terminate their inquiry with the undergraduate curriculum as it has just been set out. Many of the allegations made against the universities for their alleged neglect of science can be traced to the omission of the clause specifying mathematics as part of the B.A. curriculum in the 1558 and 1570 Cambridge statutes and its significant abridgement in the *Nova Statuta* of Oxford. As this omission in the Cambridge statutes lays the university wide open for attack, I would like to begin my discussion with Cambridge.

Hill persuasively argues that the Edwardian statutes of 1549 were the logical outcome of the radical Protestantism of the Edwardian reign, and consequently signified an introductory episode foreshadowing the blossoming of scientific enterprise in both universities during the 1640s and 1650s.

³ Heywood, *Collection*, p. 290, appendix [The 1570 Elizabethan Statutes], p. 6; Lamb, *Documents*, p. 319.
⁴ S. Gibson (ed.), *Statuta Antiqua Universitatis Oxoniensis* (Oxford, 1931), p. 390, hereafter cited as Gibson, *Statuta*.
⁵ *Oxford University Statutes*, trans. G. R. M. Ward (London, 1845), vol. 1 [The Caroline Code], pp. 275–6, 274, hereafter cited as Ward, *Statutes*; J. Griffiths (ed.), *Statutes of the University of Oxford Codified in the Year 1636* (Oxford, 1888), p. 245 for the Latin text, hereafter cited as Griffiths, *Statutes*.

In the brief radical interlude of Edward VI's reign the royal commission of 1549 tried to stimulate medical education at Cambridge, and made mathematics the subject of the first year of the arts course ... But Edward's reign was as exceptional in intellectual as in religious history. The first Elizabethan revision of the Edwardian statutes reinstated an arts course of rhetoric, logic, and philosophy; Whitgift's statutes of 1570 made no mention of mathematics at all. At Oxford the statutes of 1565 and 1586 reimposed the old subjects of the authorities. The Laudian statutes summed up this conservative trend. The bishops of 1584 opposed the making of any provision for research in the Universities.[6]

As Hill's claims have continued to influence university history of the period, it is most important that they be examined in depth. Since the curricular provisions of the 1558 statutes were adopted almost verbatim by Whitgift in 1570, for the most part I will confine my comparison to the statutes of 1549 and 1558 in my disagreement with Hill over his interpretation of the Cambridge statutes.

First, no significant distinction in terms of religious affiliation and scientific orientation can be made between the men commissioned to draw up the 1549 statutes and those summoned to revise them in 1558. Indeed two men, William Mey and Thomas Wendy, served on both commissions while Anthony Cooke served as a worthy substitute for John Cheke – who died in 1553 – both for his learning in general and his interest in mathematics in particular. Other members of the 1558 commission included Walter Haddon, Robert Horne and James Pilkington, all of whom were numbered among the most devout Protestants of the age.[7] For the above reasons, neither could the 1558 commission be termed any less zealously Protestant than the 1549 commission, nor could its members be misrepresented as opponents of science.

Second, it is simply not true that Whitgift's statutes of 1570 made no mention of mathematics. Although both the 1558 and 1570 statutes made no mention of mathematics in the article pertaining specifically to 'method of study', other articles suggest that mathematics remained an integral part of the B.A. curriculum. Thus, the 1570 statutes specify most explicitly that mathematics was one of the subjects to be disputed by undergraduates: 'No one shall be respondent except those who shall have completed their second year. He [the senior among the sophists] shall propose three principal questions – one in mathematics, the second in logic, the third in natural or moral philosophy ... The rest shall dispute against him.'[8] This

---

[6] Hill, *Intellectual Origins*, p. 311.

[7] Members of the 1549 commission included Thomas Eliens, Thomas Smith, Nicholas Roffen, John Cheke, William Paget, William Mey and Thomas Wendy. Those of the 1558 commission included, apart from Mey and Wendy, William Cecil, Anthony Cooke, Matthew Parker, William Bill, Walter Haddon, Robert Horne and James Pilkington. See C. H. Cooper, *Annals of Cambridge* (Cambridge, 1842–53), vol. 2, pp. 23, 150–1.

[8] Heywood, *Collection*, appendix, p. 13. See also pp. 11–12, 294 for the same provision in the 1549 and 1558 statutes; Lamb, *Documents*, pp. 325, 128, 284.

is not the only mention of mathematics in the 1558 and 1570 Cambridge statutes. The following provision in the 1570 statutes regulating the government of the colleges appeared almost verbatim in both previous statutes as well:

The master, the dean, and the public lecturer in the respective colleges, shall examine all who seek to be admitted into their college before their first entrance, whether they thoroughly understand grammar or not, and none shall be admitted into places of this kind who have not acquired a proficiency therein sufficient to learn mathematics and logic.[9]

Moreover, the 1570 statutes stipulate that prior to receiving his B.A. degree, every student had to pay, amongst others, the mathematical lecturer the sum of 8d.[10] Seven years after the Whitgift statutes were issued to Cambridge, William Harrison described the undergraduate studies of both Oxford and Cambridge in a way that took cognizance of mathematical instruction.

The first degree of all, is that of the generall sophisters, from whence, when they have learned more sufficientlie the rules of logike, rhetorike, and obteined thereto competent skill in philosophie, and in the mathematicals, they ascend higher unto the estate of batchelers of art.[11]

Further proof that mathematics remained part of the undergraduate curriculum is provided by a document concerning the government of Cambridge which was drawn up in 1600, most probably to be presented to Sir Robert Cecil upon his election as Chancellor. Amongst other things, this document includes a detailed description of the auditors of the various university lecturers. Under the heading 'Lecturers for the Instruction of the Younger Sort of Scholers' is listed a lecturer in rhetoric to instruct the newcomers, a reader in logic for second- and third-year students, a reader in philosophy for sophisters and bachelors and 'one Mathematical Reader to reade the Arte of Arithmeticke, of Geometry, of Cosmographie, or of Astronomy, in such sort as is fit for his Auditory, being also of Sophisters and Bacchelers of Arte'.[12] On review, then, it appears that the failure of the 1570 Cambridge statutes to mention mathematics in its single clause

---

[9] Heywood, *Collection*, appendix, p. 40. See pp. 31–2 and 319 for the same provision in the 1549 and 1558 statutes; Lamb, *Documents*, p. 346.

[10] Heywood, *Collection*, p. 34; Lamb, *Documents*, p. 346.

[11] *Harrison's Description of England in Shakespeare's Youth*, ed. F. J. Furnivall, New Shakespeare Soc., 6th Ser., vols. 1, 5, 8 (London, 1877–81), vol. 1, p. 79.

[12] *A Projecte, Conteyninge the State, Order, and Manner of Governmente of the University of Cambridge: As Now it is to be Seene in the Three and Fortieth Yeare of the Raigne of our most Gracious and Sovereigne Lady Queen Elizabeth* (Cambridge, 1769), p. 11. It might be inferred by this prescription of arithmetic and geometry for undergraduates that these disciplines were not included in the statutes for the M.A. course because they were to be fulfilled as part of the B.A. degree.

on 'method of study' is inconclusive evidence for pronouncing the absence of mathematics in the undergraduate curriculum.

Third, the last sentence in Hill's paragraph is dangerously misleading included as it is in a section dealing with science, for the 'research' in question is not mathematical research as we are led to assume, but theological research.[13]

As regards Oxford, the evidence does not justify Hill's claim that 'the Laudian statutes summed up this conservative trend' which was reintroduced with the 1565 statutes. Although the single, cryptic sentence pertaining to curriculum in the *Nova Statuta* is vague, it nonetheless assigns three terms to arithmetic and two to music.[14] Other evidence suggests that mathematics was a required course of studies for both the B.A. and M.A. degrees, and it appears more than likely that Sir Henry Savile conformed to existing practice when he stipulated that 'all scholars after the completion of the second year from their arrival at the university, down to the first year of their bachelorship completed, shall be assigned to hear the professor of geometry'.[15]

As for the Laudian statutes, the fact that they refrained from dealing with science does not necessarily mean that they censured scientific enterprise. It should be borne in mind that the Laudian statutes made mandatory all mathematical teaching as stipulated in the most satisfactory Savilian statutes. Moreover, Brian Twyne and Peter Turner, the men most responsible for drawing up the statutes, were avid mathematicians,[16] while

[13] Hill quotes Mullinger, *The University of Cambridge*, vol. 2, pp. 306–9, when he relates the incident surrounding the suggestion to 'encourage the study of divinity as a recognized pursuit among the senior members of the university'.

[14] Gibson, *Statuta*, p. 390. Much of the subject matter of music was closely related to that of arithmetic and geometry, and the university records indicate that there were teachers who received dispensations from their duties and whose students were directed to attend arithmetic lectures. In February 1580, for example, we read: 'supplicat Johannes Lant, publicus musicae praelector, ut a munere legendi liberetur et scholares illi qui teneantur interesse musicae lectioni ad arithmeticam transferantur. Causa est quod illius lectionis utilitas modica sit auditoribus, et ideo ex more haec dispensatio concedi solet.' See A. Clark, *Register of the University of Oxford*, Oxf. Hist. Soc. (Oxford, 1885–9), vol. 2, part 1, p. 100.

[15] Ward, *Statutes*, vol. 1, pp. 275–6; Griffiths, *Statutes*, p. 247. Although the *Nova Statuta*, unlike the Cambridge statutes, did not indicate the mathematical requirements for students in colleges and halls, there remains the possibility that such requirements did exist, for the Laudian statutes contain the following clause in the statutes for halls: 'every one who is to be advanced to the degree of bachelor of arts shall, before he propounds his grace, undergo a public examination in the hall by the Principal, or some other person to be appointed by the Principal, in grammar, rhetoric, logic and moral philosophy, geometry and the Greek tongue'. Ward, *Statutes*, p. 325; Griffiths, *Statutes*, p. 271.

[16] The committee that was formed in 1633 to draw up the new statutes also included: Robert Pink, Warden of New College; Peter Turner, Savilian Professor of Geometry; Thomas James, formerly Bodley's librarian; and Richard Zouch, Principal of St Alban's Hall. Twyne and Turner, however, did most of the actual work. We shall have occasion to meet all of the committee members – with the exception of Zouch – who were also scientifically oriented members of the university.

Laud himself showed his appreciation of the sciences by donating many
scientific manuscripts and instruments to the Bodleian Library and
erecting the mathematics library at St John's College, Oxford.[17]

To conclude then, there is little evidence to substantiate the claim that
all statutes subsequent to the Edwardian statutes of 1549 were detrimental
to mathematical enterprise within the universities. Generally speaking,
only two areas of university life were affected by such revisions in the
statutes: religion and government. For the most part, both Whitgift and
Laud were interested in fostering well-disciplined and tightly governed
universities which conformed to church and state. For this reason, other
than for the study of divinity, their religious bias does not appear either
to have influenced the university curriculum or to have prejudiced
scientific instruction. It has been illustrated that apart from the omission
of mathematics from the article on 'method of study' in the 1558 and
1570 Cambridge statutes and its abridgement in the *Nova Statuta*, all of
the university statutes demonstrate a significant degree of homogeneity
in their curricular provisions.

The question remains how to explain this often cited omission in the
1558 and 1570 Cambridge statutes. It is my contention that the explanation
is to be found in the changing role of the university in society. By 1558,
and even more by 1570, higher education was appealing to increasing
numbers of the upper classes who, nonetheless, still did not wish to pursue
either a university degree or an academic career. The ideal of education
which most attracted such classes and suited their needs was one founded
upon the concept of 'polite learning' which, for the most part, consisted
of dialectics, rhetoric, history and the classics. While an acquaintance with
scientific subjects was also sought by gentlemen in order to round out their
education, it was never a high priority. This position towards scientific
instruction for the higher classes is formulated by such humanists and
educationalists as Erasmus, Vives and Ascham as well as some later
commentators. Erasmus required only a smattering of knowledge in
mathematics.[18] Vives, although an adherent of the mathematical sciences,
recommended them as 'particularly disciplinary to flighty and restless
intellects which are inclined to slackness'. Nonetheless, for the most part
Vives advocated only the elements of mathematics in so far as they were
directly applicable to practical, everyday problems.[19] Although the tone
of Roger Ascham is more censorious than that of Vives, the logic behind
his remarks is similar. The mathematical sciences, warned Ascham, 'as
they sharpen mens wittes over much, so they change mens maners over

[17] W. D. Macray, *Annals of the Bodleian Library Oxford*, 2nd edn (Oxford, 1890), pp. 83–8;
J. F. Fuggles, 'A History of the Library of S. John's College, Oxford from the Foundation
of the College to 1660' (Oxford Univ. B.Litt. thesis, 1975), pp. 135ff.
[18] Quoted in Watson, *The Beginning of the Teaching of Modern Subjects*, p. 254.
[19] J. L. Vives, *On Education*, ed. F. Watson (Totowa, New Jersey, 1971), pp. 202–3.

sore, if they be not moderatlie mingled, & wiselie applied to som good use of life'.[20] In fact, some years earlier Ascham had admonished the Earl of Leicester for 'changing Tully's wisdom with Euclid's pricks and lines'.[21] It is worthy of note that over a century later Locke prescribed only a minimal knowledge of mathematics as befitting a gentleman and further limited this knowledge to such pursuits as remained practicable and enjoyable for one of this station.[22] It is against this background of the educational bias of the upper classes against overindulgence in mathematical studies that Francis Osborn's recollections should be cited:

my Memory reacheth the time, when the Generality of People thought her [mathematics] most useful *Branches*, *Spels* and her *Professors*, *Limbs of the Devil*; converting the Honour of *Oxford*, due for her (though at that time slender) Proficiency in *this Study*, to her Shame: Not a few of our then foolish *Gentry*, refusing to send their Sons thither, lest they should be smutted with the *Black-Art*.[23]

In the mid-1650s, Seth Ward, then Savilian Professor of Astronomy, formulated the ideal of education animating the upper classes to send their sons to the universities:

which of the Nobility or Gentry, desire when they send their Sonnes hither [the universities], that they should be set to Chymistry, or Agriculture, or Mechanicks? Their removall is from hence commonly in two or three years ... and the desire of their friends is not, that they be engaged in those experimentall things, but that their reason, and fancy, and carriage, be improved by lighter institutions and Exercises, that they may become Rationall and Gracefull speakers, and be of an acceptable behaviour in their Countries.[24]

The education of the upper classes will be discussed in greater detail in chapter VI. Suffice it to say that since the sons of gentlemen were unlikely to remain at university for more than two, or at most three, years, it would have been a mistake for the universities – who were interested in attracting them – to assign the first year, especially on paper, solely to mathematical instruction. For this reason the men commissioned to revise the later statutes most probably deleted the appropriate provision specifying mathematics in the article on 'method of study' as a formal, tactical manoeuvre. Nevertheless, the other articles in the statutes suggest that

[20] R. Ascham, 'The Scholemaster (1570)', *English Works*, ed. W. A. Wright (Cambridge, 1970), p. 190.

[21] *The Whole Works of Roger Ascham*, ed. J. A. Giles (London, 1864–5), vol. 2, p. 103: R. Ascham to Earl of Leicester, 5 Aug. 1564. From the letter it is clear that the advice had already been proffered some time earlier but apparently had been ignored by Leicester.

[22] *The Educational Writings of John Locke*, ed. J. L. Axtell (Cambridge, 1968), pp. 290–1, n. 2.

[23] F. Osborn, 'Advice to a son', *The Miscellaneous Works* (London, 1722), vol. 1, p. 5.

[24] S. Ward, *Vindiciae Academiarum* (Oxford, 1654), p. 50, reprinted in *Science and Education in the Seventeenth Century: The Webster–Ward Debate*, ed. Debus.

by the third year at the latest, undergraduates were expected to embark on the study of mathematics. More important than the statutes for determining the nature of mathematical instruction is the evidence of actual practice, and the purpose of the following two chapters will be to indicate that mathematical instruction continued to be conducted in the universities on lines similar to those of previous years.

Once it has been established that mathematics was not excluded as part of the official undergraduate curriculum during this period, it is necessary to assess the official opportunities available for students to obtain mathematical instruction. Such a discussion will involve an account of the various provisions for mathematical lectureships on both a university and a collegiate level.

Prior to the foundation of the Savilian professorships of geometry and astronomy at Oxford in 1619 and the Lucasian professorship of mathematics at Cambridge in 1663, the prevailing system in both institutions was that of one-year lectureships. Oxford continued the medieval tradition whereby the regent-masters lectured on mathematics – with the modification that while only a few partook in the actual teaching, the other regent-masters paid them for assuming the responsibility[25] – while in Cambridge from 1500 onward there was a university lectureship.[26]

Although this endowed mathematical lectureship in Cambridge attracted many competent men, it no doubt handicapped the university somewhat, for such a lecturer was to discourse on all branches of mathematics – astronomy, geometry, arithmetic and cosmography – four days a week.[27] On the other hand, Oxford, in line with medieval tradition, provided at least three lecturers annually, one in each of the mathematical disciplines of astronomy, geometry and arithmetic. There is evidence that at times their number was even greater. Thus, in 1563 it appears that three lecturers for each of the mathematical disciplines had been appointed.[28] On the other hand, when Queen Elizabeth visited the university there was only one lecturer indicated for each of the sciences.[29] From the formulation of the Savilian statutes, it might be inferred that in 1619 there had been four mathematical lecturers, for Savile 'deem[ed] it fair (if the University takes the same view) that the small payments which used previously to be made to the four ordinary lecturers in mathematics (which I think may

[25] Clark, *Register*, vol. 2, part 1, pp. 95, 98.
[26] M. B. Hackett, *The Original Statutes of Cambridge University. The Text and its History* (Cambridge, 1970), p. 277.
[27] Heywood, *Collection*, appendix, p. 4.
[28] Clark, *Register*, vol. 2, part 1, p. 96.
[29] Clark, *Register*, vol. 2, part 1, p. 229.

cease altogether after this foundation) should be equally divided between the above professors'.[30]

Regardless whether the university accepted Savile's suggestion, it is clear that the two Savilian scientific chairs did supersede all existing mathematical lectureships. The impact of the Savilian foundation – the first major endowed professorships in the universities since the establishment of the Regius professorships in theology, Greek, Hebrew, medicine and civil law in the first half of the sixteenth century – was felt throughout the seventeenth century. In many ways this foundation marked the culmination of numerous attempts by many men – Dee, Hakluyt, Ralegh and Hood included – to persuade the great magnates to endow mathematical chairs in the universities and/or in London. Although Gresham College was more successful in terms of attracting an earlier benefaction, it was less important in terms of the instruction it initiated. As shall be later demonstrated, it was left to the Savilian – rather than the Gresham – professors to provide the systematic, up-to-date professional scientific education needed to stimulate science in England.

The difficulties inherent in procuring a benefaction sufficiently large to establish and endow a university chair should not be underestimated. Most interested patrons shied away from large foundations, preferring instead to establish a lectureship on a collegiate level; even a modest settlement would be sufficient to augment the stipend of one of the already existing fellows. Significantly, those men who became the large benefactors of the age either remained childless or outlived their sons. Thomas Gresham, Thomas Bodley, Henry Savile, William Camden and William Laud best illustrate this point.[31]

Be that as it may, the Savilian foundation provided an important impetus for the foundation of additional chairs, both in the sciences and in the humanities. By 1625 Oxford had witnessed the foundation of a lectureship in natural philosophy by Sir William Sedley, a lectureship in anatomy by Richard Tomlins, a lectureship in moral philosophy by Thomas White and a lectureship in history by William Camden. William Heather's lectureship in music followed in 1626 and Archbishop Laud's lectureship in Arabic in 1640. In 1622 Henry Danvers, Earl of Danby, left a huge benefaction to endow the Botanical Gardens but for various reasons the work was completed only a decade later.

The situation in Cambridge contrasts sharply with that in Oxford. Apart

[30] Ward, *Statutes*, vol. I, p. 283; Griffiths, *Statutes*, p. 252. In Cambridge, however, even after the foundation of the Lucasian Chair of Mathematics in 1663 the university lecturer in mathematics continued to exist. See CUA Registry 51 for a list of these lecturers from 1668 onward.

[31] M. Feingold, 'Jordan revisited: patterns of charitable giving in sixteenth- and seventeenth-century England', *History of Education*, VIII (1979), 265, 272.

from Lord Brooke's short-lived history lectureship and Sir Henry Spelman's endowment of a lectureship in Anglo-Saxon studies in 1636, Cambridge witnessed no major foundation before 1663. To be sure, repeated attempts to that purpose were made throughout the first half of the seventeenth century. As early 1588 John Gerard had petitioned the University Chancellor, Lord Burghley, requesting the opportunity to establish a botanical garden at Cambridge. In 1621 Henry Briggs, having just been installed as Savilian Professor of Geometry, volunteered to undertake any mission that would lead to a similar benefaction for his alma mater. A few years later Francis Bacon provided in his will for the foundation of two lectureships in philosophy – one at Cambridge, the other at Oxford. Despite the terms of the will, Bacon's friend and executor, Bishop John Williams, attempted to limit the terms of the endowment to Cambridge, arguing that Oxford was already sufficiently endowed. As things would turn out, by the time Bacon's estate was settled and its debts paid, the remaining sum proved insufficient to found even one lectureship.[32]

In 1639 it appeared as if Cambridge was finally to receive an endowed professorship in mathematics. In this year Hartlib recorded in his diary:

One of Sir W. Boswell's privat friends is erecting a Mathematicua Professor Honorarius as it were in Cambridge setling a stipend for a 100 lib. per annum with a house of purpose. Only hee advances somwhat slowly in it. The founder will have the Professor of that place to take his corporal oath every 3 years to denominate the fittest successor unto him.

Unfortunately, the plans of the unnamed benefactor dragged on until the outbreak of the Civil War put an end to them. Not until 1663 did Cambridge finally establish a mathematical chair. Owing much to the persuasion of Thomas Buck (M.A. 1616, St Catharine's College and Esquire Bedell 1624–70), Sir Henry Lucas founded a professorship in mathematics, which he also augmented by his donation of a rich mathematical library.[33]

---

[32] For Gerard's petition, see BL MS Lansd. 107, fol. 155; for Briggs, see Bodl. MS Tanner 73, fol. 68; see also T. B. Mullinger, 'The relations of Francis Bacon, Lord Verulam, with the University of Cambridge', *Publ. Camb. Antiq. Soc.*, IX (1896–8), 232.

[33] Hartlib, 'Ephemerides 1639', H–JI. Could Boswell's unnamed friend possibly be William Harvey? In his Harveian oration before the College of Physicians of London in 1662, Charles Scarburgh intimated that Harvey had intended 'the setting up of a professorship of experimental philosophy at Cambridge together with a laboratory and gardens furnished with every kind of plant, for the maintenance of which he would set aside an adequate sum; but the Civil War deterred him'. *Journ. Hist. Med.*, XII (1957), 163; for Buck, see I. Barrow, *The Geometrical Lectures*, trans. E. Stone (London, 1735), pp. xviii–xix; G. J. Gray and W. M. Palmer, *Abstracts from the Wills and Testamentary Documents of Printers, Binders, and Stationers of Cambridge, from 1504 to 1699* (London, 1915), pp. 110–14.

Any attempt to resurrect the course of studies implemented by the individual colleges is complicated beyond measure by the discrepancy between the 'official' curriculum as set down in the college statutes and the 'real' course of studies as far as it can be reconstructed from contemporary evidence. Like the university statutes, most college statutes were brief to the point of being epigrammatic in their curricular provisions. More troublesome still, the statutes of most colleges failed to record changes in college curriculum and practices introduced at some later date.

Important to our appreciation of the limitations of the college statutes as regards the undergraduate curriculum is the revolutionary change in the structure and composition of the colleges which occurred during the course of the sixteenth century.[34] Of the ten medieval Oxford colleges only New College (1379) and Magdalen College (1458) provided by their statutes for the instruction of undergraduates. The statutes of the other medieval colleges – University College, Merton College, Balliol College, Lincoln College, Queen's College, All Souls College, Oriel College and Exeter College – which were geared to the studies of bachelors and masters, made little if any reference to the curriculum in general and references to the undergraduate curriculum were fewer still. It should be noted that the decision of the medieval colleges to admit undergraduates was rarely followed by any revision of the statutory requirements. Consequently, as much as this redefinition of the function of the colleges sealed the fate of the halls, which traditionally had provided for the instruction of undergraduates (by 1640, Oxford had eighteen colleges and only seven halls), for the most part it had surprisingly little effect on the college statutes.[35] This failure on the part of the statutes of the medieval colleges to keep pace with major alterations of college policy must be borne in mind if we are to draw any valid conclusions concerning those colleges whose statutes did provide for the mathematical instruction of undergraduates. As it shall presently become clear, it was precisely those colleges founded in the course of the sixteenth and seventeenth centuries whose statutes offer a clearer indication of the mathematical studies pursued by their undergraduates.

Nonetheless, even the statutes of the newer foundations cannot be relied upon totally for information concerning the official course of studies and

[34] For the medieval situation, see H. Rashdall, *The Universities of Europe in the Middle Ages*, ed. F. M. Powicke and A. Emden, new edn (Oxford, 1936), vol. 3, *passim*; Curtis, *Oxford and Cambridge in Transition*, pp. 36–40, 282; A. Emden, *An Oxford Hall in Medieval Times, being the Early History of St Edmund Hall* (Oxford, 1927).

[35] This is not to claim that some of the surviving halls – most especially Gloucester Hall and Magdalen Hall – were not important or did not continue to prosper: only that a general decline set in once the colleges assumed responsibility for undergraduate, as well as graduate, instruction.

the manner in which it was to be implemented. Usually consisting of no more than a single paragraph citing the lectures to be delivered and the exercises to be performed, their very brevity often obscures their intention. The newly founded colleges proved just as negligent as the medieval colleges when it came to altering statutes following the establishment of new lectureships or tutorials. Further to complicate the situation, it became common practice for founders of new colleges to incorporate large portions of the statutes of already existing colleges; hence, the appearance of almost identical articles in different college statutes. For all of the above reasons, the failure of the statutes of some of the newer foundations to indicate mathematical instruction for undergraduates does not preclude such a requirement. In the following pages I shall first cite those colleges whose statutes made allowances for mathematical instruction and then present whatever evidence of an official sort is at our disposal for assuming the facilities for mathematical instruction in other colleges.

At least four of the Cambridge colleges seem to have engaged mathematical lecturers; Jesus College founded in 1496, Queens' College founded in 1448, Trinity College founded in 1546 and St John's College founded in 1511. The Jesus College statutes of 1559 prescribed a weekly lecture in mathematics during term which was to be attended by undergraduate scholars as well as by fellows and bachelors.[36] The 1559 statutes of Queens' College required that one of the two censors was to read mathematics, logic and philosophy to the fellows, bachelors and scholars of the college during term, while on one feast day during term and during the long vacation he was to read mathematics in public lectures.[37] Trinity College was more generous in its provisions for mathematical instruction. The statutes, drawn up in 1560 following the refoundation of the college, provided for both a lecturer and a sublecturer in mathematics, both of whom were to offer instruction in arithmetic, geometry and astronomy.[38]

The statutes of St John's College offer the richest and most detailed example of the growing interest in mathematics. The original college statutes were set down by Bishop John Fisher in 1530, but his disgrace and subsequent execution caused the college to formulate a new set of statutes in 1545. Notwithstanding this occurrence, the new statutes of Henry VIII retained their strong mathematical bias, perhaps because the figure behind them was none other than Sir John Cheke. No fewer than four mathematical lecturers – offering instruction in arithmetic, geometry, perspective and cosmography – were to be recruited by the college.

---

[36] *Documents relating to the University and Colleges of Cambridge* (London, 1852), vol. 3, p. 109. Here and elsewhere I shall provide the date of those statutes in effect for the period under review.

[37] *Documents relating to the University and Colleges of Cambridge*, vol. 3, p. 51.

[38] The statutes are printed in Mullinger, *The University of Cambridge*, vol. 2, pp. 595–9.

Freshmen, it should be noted, were required to devote the first seven months of their university studies to geometry and arithmetic. Moreover, a mathematical examiner was designated as one of the four examiners of the college. His task was to question pupils one hour daily on the public lectures of the schools, to discourse with pupils when no public lectures took place, and to deal thrice weekly with those pupils who found the public lectures beyond their capabilities.[39]

Oxford colleges tended to be less 'professional' in their approach to mathematical instruction, and the statutes indicate few endowed lectureships in mathematics. For the most part, mathematical lectures were delivered either by lecturers in related disciplines or by bachelors and fellows of the college. A further distinction between the two universities was the Oxford tendency to schedule mathematical lectures during the long vacation, which was considered one of the four terms of the year.

The first set of statutes to make explicit mention of the mathematical sciences in its curricular provisions was that of Magdalen College. Novel both in content and manner of instruction, the Magdalen College statutes of 1487 provided for three college lecturers, two in philosophy and one in theology, who were to deliver lectures in public, free of charge, to any who wished to attend. These statutes also made specific reference to mathematics and astronomy in their articles regulating both the course of study and method of disputation of undergraduates. During the long vacation a disputation was to be scheduled at least once a week, while during the same period:

Three Times at least in every Week ... Lectures be read by the Bachelors in the Faculty of Arts, in course as they can agree, in the presence of all the Masters and Scholars of the same Faculty, when lawful impediment there is none, in the Nave of the Chapel or elsewhere ... on some useful and first-rate subject, to wit, Algebra; or on the Treatise concerning the Sphere or regarding the Motion of the Planets.

Attendance at such lectures was compulsory on the threat of subtracting daily commons for each lecture not attended.[40]

The 1517 statutes of Corpus Christi College make it clear that the lectures at Magdalen College were attended by members of other colleges. Bishop Fox, the founder of Corpus Christi, established public lectureships in Greek, Latin and theology, but none in philosophy. Hence, the following provision: 'the Bachelors of Arts shall every day ... attend, as far as they conveniently can, having respect to the public lectures read in common

---

[39] J. E. B. Mayor (ed.), *Early Statutes of the College of St John the Evangelist in the University of Cambridge* (Cambridge, 1859), pp. 105–7, 245–7.

[40] *The Statutes of Magdalen College Oxford*, trans. G. R. M. Ward (Oxford, 1840), pp. 61–2. For the Latin text, see *Statutes of the Colleges of Oxford* (London, 1853), vol. 2 [Magdalen College], p. 35.

in our college, to the two philosophical lectures read in Magdalen College, until they have acquired a thorough proficiency'.[41] Bishop Fox appears to have adopted the following provision for mathematical instruction from the Magdalen College statutes as well.

We command the Bachelors also, lest even they should become listless through idleness, and slacken overmuch, not to say give a loose to their minds and abandon their studies in the vacations, that they themselves shall thrice, at least, each week, from Relic Sunday in the month of July to the first Sunday in October, read by turns ... in the presence of the Masters and Scholars of our College, all of whom, when present in the University, except the Graduates in Theology, we would have to be present at such lectures ... Algorism, or the Treatise on the Sphere, or concerning the Motion of the Planets, or some other mathematical work, to be determined upon by the Dean of Philosophy.[42]

The statutes of Corpus Christi College served as a prototype for many subsequent college statutes and for this reason its curricular provisions are repeated. The statutes of St John's College, Oxford, drawn up by Sir Thomas White in 1556 were almost a verbatim copy of the Corpus Christi statutes, containing as they do identical provisions for lectures in the mathematical sciences during the long vacation.[43] Also modelled on Corpus Christi statutes, the Wadham College statutes of 1612 prescribed arithmetic, geometry and astronomy lectures during the long vacation.[44]

A most interesting set of statutes is that drawn up by Sir Thomas Pope following his foundation of Trinity College, Oxford, in 1556. Every morning during term the lecturer in logic was instructed to read arithmetic, logic, philosophy and geometry to members of the college – including undergraduates – while three times a week during the long vacation he was to deliver lectures in astronomy or geography. The statutes further prescribed the syllabus for these courses and the method of instruction to be followed.[45]

The new set of statutes of Exeter College drawn up in 1560 following the generous bequest of Sir William Petre was modelled, in part, on the Trinity College statutes. During term a college lecturer was to read the classical authors, while during the long vacation he was to read arithmetic, geometry or elementary cosmography.[46] The Exeter College Register provides evidence of a retrospective kind as regards the manner in which

[41] *The Foundation Statutes of Bishop Fox for Corpus Christi College in the University of Oxford A.D. 1517*, trans. G. R. M. Ward (London, 1843), pp. 111–12. For the Latin text, see *Statutes of the Colleges of Oxford*, vol. 2 [Corpus Christi College], p. 54.
[42] *The Foundation Statutes for Corpus Christi College*, trans. Ward, pp. 116–17. For the Latin text, see *Statutes of the Colleges of Oxford*, vol. 2 [Corpus Christi College], p. 57.
[43] *Statutes of the Colleges of Oxford*, vol. 3 [St John's College], p. 56.
[44] *Statutes of the Colleges of Oxford*, vol. 4 [Wadham College], p. 23.
[45] *Statutes of the Colleges of Oxford*, vol. 4 [Trinity College], pp. 44–5.
[46] Exeter College Archive A.I.(2), fol. 37.

such a provision had been complied with, for in 1737 a decree required: 'That during every long vacation the Lecturer in the classicks shall read (as the statutes require and as former lecturers always did) either arithmetick, or geometry, or the rudiments of cosmography at least four days in every week, unless such days are festivals.'[47] The following entry of 6 July 1621 taken from the same register further supports this practice: 'indulta erat venia M. Georgio Beard lectori ut abesset a Collegio usque ad festum Michaelis proxime sequentis, ea lege ut alium magistrum idoneum substitueret qui vices ejus in lectione Rhetorica et Mathematica fideliter obiret'.[48]

As it has already been explained, the statutes of the various colleges offer only the most limited scope for assessing their official provisions for mathematical instruction. Evidence garnered from other sources indicate the existence of lectureships in the mathematical sciences which were never stipulated in the college statutes. In 1616, for example, Arthur Lake, Warden of New College, Oxford, founded a lectureship in mathematics and another in Hebrew in his college.[49] Little is known of this mathematical lectureship and one of the very few references to it is contained in a letter written by the mathematician Thomas Lydiat to Thomas Man of New College in 1625. In this letter acknowledging the assistance he had received from certain fellows of New College in the transcription of manuscripts, Lydiat specifically thanked a Mr [Thomas] Miller, the mathematical lecturer, for a transcription he had made.[50] At about the same time Sir Henry Savile founded a lectureship in arithmetic in Merton College, possibly in response to the new practice of admitting under-graduates. Although this foundation is rarely mentioned, one of its first incumbents was the mathematician, Henry Briggs. Wood writes that apart from having served as Savilian Professor of Geometry, Briggs 'also read Arithmetick thrice in a week in Merton College Refectory to the Scholars thereof, being all the time of his abode in Oxford a commoner there'.[51] In the admission book of the Bodleian Library for 10 April 1611, the list of readers includes a Richard Kay, who identified himself as 'Professor Mathematicus S. Ed. H'. It should come as no surprise that the statutes and records of St Edmund Hall fail to indicate any such mathematical lectureship.[52]

[47] C. W. Boase, *Registrum Collegii Exoniensis* (Oxford, 1894), p. 355.
[48] Boase, *Registrum*, p. 97.
[49] A. Lake, *Sermons [with some Religious and Divine Meditations]* (London, 1629), 'A short view of the life and vertues of the Author', sig. *f*.
[50] J. O. Halliwell, *A Collection of Letters Illustrative of the Progress of Science in England* (London, 1841), p. 52: T. Lydiat to T. Man, 12 May 1625.
[51] A. Wood, *The History and Antiquities of the University of Oxford*, ed. J. Gutch (Oxford, 1796), vol. 1, pp. 334–5.
[52] Clark, *Register*, vol. 2, part 1, p. 270.

Statutory requirements and endowed lectureships are not our only source of information on possible opportunities for mathematical instruction. There is some evidence to suggest the instruction in mathematics by various fellows and bachelors of the college. It is most likely that such 'unofficial' lecturers either were supported by college revenues without the creation of an endowed post or included mathematics as an integral part of logic, philosophy or some other related discipline. The Magdalen College archives cite charges incurred for a lecturer in geography for the year 1540–1, even though no such lecturer is stipulated in the statutes.[53] More interesting still, they indicate that in 1591 President Bond issued a number of decrees, one of which required that all bachelors deliver lectures in geography and cosmography in a system of rotation. The stiff fines imposed upon those who failed to comply with this decree or supplied substitute lecturers make it evident that such a demand proved not to the liking of some of the bachelors.[54] Richard Hakluyt's cosmographical lectures in Christ Church in the period 1577–82 are well known.[55] An earlier indication of mathematical instruction is a list of college officers for the year 1552 which included a lecturer in mathematics.[56]

Often ignored Cambridge foundations include the two mathematical lectureships inaugurated by Sir Thomas Smith in his alma mater, Queens' College, on 2 December 1573. Bequeathing to the college the revenues of a manor in Northamptonshire (amounting to £12 7s 4d at the time of foundation) out of which £4 was designated to support a lecturer in arithmetic and £3 a lecturer in geometry, Smith's stipulations regulating this bequest suggest the direction of his mathematical interests. Smith prescribed that the reader in geometry was to lecture daily on Euclid, while the reader in arithmetic – which included algebra – was to use the textbooks of Cuthbert Tonstall, Oronce Finé or Michael Stiphelius. Smith further insisted that:

The which two lectures are not to be redd of the reader as of a preacher out of a pulpit, but 'per radium et eruditum pulverum' as it is said, that is with a penn on paper or tables, or a sticke or compasse in sand or duste to make demonstracon that his schollers maie both understand the reader and also do it themselves and so profit.

Smith even went so far as to rule that undergraduates were not to proceed

[53] W. D. Macray, *A Register of the Members of St Mary Magdalen College Oxford* (London, 1897), vol. 2, p. 69. There is no record of subsequent payments for such lectures.

[54] H. A. Wilson, *Magdalen College* (London, 1899), p. 137.

[55] *DSB*, vol. 6, p. 20.

[56] 'Dean and Chapter Book', Christ Church Lib. MS 1. b.1, fol. 7v. The College had no statutes until the nineteenth century, but was instead governed by decrees. Subsequent lists of officers do not indicate a specific mathematical lecturer, but it is possible that one of the four lecturers of dialectics taught mathematics.

for the B.A. 'before that they be well expert in the parts of Arithmatique, addition, subtraction, multiplication, division, and extraction of roots as well of whole numbers as of fractions bie the judgement of the reader of arithmetique upon the said readers oth'. Neither could a bachelor proceed for his M.A. before 'he hath redd and do understand the first six bokes of Euclide'.[57]

Although a mathematical lectureship is not stipulated in the statutes of King's College, Cambridge, the college seems to have introduced rigorous mathematical instruction during the provostship of Sir John Cheke (1548–53). Cheke, it should be noted, invited William Buckley to be the first mathematical lecturer of the college.[58] Also significant is that in 1634 Samuel Ward, Master of Sidney Sussex College, employed part of the income arising from Sir John Brereton's bequest in order to establish a mathematical lectureship at Sidney Sussex.[59]

Despite the divergent nature of the evidence under review, its cumulative effect is to suggest that most colleges stipulated either an endowed lectureship in mathematics, a rotating mathematical lectureship between college fellows and bachelors, or at the very least, lectures in mathematics during the long vacation by a college lecturer in a related discipline. Such provisions are for mathematical lectures beyond the standard provisions for lectures in natural philosophy made by all colleges. Although the Aristotelian physical treatises were usually the prescribed reading for the lectures in natural philosophy, they unavoidably had a scientific orientation, treating as they did cosmology and the life sciences.

The question remains whether we are to infer that colleges for which no formal provisions for undergraduate instruction have hitherto been uncovered, failed to provide such instruction. This possibility seems highly unlikely. At both Oxford and Cambridge the individual colleges were responsible for all aspects of undergraduate education, including the preparation of undergraduates for their public exercises. Since mathematics appears to have been a required subject in the B.A. curriculum in both Oxford and Cambridge, there is little reason to assume that the individual colleges varied greatly in their provisions for mathematical instruction. Hence, it appears likely that in those colleges for which no evidence of formal provisions for mathematical instruction has been uncovered, the lecturers in logic or philosophy had assumed the burden of mathematical instruction as well.

What might be termed an indirect proof of the homogeneity of

[57] W. Searle, *The History of the Queens' College of St Margaret and St Bernard in the University of Cambridge 1446–1662*, Camb. Antiq. Soc. Publ., vols. 9 and 13 (Cambridge, 1867, 1871), pp. 320–1.
[58] P. Rose, 'Erasmians and mathematicians at Cambridge in the early sixteenth century', *Sixteenth Century Journal*, VIII (supplement 1977), 47–59, 57 (n. 65), 58.
[59] G. M. Edwards, *Sidney Sussex College* (London, 1899), p. 93.

mathematical instruction in the various colleges is their uniformity in producing future men of science. Indeed, as it will become increasingly clear in chapters II and III, although such colleges as Merton College, Oxford, and St John's College, Cambridge, had a relatively high proportion of mathematicians, for the most part the colleges and halls varied little in the numbers of mathematicians and scientifically oriented fellows they turned out. Moreover, if no allowance is made for unrecorded, and less formal, provisions for mathematical instruction, it becomes almost impossible to explain how it could happen that precisely those Cambridge colleges which have been singled out by historians as strongholds of Puritanism and centres of scientific inquiry – Emmanuel, Sidney Sussex and Christ's – made no provisions whatever for mathematical instruction in their statutes.

Up until now our main preoccupation has been with the curricular provisions for undergraduates and only indirect mention has been made of the M.A. curriculum. Nonetheless, the curricular provisions for bachelors deserve sustained attention because of the way they often have been lumped together with the curricular requirements for undergraduates and their significance discounted. It is my contention that an understanding of the rationale behind the M.A. course of studies is vital to our grasp of the nature of scientific instruction at Oxford and Cambridge.

In contrast to the undergraduate requirements, the requirements for the master's degree remained virtually intact in the Edwardian statutes of 1549 and the 1558 and 1570 Cambridge statutes, and kept a similar orientation in the 1564/65 *Nova Statuta* of Oxford. The Cambridge statutes specify that: '[Bachelors of Art] shall be constant attendants at the lectures upon philosophy, astronomy, drawing [perspective] and the Greek language; and that, which had been before begun, they shall complete by their own industry.'[60] The *Nova Statuta* required of bachelors of art two terms of geometry, two of astronomy, three of natural philosophy, three of moral philosophy and two of metaphysics.[61] Following the implementation of the Savilian statutes in 1619, the first year of the M.A. course would have continued with geometry while the following two years would have been devoted to astronomy.[62] Apart from making attendance at lectures mandatory for the bachelor, the university statutes required his attendance at the disputations of his seniors as well as his performance of disputations which, of course, culminated in the inception declamation. Moreover, in Oxford, upon completion of these exercises and before being awarded a

---

[60] Heywood, *Collection*, p. 8, appendix, p. 7; Lamb, *Documents*, p. 320.
[61] Gibson, *Statuta*, p. 390.
[62] Ward, *Statutes*, vol. 1, pp. 245–6; Griffiths, *Statutes*, p. 247.

master's degree, the inceptor was required to deliver three lectures in natural, as well as an additional three in moral, philosophy.

As with undergraduate studies, the individual colleges provided a parallel system of instruction and exercise. Although it is beyond the scope of this study to discuss the numerous collegiate provisions for bachelors, mention should be made of those provisions directly affecting mathematical instruction. In addition to his mandatory attendance at mathematical lectures, the bachelor's performance of a set of mathematical exercises within the college was often stipulated by the statutes. In fact, the bachelor was usually required to sit for an internal examination intended to check his proficiency before he was allowed to sit for the university disputations. The following document, drawn up in 1639 by Samuel Ward, Master of Sidney Sussex College, Cambridge, confirms this rigorous routine. Those who are to commence M.A.

shall sit in the Chappel as Questionists used to do, 2 hours a day for 3 days, there to be examined for triall of their sufficiency. And because the University Statute de Bacc. Art. C. 7 requires that such be auditores Philosophicae lectionis, Astronomiae, Perspectivae et Graecae liguae; it is judged fit that triall be made of their skill therein, beside other things suited with their degree.[63]

This account of the curriculum and exercises leading to a master's degree has been brought forward in order to demonstrate that the undergraduate and graduate courses of study complemented each other. Curtis has already remarked upon the essential unity of the B.A. and M.A. courses, and the traditional concept of curriculum in the universities which 'seemed to be based on the assumption that scholars would without question continue their studies for another three years and take the master's degree in due course ... Only in that way did the statutes provide for study of all the arts and the three philosophies.'[64] As proof of the official view of the unity and continuity of instruction, Curtis goes on to quote the clause in the 1570 Cambridge statutes: 'and that, which had been before begun, they shall complete by their own industry'.[65] Building upon Curtis's argument, I should like to illustrate how such a concept influenced mathematical instruction in the universities.

Although the course of studies leading to a master's degree was similar in both universities, there is one significant difference between the statutory requirements of Oxford and Cambridge. While in Cambridge the

---

[63] Morison, *The Founding of Harvard College*, p. 76, note. Similarly, the Laudian statutes for the Oxford halls required that before any member could be advanced to the degree of master of arts, he had to be examined by the Principal of the hall or his deputies in geometry, astronomy, natural philosophy, metaphysics, and other liberal sciences. See Ward, *Statutes*, vol. I, p. 325; Griffiths, *Statutes*, p. 271.

[64] Curtis, *Oxford and Cambridge in Transition*, p. 91.

[65] Curtis, *Oxford and Cambridge in Transition*, p. 24, n. 1.

bachelor was to continue the philosophy instruction begun in his third year of the B.A., in Oxford the *Nova Statuta* made no mention of philosophy in their reference to the B.A. curriculum. The Laudian statutes appended only the study of moral philosophy to the second year of the B.A. course, while still assigning natural philosophy to the last two years of the M.A. course. Such a division is not illogical if it is borne in mind that much of the subject matter dealt with in natural philosophy was also covered by astronomy, regardless of the different orientations of the two disciplines.[66] Consequently, after 1619 there existed – at least on paper – an 'anomalous' situation whereby a student was required to follow Aristotle in the lecture in natural philosophy one day and Copernicus in the lecture in astronomy the next.

It becomes clear then, that to do justice to the various curricular requirements, it is first necessary to understand the criteria employed by those who were responsible for their formulation. Indeed, throughout the seventeenth century there were differing opinions as to the order in which the various disciplines should be approached. One such debate revolved round the question whether logic or mathematics provided the best foundation for later studies, with Newton, for one, asserting the former and Locke holding the opposite view.[67] On the other hand, there was an overall consensus that it was unwise to immerse the student in astronomy and natural philosophy before he had already acquainted himself with arithmetic and geometry. Once the reasoning behind the university curriculum is understood, the anachronism of the allegation made against the universities for their failure to introduce every freshman to Copernicus or Galileo becomes clear.

In conclusion, then, if either the university or college statutes are to be of any help at all in deciphering the situation in the universities, they must be used in conjunction with other evidence of university practices. Any explanations based on the assumption that the statutes were an exact description of reality is totally inadequate. Although the mathematical lectureships stipulated in the university and college statutes as well as less 'professional' forms of mathematical instruction whose existence has become known through other sources suggest a definite scientific bias within the universities, the extent and quality of scientific inquiry must be ascertained on the basis of other evidence. Similarly, the heavy reliance

---

[66] Indeed, the Laudian statutes substantiate this situation when they prescribe the auditors of the lecturer in natural philosophy as those 'who are to be the auditors in astronomy'. See Ward, *Statutes*, vol. I, p. 22; Griffiths, *Statutes*, p. 36.

[67] See *Unpublished Scientific Papers of Isaac Newton*, ed. A. R. Hall and M. Boas Hall (Cambridge, 1962), 'Of educating youth in the universities', pp. 369–73; *The Educational Writings of John Locke*, p. 270.

of the statutes of the newly founded colleges on those of already established colleges says more about the homogeneous structure of the colleges than about the actual teaching practices. Perhaps this point is best made by Dr Francis Bevans, Principal of Jesus College, in his remarks to the future Master, Griffith Powell. Bevans commissioned Powell in the 1590s 'to collect some statutes of other Colleges whereof he might have a view, and by or out of which he might have statutes made for the College'.[68] In order to obtain more reliable information on the actual practice of the colleges in the instruction of mathematics, it is necessary to consult the surviving accounts of lecturers, tutors and undergraduates.

[68] E. G. Hardy, *Jesus College* (London, 1899), p. 29.

II

The nature and quality of scientific instruction: the teaching community

In the previous chapter I suggested that the omission of the article prescribing mathematics to the first year of undergraduate studies in the 1558 and 1570 Cambridge statutes and its abridgement in the *Nova Statuta* of Oxford were insufficient evidence for concluding the absence of mathematical instruction in both institutions. By reference to other articles in the statutes – especially the article stipulating mathematics as a subject to be disputed as part of the B.A. requirements – and to other university and college documents, I showed that at most mathematics was reallocated to a later year in the B.A. curriculum; by the third year at the latest the student was expected to have received some instruction in mathematics. However, as any case for the existence of scientific inquiry in the universities is dependent less upon the statutes than upon evidence of adequate instruction in, and encouragement of, the mathematical sciences, the objective of the following three chapters is to assess the nature and quality of mathematical opportunities at Oxford and Cambridge.

In the first section of the following chapter I shall attempt to identify the scientific lecturers and the probable content of their lectures. Since records and official papers of the type used to document the previous chapter rarely shed light on the actual content of lectures, any such assessment must rely heavily upon more circumstantial – and one might add fragmentary – evidence, whether this be in the form of lecture notes, reputation among contemporaries or publications of a scientific nature. The second section will be devoted to a survey of scientifically minded members of the university community, whether tutors known to have instructed their charges in the mathematical sciences or 'potential tutors' – college fellows and residents of the universities – many of whom were known to have been available to the more ambitious students for advanced scientific instruction. Here again the evidence at our disposal is usually of a circumstantial nature, most often being fragments of biographical and autobiographical accounts, excerpts from personal correspondence and surviving tutorial exercises.

Before turning to a discussion of lecturers, it is necessary to deal briefly with a claim made by certain historians, namely that in the period under review university lectures had practically become obsolete, while college lectures were very meagrely attended; in their stead the college tutor became almost the sole source of instruction.[1] Without minimizing the importance of the college tutor, I shall argue that such a claim for the obsolescence of lectures is mistaken. First, attendance at lectures was compulsory under penalty of fine and the significant number of dispensations from lectures[2] being sought by students suggests that such requirements were not taken lightly. Second, although individual cases of negligence did exist, there is nothing in the various 'advice books' for students or other contemporary accounts to hint at a general relaxation of university and college discipline as regards attendance at lectures. Third, the various types of instruction took cognizance of each other, with college lectures usually scheduled between 7 and 8 in the morning, university lectures usually between 8 and 9 and tutorial instruction occupying the remainder of the hours some mornings and afternoons. Occasional references in diaries, student notebooks and testimonials to past performance further substantiate this claim. While many students did record their attendance at college and university lectures, all paid fees to lecturers.

However, a far more substantial piece of evidence shedding light on the attendance of students at university lectures does exist. Apparently each year the vice-chancellor of Cambridge recorded the names of the entire university student body as well as the lectures they attended, and submitted this document to the chancellor. Two such lists have survived, one for 1575, the other for 1588; together they clarify questions about the degree of student attendance at lectures as well as the nature of these lectures. A comparison of the names compiled by the vice-chancellor and the names contained in the registers of Gonville and Caius, Peterhouse and Christ's colleges of the identical years reveals that with few exceptions all resident students attended the university lectures. The information contained in the lists also confirms what I said earlier about the university curriculum, namely that mathematics did not disappear from the undergraduate curriculum, but instead was reallocated to the final two years of study. These lists clearly show that while first- and second-year students attended lectures in rhetoric and dialectics, 'general sophists' and bachelors both audited the lectures in mathematics and philosophy. The only discrepancy between the instruction indicated by these lists and that prescribed by the statutes is the apparent mandatory attendance of

---

[1] See, for example, Mullinger, *The University of Cambridge*, vol. 2, pp. 426–7; Curtis, *Oxford and Cambridge in Transition*, pp. 96–8.

[2] Many such dispensations can be found in the Registers of Convocation and Congregation in the Oxford University Archives.

sophisters at the Greek lectures, a subject prescribed by the statutes only
to bachelors. (Indeed, this practice is also confirmed by surviving
undergraduate notebooks.) It might be added that the Cambridge course
of study correlates closely with the Oxford practice whereby sophists also
attended lectures in mathematics, philosophy and Greek.[3] We may
assume, then, that students attended lectures, and the problem at hand is
to determine the identity of the lecturers and the probable content of their
lectures.

Among his contemporaries Sir Henry Savile had a reputation as an
eminent mathematician. Yet, if one were to rely solely upon Savile's
biographers – each of whom in turn relied heavily upon Anthony Wood
– one would evolve a distorted view of the content of Savile's lectures.
Wood delineates Savile's interests as an instructor in the following way:
'In 1570, our author Savile proceeded in his faculty [M.A.], and read his
ordinaries on *The Almagest of Ptolemy*: whereby growing famous for his
learning, especially for the Greek tongue and mathematics, (in which last
he voluntarily read a lecture for some time to the academians).'[4]
Fortunately, Savile provides one of the very rare instances in which there
are extant lecture notes to which it is possible to refer, thus liberating the
historian from sole reliance upon secondary sources. The Bodleian Library
possesses seven notebooks containing notes for the lectures Savile
delivered in Oxford. Three of the notebooks are devoted to the lectures
Savile was to read as part of his M.A. requirements, though oddly enough
these notebooks bear the dates October and November 1568.[5] Admittedly,
in corroboration of Wood's claim, the lectures consist of a Latin version
of the *Almagest*, with commentaries by Theon of Alexandria and Nicholas
Cabasilas. Yet Wood fails to make any mention of the sources consulted
by Savile in preparation for these lectures. Reading through this list of
sources is like reading through the 'Who's Who' of astronomy and
mathematics: Copernicus, Regiomontanus, Peurbach, Erasmus Reinhold,
Tartaglia, Blanchin, Werner, and Faber all are mentioned, as are the ancient
and medieval authorities. Significantly, while delivering these lectures
Savile's own convictions leaned heavily towards the new cosmology, for
at the end of the first notebook he jotted down: 'Copernicus Mathematicorū
Modernorū Prīceps'.[6] Moreover, the 'some time' denoted by Wood
consisted of almost five years – 1570–5 – while, to quote Westman, the
content of such lectures as condensed in the four notebooks

included discussion of the quadrivium with additional sections on optics, mechanics
and geography; a detailed history of Greek mathematics in the tradition of Ramus;

[3] BL MS Lansd. 20, fols. 200–15; MS Lansd. 57, fols. 213–18.
[4] A. Wood, *Athenae Oxonienses*, ed. P. Bliss (Oxford, 1813–20), vol. 2, p. 310; A. Kippis
(ed.), *Biographia Britannica* (London, 1747–66), vol. 5, p. 3598; *DNB*.
[5] Bodl. MSS Savile 26–8.
[6] Bodl. MS Savile 28, fols. 29ff; MS Savile 26, fol. 91v.

an extensive treatment of the trigonometry of Ptolemy, Regiomontanus and Copernicus; and finally, a chapter-by-chapter parallel analysis of the *Almagest* and *De Revolutionibus*. The last is comparable to the best Continental treatments of the same period, such as those of Johannes Praetorius, Tycho Brahe and Michael Maestlin.[7]

Savile's lectures demonstrate the often neglected fact that new wine can be poured into old bottles. It is noteworthy that when Savile established the chair of astronomy some fifty years later, he instructed the professor of astronomy to treat the subject in the same comparative manner: 'The professor of Astronomy is to understand that it necessarily appertains to his duty to explain the whole mathematical economy of Ptolemy, ... applying in their proper place the discoveries of Copernicus, Geber, and other modern writers.'[8] If it is borne in mind that Ptolemy provides the frame of reference for Copernicus as well as for later astronomers, such a prescription does not seem at all reactionary.

Even if Savile was a man of exceptional abilities who outstripped most lecturers both in breadth of knowledge and devotion to mathematics, there is little reason to assume that other noted men of science would not have afforded a reasonable introduction and up-to-date treatment of mathematics. For example, in 1574, when Savile was in the fourth year of his lectures, his close friend, John Chamber, was university lecturer in astronomy. Although in Chamber's case there are no extant notes of his lectures, there is an introductory lecture in the form of an appendix to his critique of judicial astrology. The lecture consists of the traditional introductory lecture of the period – devoted primarily to the defence of astronomy – but in it Chamber also warmly praises Melanchthon, Peucer, Erasmus Reinhold and Ramus. As Westman has already pointed out, the first three were the architects of the 'Wittenberg Interpretation', the men who 'helped to institutionalize the moderate, pragmatic interpretation of the Copernican theory advocated by the *Praeceptor Germaniae*'. Such evidence suggests that at least as regards up-to-date sources, the remaining lectures delivered by Chamber did not fall short of those delivered by Savile.[9]

It appears that Thomas Lydiat had also been a lecturer in astronomy at Oxford, for in the preface to his *Praelectio astronomica de natura coeli et conditionibus* (1605) he writes that the material had been delivered as a series of lectures in the university six years earlier, presumably when he

[7] Westman, 'The astronomer's role in the sixteenth century', 129; these lectures for 1570–5 are to be found in Bodl. MSS Savile 29–32. See p. 55 below.
[8] Ward, *Statutes*, p. 273; Griffiths, *Statutes*, p. 245.
[9] J. Chamber, '*Astronomiae Encomium*' appended to *Treatise against Judicial Astrologie* (London, 1601); Wood, *Athenae Oxonienses*, vol. 1, p. 744; Clark, *Register*, vol. 2, part 3, p. 33; *DNB*; R. S. Westman, 'The Melanchton circle, Rheticus, and the Wittenberg interpretation of the Copernican theory', *Isis*, LXVI (1975), 192.

was a new regent-master. Although conservative in certain matters, Lydiat
provided an up-to-date description of the body of knowledge of the field
and – as Donahue has pointed out – closely resembled Kepler in two points:
like Kepler, he wished astronomy to conform to physical principles and
was ready to abandon circularity in favour of 'oval' orbits.[10]

Unfortunately, the identity of most of the Oxford University lecturers
remains obscure. No list of lecturers is known to exist and the few odd
names that have come down to us owe their survival to their inclusion
in the occasional lists of university officials or their sporadic appearance
in the Registers of Convocation. Thus, for example, someone took the
trouble to copy the list of lecturers for 1556 no less than four times. This
list includes three lecturers for each of the seven arts and sciences as well
as for each of the three philosophies, with the exception of grammar and
rhetoric which were designated only two lecturers. Among these lecturers
we find Robert Hues (M.A. 1555, Oriel College), William Lawson (M.A.
1554) and Edward Andleser (M.A. 1555) for geometry, and John Evans
(M.A. 1555), John Restell (M.A. 1555, New College) and Thomas Nott
(M.A. 1555) for astronomy. None of these men is known to have left
evidence of subsequent scientific activity.[11] In a similar manner virtually
nothing is known of Richard Wignall (M.A. 1579, All Souls College), the
lecturer of geometry in 1580, whose name was recorded in the Register
of Convocation only because he was granted a dispensation.[12]

Another chance occurrence is responsible for bringing to light the names
of some other mathematical lecturers. In 1592, when preparations were
being made for the state visit of Queen Elizabeth and the regulations
governing the day-to-day life of the university were drawn up, a list of
lecturers accompanied such regulations. The lecturer in astronomy was
Francis Mason, a fellow of Merton College (M.A. 1590) who later was to
become a noted defender of the Church of England. An astronomical
treatise composed by Mason is the sole surviving proof of his scientific
interests.[13] The lecturer in geometry was Edward Gee (M.A. 1590,

[10] Johnson, *Astronomical Thought*, p. 321; W. H. Donahue, 'The Dissolution of the Celestial
Spheres 1595–1650' (Cambridge Univ. Ph.D. thesis, 1972), p. 83; idem, 'A hitherto
unreported pre-Keplerian oval orbit', *Journ. Hist. Astronomy*, IV (1973), 192–4. See also
ch. IV, pp. 148–52 below.

[11] OUA NEP/Supra Register I, fols. 213v–14 printed in Clark, *Register*, vol. 2, part 1, p.
97. Clark is mistaken in assigning the lectures to 1563, for only the earlier date is
compatible with the appointment of new regent-masters as lecturers. Moreover, most
of the above lecturers left Oxford before 1563. Finally, there is a separate dispensation
for William Lawson on 25 Jan. 1555/56 for intermitting his geometry lectures for ten
days. See Clark, *Register*, vol. 2, part 1, p. 98.

[12] Clark, *Register*, vol. 2, part 1, p. 99 and vol. 2, part 3, p. 52. Ten years earlier in 1569
William Kettelbie, lecturer in astronomy, received a similar dispensation. Clark, *Register*,
vol. 2, part 1, p. 99.

[13] Clark, *Register*, vol. 2, part 1, p. 229. For Mason, see *DNB*. His astronomical treatise is
in BL MS Harl. 6494, fols. 57–77v.

Brasenose College), who later gained repute as a divine and eventually was installed as chaplain to Lord-Chancellor Egerton, while the lecturer in arithmetic was George Holland (M.A. 1591, Balliol College) about whom virtually nothing is known.[14]

As regards Cambridge, we are more fortunate, for it is possible to reconstruct almost a complete list of the mathematical lecturers from the university archives. Although many of the lecturers failed to leave further testimony of their scientific interest, there are some who later became notable men of science. Lancelot Browne, who left Cambridge in 1584 in order to practise medicine in London and eventually became physician to Elizabeth and James I, had been mathematical lecturer from 1568 until 1570. It is significant that in his preface to *The Theoriques of the Seven Planets* (1602), Blundeville acknowledged assistance he had received from Browne in the compilation of the book while the mathematician Thomas Oliver dedicated his *De rectarum linearum parallelismo et concursu doctrina geometrica* (1603) to Browne.[15] The mathematical lecturer for 1574–5 was Robert Dunning (M.A. 1572), a fellow of King's College from 1567 until 1577 and a highly reputed mathematician. In 1575 he succeeded to one of the King's College fellowships in astronomy, but was expelled the following year for having falsely accused the Provost, Roger Goad, of misbehaviour.[16] Thomas Hood (M.A. 1581, Trinity College), who embarked upon a successful career as a mathematical practitioner in London, had held the appointment of mathematical lecturer for the year 1581–2.[17] More renowned still was Henry Briggs (M.A. 1585, St John's College) who was the mathematical lecturer in 1587–8. Briggs's surviving lecture notes contain a detailed exposition of Ramus's geometry, while the introductory lecture consists of a survey of the sciences, with reference to their usefulness, as well as an enumeration of the authorities in each of its faculties. Although the overall tone of the notes is traditional, significant is the reference to Copernicus in the section devoted to

[14] Clark, *Register*, vol. 2, part 1, p. 229. Gee has an entry in the *DNB*.

[15] CUA Registry 51, fols. 1–3. For Browne, who was William Harvey's father-in-law, see Cooper, *Athenae Cantabrigienses*, vol. 2, p. 421; *DNB*. Browne was also the person who advised Gabriel Harvey to choose medicine as his profession and it was to Browne's fellowship at Pembroke College that Harvey succeeded. See V. F. Stern, *Gabriel Harvey, His Life, Marginalia and Library* (Oxford, 1979), p. 75. Browne is also tentatively identified by Aquilecchia as the person who disputed against Giordano Bruno in London in 1583. G. Bruno, *La Cena de le Ceneri*, ed. G. Aquilecchia (Turin, 1955), p. 53, n. 1.

[16] CUA Univ. Acct. 2(1), fol. 256; Cooper, *Athenae Cantabrigienses*, vol. 1, p. 363; King's College Cambridge 'Liber Protocoli 1500–1578', fol. 239.

[17] J. Venn (ed.), *Grace Book* Δ (Cambridge, 1910), p. 356. For Hood, see Cooper, *Athenae Cantabrigienses*, vol. 2, p. 270; E. G. R. Taylor, *The Mathematical Practitioners of Tudor and Stuart England* (Cambridge, 1954), p. 179; Johnson, *Astronomical Thought*, pp. 196–205; F. R. Johnson, 'Thomas Hood's inaugural address as mathematical lecturer of the City of London (1588)', *Journ. Hist. Ideas*, III (1942), 94–106.

astronomy. Briggs subsequently served as mathematical lecturer and examiner at St John's College before he became successively Professor of Geometry at Gresham College and Savilian Professor of Geometry at Oxford. One of those who attended Briggs's early lectures at St John's was Thomas Gataker (M.A. 1597), who was to become a famous preacher.[18]

Briggs's successor as mathematical lecturer for the year 1588–9 was Joseph Jessop (M.A. 1587, a fellow of King's College 1582–91). Although reputed as a man of learning, little is known about Jessop's life and work. However, an interesting glimpse into his scientific attainments comes from the *Magneticall Animadversions* published by Mark Ridley in 1617. As mentioned previously, in this polemical work Ridley claims that Edward Wright, rather than William Gilbert, composed book six of the *De Magnete*. However, according to Ridley – who might well have known Jessop at Cambridge – Wright was not alone in this endeavour:

> then it was found that one Doctor *Gissope* was much esteemed by him, and lodged in his house whom he knew alwaies to be a great Scholler in the Mathematick, who was a long time entertained by Sir Charles Chandish [sic], hee was a great assistance in that matter as we judged, and I have seene whole sheetes of this mans owne hand writing of Demonstrations to this purpose and of Copernicus, in a booke of Philosophie copied out in another hand, this man should have succeeded me in Russia, had not God called him by death to a better place.[19]

Jessop died in 1599.

Two mathematicians from Gonville and Caius College served as mathematical lecturers during the 1590s: Oliver Green (M.A. 1589) in 1590–1 and Robert Wells (M.A. 1592) in 1597–8. Green certainly took his duties seriously for his stipend was increased an additional £2 13s 4d 'in regard to the extraordinary charges of his mathematical instruments'. Green remained in Cambridge until his death in 1625 and on the occasion of King James's visit to Cambridge in 1615 he repaired the college sundials.[20] Although virtually nothing is known about Wells's instruction as a mathematical lecturer, upon his death in 1632 he bequeathed to Gonville and Caius over 200 books, most of which were mathematical and medical

---

[18] From Venn, *Grace Book* Δ, p. 414, it appears that Briggs was the lecturer for 1587 as well, for he was substituted for a short while by William Rowley. For the lecture notes see BL MS Harl. 6796, fols. 81–146; fols. 147–54 are the notes for the introductory lecture. *Thomas Gataker D.D. his Vindication of the Annotations by him published upon ... Jer.10.2 against Mr William Lillie ... and Mr John Swan* (London, 1653), p. 87. See pp. 68, 138–43 below.

[19] Cooper, *Athenae Cantabrigienses*, vol. 2, p. 241; King's College Cambridge 'Liber Protocoli 1578–1627', pp. 13, 31; Ridley, *Magneticall Animadversions*, pp. 9–10. CUA Univ. Acct. 1(1), 'Vouchers for the Accounts 1588–9'.

[20] J. Venn, *Biographical History of Gonville and Caius College 1349–1897* (Cambridge, 1897–1912), vol. 1, p. 114; CUA Univ. Acct. 2(1), fol. 314.

volumes.[21] We also know that Wells's tutor during his student years had been the renowned Richard Swale (M.A. 1572), President of Gonville and Caius College from 1582 until 1589 and himself a mathematical lecturer for four years, 1573–4 and 1575–8.[22]

Other notable men include William Rawley (M.A. 1608, Corpus Christi College), the mathematical lecturer in 1610–11, who later was appointed chaplain and secretary to Francis Bacon as well as his literary executor,[23] and John Rant (M.A. 1634, Gonville and Caius College), the mathematical lecturer in 1636, whose scientific interests are indicated by the astronomical and mathematical manuscripts he bequeathed to the Cambridge University Library.[24]

Certain other mathematical lecturers at Cambridge gained repute in fields other than mathematics. Barnabas Gooch (M.A. 1590), Master of Magdalene College from 1604 until 1626, shared the mathematical appointment in 1593–4 with William Alabaster (M.A. 1591, Trinity College), the neo-Latin poet. Like Green before them, both men were paid an additional sum – this time £14 13s 4d – in view of the expenses they had incurred for their mathematical instruments.[25] Still another man who was later to become head of a house was William Beale (M.A. 1613, Jesus College), the mathematical lecturer in 1615–16. Elected Master of Jesus College in 1632, two years later he exchanged this mastership with the mastership of St John's College, where he remained until 1642.[26]

During the 1640s three Cambridge Platonists – all of whom came up to Emmanuel College during the previous decade – served as mathematical lecturers. The first was Ralph Cudworth (M.A. 1639) who held the office in 1641–2, by which time he was clearly conversant in the most recent astronomical and philosophical discoveries. An examination of the sale catalogue of Cudworth's library confirms the breadth of his reading. Of the approximately 2500 volumes, about a third consist of mathematical, medical and philosophical books, including almost complete runs of works by Brahe, Kepler, Descartes, Gassendi, Bacon and Boyle as well as additional works by Lansberg, Briggs, Mydorg, Boulliau, Harriot, Harvey, Torricelli, Wallis, Spinoza and Newton.[27] Two years later Nathaniel

[21] Venn, *Biographical History of Gonville and Caius College*, vol. 1, p. 122; CUA Univ. Acct. 2(1), fol. 348.

[22] CUA Univ. Acct. 2(1), fols. 251, 259, 262, 266; Cooper, *Athenae Cantabrigienses*, vol. 2, p. 492; B. P. Levack, *The Civil Lawyers in England 1603–1641* (Oxford, 1973), p. 373.

[23] CUA Univ. Acct. 2(1), fol. 433; *DNB*; Hartlib, 'Ephemerides', entries for 1634–40.

[24] CUA Univ. Acct. 2(1), fol. 661. Rant's manuscripts are in CUL MSS Ii.i.1, 15, 16; MS Ii.iii.17. Venn, *Biographical History of Gonville and Caius College*, vol. 1, p. 276.

[25] CUA Univ. Acct. 2(1), fol. 325. For Gooch, see Venn, *Alumni Cantabrigienses*, vol. 2, p. 231. For Alabaster, see *The Sonnets of William Alabaster*, ed. G. M. Story and H. Gardner (Oxford, 1959). See also p. 92 below.

[26] CUA Univ. Acct. 1(3), 'Vouchers for the Accounts 1615–16', fol. 11. For Beale, see *DNB*.

[27] CUA Univ. Acct. 2(1), fol. 694; *DNB*; E. Millington, *Bibliotheca Cudworthiana* (London, 1691); J. A. Passmore, *Ralph Cudworth, An Interpretation* (Cambridge, 1951); L. Gysi, *Platonism and Cartesianism in the Philosophy of Ralph Cudworth* (Bern, 1962).

Culverwell (M.A. 1640) was elected lecturer. Little is known about Culverwell's activities during this period. However, he was probably already engaged in the composition of *An Elegant and Learned Discourse of the Light of Nature*. Completed in 1646 but published only posthumously in 1652, the discourse displays Culverwell's familiarity with the recent astronomical and physical discoveries of Bacon, Descartes, Galileo and Digby.[28] Another gifted Platonist who developed his mathematical skills at Emmanuel College was John Smith (B.A. 1640, M.A. 1644). In Smith's case we know for a fact that Benjamin Whichcote served as his tutor. Like Wallis, Smith had no hope of attaining a fellowship at Emmanuel (the statutes limited the number of fellows from each county to two and the relevant fellowships were already filled), and in 1644 the two migrated to Queens' College. Smith was made mathematical lecturer in his new college that year and University lecturer three years later. We are fortunate to possess a catalogue of Smith's library – containing some 600 volumes – which was bequeathed to Queens' College following his untimely death in 1652. A large proportion of the library consisted of mathematical and astronomical books, including almost complete runs of the works of Galileo, Kepler, Descartes and Gassendi.[29]

Certain college lecturers gained sufficient repute by their lectures to advance their fortunes. Peter Heylin's lectures in cosmography at Magdalen College, Oxford, during every long vacation of his M.A. studies from 1617 until 1619 brought him a fellowship at that college,[30] while William Wilkinson's lectures at St John's College, Cambridge, brought him the recommendation of Robert Bennett to Lord Burghley, who in 1582 was in need of a tutor for his son. In his recommendation Bennett described Wilkinson as one who had a 'good sight in the mathematical sciences, especially cosmography, where he hath read in the House'.[31] Wilkinson eventually served in the capacity of chaplain to Burghley. In addition to

---

[28] CUA Univ. Acct. 2(1), fol. 710; N. Culverwell, *An Elegant and Learned Discourse of the Light of Nature*, ed. R. A. Greene and H. MacCallum (Toronto, 1971).

[29] J. E. Saveson, 'Some Aspects of the Thought and Style of John Smith, the Cambridge Platonist' (Cambridge Univ. Ph.D. thesis, 1955); idem, 'Descartes' influence on John Smith, Cambridge Platonist', *Journ. Hist. Ideas*, xx (1959), 258–63; idem, 'The library of John Smith, the Cambridge Platonist', *Notes & Queries*, cciii (1958), 215–16; CUL MS Dd.ix.44 contains historical and cosmographical notes by Smith. M. Micheletti, *Il Pensiero Religioso di John Smith Platonico di Cambridge* (Padua, 1976); Rigaud, *Correspondence of Scientific Men*, vol. 2, pp. 475–9.

[30] Among the authorities cited by Heylin are Keckermann, Magirus, Frigius, Maginus, Ortelius, Mercator, Blundeville as well as Bacon's *Advancement of Learning*. For Heylin, see G. Vernon, *Life of the Learned and Reverend Dr. Peter Heylin* (London, 1682); J. Barnard, *Theologo-Historicus or the True Life of the most Reverend Divine, and Excellent Historian Peter Heylin* (London, 1683). Heylin's autobiographical fragments were prefaced to his *Memorial of Bishop Waynflete*, ed. J. R. Bloxam (London, 1851), pp. x–xxiv; Wood, *Athenae Oxonienses*, vol. 3, pp. 552–68; DNB.

[31] *Hist. MSS Comm.*, *Salisbury MSS*, vol. 2, p. 524: R. Bennett to Lord Burghley, 8 Oct. 1582.

Henry Briggs, mathematical lecturers at St John's College, Cambridge, included William Gilbert (M.A. 1564) who served as mathematical examiner in 1565 and 1566; Thomas Randall (M.A. 1565) who was lecturer in 1567 and took his M.D. in 1577, becoming a fellow of the College of Physicians of London in 1584; and William Holland (M.A. 1583), who was mathematical examiner in 1588 and a fellow from 1584 until 1608. With the exception of Gilbert, nothing is known of the scientific interests of these lecturers.[32]

To conclude, then, although too little is known of the identity of the various mathematical lecturers and the content of their lectures to make sweeping generalizations, the little we do know suggests that many of these men manifested more than cursory interest in the mathematical sciences.

Despite the ever-increasing trend from early in the sixteenth century to effect a greater professionalization in the teaching system in the form of endowed lectureships and specialization of subject, the tutor was still expected to instruct his pupils in the entire range of curricular subjects. The tutorial system – which some historians date to the late medieval period of university history – expanded rapidly during the sixteenth century until it came to exercise the highest degree of influence over every sector of student life. Curtis has summed up this influence in the following way: 'The work of the college tutors rather than the reading of the college lectures was probably in the sixteenth century and was definitely in the seventeenth century the most important influence on a scholar's education.'[33] As a fellow of the same college, the tutor not only supervised his pupil's studies, but was originally responsible for his admission to the university, kept a vigilant eye on his expenses and social behaviour and, in cases in which the student was of noble or wealthy parentage, reported to his family at regular intervals. Given this role played by tutors in the education of youth, it is essential to determine the nature and quality of instruction they might have provided to their charges.

While the quality of a university or college lecturer can be determined almost solely on the basis of his competence in handling a particular subject, the quality of a college tutor varies to some extent with the ability, determination and social position of his student. If we are to correctly assess the image of the tutor as it has been passed down to us, we must always bear in mind the reciprocal nature of this relationship. If no allowance is made for the variability and flexibility in this relationship, then many tutors might be unjustifiably judged lax in carrying out their responsibilities. For this same reason a certain discretion must be exercised

[32] Cooper, *Athenae Cantabrigienses*, vol. 2, pp. 553, 356–8 for Gilbert; vol. 2. pp. 203 and 548 for Randall; and vol. 2, p. 473 for Holland.
[33] Curtis, *Oxford and Cambridge in Transition*, p. 107.

when reading contemporary accounts of tutors. Often a close examination of a slanderous account of a particular tutor reveals that the author, often a former pupil, was biased by dissenting religious opinions, a natural antipathy, or the need to justify his own negligence or incompetence. This is not to deny the presence of some negligent tutors within the universities, but only to emphasize that the close, sometimes even intense, nature of the relationship often nurtured a very personal assessment. Moreover, it should be remembered that the position of a tutor was greatly determined by his reputation; the more the tutor was esteemed by former students, the more likely it was that new students, and wealthy students especially, would be entrusted by parents to his care.

Heads of colleges or halls should be considered chief among tutors, and their importance cannot be overstressed. Not only did they provide the ultimate authority in the colleges regarding all matters of lectures, exercises and examinations but, according to the statutes, they were the only tutors allowed to supervise more than four or five students at a time. They were further entrusted with the education of students from the more distinguished families and proved the natural patrons for poor, but promising, youths. Indeed, many preferments to scholarships and fellowships can be attributed to the patronage of heads of college. Such being the case, it is instructive to establish the views of many heads of house towards mathematics and scientific enterprise.

Mention has already been made of two Oxford heads of house who established mathematical lectureships in their respective colleges. As autocratic warden of Merton College for thirty-six years (1585–1621), Sir Henry Savile not only established his arithmetic lectureship, but was responsible for attracting many of the most promising youths to Merton as well as enlarging the college library and furnishing it with many mathematical and astronomical works.[34] Although Arthur Lake served for only four years as Warden of New College (1613–17), his foundation of the mathematical lectureship coincided with the election of a most worthy successor, Robert Pink (M.A. 1601, B.Med. 1612, New College), who served from 1617 until 1647. Pink's scientific propensity is revealed in his correspondence with the mathematician Thomas Lydiat to whom he served as patron. He was also instrumental in raising funds to pay off Lydiat's debts and effect his release from prison, and on a more

[34] Wood, *Athenae Oxonienses*, vol. 2, pp. 310–16; J. M. Fletcher (ed.), *Registrum Annalium Collegii Mertonensis, 1567–1603*, Oxf. Hist. Soc., New Ser., vol. 24 (Oxford, 1976), *passim*; H. W. Garrod, 'Sir Henry Savile: 1549–1949', *The Study of Good Letters*, ed. J. Jones (Oxford, 1963), pp. 101, 119; J. R. L. Highfield, 'An autograph manuscript commonplace book of Sir Henry Savile', *Bodl. Lib. Rec.*, VII (1963), 73–83. See also ch. IV, pp. 124–30.

professional level he transcribed manuscripts for Lydiat's use. Pink was also an early patron of Isaac Barrow as well as a close associate of both John Bainbridge and James Ussher, and from the Bainbridge and Ussher correspondence it appears that at times their meetings were devoted to discussions of a scientific nature.[35] The long presidency of Nicholas Bond (1589–1618) of Magdalen College witnessed his decree that all bachelors lecture on cosmography and geography during the long vacation. Bond (B.A. 1563/64, St John's College, Cambridge, M.A. 1574, Magdalen College, Oxford) left additional evidence of his scientific interests. An inventory of his household includes two globes as well as various mathematical instruments valued at 40s.[36]

From 1613 until 1620 Jesus College, Oxford, had for its Principal Griffith Powell (M.A. 1589, Jesus College), who had been an important figure in the college for the previous twenty years or so. His treatise on logic – *Analysis analyticorum posteriorum sive librorum Aristotelis de demonstratione* (Oxford, 1594) – was based on Zabarella but laid greater emphasis upon geometry as the appropriate tool for approaching the subject.[37] William Laud (M.A. 1598, St John's College, Oxford) was not only a benefactor of the mathematics library at St John's, but just before his rise in the Church he served as President of the college for ten years (1611–21). Laud's correspondence with his former college includes many references to the mathematics library, and on one occasion he states his intention of encouraging the 'younger Fellows and students there to give themselves more to those studies [mathematics] than they have formerly done'. Laud also served as patron to many men of science, including John Greaves, Peter Turner and Brian Twyne.[38]

William Juxon (B.C.L. 1603, St John's College, Oxford) succeeded William Laud as President of St John's and, like his predecessor, patronized scientific activity. In fact, Juxon, who served as President for twelve years (1621–33), appears to have been even more committed to scientific endeavours than Laud. In 1635 Hartlib recorded in his diary that Juxon, by then Bishop of London, 'hase great delight to all experimental

---

[35] *DNB*; Pink's correspondence with Lydiat is found in Bodl. MS Bodley 313; H. Rashdall and R. S. Rait, *New College* (London, 1901), pp. 146–69.

[36] Cooper, *Athenae Cantabrigienses*, vol. 2, pp. 466–7; Macray, *Register of Magdalen College Oxford*, vol. 2, p. 180.

[37] Wood, *Athenae Oxonienses*, vol. 2, p. 283. For a discussion of the *Analysis*, see C. B. Schmitt, *John Case* (forthcoming).

[38] *The Works of the most Reverend Father in God William Laud D.D. sometime Lord Archbishop of Canterbury*, ed. W. Scott and J. Bliss (Oxford, 1847–60), vol. 7, p. 192: W. Laud to the President and Fellows of St John's College, 16 Oct. 1635; Macray, *Annals of the Bodleian Library*, pp. 83–8; Fuggles, 'A History of the Library of S. John's College, Oxford', p. 135; H. R. Trevor-Roper, *Archbishop Laud*, 2nd edn (London, 1965); I. Adamson, 'The Foundation and Early History of Gresham College, London 1596–1704' (Cambridge Univ. Ph.D. thesis, 1975), p. 135.

philosophy and mathematical–mechanical inventions ... Hee commended highly a colledge for inventions.' Two years later, Juxon wrote to the committee of Gresham College in support of John Greaves's proposed astronomical expedition to the Near East: 'This worke I find by the best astronomers, especially by Ticho Brache and Kepler, hath bynn much desired as tending to the advancement of that science, and I hope it will be an honour to that nation and prove ours if we first observe it.'[39]

Thomas Clayton (B.A. 1594, Balliol College, M.A. 1599, M.D. 1611, Gloucester Hall), Gresham Professor of Music 1607–10, Regius Professor of Medicine 1611–49 and Principal of Broadgates Hall 1620–4, became the first Master of Pembroke College when the latter institution replaced Broadgates in 1624. His mastership, a post he retained until 1649, witnessed the establishment of Pembroke College as a centre for the medical and natural sciences. Thomas Browne, Thomas Lushington, George Jollife and John Wyberd were numbered among his students. In 1633 another of Clayton's students, Edward Dawson, was the first at Oxford to defend Harvey's circulation of the blood. Clayton was also a friend of the mathematicians Thomas Allen, John Bainbridge and Henry Briggs as well as a contributor to Hakewill's *Apologie*.[40]

From his early days at Balliol College where he proceeded M.A. in 1585, George Abbot – Master of University College, Oxford, from 1597 until 1610 – was known to be an avid geographer and he composed *A Briefe Description of the Whole World* (1599) for the use of his pupils. Abbot also had been acquainted with John Dee from at least as far back as 1594 and during his later career as Bishop of London and Archbishop of Canterbury, he served as patron to a new generation of geographers and mathematicians including Samuel Purchas and John Greaves. His scientific inclinations are also evident from the numerous astronomical and geographical books he bequeathed to the Lambeth Palace Library.[41] Another noted geographer was John Prideaux, Rector of Exeter College from 1612 until 1642. As one of the more eminent and successful

[39] *DNB*; Hartlib, 'Ephemerides 1635', D–EIO; PRO T.56/13, fol. 2v quoted by Tyacke, 'Science and religion at Oxford before the Civil War', p. 84.

[40] J. Ward, *The Lives of the Professors of Gresham College* (London, 1740), pp. 208–11; Webster, *The Great Instauration*, pp. 125–6, 128; F. L. Huntley, *Sir Thomas Browne: A Biographical and Critical Study* (Ann Arbor, 1968), pp. 40–3.

[41] By 1636 the *Description* had gone through nine editions. E. G. R. Taylor, *Late Tudor and Early Stuart Geography 1583–1650* (London, 1934), pp. 37, 55, 213; E. W. Gilbert, *British Pioneers in Geography* (Newton Abbot, 1972), pp. 43–5; *The Private Diary of Dr John Dee and the Catalogue of his Library of Manuscripts*, ed. J. O. Halliwell, Camden Soc., vol. 19 (London, 1842), p. 49; Adamson, 'The Foundation and Early History of Gresham College', p. 135; G. Bill, 'Lambeth Palace Library', *The Library*, 5th Ser., XXI (1966), 192–206; P. A. Welsby, *George Abbot. The Unwanted Archbishop, 1562–1633* (London, 1962); A. Cox-Johnson, 'Lambeth Palace Library 1610–1669', *Trans. Camb. Bibl. Soc.*, II (1955), 105–26.

seventeenth-century tutors, Prideaux (M.A. 1601, Exeter College) brought Exeter College to unprecedented fame and imbued many of its students with his keen geographical interest. Prideaux was a close friend of the famous geographer Philip Cluvier who, owing to the Rector's prodding, came to Exeter College in 1619. Prideaux also acted as tutor to Cluvier's son who eventually became a geographer as well. Another foreign geographer trained by Prideaux was James d'Orville who, together with his brother Frederick, had been entrusted to Prideaux. Walter Charleton, while a student at Magdalen Hall, Oxford, under the supervision of John Wilkins, is said to have had Prideaux as his mentor. Wood also relates that Prideaux had a large share in the compilation of *A Geographicall and Anthologicall Description of all the Empires and Kingdomes, both of Continents and Islands in this Terrestriall Globe, etc.* (1608) by Robert Stafford who, it appears, had been his pupil for a few years beginning in 1604.[42]

John Rainolds (M.A. 1572), President of Corpus Christi College from 1598 until 1607, is remembered chiefly as the leader of the moderate Elizabethan Puritans. However, Rainolds was one of the foremost intellectuals of the sixteenth century whose wide range of knowledge included scientific and occult studies. Already as a young bachelor, he delivered an oration 'In Praise of Astronomy' as part of his M.A. exercises. Apart from legitimizing the study of astronomy, the oration – which is remarkable for its deeply Platonic and Hermetic character – indicates Rainolds's close familiarity with the 'occult tradition'. A study of the surviving catalogue of Rainolds's magnificent library – which included some 2500 volumes – reinforces his breadth of knowledge. Included are the occult texts of Plato, Plotinus, Lucretius, Hermes Trismegistus, Ficino, Reuchlin, Trithemius, Agrippa and della Porta as well as the works of Sextus Empiricus, Nicholas of Cusa and Telesio. Among the scientific authors we find Gemma Frisius, Dasypodius, Peucer, Clavius, Ramus, Praetorius, Apian, Mercator, Ortelius, Magini, Lydiat, Hakluyt, Euclid, Archimedes, Vitruvius, Agricola, Vesalius, Valverde, Columbus, Aldrovandus, Fernel, Fuchs, Gesner, Paracelsus, Libavius as well as Francis Bacon's *Advancement of Learning* published two years before Rainolds's death.[43]

Thomas Jackson (M.A. 1603), who served as President of Corpus Christi College from 1630 until 1640, was Rainolds's friend and disciple as well

---

[42] Boase, *Registrum*, pp. 89–90, 95; *DNB*; Taylor, *Late Tudor and Early Stuart Geography*, p. 136; L. Sharp, 'Walter Charleton's early life, 1620–1659, and relationship to natural philosophy in mid-seventeenth century England', *Annals of Science*, xxx (1973), 314; Wood, *Athenae Oxonienses*, vol. 2, p. 291.

[43] *DNB*; Queen's College Oxford MS 241, fols. 151–5; Bodl. MS Wood D.10. For a biographical study of Rainolds together with an edition of his library catalogue, see M. Feingold, *An Elizabethan Intellectual: John Rainolds, the Man and his Books*, Oxford Bibl. Soc., occasional publications (forthcoming).

as the executor of his will. He also shared Rainolds's interest in the mathematical and occult sciences. 'The ornament of the university in his time' – as Wood termed him – by the time he was elected a fellow of Corpus Christi College in 1606, he had already 'laid the grounds carefully in arithmetic, grammar, philology, geometry, rhetoric, logic, philosophy, Oriental languages, histories &c'. Jackson's writings suggest the strong influence of Neoplatonism and the 'ancient theology', both of which undoubtedly contributed to his frequently expressed disdain for Aristotelianism and scholasticism.[44]

Another head of hall with mathematical interests was John Budden (M.A. 1589, Trinity College), Principal of New Inn Hall from 1609 until 1618, and Broadgates Hall from 1618 until 1620. Having begun his career as a student of Thomas Allen, in 1597 Budden was an unsuccessful candidate for both the newly founded astronomy and geometry professorships at Gresham College. Instead he continued on in the faculty of civil law where he received his D.C.L. in 1602. Budden retained his interest in science, however, and was appointed reader of philosophy in Magdalen College (c. 1601–7), despite the fact he had never been a fellow of that college.[45]

Among the Cambridge heads of college mention should be made of Andrew Perne, Master of Peterhouse from 1554 until 1580 who, judging from the collection of astronomical instruments and maps he bequeathed to his college library, was a keen mathematician and astronomer.[46] Pembroke College had in succession two masters interested in science. In 1578 William Fulke (M.A. 1563, St John's College) was elected Master. Earlier in his life, Fulke, in defiance of his father who had wished him to embark upon a career in law, pursued first mathematics and then divinity, and his first publications included astrological and astronomical tracts as well as tracts on mathematical games. There is an anecdote that while still a fellow at St John's, Fulke was accused of keeping 'in his chamber conies, dogs, rats, birds, virginals: and useth to go a birding with his boys'.[47] Lancelot Andrewes (M.A. 1578 and a fellow from 1576)

[44] Wood, *Athenae Oxonienses*, vol. 3, pp. 664–70; *DNB*; S. Hutton, 'Thomas Jackson, Oxford Platonist and William Twisse, Aristotelian', *Journ. Hist. Ideas*, XXXIX (1978), 635–52.

[45] Wood, *Athenae Oxonienses*, vol. 2, pp. 282–3; Clark, *Register*, vol. 2, part 1, p. 233; *DNB*; Levack, *Civil Lawyers in England*, p. 214.

[46] Perne's instruments included astrolabes, quadrants, globes and dials. Among the books in the library, we find Euclid, Gemma Frisius, Ortelius, Mercator, Peurbach, Finé, Peucer, Digges and Copernicus. I am grateful to Dr S. E. Leedham-Green, Assistant Keeper of the University Archives, for allowing me to consult her transcript of Perne's inventory as well as other inventories in the Cambridge University Library. For Perne, see Cooper, *Athenae Cantabrigienses*, vol. 2, pp. 45–7; *DNB*.

[47] Quoted in H. C. Porter, *Reformation and Reaction in Tudor Cambridge* (Cambridge, 1958), p. 128. For a recent study of Fulke, see R. Bauckham, 'The Career and Thought of Dr William Fulke 1537–89' (Cambridge Univ. Ph.D. thesis, 1973); idem, 'Science and religion in the writings of Dr William Fulke', *Brit. Journ. Hist. Science*, VIII (1975), 17–31.

assumed the mastership of Pembroke College upon the death of Fulke in
1589 and relinquished the position in 1605 when he was elevated to the
bishopric of Chichester. Andrewes was singled out for praise by Francis
Bacon, who regarded him as a potential supporter of the Great Instauration.
Indeed, in 1606 Bacon wrote to Tobie Matthew to whom he had forwarded
a copy of the *Advancement of Learning*, insisting that Matthew had 'more
right to it than any man, except Bishop Andrewes, who was [his]
inquisitor'. A partial reconstruction of Andrewes's library – which
included the works of Mercator, Hakluyt, Agricola, Schoener, Copernicus
and Gilbert – confirms his scientific inclinations.[48]

Samuel Ward (M.A. 1596, Christ's College), Master of Sidney Sussex
College from 1610 until 1643, had proved himself of a mathematical cast
of mind ever since his student days. The diary he kept indicates his interest
in the mathematical sciences and botany as well as his association with
Henry Briggs and other scientifically oriented members of the college and
university. Some time before his election to a fellowship in Emmanuel
College in 1596, he had contemplated accepting the university mathematical lectureship.[49] Samuel Collins, a fellow of King's College from 1595
until 1615 and Provost from 1615 until 1644, also seems to have been
receptive to scientific ideas. William Rawley recounted that Collins, 'A Man
of no vulgar Wit ... affirmed unto [him]; That when he had read, the Book
of the Advancement of Learning; He found Himself in a case, to begin
his Studies anew; and that he had lost, all the Time, of his Studying before'.
A further indication of Collins's scientific curiosity was his request to Sir
William Boswell to acquaint him with his opinion of Campanella's defence
of Galileo, a request which was recorded only because of Boswell's reply.[50]

In 1616/17 Edward Martin (M.A. 1612) was elected a fellow of Queens'
College as well as the college lecturer in geometry, an appointment he held
until 1621. For the year 1623–4 Martin was mathematical examiner and
from 1631 until 1643 he served as President. Martin's mathematical bent

[48] Bacon, *Works*, vol. 10, p. 256, vol. 11, pp. 23, 141; H. Isaacson, *An Exact Narration
of the Life and Death of the Reverend and Learned Prelate, and most Painfull Divine Lancelot
Andrewes late Bishop of Winchester* (London, 1650); D. D. C. Chambers, 'A catalogue
of the library of Bishop Lancelot Andrewes 1555–1626', *Trans. Camb. Bibl. Soc.*, v
(1969–71), 99–121. Andrewes donated the Copernicus volume to Pembroke College
upon his election as Master in 1598.

[49] M. M. Knappen (ed.), *Two Elizabethan Puritan Diaries by Richard Rogers and Samuel Ward*
(Chicago, 1933), pp. 107, 112, 128 for entries for 11 June 1595, 19 Feb. 1595/96 and
Jan. 1597/98, respectively. For other references, see entries for 17 May 1595 (pp. 103–4);
2 June 1595 (p. 106); 6 Nov. 1595 (p. 111); 28 July 1596 (p. 113); 21 Aug. 1596
(p. 114); 3 April 1614 (p. 131). For Ward, see *DNB*.

[50] F. Bacon, *Resuscitatio, or, Bringing into Publick Light Severall Pieces, of the Works, Civil,
Historical, Philosophical, & Theological, hitherto Sleeping*, ed. W. Rawley (London, 1657),
'The Life of the Author', King's College Cambridge, 'Provost's Letter Book', vol. 4, fols.
63–4. All four volumes contain the correspondence of Collins relating mainly to college
business. See also *DNB*.

was described by Lloyd in the following way: 'his parts, as his nature, inclining to Solidity, rather than Politeness; he was for the exact Sciences, Logick and Mathematics in his Study, as he was for strict Rules in his Conversation'.[51] John Gostlin, Master of Gonville and Caius College from 1619 until 1626, was a popular Regius Professor of Medicine as well as a student of astronomy, whose short treatise on comets, now lost, was dedicated to James I.[52] From 1622 until 1628 Emmanuel College was under the mastership of John Preston (M.A. 1611) who is known to have displayed interest in the sciences before he committed himself to theology. His biographer describes his diligent pursuit of botany, philosophy, astrology and medicine and even goes so far as to suggest that his reputation in medicine was comparable to that of the famous physician and alchemist, William Butler of Clare College.[53]

Given this position of heads of colleges and halls as cornerstones of their institutions, the fact that a significant number were associated with scientific enterprise no doubt influenced the quality of scientific instruction in their respective institutions. With some degree of certainty it can be claimed that they encouraged mathematical instruction both for students in general and for those keen and gifted students to whom they served as tutors and patrons.

It is not surprising that much of the evidence at our disposal for evaluating the nature and quality of mathematical instruction in the universities portrays the association of tutors with the upper classes. Not only were the tutors for gentlemen in continual correspondence with the respective families – reporting on behaviour and progress in studies – but such correspondence was more likely to survive. Equally important, as a modicum of scientific knowledge was usually deemed beneficial to a young gentleman's education, the nature of mathematical instruction is often made evident in the surviving correspondence.

Often tutors for the upper classes evolved a more personal relationship with their charges and, like private tutors, extended their tuition beyond term or, indeed, even beyond the walls of the university, travelling long

---

[51] Searle, *Queens' College*, p. 465; D. Lloyd, *Memoires of the Lives, Actions, Sufferings & Deaths of those Noble, Revered and Excellent Personages, that Suffered by Death, Sequestration, Decimation, or otherwise, for the Protestant Religion and the Great Principle thereof, Allegiance to their Soveraigne, in our late Intestine Wars from the year 1637, to the year 1660* (London, 1668), p. 461.

[52] Venn, *Biographical History of Gonville and Caius College*, vol. 3, pp. 74–85; idem, 'Dr Gostlin', *The Caian*, III (1894), 86–92.

[53] T. Ball, *Life of the Renowned Doctor Preston Writ by his Pupil Master Thomas Ball in the year 1628*, ed. E. W. Harcourt (Oxford and London, 1885). Preston was similarly credited by George Atwell with being 'the best skild in Astrology of all that ever wrote against it'. G. Atwell, *An Apology, or, Defence of the Divine Art of Natural Astrologie* (London, 1660), p. 42.

distances to the student's own residence. The following letter, written by John Crowther, a tutor at Magdalen Hall, Oxford, to Ralph Verney, his student for two years (1631–2), on 6 November 1631 indicates that Verney was being instructed in astronomy:

I have sent you the astronomy notes, which I have now brought to a perfect and compleate head, save only one sheete containing the differences and computes of time, which I had not time to finish. Had not I watched it late at night, I could hardly have despatched these. But You shall receive it also, with my intended method, as soon as possible I may. I have made it as yet my only studdy, at those times I am vacant from reading to schollers, and will not (God willing) take any other thing in hand till I have finished it. In the interim, I shall desire your paines in the reading of what you have already. I desire, till you heare againe from me, that you only studdy your logicke and astronomy notes.

Five weeks later, on 18 December, Crowther once again addresses his charge, this time concerning his intention of instructing him in geography. Most interestingly, this letter also provides a glimpse into the nature of the relationship between tutor and student.

There's one maine thing especially, and which I know You'le account most necessary and willingly embrace, which I have not as yet initiated you in, *scilicet*, the grounds of geography. When your strangers are gone, if you cannot have the leisure to come over hither, send but me word, and I'le attend you for a weeke or soe at Claydon till I have shewed you the principall grounds in that science, and shewed you by my former directions how you may make further progresse yourselfe.[54]

The evolution of a relationship in which the tutor became both instructor and friend is also apparent in the tutorship of Justinian Isham of Christ's College, Cambridge (1627–8), by the eminent tutor Joseph Mede. Mede nurtured Isham's scientific inclinations while he was a student and soon became a friend who was entertained 'rather overwhelmingly' at the family residence. Isham's more elaborate mathematical reading is made apparent by the fact that he was the only one of Mede's students to have purchased Leonard Digges's *A geometrical practise named pantometria* (London, 1571, 1591).[55] The sons of Sir John Eliot, John and Richard, who matriculated at Lincoln College, Oxford, in 1629, were contemporaries of

[54] *The Verney Papers*, ed. J. Bruce, Camden Soc., 1st Ser., vol. 56 (London, 1853), pp. 150–1. John Crowther was probably that member of Magdalen Hall who matriculated in 1581, aged 17, and remained there for over fifty years until he was presented with a living by the Verney family in 1634. See F. P. Verney, *Memoirs of the Verney Family during The Civil War* (London, 1892), vol. 1, pp. 117–22, 143–5.

[55] Christ's College Cambridge, 'Account Books of Joseph Mede', vol. 3, fol. 90v. For Isham's life and intellectual milieu, see *The Correspondence of Bishop Brian Duppa and Sir Justinian Isham, 1650–1660*, ed. G. Isham, Northamptonshire Rec. Soc., vol. 17 (Lamport Hall, Northamptonshire, 1955). The story of Mede appears on p. xxxiii. For Mede's scientific interests see *The Works of the Pious and Profoundly Learned Joseph Mede*, ed. J. Worthington (London, 1677). See pp. 96–8 below.

Verney who also experienced a particularly close bond with their tutor, one Thomas Knightley. Although it is apparent that Knightley accompanied his charges beyond the university gates, there is little evidence shedding light on the exact nature of his instruction. Nonetheless, it is worthy of note that when the tutor forwarded to Sir John the final bill for his sons' education at Oxford, the following item is specified: 'Item Introduction to Astronomie left unpaid to ye bookbinder 3[d]'.[56]

Henry Oxinden was another gentleman who appears to have received mathematical instruction during his stay at university, although no trace of this instruction is apparent in his later career. Oxinden matriculated at Corpus Christi College, Oxford, in 1626 under the tutorship of the mathematician Robert Hegge, but had commenced his studies as early as 1624. Our insight into Oxinden's mathematical instruction derives from a letter addressed to him by James Holt, a fellow of Corpus Christi College, some years later in conjunction with their joint efforts to procure a fellowship for Oxinden's brother, James. On 25 May 1631, Holt wrote: 'I had sent ere this some Mathematicall bookes which you did once affect, could I have had a convenient messenger, but I doubt not but I shall have both leasure and opportunity hereafter to send them to thee.' During his stay at Oxford Oxinden also appears to have forged friendly relations with John Bainbridge, Savilian Professor of Astronomy, for three weeks later Holt advised Oxinden: 'It [would] not be amiss for you to write to Dr. Bambridge [*sic*] to solicite Mr. President [Thomas Jackson] in your Brother's behalfe.'[57] As already noted, Peter Heylin was a tutor and a fellow of Magdalen College, Oxford, from 1618 until 1629, the first two years of which he delivered his successful cosmography lectures. Of the students under his supervision we know only of George Digby, the future 2nd Earl of Bristol, who was admitted to Magdalen College in 1626 and quickly gained Heylin's favour. Inspired by Heylin's scientific enthusiasm, the Earl remained a passionate student of astrology throughout his life.[58]

Occasionally students of noble birth brought along with them their own tutors, as was the case with Robert Dudley, the son of the Earl of Leicester. Instructed for a year or two (*c.* 1588–9) at Christ Church, Oxford, by Sir Thomas Chaloner, an ardent natural philosopher, Dudley was imbued by his tutor with a love of science which distinguished him later in life.[59] In a similar manner Robert Hues (B.A. 1578, Magdalen Hall, Oxford)

[56] J. Forster, *Sir John Eliot: A Biography* (London, 1864), vol. 2, p. 589.
[57] *The Oxinden Letters, 1607–1642*, ed. D. Gardiner (London, 1933), pp. 64–5, 68.
[58] For Digby, see *DNB*.
[59] Wood, *Athenae Oxonienses*, vol. 3, pp. 258–62. For Chaloner, who was a student of Magdalen College, Oxford, but left without a degree, see *DNB*. The most recent biography of Dudley is by A. G. Lee, *The Son of Leicester: The Story of Sir Robert Dudley, Titular Earl of Warwick, Earl of Leicester, and Duke of Northumberland* (London, 1964); see also A. M. Crino, 'Il Duca di Northumbria in Toscana', *English Miscellany*, XXVIII–XXIX (1979–80), 19–59.

followed Algernon Percy, the son of his patron, Henry Percy, 9th Earl of Northumberland, to university where for two years he instructed him in mathematics and cosmography.[60]

Correspondence between tutors and students or their parents was rarely a one-way affair and the instructions penned by concerned fathers often illuminate the course of studies pursued by their sons. On 27 August 1646 Francis Gardiner wrote to William Sancroft, tutor at Emmanuel College, Cambridge, communicating the course of study he wished his son to pursue. He desired to have him diligent in logic, philosophy, Greek, Hebrew and French, and of course theological studies, adding that: 'For his geometry and arithmetic, his fancy tending that way, may happily cause him to spend some hours in those studies, (I would not have any trifled away.)'[61] Another father, voicing his concern to Sancroft's friend, Richard Holdsworth – President of Emmanuel College – asserts that he did not wish his son to be a great scholar but only to acquire such gentlemanlike accomplishments as the study of the globe. Holdsworth is certain that Sancroft was most capable of performing this task.[62] In the first chapter I mentioned that the curriculum followed by members of the upper classes – especially as regards scientific instruction – differed somewhat from that followed by the ordinary student, generally because of the brevity of their stay in university, but also because of the different roles that most were to assume later in life. Indeed, chapter VI will be devoted in part to an examination of the ways in which the education of the upper classes deviated from that of the majority of students. At this time I merely wish to emphasize that scientific instruction was not limited to members of the upper classes and there are numerous examples worth citing of tutors who instructed their charges in the various mathematical disciplines. Thomas Lushington (M.A. 1618, Lincoln College), tutor in Broadgates Hall – later Pembroke College – from 1619 until 1631, is remembered chiefly because he served in that capacity to Sir Thomas Browne. Both an amateur mathematician and a Neoplatonic divine, Lushington continued to exert a strong influence over his pupil even after the latter received his medical

---

[60] Confusion surrounds the university career of young Percy. He matriculated at St John's College, Cambridge, in Easter 1615, entered the Middle Temple in August of that year and proceeded M.A. at Cambridge in 1616; by July 1617 he had subscribed at Christ Church, Oxford. Venn, *Alumni Cantabrigienses*, vol. 3, p. 346. For Hues, see Wood, *Athenae Oxonienses*, vol. 2, pp. 534–5; Taylor, *Mathematical Practitioners*, p. 178.

[61] H. Cary (ed.), *Memorials of the Great Civil War in England from 1646 to 1652* (London, 1842), vol. 1, p. 152. Thomas Gardiner matriculated in July 1646 and left two years later for Gray's Inn. Venn, *Alumni Cantabrigienses*, vol. 2, p. 194.

[62] Cary, *Memorials*, vol. 1, p. 14: R. Holdsworth to W. Sancroft, 30 April 1646. Holdsworth did not exaggerate Sancroft's qualifications. The catalogue Sancroft compiled of his library while a fellow of Emmanuel College (1642–51) included Scheiner's optics; three works of Bacon; Keckermann's mathematics; Carpenter's *Philosophia libera* and Gilbert's *De Magnete*. Bodl. MS Sancroft 122.

degree abroad. In fact, it was owing to Lushington's prodding that Browne later followed his old tutor and settled in Norwich.[63] Abraham Woodhead (M.A. 1631) was a fellow and a tutor of University College, Oxford, from 1633 until 1648, and among his University students were Thomas Henshaw and Thomas Strode, the latter of whom became a mathematical writer after the Restoration. As for Woodhead, after he had been deprived of his fellowship in University College by the Parliamentary Visitors he was asked by Sir Thomas Aylesbury, the great patron of mathematics, to act as mathematical tutor to George, Duke of Buckingham, and his brother Francis. From late 1648 until 1652 he served in the capacity of private mathematical tutor to Arthur, Lord Capel.[64] Although there is no record of Nathaniel Simpson's students, according to Wood his *Arithmeticae Compendium*, published in 1622, was written purposely for the use of the junior students of Trinity College, Oxford.[65]

The diary of Thomas Crosfield might well afford some insight into the intellectual pursuits of a man who, in many ways, may have typified the average university tutor. The diary begins in 1626 – a year after Crosfield graduated M.A. from Queen's College, Oxford – and continues until 1640, with some additional entries for the 1650s. Although Boas edited selections from Crosfield's diary some fifty years ago, he was more interested in Crosfield's comments upon current political and religious affairs – as well as university politics – than in his intellectual pursuits. For a glimpse into the scope of Crosfield's scientific studies, therefore, we must return to the manuscript.

Although there were no requisites that a fellow continue his studies of the arts curriculum beyond the M.A., Crosfield nonetheless opted to attend lectures. These included not just theological lectures, but lectures in music, history and moral philosophy. For example, in 1626 Crosfield enrolled in the private Arabic lectures initiated by Mathias Pasor. His diary also records his occasional attendance at the medical and anatomical lectures of Thomas Clayton, the lectures in natural philosophy of Edward Lapworth, the astronomy lectures of John Bainbridge and the geometry lectures, first of Henry Briggs and, after 1631, of Peter Turner. Unfortunately, Crosfield's entries are brief, usually telling us little more than the

[63] For Lushington, see Wood, *Athenae Oxonienses*, vol. 3, pp. 526–31; *DNB*; *The Works of Sir Thomas Browne*, ed. G. Keynes (London, 1964), vol. 4, pp. 375–6; Huntley, *Sir Thomas Browne*, pp. 43–5, 251–2. BL MS Sloane 1838 is a short commentary by Lushington on Proclus's theology.

[64] In 1645 Woodhead left for the Continent with some students, including Thomas Radcliff (son of Sir George), Thomas Culpeper and Thomas Strode. Strode matriculated in 1642 and following his return from France retired to his home where he devoted himself to mathematics. See *DNB*; M. Slusser, 'Abraham Woodhead (1607–78): some research notes, chiefly about his writings', *Recusant History*, xv (1981), 406–22.

[65] Wood, *Athenae Oxonienses*, vol. 3, p. 37.

title of the lecture. Even so, we learn that Briggs taught geometry and algebra, Bainbridge lectured on the calendar and Turner lectured on magnetism and electricity.

Also noteworthy in the diary are Crosfield's personal notes drawn from such books as Mercator's *Geography*, Bacon's *Advancement of Learning* and *Natural History*, Magini's *Isagoge Astronomia*, Kepler's *Somnium* and Hakewill's *Apologie* as well as his recorded purchases of a globe, a dial and a pair of compasses. Crosfield's meetings and discussions with scientifically oriented members of the university are also illuminating. Thus we learn that both Briggs and Bainbridge were his friends and that Henry Jacob of Merton College assisted him in his study of Semitic languages. Also recorded is an invitation of 1633 to Crosfield – together with Mr Clayton – by one Mr Wells to attend an evening with a visiting Danish scholar. The discussion on that occasion gravitated towards mathematics, concentrating on Briggs, Longomontanus and Ramus. Two years later we learn of a discussion – or an informal study – of the theories of Lansberg, Hortensius, Copernicus and Fromondus concerning the motion of the earth. Finally, in 1637 Crosfield jotted down certain of his ideas concerning the well-known 'Ancients and Moderns' debate, in the course of which he listed some of the new inventions of the day – including Comenius's pansophic ideas and didactics, the *perpetuum mobile* and the telescope – as well as the recent discoveries in navigation, the new algebra and Galileo's new astronomy.[66]

As regards two Oxford tutors, we possess more than cursory information on the texts they prescribed for their pupils. Although the few extant commentaries prepared by the most successful Queen's College tutor, Richard Crakanthorpe (fellow from 1598 until 1624), for the use of his students adopt the Aristotelian framework of the books to which they refer, they nonetheless contain much up-to-date scientific information. For example, when he discusses Aristotle's *De coelo*, Crakanthorpe narrates in detail some of the more recent astronomical discoveries, including the new star of 1572, the comets of 1577 and 1580 as well as the 1610 telescopic observations of Galileo. The sources consulted by Crakanthorpe are equally illuminating, including as they do Thomas Hood's *The Use of both the Globes* (1592), Digges's *Alae seu scalae mathematicae* (1573), Clavius's *In Ioannis de Sacro Bosco Commentarius* (1581) and Thomas Lydiat's *Praelectio astronomica* (1605) as well as Galileo's *Sidereus Nuncius* (1610) and Kepler's commentary on Galileo's book, *Dissertatio cum nuncio sidereo*.[67]

In the case of Thomas Sixsmith (M.A. 1625) of Brasenose College, only

[66] Queen's College Oxford MS 390, fols. 16–22, 57v, 61v, 65, 175v, 177, 177v. F. S. Boas, *The Diary of Thomas Crosfield* (London, 1935).
[67] Queen's College Oxford MS 196, fols. 118–33; see also MS 224, fols. 130–81v.

the list of books he prescribed for his pupils has survived. As with Crakanthorpe, although the framework of such a list is determined by Aristotle's works, the texts recommended by Sixsmith are diverse. Under the heading *De coelo*, Sixsmith prescribes 'Clavius and other commentators upon Johannes de Sacrobosco' as well as Maestlin's *Epitome astronomiae* (1582). Sixsmith also prescribes 'Fernelius with other Physicians and Anatomists' under the heading 'De Generatione et Corruptione'.[68]

One of the more popular tutors at Cambridge during the first half of the seventeenth century was William Moore (M.A. 1613 and a fellow of Gonville and Caius College from 1613 until 1647). According to his biographer, Moore – who tutored more than 300 students – was 'one of the ablest that ever I met with, not onely in ... Divinity ... and *Chronologie* ... but also in *Anatomy*, *Physic*, *Mathematicks*, and the like. Those who are the most eminent for all these now in *England* being of his education.' One of these eminent students was Charles Scarburgh to whom Moore's biography is dedicated. Robert Wells (admitted to Gonville and Caius in 1641) was another. In 1643 Wells donated to Gonville and Caius College a series of mathematical and astronomical books 'as a token of gratitude, and to encourage mathematical studies'. Moore, in turn, bequeathed to the college a splendid collection of some 135 manuscripts, many of which reflect his interest in astronomy and medicine.[69]

In Magdalen Hall, Oxford, there existed an extraordinary chain of scientifically minded tutors. We have already had occasion to note John Crowther's instruction of Ralph Verney. Mention should also be made of William Pemble (M.A. 1618), a fellow and a successful tutor from 1614 until his death in 1622, aged 31. Apart from the eminence Pemble achieved as a divine, he was also renowned for his interest in science. John Geree (M.A. 1621, Magdalen Hall), a friend of Henry Briggs and possibly a student of Pemble, credited him with gaining eminence 'even in those sublimer speculations of which all are not capable, few search after: For he was expert in the *Mathematicks* both mixt, and pure'. The direction of Pemble's instruction is suggested by his *A Briefe Introduction to Geography* which, like all his works, was published posthumously. Clearly intended as a manual for the use of his students, the text introduces cosmography,

---

[68] Brasenose College Oxford MS 80, unpaginated. Two copies of this 'A direction for my schollers, what boockes to buy' are in this manuscript. Sixsmith also published two of the manuscripts of Edward Brerewood, Gresham Professor of Astronomy, who died in 1614: *Tractatus quidam logici de praedicabilibus, et praedicamentis* (Oxford, 1628) and *Tractatus duo: quorum primus est de meteoris, secundus de oculo* (Oxford, 1631).

[69] Venn, *Biographical History of Gonville and Caius College*, vol. 1, pp. 192–3, 341; T. Smith, *The Life and Death of Mr William Moore, Late Fellow of Caius Colledge, and Keeper of the University Library* (Cambridge, 1660); for a description of his manuscripts, see M. R. James, *A Descriptive Catalogue of the Manuscripts in the Library of Gonville and Caius College* (Cambridge, 1907–8), *passim*. One of Moore's own medical notebooks is in CUL MS Dd.iv.81 and a catalogue of his library is in CUL MS Dd.iv.5.

assuming no previous knowledge on the part of the student. Yet even at this elementary level Pemble includes an impartial account of the reasons for and against the motion of the earth.[70]

A student of Pemble and a successful tutor from 1624 until 1630 was John Tombes who served in this capacity to John Wilkins (M.A. 1634). Wilkins himself acted as a college tutor – to Walter Charleton (M.D. 1643) among others – before leaving Oxford some time between 1638 and 1640. It was during his abode at Magdalen Hall that Wilkins first contracted his life-long friendship with Jonathan Goddard (matriculated 1632) as well as composed all of the scientific works that were to see publication between 1638 and 1648.[71]

Owing perhaps to the fact that many scientists were not at university when they published their work, there seems to exist an impression among historians that Oxford and Cambridge lacked the more celebrated men of science altogether. This is certainly not the case. Although certain mathematically minded men left the universities after obtaining a degree, usually an M.A., many held college fellowships at some time during their careers.[72]

It is often ignored that all of the professors recruited by the newly founded Gresham College in London had been fellows at either Oxford or Cambridge prior to their appointments. When he was elected first Gresham Professor of Geometry, Henry Briggs – one of the most important men in English mathematics in the first quarter of the seventeenth century – had been a fellow of St John's College, Cambridge, for ten years (1587–97), where he had also served as mathematical examiner in 1592. Having gained much repute in London, Briggs surrendered his chair at Gresham College in 1620 and moved to Oxford to become the first Savilian Professor of Geometry.[73] Edward Brerewood had been a member of St Mary's Hall, Oxford, for seven years (1590–7) before serving as Professor of Astronomy

[70] *A Briefe Introduction to Geography* (Oxford, 1630). *The Workes of that Late Learned Minister of God's Holy Word Mr William Pemble*, 4th edn (Oxford, 1659), p. 145. See also Wood, *Athenae Oxonienses*, vol. 2, p. 330; *DNB*.

[71] For Wilkins, see *Biog. Brit.*, vol. 6, pp. 4266–75; B. J. Shapiro, *John Wilkins 1614–1672. An Intellectual Biography* (Berkeley and Los Angeles, 1969); *DSB*. For Charleton, see R. H. Kargon, *Atomism in England from Hariot to Newton* (Oxford, 1966); N. R. Gelbart, 'The intellectual development of Walter Charleton', *Ambix*, XVIII (1971), 140–68; Sharp, 'Walter Charleton's early life', 311–40.

[72] For those men of science that left after taking their B.A. and M.A., see ch. III.

[73] Wood, *Athenae Oxonienses*, vol. 2, pp. 491–2; *Biog. Brit.*, vol. 2, pp. 979–81; Briggs's life by Dr Thomas Smith in *Vitae quorundam eruditissimorum et illustrium virorum* (London, 1707); Ward, *The Lives of the Professors*, pp. 120–9; D. M. Hallowes, 'Henry Briggs, mathematician', *Trans. Halifax Antiq. Soc.* (1962), 79–92; D. W. Waters, *The Art of Navigation in England in Elizabethan and Early Stuart Times*, 2nd edn (Greenwich, 1978), *passim*; Taylor, *Mathematical Practitioners*, *passim*; Adamson, 'The Foundation and Early History of Gresham College', pp. 128–33.

at Gresham College. A general scholar with a retiring nature well suited
to Gresham College, Brerewood published nothing during his life-time, but
his manuscripts in astronomy, logic, theology and linguistics were published
posthumously by his nephew and others. Mersenne, after reading
Brerewood's *Enquiries Touching the Diversities of Languages and Religions*
(London, 1614), recorded the following opinion: 'I believe that whatever
may come from his hand will be excellent.'[74]

Edmund Gunter had been a fellow of Christ Church, Oxford, for thirteen
years (1606–19) prior to his appointment as Gresham Professor of
Astronomy. Having embarked upon his mathematical studies as a student,
by 1607 Gunter had completed his *De Sectore* which, although widely
circulated in manuscript form, was published only in 1623. In 1614
Gunter had been a contender for the Gresham chair of astronomy, but
the position was awarded to his fellow member of Christ Church, Thomas
Williams. Gunter's reputation as a mathematician nevertheless continued
to flourish and when Sir Henry Savile was contemplating his choice for
the first incumbent of the chair of geometry, he arranged a meeting with
Gunter. Gunter's interest in scientific instruments, however, was
considered somewhat excessive by Savile and caused the latter to retract
his earlier choice and opt for a more 'theoretical' mathematician: Henry
Briggs.[75]

Peter Turner (M.A. 1611/12, Merton College), who was appointed
Gresham Professor of Geometry in 1620 following the recommendation
of Briggs and Bainbridge, had been a fellow of Merton College since 1607.
This Gresham appointment, however, did not cause Turner to relinquish
his Merton fellowship and in 1631 he returned to Oxford as Savilian
Professor of Astronomy. Turner failed to leave any publications for
posterity, perhaps for the very reason suggested by Wood; although Turner
authored 'many admirable things, ... being too curious and critical, he
could never finish them according to his mind, and therefore cancell'd
them'. Whatever the reason, only the barest evidence of Turner's

[74] Wood, *Athenae Oxonienses*, vol. 2, pp. 139–41; Ward, *Lives of the Professors*, pp. 74–6;
Adamson, 'The Foundation and Early History of Gresham College', pp. 140–2; H. Brown,
Scientific Organizations in Seventeenth-Century France (1620–1680) (New York, 1934),
pp. 52–3; M. Mersenne to T. Haak, 15 Jan. 1639/40.
[75] Wood, *Athenae Oxonienses*, vol. 2, pp. 405–6; J. Aubrey, *Brief Lives*, ed. A. Clark (Oxford,
1898), vol. 1, p. 276, vol. 2, p. 215; Ward, *Lives of the Professors*, pp. 77–81; Taylor,
Mathematical Practitioners, p. 196, *et passim*; Waters, *The Art of Navigation, passim*;
Adamson, 'The Foundation and Early History of Gresham College', pp. 142–3. Thomas
Williams, Gunter's predecessor (M.A. *c.* 1605, Christ Church), also served as a
mathematics tutor to Prince Henry, for whom he translated the *Sphaera* of Sacrobosco.
See Ward, *Lives of the Professors*, pp. 76–7; Clark, *Register*, vol. 2, part 3, p. 233; 'J.
H. Halliwell Sale Catalogue', MS 23, printed as an appendix to A. N. L. Munby, *The History
and Bibliography of Science in England: The First Phase, 1833–45* (Los Angeles, 1968),
p. 34.

mathematical activities survive. We know that in 1627 Turner transcribed certain Greek musical tracts for John Selden. Our glimpse into Turner's activities while Savilian Professor of Geometry derives only from Thomas Crosfield whose diary entry of 1632 mentions briefly Turner's lecture on the magnetic and electrical theories of the Jesuit Niccolo Cabeo, as propounded in the latter's *Philosophia Magnetica* (1629). Later in the decade we also hear of Turner's controversy with Francis Potter over the mathematical basis of the latter's book, *An Interpretation of the Number 666*, published only in 1642. Tyacke has also suggested that Turner, who was one of the moving forces behind the formulation of the Laudian statutes, was also responsible for the Copernican diagrammatic form of the new university syllabus.[76]

As a result of Turner's influence, his successor to the Gresham professorship was another Mertonian, John Greaves (M.A. 1628) who, like his predecessor, retained his college fellowship together with the chair of geometry in London. A keen astronomer and orientalist who was trained by John Bainbridge, Greaves pursued both disciplines during his long expedition to the Near East between 1637 and 1640. In 1643 Greaves succeeded Bainbridge as Savilian Professor of Astronomy without, however, relinquishing his post at Gresham College.[77]

Additional examples abound of scientists who at some time during their careers had been college fellows. Upon his death in 1616, Richard Forster (M.A. 1567, All Souls College and a fellow until the late 1570s) was termed 'medicinae doctor et nobilis Mathematicus' by William Camden. Indeed, Forster's mathematical, astronomical and astrological skills were highly regarded by many. Already in 1567, the year he proceeded M.A., Forster dedicated an astrological tract, 'Praedictio solaris deliquii quod incidit in annum domini 1567, cuius tamen effectus durobit ad annum domini 1570', to Henry Fitzalan, Earl of Arundel. Two years later he gave Arundel's daughter Jane, Lady Lumley, a 'table of the Right Ascension of about 130 fixed stars' as a new year's gift. By 1575 Forster had become physician to the Earl of Leicester, to whom he also dedicated his only published work, *Ephemerides Meteorographicae* (1575). Forster later became a fellow and eventually the President of the College of Physicians of

[76] Wood, *Athenae Oxonienses*, vol. 2, pp. 306–7; Ward, *Lives of the Professors*, pp. 129–35; Adamson, 'The Foundation and Early History of Gresham College', p. 134; Bodl. MS Selden Supra 108, fols. 180, 228 (summarized in Ward, pp. 134–5); Queen's College Oxford MS 390, fol. 61v; Mede, *Works*, ed. Worthington, pp. 852–9; Tyacke, 'Science and religion at Oxford before the Civil War', p. 89.

[77] T. Smith's life of Greaves in *Vitae quorundam*; T. Birch (ed.), *The Miscellaneous Works of John Greaves* (London, 1737); Ward, *Lives of the Professors*, pp. 135–53; *Biog. Brit.*, vol. 4, pp. 2267–79; Adamson, 'The Foundation and Early History of Gresham College', pp. 134–9; Tyacke, 'Science and Religion at Oxford before the Civil War', pp. 83–4. See pp. 147, 187 below.

London. A close associate of Christopher Heydon and Edward Wright, Forster also corresponded with Christopher Clavius and Johannes Antonius Magini.[78]

Another fellow of All Souls College was Thomas Heth (M.A. 1573 and a fellow from 1567 until c. 1583) who acquired a reputation 'for his admirable skill in astronomical and physical affairs' and included Thomas Allen and John Dee among his admirers. The last record of Heth dates from March 1583 when he published a small tract refuting Richard Harvey's astronomical predictions for the conjunction of Saturn and Jupiter about to take place the following month. Heth's criticism was directed, not against astrology *per se* – of which he himself was a devoted follower – but against the overwhelming mathematical and astronomical ignorance of many astrological practitioners. The careless predictions of these men, argues Heth, reveals them 'to be but ... simple Astrologian[s], not seene at all in the *Theory* of the Planettes, nor well acquainted with *Copernicus* his *Hypotheses*, *Reinholts* observations, or *Peurbachius*'. In addition to these authorities Heth also cites Maestlin, Stadius, Gemma Frisius and the Alphonsian tables.[79]

Among Oxford men note can also be made of Charles Turnbull (M.A. 1581 and a fellow of Corpus Christi College from 1579) who practised medicine in Oxford until his death in 1605; it is unclear, however, whether he retained his fellowship at Oxford for the entire period. Turnbull had a reputation as an extremely competent mathematician and astronomer, which was boosted by his publication of *A Perfect and Very Easy Treatise of the Use of the Celestiall Globe* in 1585 and his construction of dials for his college.[80] Some years later, another prodigy of Corpus Christi College, Robert Hegge (M.A. 1620), wrote a description of the dial in his elaborate essay on dials and dialling, c. 1624. Hegge, who died suddenly in 1629 in his thirtieth year, was described by Wood as 'the best in the University for the mathematical faculty history and antiquities (and

---

[78] Camden, *Epistolae*, appendix, p. 17; *DNB*; BL MSS Royal 12.B.XI, 12.E.II; Bodl. MSS Ashmole 209, fols. 131–203; 242, fols. 1–19v; 576; C. Heydon, *An Astrological Discourse with Mathematical Demonstrations proving the Powerful and Harmonical Influence of the Planets and Fixed Stars upon Elementary Bodies, in Justification of the Validity of Astrology* (London, 1650), 'To the Reader'; Gregorian Univ. Rome MS 529, fol. 66; A. Favaro, *Carteggio inedito di Ticone Brahe, Giovanni Keplero e di altri celebri astronomi e mathematici dei secoli xvi. e xvii. con Giovanni Antonio Magini* (Bologna, 1886), pp. 242–3, 246–8, 317–21, 335–6.

[79] Wood, *Athenae Oxonienses*, vol. 1, p. 498; T. Heth, *A Manifest and Apparent Confutation of an Astrologicall Discourse ... with a Briefe Prognostication, or Astrologicall Prediction, of the Conjunction, of the Two Superiour Planets, Saturn and Iupiter* (London, 1583), sig. B7 et passim.

[80] Wood, *Athenae Oxonienses*, vol. 1, p. 755; Taylor, *Mathematical Practitioners*, pp. 179–80. P. Pattenden's *Sundials at an Oxford College* (Oxford, 1979), which only came to my notice while this book was in press, contains the fullest account of Turnbull. Pattenden speculates that Turnbull might still have been alive in 1625.

therefore much beloved by Tho. Allen)'. A few of Hegge's historical and theological writings, most of which were composed during his last years, have survived as well as a few fragments of his mathematical manuscripts. As it has already been shown, at least one student in the college, Henry Oxinden, received his mathematical instruction from Hegge.[81]

In Merton College we find Thomas Savile (M.A. 1585), a younger brother to Henry and a fellow from 1580 until 1593, whose career was cut short by his untimely death in 1593. As one of the most learned young men of his time, Thomas appears to have rivalled his brother in the extent of his mathematical knowledge. On his trip to the Continent from 1588 until 1591 Savile became acquainted with many of the foremost men of science and intellectuals, and corresponded with Johannes Praetorius, Thadeus Hajec and Tycho Brahe.[82] Lawrence Keymis (M.A. 1586), a fellow of Balliol College from 1582 until 1591, was reportedly well versed in geography and mathematics, and after resigning his fellowship, with the help of Harriot he entered the service of Ralegh and later became a successful sea captain.[83] A distinguished member of New College was Thomas Lydiat (M.A. 1599), who was a fellow from 1593 until 1603. His intention to become a divine was hindered by a defect in his memory and utterance and consequently he resigned his fellowship and devoted himself to chronology, astronomy and mathematics. Appointed Prince Henry's cosmographer in 1609 and elected a fellow of Trinity College, Dublin, in 1610, Lydiat later accepted the family living near Oxford where he continued his chronological and astronomical studies, which involved him in a long and bitter debate with Scaliger.[84] In Exeter College we encounter George Hakewill, a fellow from 1596 until 1611, whose chief fame rests on his *Apologie*, first published in 1627 'although begun long previously'. In this work – which was a bitter attack on the theory of the decay of nature and its latest propagandist Godfrey Goodman (*The Fall of Man*, 1611) – Hakewill employed as ammunition the latest developments in the mathematical and life sciences as well as the mechanical arts.[85]

---

[81] For Hegge, see Wood, *Athenae Oxonienses*, vol. 2, pp. 456–8; *DNB*. The treatise on dials is in Corpus Christi College MS 40. Another copy entitled 'Heliotropium Sciotericum' is in Corpus Christi College MS 430, fols. 16–34. The same manuscript also includes a mathematical fragment 'De minutiis seu integrorum partibus' (fols. 2v–4v) and 'De iride' (fol. 81v). See also P. Pattenden, 'Robert Hegge, an Oxford antiquary', *Oxoniensia*, XLV (1980), 284–99.

[82] For Thomas Savile, see pp. 130–3 below.

[83] Wood, *Athenae Oxonienses*, vol. 2, pp. 230–1.

[84] See TCD MS 388, fol. 96 for autobiographical information included in Lydiat's dedication of a sermon to John Bancroft, Bishop of Oxford. See also Wood, *Athenae Oxonienses*, vol. 3, pp. 185–9; R. Plot, *Natural History of Oxford-Shire* (Oxford, 1677), pp. 222–4; *DNB*. See pp. 48–9 above and pp. 148–52 below.

[85] Wood, *Athenae Oxonienses*, vol. 3, pp. 253–7; Boase, *Registrum*, pp. 87–8, 107; *DNB*; Jones, *Ancients and Moderns*, pp. 29–40; R. W. Hepburn, 'George Hakewill: the virility of nature', *Journ. Hist. Ideas*, XVI (1955), 135–50.

Christ Church is represented by Robert Burton, who was a fellow for forty-one years (1599–1640). Burton's grasp of scientific matters is clearly evident in his *Anatomy of Melancholy* (1621) as well as in the large and at times heavily annotated collection of books he bequeathed to the Bodleian Library and the library of Christ Church.[86] Another long-standing member of the university was Brian Twyne, a fellow of Corpus Christi College from 1605 until 1623, and thereafter a resident of Oxford. Twyne was a pupil of Thomas Allen, and his voluminous papers as well as his library attest to his extensive and up-to-date knowledge of the mathematical sciences. Twyne read various works of Kepler and was also one of the first Englishmen to mention in print Galileo's telescopic observations, the occasion being the verses he composed commemorating Sir Thomas Bodley's death. Twyne served as a tutor as well. In one of his notebooks he records that he had lent a table of multiplication to a Mr Elyott; as Curtis has pointed out, this is most likely a reference to Benjamin Elyott (M.A. 1620). Evidence of a more conclusive nature appears elsewhere in the same manuscript. There are a number of pages penned in a clear, even hand, which contain a detailed exposition – in English – of Euclid's theorems and utilize Ramus's and Billingsley's English translations as textbooks. Most probably this exposition was intended for the instruction of students.[87]

Richard James (M.A. 1615, Corpus Christi College) was one of Oxford's foremost scholars in the first half of the seventeenth century. A resident of the university until his death in 1638, James included Thomas Allen, Sir Kenelm Digby, Brian Twyne, Sir William Boswell, Sir Henry Wotton and John Selden among his associates. James was interested in geography and botany, both of which he pursued during his extensive periods of travel in England and on the Continent. James's scientific interests must also have included astronomy, for once again back in Oxford in 1632, he wrote the following to Sir Robert Cotton: 'so soone as I may sett warme, & have

---

[86] For a bibliography of Burton, see *New Cambridge Bibliography of English Literature* (Cambridge, 1974), vol. 1, pp. 2219–21; for Burton's library, see 'Robert Burton and the Anatomy of Melancholy', ed. F. Madan, *Oxf. Bibl. Soc.*, 1 (Oxford, 1925), 222–46. See also J. B. Bamborough, 'Robert Burton's Astrological Notebook', *Rev. Eng. Stud.*, New Ser., XXXII (1981), 267–85. See pp. 148–52 below.

[87] Bodl. MS Corpus Christi College 254, fol. 23 for Elyott (Curtis, *Oxford and Cambridge in Transition*, pp. 121–2), fols. 90–105v for the notes on Euclid. Other subjects included in the volume are navigation and astronomy; see fols. 86–9, 106–7v. Many other mathematical, astronomical, astrological and chemical notes may be found among the fourteen notebooks of Twyne comprising Corpus Christi College MSS 254–65, 279–80. All but MS 280 are deposited in the Bodleian Library. For Twyne, see Wood, *Athenae Oxonienses*, vol. 3, pp. 108–11; 'Some correspondence of Brian Twyne', ed. H. G. S., *Bodl. Lib. Rec.*, V (1926–8), 213–18, 240–6, 269–72 for his correspondence with his father while a student; S. Gibson, 'Brian Twyne', *Oxoniensia*, V (1940), 94–114; F. Ovenell, 'Brian Twyne's Library', *Oxf. Bibl. Soc.*, New Ser., IV (1952), 1–42; *Justa Funebria Ptolemaei Oxoniensis* (Oxford, 1613), p. 115. I owe this reference to Dr Nicholas Tyacke.

satisfied my self in somme fewe other readings, thether I purpos à previall ascent by earnest contemplation of Astronomye tille the swallowe returnes and brings a fitter season for travaill'.[88] Nathaniel Carpenter (M.A. 1613), a fellow of Exeter Collège from 1607 until 1626, was a protégé of Ussher who served as the Archbishop's chaplain for the two years preceding his own death. According to Wood 'by a virtuous emulation and industry' Carpenter became 'a noted philosopher, poet, mathematician and geographer'. His scientific publications include *Philosophia libera* (1621), *Geography Delineated Forth in Two Bookes* (1625) and a work on optics, the original of which was lost but of which a copy has survived.[89]

In Lincoln College Gilbert Watts was a fellow from 1616 until 1642. Known chiefly as one of the earlier ardent Baconians, Watts translated Bacon's *De augmentis scientiarum* into English in 1633 and upon his demise left some unpublished manuscripts, including 'Digressions on the Advancement of Learning' and 'An Apology for the Instauration of Sciences'.[90] Another ardent Baconian was William Gilbert, who for many years was a resident of Gloucester Hall where he incepted M.A. in 1623. In 1634 Hartlib commends Gilbert who 'spends himselfe in a Verulamian Philosophy for the Natural Part. Hase many brave Experiments et if any understands Verulam.' Thereafter Gilbert frequently appears in Hartlib's diary as a commentator and informer on scientific subjects. During this period he also corresponded with Gellibrand on mathematical subjects. By 1638 Gilbert was residing in Dublin from which place he wrote to Archbishop Ussher about the progress of his astronomical observations. Having related that his attempt to observe a lunar eclipse was frustrated by inclement weather, Gilbert goes on to comment at length upon Galileo's telescopic observations of Jupiter, Saturn and the sunspots. Appearing to favour a heliocentric cosmology, Gilbert reflects upon the possibility of an infinite universe and a plurality of worlds.[91]

Robert Payne is remembered chiefly because of his association with the

[88] DNB; *The Poems of Richard James, B.D.* (1592–1638), ed. A. B. Grosart (London, 1880), introduction. The letter is quoted on p. xxxiv. See also pp. xxxix, 266–7.

[89] On his deathbed Carpenter is said to have repented for having courted 'the maid instead of the mistress', i.e., philosophy and mathematics instead of theology. Wood, *Athenae Oxonienses*, vol. 2, pp. 421–2; Boase, *Registrum*, pp. 92–3; Jones, *Ancients and Moderns*, pp. 65–71, 288–9; Bodl. MS University College 153 is a copy of Carpenter's 'Systema opticum'.

[90] Wood, *Athenae Oxonienses*, vol. 4, pp. 433–4; Webster, *The Great Instauration*, pp. 49, 127–8. Among the 150 volumes bequeathed by Watts to Lincoln College we find works by Bacon, Euclid, Witelo, Peucer, Gilbert, Harvey and Digby. Lincoln College, Oxford, Benefactors' Book, unpaginated entry under the year 1657.

[91] Clark, *Register*, vol. 2, part 3, p. 38; Hartlib, 'Ephemerides 1634', C–D 15; Webster, *The Great Instauration*, p. 128; R. Parr, *The Life of the Most Reverend Father in God, James Ussher Late Lord Arch-Bishop of Armagh, Primate and Metropolitan of all Ireland with a Collection of 300 Letters* (London, 1686), pp. 492–4.

Cavendish circle in the 1630s, but his scientific interests can be traced back to his student years at Christ Church, Oxford, where he incepted M.A. in 1617. Three notebooks composed by Payne during his graduate study indicate an avid interest in the writings of Roger Bacon. Noteworthy is Payne's consultation of diverse manuscripts in the possession of Thomas Allen, Brian Twyne and John Prideaux in the process of compiling these notebooks. In 1624 he was elected a founding fellow of Pembroke College and it is possible that he was the 'Mr Paine' who in the same year was an unsuccessful contender for the Gresham chair of astronomy, losing to Henry Gellibrand. By 1631, if not earlier, Payne had become acquainted with Sir Charles Cavendish, for that year Cavendish presented him with a copy of Harriot's recently published *Artis analyticae praxis*. Payne's association with the Cavendishes continued during the 1630s; he served both as chaplain and alchemist to William Cavendish, Duke of Newcastle, and rallied around Sir Charles Cavendish, who became the pivotal member in a circle that included Thomas Hobbes and Walter Warner. In 1638 Payne was elected a canon of Christ Church, an appointment he held until his ejection from the university in 1648. During Payne's last years, which were spent in the environs of Oxford, he corresponded frequently with Gilbert Sheldon, the future Archbishop of Canterbury, their discussions occasionally revolving around the scientific works of Gassendi, Kircher and Hobbes.[92]

A younger contemporary and life-long friend of Payne was George Morley, the future Bishop of Winchester. Like certain of his contemporaries at Christ Church, Morley developed his scientific interests during his student years; by the time he graduated M.A. in 1621 he was already acquainted with Thomas Harriot, who died in that year. Morley also befriended Harriot's associate, Walter Warner, who intimated to him that it was he who first discovered the circulation of the blood and conveyed his ideas to William Harvey. Morley was a most successful tutor during the 1620s and 1630s and included John Gregory among his students. He was also part of the group – which included Payne, Chillingworth and Hobbes – that gathered round Lucius Cary, Lord Falkland, at Great Tew.[93]

[92] J. Foster, *Alumni Oxonienses 1500–1714* (Oxford, 1891), vol. 3, p. 1129; Adamson, 'The Foundation and Early History of Gresham College', p. 279; Bodl. MSS University College 47–9. Harriot's book is Bodl. sig. Savile O.9. Margaret Cavendish, Duchess of Newcastle, *The Life of William Cavendish, Duke of Newcastle*, ed. C. H. Firth (London, no date), p. 108, n. 1; Hist. MSS Comm. Welbeck Abbey MSS, vol. 2, pp. 125–30; G. Halliwell, *A Collection of Letters Illustrative of the Progress of Science in England* (London, 1841), pp. 65–9, hereafter cited as Halliwell; BL MS Harl. 6796, fols. 317–39 (translation made in 1636 of Galileo's *Le meccaniche*); MSS Lansd. 93, fol. 179; 841, fols. 21–2, 92–92v; *The Theologian and Ecclesiastic*, VI (1848), 165–74, 217–24.
[93] *DNB*; Aubrey, *Brief Lives*, vol. 2, pp. 15–16; K. Weber, *Lucius Cary, Second Viscount Falkland* (New York, 1940), pp. 99–109.

Another Christ Church member, Edmund Chilmead (M.A. 1632), was a versatile scholar reputed to have excelled in mathematics, Greek and music. In 1639 he published his translation from the Latin of Hues's *Treatise of the Globes*, while his interest in astrology may be inferred by his translation of Gaffarel's *Unheard of Curiosities concerning the Tallismatical Sculptures of the Persians*. Chilmead's chief interest, however, was music. In the 1640s he composed an extremely interesting treatise criticizing Bacon's theory of sounds as expressed in the latter's *Sylva Sylvarum*, while making extensive reference to the recent ideas on harmony of Mersenne. The treatise was dedicated to Henry King, Bishop of Chichester, and in the dedication Chilmead maintained that the treatise would never see publication owing to its criticism of Bacon. Chilmead also wrote commentaries on ancient Greek musical tracts as well as organized weekly music sessions in London after his ejection from Christ Church.[94]

A younger contemporary of Crosfield at Queen's College, Oxford, was Thomas Barlow (M.A. 1633) who became Bishop of Lincoln after the Restoration. At least one of Barlow's students – John Owen – learned mathematics and philosophy under Barlow's tutorship. As far back as the 1630s Barlow was also a friend and associate of John Gregory of Christ Church and Obadiah Walker of University College, while in the 1650s he was a member of the Oxford scientific club and included John Wilkins and Robert Boyle among his friends. Although mathematical books are not specified in his 'A Library for Younger Schollers' – a study guide which will be discussed in greater detail in chapter III – noteworthy is the inclusion of works by Gassendi, Bacon, Descartes and Digby in the section devoted to philosophy.[95]

Two additional members of the Greaves family who expressed enthusiasm for science were Edward (elected a fellow of All Souls College in 1634) and Thomas, chosen a scholar of Corpus Christi College in 1627 and elected a fellow in 1636. Edward chose to study medicine in which

---

[94] Wood, *Athenae Oxonienses*, vol. 3, pp. 350–1; *DNB*; Hartlib, 'Ephemerides 1651', EE2–EE3; Bodl. MS Tanner 204, 'An examination of certaine experiments in the second & third centuries of the natural history of ... Francis L. Verulam ... touching the nature of sounds'. See also M. Feingold and P. M. Gouk, 'An early critique of Bacon's *Sylva Sylvarum*: Edmund Chilmead's treatise on sound', *Annals of Science*, XL (1983), 139–57.

[95] *DNB; The Genuine Remains of that Learned Prelate Dr Thomas Barlow late Lord Bishop of Lincoln* (London, 1693); W. Orme, *Memoirs of the Life, Writings and Religious Connexions of John Owen, D.D.* (London, 1820), p. 12; *Gregorii Posthuma: or Certain Learned Tracts Written by John Gregorie M.A. and Chaplain of Christ-Church in Oxford* (London, 1650), p. 119; Boyle, *Works*, vol. 6, p. 317; '*A Library for Younger Schollers' Compiled by an English Scholar Priest about 1655*, ed. A. De Jordy and H. F. Fletcher (Urbana, 1961), p. 4. Owen (M.A. 1635) continued in diligent pursuit of the sciences, mainly mathematics and astronomy. He was also a member of the Oxford scientific club of the 1650s and his library catalogue included works of Bacon, Descartes, Galileo, Mersenne, Gassendi, Seth Ward, John Wallis, Snell and Kircher. E. Millington, *Bibliotheca Oweniana* (London, 1684). For Barlow's 'A Library for Younger Schollers', see pp. 94–5 below.

he excelled and was created baronet. Although Thomas was an able mathematician who annotated a copy of Henry Savile's *Praelectiones tresdecem in principium elementorum Euclidis* (Oxford, 1621), his chief interest lay in Oriental languages, in the study of which he was greatly esteemed.[96] Finally, mention should be made of Thomas Powell (M.A. *c.* 1634 and a fellow of Jesus College from 1632 until 1640), who was both a versatile scholar and man of science. A close friend of the Vaughan twins, Henry and Thomas, who matriculated at Jesus College in 1638, it is quite possible that Powell acted as their tutor; in any case, both brothers prefaced commendatory verses to Powell's *Elementa opticae: nova, facili & compendiosa methodo explicata* (London, 1651). In 1661 Powell also published an interesting volume entitled *Human Industry: or a History of the most curious manual Arts* (London, 1661).[97]

Cambridge numbered several men of science among its fellows. Elected a fellow in 1561, William Gilbert retained his fellowship until 1573 at which time he moved to London to begin a successful career as a physician. As far as I know Gilbert was the only scientist to have obtained a pension from the Queen, whom he also attended, to enable him to pursue his scientific experiments.[98] In Trinity College we find Thomas Bedwell (M.A. 1570), one of the best mathematicians of the last quarter of the sixteenth century. Referred to as 'Our English Tycho' by his nephew, the orientalist and mathematician William Bedwell, Thomas was elected a fellow in 1568 and held the appointment until he moved to London some years later where he applied himself to civil and military engineering. His publications include an English translation of Lazarus Schonerus's *De numeris geometricis* (1614) as well as two practical tracts concerning building, all of which were published posthumously by his nephew.[99]

The 1570s and 1580s witnessed the three Harvey brothers serving as Cambridge fellows: Gabriel and Richard as fellows of Pembroke Hall from 1570 and 1582, respectively, and John as a fellow of Queens' College from 1584. All three were scientific enthusiasts with strong astrological

---

[96] For Edward Greaves, see Wood, *Athenae Oxonienses*, vol. 3, p. 1256. Thomas Greaves's tombstone reads: 'Thomas Gravius ... in Philosophicis paucis secundus, in Philologicis peritissimis par; in Linguis Orientalibus plerisque major; quarum Persicam notis in appendice ad *Biblia Polyglotta* doctissime illustravit. Arabicam publice in Academia Oxon, professus est; dignissimus etaim, qui & Theologiam in eodem loco profiteretur. Poeta insuper & Orator insignis, atque in Mathematicis profunde doctus.' Wood, *Athenae Oxonienses*, vol. 3, pp. 1061–2; *DNB*.

[97] Wood, *Athenae Oxonienses*, vol. 3, pp. 507–8.

[98] The most recent study of Gilbert is the thesis of Abromitis, 'William Gilbert as Scientist'. See also D. H. D. Roller, *The De Magnete of William Gilbert* (Amsterdam, 1959); S. Kelly, *The De Mundo of William Gilbert* (Amsterdam, 1965), the second volume of which consists of a reprint of the first, 1651, edition of *De Mundo*.

[99] Cooper, *Athenae Cantabrigienses*, vol. 2, pp. 539–40; *DNB*; Taylor, *Mathematical Practitioners*, p. 177.

inclinations and equally strong opinions, the result of which was to entangle the brothers in endless heated controversies. In 1583 Richard and John collaborated to publish their astronomical/astrological predictions concerning the great conjunction that was to occur that year. John Harvey vacated his fellowship around 1580 in order to become a physician in Norfolk, while Richard vacated his a few years after his election in order to marry. The more famous and eccentric Gabriel, although better known for his oratory and literary quarrels with Greene and Nash, was also a great admirer of the mathematical and physical sciences. Gabriel failed to renew his fellowship at Pembroke Hall when it terminated in 1578 and through the assistance of the Earl of Leicester he was elected a fellow of Trinity Hall. In 1584 he returned to Pembroke Hall where he succeeded Lancelot Browne to the medical fellowship. Although from the late 1590s until his death in 1631 Gabriel practised medicine and astrology, he earlier wrote against judicial astrology.[100]

Edward Wright (M.A. 1584), the mathematician and writer on navigation, was a fellow of Gonville and Caius College from 1587 until 1596. Wright embarked upon his mathematical and astronomical studies while he was still an undergraduate, and his early collaborators included his fellow college member, John Fletcher, as well as the mathematician from St John's, Henry Briggs. Another associate of Wright's was Mark Ridley – an exact contemporary at Cambridge – who later described him to be 'most perfect in Copernicus from his youth'. Later, as a fellow, Wright accompanied the Earl of Cumberland on his voyage to the Azores in 1589 and upon his return to Cambridge he composed the draft of what was later to appear as *Certaine Errors of Navigation* (1599). In 1592 Wright greatly assisted Emery Molyneux in his construction of the first English globes. It was also during the 1590s that Wright communicated with Jodocus Hondius, Thomas Blundeville and William Barlow, all of whom incorporated various aspects of Wright's discoveries into their own work. Upon resigning his fellowship in 1596, Wright moved to London where he became a lecturer in navigation to the East India Company and a tutor to Prince Henry, for whom he also constructed a magnificent mechanical sphere.[101]

[100] Cooper, *Athenae Cantabrigienses*, vol. 2, pp. 126–7, 182–3; *Gabriel Harvey's Marginalia*, ed. G. C. Moore Smith (Stratford-upon-Avon, 1913); Stern, *Gabriel Harvey*.

[101] For Wright's early scientific studies, see p. 161 below. Ridley, *Magneticall Animadversions*, pp. 9–10; Taylor, *Mathematical Practitioners*, pp. 181–2; E. J. S. Parsons and W. F. Morris, 'Edward Wright and his work', *Imago Mundi*, III (1939), 61–71; J. Venn, *Annals of Gonville and Caius College*, Camb. Antiq. Soc. Octavo Public., vol. 40 (Cambridge, 1904), pp. 242–5; Waters, *The Art of Navigation*, passim; H. M. Wallis, 'The first English globe: a recent discovery', *Geographical Journal*, CXVII (1951), 275–90; Sherburne, *The Sphere of Marcus Manilius*, appendix, p. 86; BL MS Sloane 651, fols. 39–51v contain a description of Wright's sphere; see p. 201 below. See also H. C. King and J. R. Millburn, *Geared to the Stars: The Evolution of Planetariums, Orreries, and Astronomical Clocks* (Toronto, 1978), pp. 96–7.

As early as 1580, the year before he graduated B.A., John Fletcher (M.A. 1583 and a fellow of Gonville and Caius College from 1581 until 1613) was singled out by Gabriel Harvey as one of the most promising mathematicians of the day. Ten years later, when Sir Thomas Tresham was in need of a good mathematician, John Fletcher was recommended to him as 'one of the cunningest we have in that faculty'. A college tutor, Fletcher is credited with having instructed such Cambridge mathematicians as Henry Briggs and Sir William Boswell as well as with having acted as the moving force behind the writing and publishing of Sir Christopher Heydon's *Defense of Judicial Astrology*. It might be mentioned that Fletcher's astrological pursuits once involved him in a law suit.[102]

Archbishop Ussher's enthusiasm for chronology and astronomical calculations was responsible for bringing to light a little-known astronomy enthusiast, Thomas Whalley (M.A. 1592 and a fellow of Trinity College, 1591–1637). While Whalley's correspondence with Ussher reveals his grasp of astronomy and mathematics, his bequest of manuscripts to his college library indicates his chemical interests.[103] Sir William Boswell, a fellow of Jesus College from 1606 until 1629, was one of the most important patrons of science in the first half of the seventeenth century; Joseph Mede, Thomas Lydiat, John Pell and Samuel Hartlib were among those who enjoyed his patronage. For this reason it is unfortunate that there exists no adequate biography of the man. Boswell is frequently mentioned in Hartlib's diary both as a conduit for the most recent scientific news and as the author of various mathematical and astronomical treatises, none of which were ever published. One of the few Englishmen to have corresponded with Galileo, Boswell served as an important avenue for the dissemination of Galileo's ideas in England. Unfortunately, his vast library – which included unpublished papers of Dee, Gilbert and Bacon – was lost and only a copy of Gilbert's manuscript of *De Mundo* (1651) was published from Boswell's copy.[104]

---

[102] Venn, *Biographical History of Gonville and Caius College*, vol. 1, p. 95; idem, 'An astrological fellow', *The Caian*, VI (1897), 28–36; idem (ed.), *Annals of Gonville and Caius College*, pp. 232–3; Stern, *Gabriel Harvey*, p. 168 (the author mistakenly ascribes the reference to Giles Fletcher); *Hist. MSS Comm. Various Collections*, vol. 3, p. 59; Gonville and Caius College MS 73, fols. 348–88, contain eighteen letters written by Heydon to Fletcher between 1597 and 1605. A fragment of Fletcher's medical studies can be found in BL MS Sloane 2563, fols. 71–92, which consist of a treatise on urines.

[103] Venn, *Alumni Cantabrigienses*, vol. 4, p. 377; *The Whole Works of James Ussher*, ed. C. R. Elrington (Dublin, 1847–64), vol. 16, pp. 269–74; Trinity College Cambridge MSS R. 14: 38, 39, 44, 45, 56, 57. Whalley also bequeathed to the college his copy of the 1566 edition of Copernicus which is now housed in Leeds University Library.

[104] Apart from the short notice in the *DNB* and the correction of it in the *Bull. Inst. Hist. Res.*, X (1932/33), 58–9, the only biography of Boswell is the short article by G. Davies in his edition of *Autobiography of Thomas Raymond and Memoirs of the Family of Guise*, Camden Soc., 3rd Ser., vol. 28 (London, 1917). At least on one occasion we know that Boswell acted as a tutor. See his letters to Sir William Waldegrave concerning his tutorship of the latter's grandchild, William Clopton. BL MS Harl. 374, fols. 36–44, letters

In King's College we find another member of the Savile clan, this time Samuel Savile (M.A. 1615 and a fellow from 1610 until 1623). A relative of Sir Henry, under whom he received his education at Eton, Samuel became a competent mathematician and philosopher. Despite his scholarly attainments, however, Savile chose to follow the life of a courtier and, after having served as secretary to the Earl of Carlisle, he became Esquire to the Body Extraordinary of Charles I.[105] Almost forgotten today but highly regarded by his contemporary mathematicians was Edward Davenant, D.D. (M.A. 1617 and a fellow of Queens' College from 1615 until 1625). Upon receiving a living at Gillingham, Davenant retired from academic life but continued to pursue mathematics for an additional fifty-five years. He was the inventor of a trigonometrical problem which bears his name – and which Newton, among others, managed to solve – as well as the man who first introduced John Aubrey to mathematics.[106] Walter Foster (M.A. 1621), a fellow of Emmanuel College from 1622 until 1632 and brother to the Gresham professor Samuel Foster, was a mathematician who was highly commended by John Twysden, the editor of Samuel Foster's papers published posthumously.[107]

By the time Ralph Winterton graduated M.A. in 1624 from King's College, he was an ardent student of the mathematical sciences. According to his own testimony, he pursued mathematics with such intensity that he suffered from sleeplessness and melancholy. Having related his problem to John Collins, who became Regius Professor of Medicine in 1626, the latter advised him to give up mathematics and instead apply himself to medicine. Winterton duly followed this advice, the first fruits of his studies being two consecutive editions of Hippocrates's *Aphorisms* (1631 and 1633). For the second edition he solicited verses from colleagues and friends, including John Collins, Thomas Clayton, Edward Lapworth, John Bainbridge, Francis Glisson, Henry Jacob, Herbert Thorndike and James Duport. In 1635 Winterton replaced Collins as Regius Professor and hoped to use his new office to improve medical studies at Cambridge. However, his untimely death in September 1636 put an end to all such plans.[108]

for the years 1607–8; Hartlib, 'Ephemerides 1634–40', *passim*; N. Tyacke, 'Arminianism and English culture', *England and the Netherlands*, ed. A. C. Duck and C. A. Tamse (The Hague, 1981), vol. 7, pp. 109–10. See also pp. 96, 152 below.

105 Venn, *Alumni Cantabrigienses*, vol. 4, p. 231; W. Sterry, *The Eton College Register 1551–1698* (Eton, 1943), p. 297.

106 For Davenant's mathematical notebooks, see Exeter College Oxford MSS 73–5; Worcester College Oxford MS 5.5. For Davenant, see Venn, *Alumni Cantabrigienses*, vol. 2, p. 13; Aubrey, *Brief Lives*, vol. 1, pp. 198–203; Rigaud (ed.), *Correspondence of Scientific Men*, vol. 1, pp. 155, 212, vol. 2, pp. 3, 5, 15, 260, 276; Elrington, *The Whole Works of Ussher*, vol. 16, pp. 75–7, 114–15; M. Hunter, *John Aubrey and the Realm of Learning* (London, 1975), pp. 48–50.

107 S. Foster, *Miscellanies, or, Mathematical Lucubrations*, ed. J. Twysden (London, 1659), preface; Ward, *Lives of the Professors*, pp. 87–8.

108 DNB; R. Winterton (trans.), *The Considerations of Drexelius* (Cambridge, 1636); idem, *Hippocratis magni aphorismi soluta et metrici* (Cambridge, 1633).

In addition to Mede, Christ's College had at least two other fellows who manifested a keen interest in science. Robert Gell (M.A. 1621 and a fellow 1623–38) was a mathematician and astrologer who preached at least two sermons before the newly founded society of astrologers in the 1640s.[109] The engagement of Nathaniel Tovey (M.A. 1619 and a fellow from 1621 to 1634) as co-editor with Herbert Thorndike (M.A. 1620, a fellow of Trinity College 1620–45) – another mathematician almost entirely neglected today – for the projected publication of Walter Warner's papers attests to the scientific interests of both men. Thorndike was credited by Seth Ward and others with being 'one of the best scholars and mathematicians of his age' and in 1643 Seth Ward tried to procure his election as Master of Sidney Sussex College following the resignation of Samuel Ward, only to be thwarted by Cromwell who ordered the arrest of one of the fellows supporting Thorndike. The project for the edition of the Warner papers came to a halt when it was discovered that much of the material was incomplete and Thorndike subsequently gave the papers in his possession to John Collins, the great popularizer of science from the 1650s onward.[110]

Lastly, mention should be made of James Duport, a fellow of Trinity College from 1630 until 1664, if only because of his 'negative' approach to science. Having professed a preference for Aristotle, Duport composed some poems attacking the new science in his *Musae subsecivae* (1676). Notwithstanding his scientific stance, Duport was a most popular tutor who numbered the celebrated mathematician Isaac Barrow and the naturalists John Ray and Francis Willoughby among his pupils, once again attesting to the interest generated in a subject as much by its detractors as by its defenders.[111]

Like so many other mathematicians William Oughtred combined the theoretical study of mathematics with the practical construction of mathematical and astronomical instruments. By the time he graduated B.A. from King's College, Cambridge, in 1596, he had already circulated his 'Easy Method of Geometrical Dialling' which brought him into contact with many mathematicians. Shortly after proceeding M.A. in 1599, Oughtred invented the horizontal instrument, a description of which was published by one of his students three decades later. One of these instruments of Oughtred's own making was presented to his patron Thomas Bilson, Bishop of Winchester, in 1603. Although we are never given the names of any students tutored by Oughtred during the time of his fellowship (1596–*c.* 1606), later in life he wrote of the efforts he had

[109] H. F. Fletcher, *The Intellectual Development of John Milton* (Urbana, 1956–61), and references cited therein.
[110] For Tovey, who was a most successful tutor, see Fletcher, *The Intellectual Development of John Milton*, vol. 2, pp. 33, 39, 312. For Thorndike, see Aubrey, *Brief Lives*, vol. 2, p. 257; Halliwell, pp. 94–5; *DNB*.
[111] *DNB*.

made in the mathematical sciences, seeking not only '[his] private content, but the benefit of many: and by inciting, assisting, and instrumenting others, brought many into the love and study of those Arts, not only in [his] own, but in some other Colledges also'. After leaving Cambridge and settling in his vicarage at Albury, he continued to serve as mathematical instructor to many gifted university students, including Seth Ward and Charles Scarburgh of Cambridge and Thomas Henshaw of Oxford.[112] This service on the part of Oughtred brings us to the point that has been consistently over-looked concerning the significance of men of science as college fellows. Although there is little surviving evidence to indicate that the majority ever served as tutors, as fellows of college they were all what might be termed 'potential tutors': that is, as members of the academic community these men were in a position to be sought out by the more ambitious students who had outgrown their tutors in their pursuit of scientific knowledge.

Such a possibility is enhanced by the example of the great Oxford mathematician Thomas Allen who was a member of Gloucester Hall for over sixty years (1570–1632). Allen gained a reputation as the 'high priest' of English mathematics, not necessarily because of his mathematical superiority – for his skill as a mathematician was at least matched by that of such men as Dee, Harriot and Briggs – but because he fulfilled the important function of friend and instructor to the most promising mathematical talents. Sir Philip Sidney, Brian Twyne, Robert Hegge, Robert Fludd, Sir Kenelm Digby, Sir John Davies and John Budden were all numbered among Allen's students. Indeed, Allen never published his work and he seems to have been content to provide instruction, information and encouragement to others. In fact, all the dignities of high office offered him – a bishopric included – could not draw him away from his beloved Oxford.[113]

---

[112] See p. 172 below. W. Oughtred, *To the English Gentrie, and all others Studious of the Mathematicks which shall be Readers hereof. The just Apologie of Wil: Oughtred, against the Slaunderous Insinuations of Richard Delamain, in a Pamphlet called Grammelogia* (London, 1632), sig. A4v-B, B3v; *Biog. Brit.*, vol. 5, pp. 3278–98; F. Cajori, *William Oughtred, A Great Seventeenth-Century Teacher of Mathematics* (Chicago and London, 1916).

[113] Wood, *Athenae Oxonienses*, vol. 2, pp. 541–4 and index sub Allen; T. Fuller, *The History of the Worthies of England*, ed. P. A. Nuttall (London, 1840), vol. 3, pp. 137–8; Aubrey, *Brief Lives*, vol. 1, pp. 26–8; for Allen's teaching of Fludd, see R. Fludd, *Integrum morborum mysterium: sive medicinae catholicae* (Frankfurt, 1631), I. ii. sectio secunda, p. 234. William Burton, in his funeral oration for Allen, also mentioned that at some unspecified date Allen had delivered highly successful lectures at the university which 'were so popular that it was feared the rooms would burst'. See W. Burton and G. Bathurst, *In viri doctissimi, clarissimi, optimi, Thomae Alleni ... orationes binae* (London, 1632), p. 5. The translation is given in the recent article by M. Foster, 'Thomas Allen (1540–1632), Gloucester Hall and the survival of Catholicism in Post-Reformation Oxford', *Oxoniensia*, XLVI (1981), 127. See also A. G. Watson, 'Thomas Allen of Oxford and his manuscripts', *Medieval Scribes, Manuscripts and Libraries: Essays Presented to N.*

There were also some eminent foreigners who were invited to the universities where they lectured in their respective disciplines as well as offered mathematical tuition to the more gifted students. In 1580 the celebrated Italian lawyer Albericus Gentili arrived in England and, owing to the warm recommendation of the Chancellor of Oxford, the Earl of Leicester, he was offered first lodgings at New Inn Hall and eventually the Regius Professorship of Civil Law. Yet Gentili also proved himself a most capable mathematician who numbered Thomas Savile and William Camden among his friends and Henry Wotton of Merton College among his students. Upon taking his B.A. in 1588 Wotton chose to deliver three lectures entitled 'De oculo' concerning 'the *Form*, the *Motion* [and] the curious *composure* of the *Eye*'. Throughout his life Wotton retained his interest in mathematics. He both visited Kepler and observed some of his experiments as well as helped disseminate Galileo's observations in England. His treatise, *Elements of Architecture*, is additional proof of his scientific inclinations as is the lively correspondence he carried on with Sir Edmund Bacon of Redgrave. Wotton also purchased a mathematics library for his patron, Edward, Lord Zouch.[114]

Another foreigner with scientific leanings was Mathias Pasor, the eminent Arabist who resided in Oxford from 1625 until 1629, during which time he was instructor of Hebrew and mathematics. Pasor's instruction in Arabic has already been cited in connection with Thomas Crosfield. But Pasor's most brilliant Arabic student was Edward Pocock (M.A. 1626, Corpus Christi College) who eventually became Laudian Professor of Arabic. Most probably Pocock was also aided by Pasor to perfect his knowledge of mathematics. At the same time, Pasor served as mathematical tutor to Richard Robarts, Lord Randor, and by 1626 he was also corresponding with Samuel Hartlib.[115]

Any discussion of the academic opportunities to pursue science would be incomplete without some mention of the practice of private tuition. Throughout the sixteenth and seventeenth centuries, whether in the universities, London or the provinces, as men attempted to master new

R. Ker, ed. M. B. Parks and A. G. Watson (London, 1978), pp. 279–314. See pp. 157–8 below.

[114] I. Walton, *The Lives of John Donne, Sir Henry Wotton, Richard Hooker, George Herbert and Robert Sanderson* (repr. London, 1973), p. 100; L. P. Smith, *The Life and Letters of Sir Henry Wotton* (Oxford, 1907), *passim*. For Gentili, see *DNB*; G. van der Mollen, *Alberico Gentili and the Development of International Law* (Amsterdam, 1938); Levack, *Civil Lawyers in England*, p. 232.

[115] Wood, *Athenae Oxonienses*, vol. 3, pp. 444–6; *DNB*; L. Twells (ed.), 'The Life of the Reverend and most Learned Dr. Edward Pocock', *The Theological Works of the Learned Dr. Pocock* (London, 1740), vol. 1, p. 2; G. H. Turnbull, *Hartlib, Dury and Comenius, Gleanings from the Hartlib Papers* (London, 1947), pp. 13–16. For Pasor's friendship with Henry Briggs and Thomas Lydiat, see pp. 139, 152 below.

subjects and broaden their knowledge of others, there occurred an increasing demand for private tuition. Private tuition in Oxford and Cambridge embraced the entire spectrum of learning and recreation, and teachers were available for instruction in dancing, fencing and riding, in French and other languages, as well as in subjects that were part of the official curriculum. Simonds D'Ewes, for example, relates how after one of his Greek public lectures he was approached by the lecturer, Andrew Downes, who offered his services to D'Ewes in the capacity of private tutor, an offer the student refused for lack of funds.[116]

Among the private teachers who offered instruction in the sciences was Richard Holland, who spent most of his long life (1596–1677) in Oxford where – according to Wood – he taught 'geography and mathematics among the young scholars for about 50 years, grew wealthy and being always sedulous in his employment, several afterwards became eminent by his instruction'.[117] Another Oxford teacher who took on private students during much the same time was John Hulett. Having received his education at New Inn Hall, Oxford (M.A. 1633), Hulett returned to Oxford after a European tour and offered private tutorials from the late 1630s until his death in 1663. According to Wood, in addition to *The Description and Use of a Quadrant* and several ephemerides, Hulett left behind some manuscripts which were subsequently lost.[118]

Robert Hues, the eminent astronomer mentioned earlier in connection with Algernon Percy to whom he acted as tutor, chose to spend his later years in retirement in Oxford from which place he became a type of private tutor to Oxford men. Thomas Browne recorded in a letter to his son many long conversations with the old astronomer and cosmographer who died in 1632, four months before his friend Thomas Allen.[119] But Browne should not be viewed as an isolated instance. Owing to Wood's probe for information about Nicholas Hill, there exists an intriguing letter to Wood from Obadiah Walker, then Master of University College, disclosing information on Hill. In this letter Walker relates information previously related by Hues to Joseph Maynard, and disclosed by Maynard years later when he was already Rector of Exeter College. Maynard was senior to Browne by only a few months when he matriculated at Exeter College in 1622, and the example of these two suggests that there might have been other students and fellows who also became acquainted with Hues during the latter's residence in Oxford.[120]

[116] *The Autobiography and Correspondence of Sir Simonds D'Ewes*, ed. J. O. Halliwell (London, 1845), vol. 1, p. 120.
[117] Holland could be the Holland who matriculated at Brasenose College in 1615. Clark, *Register*, vol. 2, part 2, p. 343; Wood, *Athenae Oxonienses*, vol. 3, p. 1109; *DNB*.
[118] Wood, *Athenae Oxonienses*, vol. 3, p. 649.
[119] *The Works of Sir Thomas Browne*, ed. G. Keynes (London, 1964), vol. 4, pp. 95–6: T. Browne to E. Browne, 13 June [1678].
[120] Bodl. MS Wood F.45, fol. 77: O. Walker to A. Wood, 11 April 1690. See Wood, *Athenae Oxonienses*, vol. 2, p. 87.

In Cambridge George Atwell, who began his career as a surveyor but by 1624 had settled in Cambridge, offered his services as a teacher of mathematics, an instrument-maker, an astrologer and a surveyor for a quarter of a century. Although unlike his Oxford counterparts Atwell was not a university graduate, he nonetheless forged close relations with at least one college. There is a letter of 1624 from Atwell to John Tapp composed in Trinity College. Apparently, Atwell was also befriended by John Pell during the latter's undergraduate stay at Trinity, for Pell's papers include some fragments of Atwell's work on dialling dating from 1629. Years later Atwell was enabled to publish his *The Faithful Surveyor* (1658) as a result of the financial aid given to him by Nathaniel Rowns, Master of Emmanuel College.[121] During the Interregnum Bassingbourne Gawdy asked his father for permission to attend a private teacher in the mathematics, one 'who makes it his whole profession and hath teached very many',[122] and although the teacher remains unnamed, it might very well have been Atwell.

It is believed that this survey is sufficient to refute the claim that there were very few scientifically minded men who could have provided instruction in the universities. The least a student could derive from the average tutor was a reasonable introduction and guideline for further mathematical pursuits. For those who outgrew their tutors the road was open to seek the acquaintance of the more distinguished members of the scientific community, scientific enthusiasts who were also heads of college and professional instructors.

[121] BL MS Addit. 5387, fols. 1–6; BL MS Addit. 4431, fols. 70–4v; Taylor, *Mathematical Practitioners*, pp. 199, 360.
[122] J. Venn, *Early Collegiate Life* (Cambridge, 1913), p. 212: B. Gawdy to his father, c. 1655.

III

The nature and quality of scientific instruction: the student community

While the evidence of a significant number of scientifically oriented members of the university community suggests the existence of adequate opportunities for mathematical instruction on various levels, we must turn to the evidence of the students themselves for corroboration of such instruction. Individual statements by students, manuals of advice for students, lists of book purchases, student notebooks and probate inventories of private libraries and university booksellers are a valuable source of information on the university curriculum as are biographical accounts of those students known to have attained some degree of scientific proficiency while at university, especially as undergraduates.

As there are so few contemporary documents shedding any light on the state of science in pre-Civil War England, the few at our disposal have become the cornerstones of our knowledge. The accounts of such eminent men of science as John Wallis, Seth Ward and William Gascoigne have been cited as evidence of the hostility of the universities towards the new science and the absence of mathematics in their curriculum during the first half of the seventeenth century. What occurred though, especially in the nineteenth century when such documents were first brought to the attention of historians, was that while the piquant sentences were isolated for examination, little or no reference was made to the document as a whole; the reason why its author committed such thoughts to paper or biographical details which might have helped historians to elucidate its meaning are never brought out. Although most such accounts are of events recollected after a lifetime devoted to extending the frontiers of a scientific field, no allowance is made for selective memory, the inevitable ignorance of youth when compared with the wisdom of old age, or the not infrequent tendency towards self-aggrandizement or aggrandizement of a famous figure. Rare indeed is the man who in old age does not choose to envisage himself or his hero as the impatient youth stubbornly rejecting all authority as he single-handedly carves out for himself an as yet unexplored territory.

A case in point is the often quoted account by John Wallis, Savilian Professor of Geometry from 1649 until his death in 1703, of his initial encounter with mathematics. The fact that Wallis was esteemed as one of the more gifted mathematicians of the age and that his autobiography provides one of the most detailed accounts of the origins of the Royal Society has made this recollection a key reference. For this reason I shall first quote the appropriate passages in full and then place them within the context of his autobiography as a whole:

I did thenceforth prosecute it [mathematics], (at School and in the University) not as a formal Study, but as a pleasing Diversion, at spare hours; as books of *Arithmetick*, or others *Mathematical* fel occasionally in my way. For I had none to direct me, what books to read, or what to seek, or in what method to proceed. For Mathematicks, (at that time, with us) were scarce looked upon as *Accademical* studies, but rather *Mechanical*; as the business of *Traders, Merchants, Seamen, Carpenters, Surveyors of Lands*, or the like; and perhaps some *Almanak-makers in London*. And amongst more than Two hundred Students (at that time) in our College, I do not know of any Two (perhaps not any) who had more of *Mathematicks* than I, (if so much) which was then but little; And but very few, in that whole University. For the Study of *Mathematicks* was at that time more cultivated in *London* than in the Universities.

A few paragraphs later Wallis recalls the beginnings of the scientific meetings in London of 1645 which eventually led to the founding of the Royal Society:

About the year 1645, while I lived in *London* ... I had the opportunity of being acquainted with divers worthy Persons, inquisitive into Natural Philosophy, and other parts of Humane Learning; And particularly of what hath been called the *New Philosophy* or *Experimental Philosophy*.[1]

The first passage needs some elaboration. Mention should be made of Wallis's age when he composed his autobiography and his somewhat arrogant and conceited nature which, by all accounts, led him from one controversy to another throughout his long life. Even in this autobiography modesty does not emerge as one of Wallis's virtues. In a draft version we read:

I came well grounded to the University, and had all along the good hap (both at the school and the University,) to be reputed one of the best scholars of my rank.[2]

Written when Wallis had served as Savilian Professor of Geometry for some fifty years, his autobiography recollects a period during which mathematics was far from being his main preoccupation. He pursued mathematical studies as 'a pleasing Diversion', while his intention was to concentrate on divinity, 'on which [he] had an eye from the first'.[3] It

---

[1] C. J. Scriba, 'The autobiography of John Wallis F.R.S.', *Notes and Records of The Royal Society*, xxv (1970), 27, 39.
[2] Scriba, 'The autobiography of John Wallis', 28.
[3] Scriba, 'The autobiography of John Wallis', 30.

should be emphasized that a career as a divine necessitates no more than a general knowledge of mathematics. Such a description, however, is in no way indicative of the instruction received by those who wished to cultivate the mathematical sciences in a more serious manner. Moreover, Wallis's claim that there was little knowledge of the sciences in Cambridge and that he alone was a prodigy of Emmanuel in particular and the university in general is a flagrant exaggeration. In the 1630s Emmanuel produced such men as Jeremiah Horrox, an exact contemporary of Wallis, John Sadler and the Cambridge Platonists Benjamin Whichcote, John Smith and Ralph Cudworth. In the university as a whole we find Charles Scarburgh, John Beale, William Holder and Seth Ward. At least as regards Whichcote, we know that an association did exist, for the Platonist acted as Wallis's tutor. As for the others, it appears that either Wallis did not associate with them, his interests at the time lying elsewhere, or he is distorting the facts to make a point.

The second paragraph quoted from Wallis's autobiography deals with his newly formed associations in London and serves as the basis for Hill's claim that 'Wallis never heard of the "new experimental philosophy" until years after he had left Cambridge'.[4] Certainly if this ambiguous sentence proves anything, it is that Wallis had some acquaintance with such studies and was fortunate enough to meet people with similar interests. But there is no need to bicker about semantics. In this same autobiography Wallis attests to the fact that he took himself to the 'Speculative part of *Physick and Anatomy*' and was the first 'who (in a publick Disputation) maintained the Circulation of the Bloud', as part of his B.A. exercises it should be added. Moreover, he 'had then imbib'd the Principles of what they {now} call the *New Philosophy*'. He 'diverted also to *Astronomy and Geography* (as parts of *Natural Philosophy*) and to other parts of Mathematicks; though, at that time, they were scarce looked upon, with us, as Accademical Studies then in fashion'.[5] Thus, in contradiction to Hill's claim, it appears that Wallis was certainly familiar with, and capable of handling, up-to-date sources of scientific knowledge. Other evidence, which will be presented in the course of this chapter, should make it clear that Wallis was not the only student capable of scientific sophistication. As for Wallis's concluding remark that these studies were not looked on 'as Accademical Studies then in fashion', it means not that they were despised or censured, but simply were without an endowed chair and as yet had not gained the full autonomy with which they were to be endowed with the introduction of the tripos in the late seventeenth and early eighteenth centuries.

The anecdote related by Walter Pope in his biography of Seth Ward (M.A. 1640, Sidney Sussex College, Cambridge), Savilian Professor of

    4   Hill, *Intellectual Origins*, p. 64.
    5   Scriba, 'The autobiography of John Wallis', 29–30.

Astronomy at Oxford from 1649 until 1660 and one of the most important members of the Royal Society, also deserves to be closely scrutinized, for it has been brought as proof of the impoverished state of mathematics in early-seventeenth-century Cambridge.

In the College Library he found, by chance, some Books that treated of the Mathematics, and they being wholly new to him, he inquired all the College over for a Guide to instruct him that way, but all Search was in vain, these Books were *Greek*, I mean unintelligible, to all the Fellows of the College. Nevertheless, he took courage, and attempted them himself, *proprio Marte*, without any Confederates, or Assistance, or Intelligence in that Countrey, and that with so good Success, that in a short time he not only discovered those *Indies*, but conquer'd several Kingdoms therein, and brought thence a great part of their Treasure.[6]

This passage, interpreted in conjunction with Ward's visit to Oughtred in 1644, has caused Hill and Webster to conclude that it was this last association that introduced Ward to mathematics.[7] However, a citation of this passage without reference to what follows does great injustice to its meaning. Ward embarked upon these studies in his first, or at most second, year at university, for by the time he had become a sophister in his third year 'he disputed in those Sciences, more like a Master than a Learner'. These preliminary exercises were greatly esteemed by the then Savilian Professor of Astronomy, John Bainbridge, who happened to attend them. Significantly, one of the topics disputed by Ward as part of his B.A. requirements was astronomy, a subject usually assigned only to M.A. students. In fact, Ward's topic was drawn from the controversy over the Julian and Gregorian versions of the calendar and – by Pope's own account – his performance gained Ward high repute.[8] More important still, Ward's sojourn with Oughtred in 1644 was not his first, for as early as 1640 or 1641 Ward, together with Charles Scarburgh, had visited the renowned teacher. By 1642 Ward was already a college lecturer in mathematics at Sidney Sussex College, teaching Oughtred's famous *Clavis*.[9] Pope's rendering of Ward's initial encounter with mathematics and his inability to find a knowledgeable guide appears to be flawed for another reason. Ward was under the special tutorship of the then Master of Sidney Sussex College, Samuel Ward, who – as has been shown in chapter II – was himself a scientific enthusiast and a keen mathematician.[10] If no one else then, he alone could have assisted his charge in his pursuit of mathematical

---

[6] W. Pope, *The Life of the Right Reverend Father of God, Seth, Lord Bishop of Salisbury*, ed. J. B. Bamborough (Oxford, 1961), p. 10.

[7] See, for example, Hill, *Intellectual Origins*, p. 53; Webster, *The Great Instauration*, p. 120; Curtis, *Oxford and Cambridge in Transition*, p. 245; Costello, *The Scholastic Curriculum*, pp. 102–3.

[8] Pope, *The Life of Seth*, pp. 10–12.

[9] *Biog. Brit.*, vol. 6, appendix 158–9; Wood, *Athenae Oxonienses*, vol. 4, p. 247.

[10] Samuel Ward, *Opera nonnulla*, ed. Seth Ward (London, 1658), 'Ad lector', sig. A2. See above, p. 60.

knowledge. It becomes increasingly apparent, therefore, that neither Wallis nor Ward had to leave Cambridge in order to embark upon what eventually became a life-long study of mathematics. Such accounts of the early encounters of scientists with mathematics should be understood more as proof of the initiative of men who have been held up as models of progressive thought than as exposés of the universities.

And what about others? William Gascoigne, a brilliant young astronomer, wrote to Oughtred somewhere between 1640 and 1641 that he had left both Oxford and London before he knew 'what any proposition in geometry meant'. A piece of information not related is that Gascoigne probably stayed only a short while in Oxford on account of his Catholicism, and his name is not recorded in any of the registers.[11] In any case, if this was the situation in 'unreformed' Oxford of the pre-Civil War era, how are we to explain that as late as 1652 another correspondent of Oughtred, Robert Austin, wrote: 'I am now at Cambridge, but methinks, I do but lose my time here, when I compare my gains here with those at Albury.'[12] Austin's letter is conveniently ignored by historians who assign the utmost importance to the Puritan hegemony for the introduction of proper scientific instruction. But in Austin's case, as in the case of others, allowance should be made both for the proliferation of flattering figures of speech in addresses to eminent mentors as well as the scarcity of tutors and lecturers capable of rivalling in knowledge and in dedication a private instructor of the calibre of Oughtred.

Research provides examples of other sentences which, if viewed uncritically and taken out of context, could leave the reader puzzled as to the reality they are intended to portray. I should like to instance my point with two testimonials of noted adherents of the new science in the second half of the seventeenth century, both of which are intended to reflect the state of scientific instruction in Cambridge in the 1650s. The first was made in a lecture delivered by the eminent naturalist John Ray around 1660; he was 'sorry to see so little account made of real Experimental Philosophy in this University and that those ingenious sciences of the Mathematics are so neglected by us'.[13] On the other hand, Joseph Glanvill, who matriculated at Exeter College, Oxford, in 1652 during the heyday of the Wadham group, lamented that his friends did not first send him to Cambridge because the 'new philosophy and art of philosophising' were better developed there.[14] Whose word, then, is to be believed?

---

[11] Rigaud, *Correspondence of Scientific Men*, vol. I, p. 35: W. Gascoigne to W. Oughtred, Feb. 1640/41.

[12] Rigaud, *Correspondence of Scientific Men*, vol. I, p. 73: R. Austin to W. Oughtred, 3 Dec. 1652.

[13] Quoted by C. E. Raven, *John Ray, Naturalist*, 2nd edn (Cambridge, 1950), p. 14, n. 5.

[14] Quoted by Webster, *The Great Instauration*, p. 134.

An interesting and hitherto unexplored source of information on the university curriculum in general and mathematical instruction in particular is the *Responsa Scholarum*: it consists of the autobiographical statements of English Catholics wishing to enter the English College at Rome and includes information on family, upbringing, religious beliefs and education. Although almost 600 such responses are recorded for the period 1598–1685, only about 150 refer to the English universities. No doubt in part this is because Oxford and Cambridge severely restricted the entrance of Catholics and more than half of the scholars had attended the Jesuit college of St Omers; indeed, many of the candidates for the English College with any English university background had been Protestants before their arrival in Rome. Of those who did indicate some previous university training, the vast majority referred to their education in the most general terms, either failing to specify their course of studies altogether or limiting their curricular descriptions at most to rhetoric, dialectics and philosophy. This might be explained by the fact that most of the students who filled out the questionnaire showed no particular interest in enumerating their previous course of studies and lumped together the various disciplines under their general headings. It should be borne in mind that rhetoric usually embraced poetry, history, grammar and sometimes even geography, while philosophy embraced natural philosophy, ethics and metaphysics as well as the various mathematical sciences. Fortunately though, a few responses were more detailed, thus offering a rare glimpse into the nature of the university curriculum in our period.

John Greaves, who matriculated at Trinity College, Oxford, in 1590 and took his B.A. in 1593/94, specifies that his course of studies included natural and moral philosophy, dialectics, astronomy, geometry, speculative arithmetic, geography, history and poetry. It is not at all surprising that as a convert wishing to enrol in a Catholic college he deemed his course of studies unsatisfactory.[15] Charles Waldegrave, the son of a wealthy family who matriculated as a fellow-commoner at Gonville and Caius College, Cambridge, in May 1598 and left two years later for Flanders, records that his studies consisted of logic and cosmography 'with little progress'.[16] At about the same time John Smith alias Carrington spent three years at St Mary's Hall and Gloucester Hall, Oxford. According to his statement he studied logic and the first part of dialectics, dabbled in

[15] *The Responsa Scholarum of the English College, Rome*, ed. A. Kenny, Catholic Rec. Soc., vol. 54 (Newport, Mon., 1962), vol. 1, p. 9. Greaves – not to be confused with his namesake the Gresham Professor of Geometry – left Oxford shortly after taking a B.A. Foster, *Alumni Oxonienses*, vol. 2, p. 596.
[16] *Responsa Scholarum*, vol. 1, p. 89; Venn, *Alumni Cantabrigienses*, vol. 4, p. 315.

philosophy, medicine, cosmography, history, rhetoric and poetry, all of which 'bore no more fruit than an often transplanted shrub'.[17]

Four other candidates for the English College had gone beyond the B.A. Francis Young was admitted to St Mary's Hall, Oxford, in 1585 and transferred to Trinity College, Oxford, two years later where he took his B.A. in 1589/90 and M.A. in 1593/94. In his statement he indicates a university education which included grammar, poetry, rhetoric, a little Greek, geography, arithmetic, some astronomy, very little dialectics and philosophy.[18] Another entry provides an autobiographical fragment on the neo-Latin English poet William Alabaster, whom we have had occasion to mention as a mathematical lecturer. Alabaster, who had been educated at Trinity College, Cambridge, for fourteen years (1584–97), relates that his studies consisted of grammar, poetry, rhetoric, logic, philosophy, mathematics, history, criticism, philosophy and almost all the Greek and Latin authors in so far as they were relevant to theology; he then goes on to elaborate his theological studies.[19] Mention should also be made of Thomas Hodgson who in 1581 matriculated at Gloucester Hall, Oxford, where he remained for seventeen years, devoting his time mostly to astronomy and judicial astrology, before he was licensed to practise medicine.[20]

Yet by far the most communicative response was made by John Everard who entered Clare Hall, Cambridge, in 1598, aged 12, under the tutorship of the Master, Dr Byng. As Everard enumerates his course of studies for the seven years he spent at Cambridge until he proceeded M.A., often citing the texts used, it is worth quoting the entire section pertaining to his university education.

Suscipit tutelam mei Dr BINGUS, tunc temporis Collegii praefectus: Initior sacris, et impiis nescio quibus votis, iam tum obstringor, puer trimestris scilicet, et qui ne vapulem centies iuremque peieremque, sed istud ἀπροσδιονυσον et extra oleas: Enimvero Poeticam, Rhetoricam, et Graecas litteras edoctus antehac, primo quod fieri solet anno vacabam Logicae, Ibi mihi familiares SETONUS, AGRICOLA, TITELMANNUS, FLAVIUS, PACIUS; dein producto ad umbilicum anno, innotescit paulatim ZABARELLA, PORPHYRIUS, ALEXANDER APHRODISIUS, ac ipse ARISTOTELES, cuius οργανον ut moris est ter quater revolvi, paratus, quod et hic usuvenit, in quodvis Magistri verbum iurare tametsi ipse sibi mentiendi conscius esset, et plurima praesertim in Topicis loca aspergeret, quae non ad veritatem sed ad victoriam facerent, attestante D. THOMA, et Alexandro Aphrodysio comment. in Top. lib. 6.c.3. Elapso anno, instauravit mihi studia subsequens annus, cum ad

[17] *Responsa Scholarum*, vol. 1, p. 89. There is no John Smith or Carrington who matriculated at either of the above-mentioned halls in the 1590s referred to in Clark's *Register*.

[18] *Responsa Scholarum*, vol. 1, pp. 6–8; Foster, *Alumni Oxonienses*, vol. 4, p. 1704.

[19] *Responsa Scholarum*, vol. 1, pp. 1–3; Venn, *Alumni Cantabrigienses*, vol. 1, p. 11; *DNB*.

[20] Hodgson proceeded M.A. in 1594. *Responsa Scholarum*, vol. 1, pp. 90–3; Clark, *Register*, vol. 2, part 3, p. 146.

Aristotelis, Ethicam philosophiam ad Nichomachum inscriptam, ad Politicam etiam conversus, opera ut plurimum DONATI, MARTYRIS, CASI, et FOORTHI usus sum, admistis quotidie lectionibus Graeca, Rhetorica, Logica, Philosophica, Mathematica, disputationibus, declamationibus, oratiunculis, sophismatis, problematibus,aliisque item exercitiis, quibus ex Academiae statutis et Collegii regulis interesse tenemur. Irrepsit demum tertius annus, cuius cum quarto communia fuere studia, Naturalis philosophia, ex naturae Genio praecipue, dein etiam ex probatissimis interpretibus petenda, quos mihi adscivi praeter supra commemoratos TOLLETUM, SCALIGERUM et CARDANUM, nec caeteros contempsi quoscunque mihi fors vel casus obvios dabat. Sub finem quarti anni, post ter publice defensas, et novies oppugnatas theses, factus sum Baccalaureus in artibus, et non ita multo post in Collegii societatem adscitus, assumpto gradu, et illato turgido honore, ovans incedebam. Iamque rebus ad voluntatem propriam gerendis, etsi meae ipsius προαιρεσι derelictus plurimum de anteacti temporis intensione remittebam, succisivis tamen horis et priora studia recolebam, et addebam indies metaphysices, mathematicesque aliquid, dum prioribus quatuor, tribus ulterius additis annis, tandem Magister in artibus evaderem.[21]

This last entry offers a rare insight into the educational practices of the universities not only because Everard was most elaborate in his statement, but because apart from his religious concerns, he appears to typify the average student of whom so few records exist. There is no evidence whatsoever to indicate that Clare Hall implemented a more rigorous course of scientific instruction than other colleges; in fact, its statutes make no reference to mathematics. Such being the case, it is noteworthy that by his second year Everard had been attending daily lectures in mathematics, while as a bachelor he studied metaphysics and astronomy for three years; unfortunately, in neither case did Everard indicate the textbooks used.

Most significantly, although the candidates cited above wrote somewhat disparagingly of the education they had received in the 'heretic' universities, their statements reveal a similar pattern. With minor variations, as undergraduates they pursued a course which consisted of logic, rhetoric, history, poetry and mathematics – often including cosmography, geometry or geography – while as bachelors they studied philosophy and astronomy. There appears, then, to have existed a theory of education common to both universities which manifested itself in a similar course of instruction.

The various schematic outlines of studies – often in the form of manuals of advice for students – substantiate the evidence already provided by those candidates for the English College who set down more detailed descriptions of their university course of studies. Although for the most part these

---

[21] *Responsa Scholarum*, vol. I, pp. 225–6; Venn, *Alumni Cantabrigienses*, vol. 2, p. 110; *DNB*. Thomas Byng, who served as Master of Clare Hall from 1571, died in December 1599, some two years after Everard's admittance. Nothing is known about who replaced Byng as Everard's tutor. For Byng, see Cooper, *Athenae Cantabrigienses*, vol. 2, pp. 279–80, 551.

manuals date from the middle and second half of the seventeenth century, they show little variation in either the courses they suggest or the order in which they were to be studied; what did change was the recommended list of books which was continually being updated throughout the century, or, more accurately, being added to the existing corpus.

The course of studies implemented by Henry Dunster at Harvard College in 1642 – and described in a pamphlet circulated in order to drum up support for the college in England – appears to have differed from that of the universities only in so far as it was compressed into three years instead of four and put a pronouncedly stronger emphasis upon religious studies. As undergraduates, the Harvard students were expected to attend lectures and tutorials in grammar, Greek, moral and natural philosophy, arithmetic, geometry, astronomy, poetry, rhetoric and history. Most likely the type of education instituted by Dunster reflected his own experience as a student at Magdalene College, Cambridge, where he had proceeded M.A. in 1634.[22]

A pamphlet of 1660 entitled 'An Oxford Conference of Philomathes and Polymathes' presents the course of studies pursued by first-year students at Oxford. The speaker, Philomathes, describes his studies with his tutor in the following way: 'I am, this my first year, to let Logick alone, and employ my time in Classick Authors, Greek & Latine, with a little mixture of Arithmetick and Geometry, and the use of the Globe, and a little of Musick, both vocal and instrumental. But next year, have at your Logick.'[23] Although the 'Directions for a Student in the Universitie' (*c.* 1640) attributed to Richard Holdsworth makes no mention of mathematics, this does not necessarily mean that he did not teach mathematics to his students.[24] For the most part mathematics was discussed in a separate chapter only late in the seventeenth century and the early manuals sometimes glossed over the subject or referred the student to the tutor or other professional instructors for such information. For example, the only time the extremely detailed 'A Library for Younger Schollers' – compiled by Thomas Barlow, Provost of Queen's College, Oxford, during

[22] Morison reprinted this pamphlet as appendix D to *The Founding of Harvard College*, where the relevant sections concerning curriculum are to be found on pp. 535–6. For Dunster, see also S. E. Morison, *Harvard College in the Seventeenth Century* (Cambridge, Mass., 1936), *passim*. Dunster's copy of Ramus's arithmetic and geometry textbook, bought while he was an undergraduate, is in the Boston Public Library. See Morison, *The Founding of Harvard College*, p. 112.

[23] C. Barksdale, *An Oxford Conference of Philomathes and Polymathes* (London, 1660), p. 4.

[24] The 'Directions' were printed by Fletcher as appendix II to *The Intellectual Development of John Milton*, vol. 2, pp. 623ff. Noteworthy is Holdsworth's failure to make adequate mention of natural philosophy – citing only a few textbooks – although it played a major role in the curriculum. See J. A. Trentman, 'The authorship of "Directions for a Student in the Universitie"', *Trans. Camb. Bibl. Soc.*, VII (1978), 170–83.

the 1650s and later Bishop of Lincoln – is incommunicative is when it pertains to mathematical instruction:

5 For Mathematics, I referre you to the Professers of those Sciences, who, as their knowledge is more, soe (I am confident) their Charitie will not bee lesse, in communicateing their Directions in this particular.

In their foreword to this edition of the manuscript, De Jordy and Fletcher write: 'These lists of books display the scholarly interests of their time, the next subject after metaphysics being "Mathematicks", but, once listed, it was dropped, the reader being directed to "the Professers [sic] of those Sciences".' Such an omission might be explained by the fact that this extant manuscript appears to be a copy of an original of which no trace remains. It seems highly probable that the later compiler and transcriber, aware of the new scientific developments, dropped the section, referring the student elsewhere.[25] For interestingly enough, an anonymous advice, probably penned in the late 1680s, is just as reticent when it comes to scientific instruction. Although the author does not deal with mathematics, when it is time to treat astronomy, he writes: 'That part which treats of Celestiall bodyes belongs properly to Astronomy, & is therefore to be refferred to Mathematics.'[26] It was only during the last decade of the seventeenth century and the early eighteenth century that elaborate discussions of mathematics began to appear in student manuals. Daniel Waterland's manual of the first decade of the eighteenth century propounds the same basic educational views held by earlier writers with the difference that he prescribes the necessary scientific texts under the heading 'philosophical authors'.[27]

Consequently, as with individual accounts, the occasional omission of mathematics in student manuals is insufficient evidence for concluding that mathematics was absent from the undergraduate course of studies. I would explain such an omission by reference to the increasing awareness

[25] *A Library for Younger Schollers*, ed. De Jordy and Fletcher, pp. 4, v–vi. At any rate, after listing the scholastic texts for natural philosophy, the author cites the works of Gassendi, Descartes, Bacon, Digby and White.

[26] It begins, 'In order to ye attainment of learning & increase in knowledge, 'tis highly necessary ...' Bodl. MS Rawl. D 188, fol. 5. The author similarly avoids discussing chemistry, for it is to be learned through 'a course in the Laboratory', but dwells on the new philosophy, recommending Bacon, Sprat, Boyle and the various Cartesians. See fols. 5–6. The 'Rules to be observed by young pupils & schollers in the university' (printed by G. Trevelyan under the title 'Undergraduate life under the Protectorate', *The Cambridge Review*, LXIV (1943), 328–30) drawn up by James Duport in the 1650s is even less informative as regards curriculum, consisting mostly of rules of conduct.

[27] D. Waterland, *Advice to a Young Student* (London, 1730). In the advertisement preface the author states that the manual had been drawn up over twenty years earlier by a tutor for the private use of students. Waterland (M.A. 1706, Magdalene College, Cambridge) became Master of the College in 1714 where he remained until 1740. *DNB*.

of scientific developments and what may be termed the increasing professionalization of the sciences. The middle of the seventeenth century was a period of transition in which on the one hand the educated man was made increasingly aware of the inadequacy of traditional mathematical texts, but on the other had not as yet acquired the tools to handle with ease, still less to judge, the newer works that were continually making their appearance. Like most critics whose task it is to recommend the best books available, they preferred to shy away from such subjects and defer judgement until the books had been judged by more knowing minds. Hence, it was not before the turn of the eighteenth century that the compilers of student manuals gave their approval to such works as had already been assimilated by the universities.[28]

The account books of Joseph Mede, a tutor and a fellow of Christ's College, Cambridge, from 1613 until 1638 who has already been mentioned in connection with his tutorship of Justinian Isham, are also a valuable piece of information for determining the nature and quality of mathematical instruction. Mede, it should be noted, was interested in a broad spectrum of scientific subjects. Late in life he spoke of his mathematical studies pursued in his 'younger time' and John Worthington, Mede's biographer, attributed to him a close study of astrology. In addition to his interest in mathematics, Mede retained a life-long interest in medicine and anatomy, 'being usually sent for when they had any Anatomy in Caius College'. Mede also seems to have carried on a scientific correspondence with his friend and patron Sir William Boswell in which he discussed such issues as ' *De motu Gravium & Levium* ... the *Equality of Natural Motions*, with some reflexions upon the common opinion of their being *velociores in sine quam in principio*; others about the Nature of *Comets*, particularly about the *Comet* in 1618'.[29]

The account books in which Mede recorded the expenses of his students were used extensively by Fletcher in his *Intellectual Development of John Milton*, but as Fletcher was not primarily interested in the study of mathematics, his findings can be supplemented. An examination of these account books indicates that Mede not only provided his students with such

[28] When Joshua Barnes came to revise Holdsworth's *Directions*, he left intact most of the scholastic texts but ordered that 'because the course of philosophical studies is now altered', a student 'may make use of Des Cartes his Book of Meteors, also his De Passionibus and etc; as also of Le Grand, Regius and other Cartesians e.g. Rohault and others'. Emmanuel College Cambridge MS 179, fol. 56.

[29] The four volumes of Mede's account books are housed in the library of Christ's College, Cambridge. For Mede's scientific interests, see *Works*, ed. Worthington, 'The General Preface'; T. Birch (ed.), *The Court and Times of Charles the First* (London, 1848), vol. I, pp. 117, 329; J. Looney, 'Undergraduate education at early Stuart Cambridge', *History of Education*, x (1981), 9–19.

sums as were necessary to purchase books in the Cambridge bookstores, but that he also sold the newcomers texts he had acquired from departing students; this practice is especially discernible as regards the basic undergraduate textbooks. It is also evident that not all of Mede's students purchased books or that at least their purchases went unrecorded. No doubt some brought the required works with them to university; in this context it should be noted that Mede often instructed successive members of the same families who could easily have passed along their books. Nonetheless, of a total of 95 students supervised by Mede between 1618 and 1636, 29 acquired at least one of the three basic mathematical texts used by Mede: Ryff's *Geometry*, Keckermann's *Mathematics* and Blundeville's *Exercises*. From the accounts it appears that Ryff's *Geometry* – which at times had been assigned together with Gemma Frisius's *Arithmetic* – was increasingly replaced by Blundeville's and Keckermann's texts which were more up-to-date and covered a wider range of topics. Blundeville's *Exercises*, first published in 1594 and brought out in at least six additional editions by 1638, treated arithmetic, cosmography and astronomy as well as included treatises on the globe and navigation. In addition to the twenty-nine students who acquired these mathematical texts, two students purchased Keckermann's *Systema compendiosum totius mathematices, hoc est: geometriae, opticae, astronomicae, et geographicae* (1617), two more acquired Alsted's *Encyclopedia* (1620) which also included mathematics and astronomy, and, as mentioned previously, Justinian Isham acquired Digges's *Pantometria* (1571). An additional seven students purchased one of the following cosmographical texts: Sebastian Munster's *Cosmography* (1572), Robert Hues's *Tractatus de Globis* (1594), George Abbot's *A Briefe Description of the Whole Worlde* (1599), Abraham Ortelius's *Theatrum orbis terrarum* (1606) and Peter Heylin's *Microcosmus* (1621). It should be noted that the entries are occasionally illegible, thus obscuring certain purchases. Especially as regards Keckermann, it is extremely difficult to ascertain which of the author's texts is being indicated. A further factor which might affect the validity of the account books as a true description of Mede's mathematical instruction is that by the late 1620s there occurs a definite decrease in the number of entries for all books, including mathematical books. Whereas of the 59 students whom Mede instructed from 1618 until 1626 there are 23 entries recording the purchase of one of the three mathematical texts, of the 36 students tutored by Mede from 1626 onward, there are only six entries for these texts. This significant decrease can be explained either by a growing carelessness on the part of Mede or an increasing tendency among students to acquire texts independently.

Nevertheless, the cumulative effect of these account books is to suggest that for Mede's students mathematical instruction played a significant role in their undergraduate education. While Mede probably provided at least minimal mathematical instruction to all of his students – even those students whose purchases of mathematical texts are not recorded – those keener students who acquired the more advanced mathematical works most likely received further instruction. This last point brings us back to one of the conclusions of the last chapter, namely, that although all students appear to have received some grounding in mathematics, only a minority wished to receive a more elaborate and penetrating instruction.

Although student notebooks of the sixteenth and seventeenth centuries are a potentially valuable source of information on the university curriculum, a certain degree of caution should be exercised when dealing with them. Two related factors, the first concerning the circumstances of their preservation and the second, their content, should be borne in mind in any attempt to assess their significance. Of the relatively few extant student notebooks scattered in various libraries, the circumstances of their preservation – including the way in which they made their appearance in libraries – usually cannot be ascertained. Some notebooks were passed down from one member of a family to another or from one colleague to another until the papers were entrusted to a library or collected by some antiquarian such as Rawlinson or Harley. And this brings us to the question of content, or why certain notebooks were more likely than others to survive. As regards the few extant undergraduate notebooks of our period, it was more probable that notebooks containing the backbone of the curriculum – that is to say logic and philosophy – would be preserved by their original owners and passed on to others. Not only were the B.A. and M.A. exercises heavily oriented towards these subjects, but they were viewed by most educated men as the cornerstones of later intellectual pursuits. Given this situation, it might be argued that only a true mathematical enthusiast would have been likely either to devote an entire notebook to mathematics or to have clung to it over the years. More important still, much of the material found in such notebooks is presented in the form of questions – either mock or real – which were intended to aid the student in his preparation for his final exercises, whether B.A. or M.A. It is easy to understand, then, why notebooks devoted entirely to mathematics are a rarity and 'miscellaneous' notebooks treating a wide gamut of subjects are the rule.

Once the above-mentioned factors influencing the nature of extant student notebooks are taken into account, the state of science in the universities as reflected in such notebooks is nowhere as bleak as it has been portrayed. For example, the argument of Costello that no mathematical instruction took place in Cambridge during the first half of the seventeenth century because he had found no student notebooks of that era treating mathematics is seriously flawed. He not only ignored the factors that would influence the nature and content of those notebooks that would have been likely to survive, but implicit in his argument is the assumption that the notebook under examination was the student's sole notebook and the subjects treated therein the only ones in which he received instruction. Moreover, his sample is far from representative.[30] My own examination of student notebooks of the period suggests that the student community was provided with mathematical instruction on various levels and was more aware of the recent scientific notions than is often assumed.

Curtis has already made mention of John Stay's 'Tome the Second, of Schoolle Exercises' which characterizes student mathematical studies around 1634 and attests to Stay's familiarity with Briggs's work on logarithms and his approval of the Copernican system.[31] There are, however, other notebooks treating mathematics, even if at times only the most fragmentary evidence of a student's mathematical instruction has survived. Although the notebook of the Carnsew brothers, who matriculated at Broadgates Hall, Oxford, in 1572, is for the most part devoted to logic, history and theology, it nonetheless indicates their knowledge of the extraction of the cube and the quadrant.[32] A student of Christ Church, Oxford, in 1581 appears to have been instructed in the elements of astronomy[33] while an anonymous notebook – perhaps of a Cambridge undergraduate in the late sixteenth century – reveals the strong influence of Ramus and occasionally branches out to arithmetic and geometry.[34] Even Simonds D'Ewes, who not once mentioned his study of mathematics in any of his autobiographical tracts, appears to have received some mathematical instruction, for one of his student notebooks from 1619 contains a fragment of a geometrical problem.[35]

Other undergraduates afford us with more substantial evidence of their mathematical instruction. An anonymous notebook of the early seventeenth century includes basic arithmetical and geometrical propositions as well as directions for the use of the quadrant.[36] An interesting notebook was composed by Samuel Brown (M.A. 1605, All Souls College, Oxford) some time during his student years and includes, among other things, notes on chronology, astronomy, geometry and cosmography. In 1619 Brown bestowed the notebook upon John Cotton who was about

[30] Costello, *The Scholastic Curriculum*, passim.
[31] CUL MS Dd.III.17; Curtis, *Oxford and Cambridge in Transition*, p. 244.
[32] PRO SP 46/15, fol. 213.
[33] BL MS Harl. 4048, fols. 78v–75v (reverse).
[34] BL MS Harl. 3230, fols. 2, 112, 180–1.
[35] BL MS Harl. 191, fol. 1v.
[36] Bodl. MS Jesus College 87.

to matriculate at Christ Church, Oxford, apparently assuming that the material would be of some assistance to an undergraduate.[37] The surviving commonplace book of John Ramsey, who resided for two years (1601–3) at Peterhouse, Cambridge, suggests that he was tutored in both mathematics and cosmography by Dr Soame. Clearly indicated in the notebook is Ramsey's acquaintance with the work of most of the contemporary English mathematicians and instrument-makers, including Briggs, Hood, Blagrave, Blundeville, Norden and Elias Allen.[38] In 1607 one Edmund Lee composed a commonplace book which includes lengthy commentaries on the various scientific disciplines. Lee devotes a section to geometry, elaborating on the problem of the quadrature of the circle, as well as to optics and astronomy. He also shows signs of interest in the works of Roger Bacon and John Dee. Other sources consulted by Lee include Euclid, Ptolemy, Stifelius and Kepler, and it is noteworthy that the notions of a moving earth and the earth as a magnet are both discussed favourably.[39]

Other evidence of undergraduate mathematical instruction includes an anonymous notebook, most probably of a Cambridge student, c. 1610–12, which treats arithmetic as well as containing biographical information on 'Copernicus Nicholaus mathematicus Germanus statuit terram moveri ex nat. 1473 mort. 1543 aetat 70'.[40] Another anonymous commonplace book of the 1630s contains, in addition to a thesis on natural and moral philosophy, notes on astronomy, astrology and alchemy. Indeed, it begins with an oration entitled 'Oxonii in schola astron. cum nobiliss. dominus Carolus Herbertus altera vice sub baccalaureu responderet'.[41] A notebook of Thomas Chasey, probably of the late 1630s or 1640s, discourses on the trigonometrical canons of Pitiscus, and quotes from Wingate, Briggs and Gellibrand.[42] In 1640 Henry Ford appears to have received instruction similar to that received by Edmund Lee, but in his case there is less willingness to accept the recent scientific notions. In this notebook, which includes arithmetic, ethics, physics, geography and optics, Ford comments briefly on the nature of comets and answers in the negative the question 'Luna sit habitabilis?' The question 'Sit naturae magneticae?' is also answered in the negative, with Ford arguing 'contra Gilbertum', while the question 'Quiescente coelo moveatur?' is answered in the negative as a direct refutation of Copernicus.[43]

Other students revealed more specialized interests. William Camden,

---

[37] Bodl. MS Jesus College 92. For Brown, see Wood, *Athenae Oxonienses*, vol. 2, p. 531. For Cotton, see Foster, *Alumni Oxonienses*, vol. 2, p. 334.

[38] Bodl. MS Douce 280, fols. 1–4v, 91v, 103v–4.

[39] CUL MS Addit. 102, fols. 4v, 114v, 207–9, 239v, 241v–2.

[40] Bodl. MS Lincoln College 124. The reference to Copernicus appears on fol. 5.

[41] Bodl. MS Rawl. D. 1147.

[42] Bodl. MS University College 175.

[43] CUL MS Dd.III.24. The questions appear on fols. 18v, 19v.

who was a student at Broadgates Hall and Christ Church, Oxford, from
c. 1566 until 1573, has left some evidence of his scientific pursuits while
a resident of the university. Camden's life-long friendship with Henry
Savile began at Oxford and Camden probably attended Savile's renowned
lectures. Writing to Camden many years later, Savile informed him that
he had deposited his lecture notes – 'many of them ... as old as [their]
acquaintance ... when [he] read in the schools as Regent-master' – in the
mathematical library he had founded at Oxford. Quite possibly Camden
also acquired his copy of the 1566 edition of Copernicus during these
Oxford years, for he developed his astronomical interests at Oxford and
later in life he recorded the diligence with which he had observed the new
star of 1572. Camden's life-long interest in astrology also dates back to
this Oxford residence. A notebook containing assorted astrological notes
still survives as does Camden's copy of Cyprian Leowitz's *De coniunctionibus*,
purchased on 18 April 1573. Aubrey also records his having seen
Camden's copy of Stadius's *Ephemerides* with Camden's notes 'by which
[he] find[s] he was astrologically given'. Worthy of note is the possibility
that Camden's acquaintance with Dee began during this Oxford stay, for
by August 1574 Dee had written Camden a long letter in which he
discoursed on various antiquarian subjects as well as defended his
Propaedeumata aphoristica.[44]

Camden's fellow antiquarian, Henry Spelman, shared his interest in
astrology. Although Spelman remained in Trinity College and Trinity Hall,
Cambridge, for only eight terms, 1580 through 1581, his notebook from
that period indicates an avid interest in judicial astrology and refers to the
work of Ptolemy, Cardan and Bonatus. During the same period Spelman
purchased a copy of Maestlin's *Ephemerides novae ab anno 1577 an annum
1590*.[45]

Although they are of a somewhat later date, the following notebooks
nonetheless suggest a similar pattern of instruction. The commonplace
book of Nicholas Tufton (1649) included rhetoric, logic and arithmetic,[46]
while that of Benjamin Gostlet, another undergraduate of Christ Church,

[44] Camden, *Epistolae*, p. 315: H. Savile to W. Camden, 3 Nov. 1621; W. Camden, *Annales.
The True and Royall History of the Famous Empresse Elizabeth* (London, 1625), p. 319.
Camden's copy of Copernicus is at Brown University, sig. *QB41 C76; BL MS Cotton Julius
F.XI, fols. 70v–1, 151v–2v; his copy of Leowitz is in the Huntington Library. See M. Aston,
'The fiery trigon conjunction: an Elizabethan astrological prediction', *Isis*, LXI (1970),
165, n. 15; Aubrey, *Brief Lives*, vol. I, p. 144; Bodl. MS Ashmole 1788, fols. 70–6:
J. Dee to W. Camden, 7 Aug. 1574. For Camden's interest in astrology and the occult,
see also F. J. Levy, 'William Camden as a Historian' (Harvard Univ. Ph.D. thesis, 1959),
pp. 114–19.
[45] BL MS Harl. 6360, fols. 1–31; C. H. Cooper, 'An early autograph of Sir Henry Spelman',
Camb. Antiq. Soc. Commun., II (1860–4), 101–3. See pp. 151–2 below.
[46] Bodl. MS Rawl. D. 746.

Oxford (*c.* 1650), included the elements of geometry, astronomy and physics.[47]

For some other students, their surviving notebooks belong to the time of their M.A. studies. Around 1600 while enrolled in his M.A. course at Balliol College, Oxford, John Goodridge composed a notebook devoted to astronomy. Although the material is Aristotelian in orientation, it makes frequent use of the ever popular *Exercises* of Thomas Blundeville. Goodridge's continuing interest in mathematics is evident from his endowment at Wadham College of a 'lecturer in the long vacation provided he expounds mathematics' as well as from a number of his mathematical and astrological books now housed in the college library.[48] At about the same time (*c.* 1602–5) another Oxford student, Daniel Featley (Fairclough) was engaged in preparing for his M.A. exercises in Corpus Christi College. One of his exercises was to answer the question 'An terra moveatur, coelum quiescat?' Although Featley was expected to answer such a question in the negative, his short composition cited Copernicus as the authority against whom he argued, once again revealing knowledge – or at least awareness – of the alternative system.[49] Another student appears to have been bolder. When John Mansell – later Master of Queens' College, Cambridge – was preparing for his exercises which took place in 1601, he responded to an astronomical question on the nature of the planetary system. Mansell, however, chose to support the Copernican system and began his composition thus: 'Terra est corpus mobilissimum motum terrae circularem, asseruit olim pythagoras, demonstravit nuper Copernicus, at Mathematice pro suo instituto reformand hypothese Astronomiae.' He then continued with a relatively detailed technical account of the heliocentric theory. Another of Mansell's exercises took the form of an oration entitled 'optimus mathematicus, optimus polyticus' and included a customary defence of mathematical studies.[50]

The questions issued by the universities annually for the disputations of their students provide a good test-case for the argument, for many of the mock questions in the notebooks find their correlation in the official exercises. It is necessary to cite only the questions for Oxford to make this point. As early as 1576 there occurred the question 'An terra quiescat in medio mundi?' which, as was seen in the two previously cited student notebooks, was answered both in the affirmative and in the negative. In the 1580s questions relating to the possibility of a plurality of worlds appear twice. In 1581 we find 'An plures sint aut esse possint mundi?'

[47] Bodl. MS Rawl. D. 233.
[48] Wadham College Oxford MS A4/24; Ward, *Lives of the Professors*, pp. 314–17; H. A. Wheeler, *A Short Catalogue of Books Printed in England, and British Books Printed Abroad before 1641 in the Library of Wadham College Oxford* (London, 1929), p. 27.
[49] Bodl. MS Rawl. D. 47, fol. 109v.
[50] Bodl. MS Don. D. 152, fols. 41–41v, 29v–30v.

and seven years later 'An sint plures mundi?' It is tempting to interpret the 1611 question 'An luna sit habitabilis?' as an immediate response to Galileo's lunar observations published only the previous year.[51] Proof of the relevance of the examination questions to contemporary events can be found in the question for 1608: 'An terra sit naturae magneticae?' This is one of the rare instances in which there is external evidence. In a letter to John Chamberlain on 14 July 1608, Dudley Carleton writes: 'In the Monday exercise there were likewise many invectives, as the philosophers in the question *an terra sit naturae magneticae*, against Dr. Gilbert and all his secretaries, which they called Gilbertinos, where *il y va de votre* interest.'[52] Other evidence suggests even a greater licence for novelty. In 1640, for example, Samuel Hartlib received the following account – possibly from Joachim Hubner who was then at Oxford – of exercises performed by students in their college. 'One of the best exercises at Oxford is their declamations against Aristotle, which are kept yearly at a certain time. Their speeches for the most part are most accurately elaborated wherein Aristotle is mightily towsed.' Several pages later in the diary the place of such disputations is identified as Merton College. The performance of these exercises did not represent a break with tradition at Merton. To the contrary, the custom originated in the sixteenth century. In fact, the exercises designated by Hartlib are the very exercises outlined in the Merton College statutes according to which every master of arts of two years' standing was required to propose or defend six different theses. We do not know exactly when these college exercises became anti-Aristotelian in their thrust, but we do know that such a tradition dates back to at least the second half of the sixteenth century. It was during such a declamation, for example, that in 1573 Henry Savile argued 'Terra movetur circulariter' and that in 1594 Richard Trafford argued 'Aristotelis obscuritas in philosophia naturali tradenda reprehendenda est'. In 1599 and again in 1602 there were posed a series of questions drawn from Aristotle's *Rhetoric*, *Politics*, and *Ethics*, against which the disputants were specifically instructed to argue. We also know that in 1632 Hugh Cressey answered in the affirmative the question 'An scepticorum dubitantia praeferenda sit peripateticorum thesibus?'[53]

At least one other college displayed a similar flexibility in the topics they assigned their graduates for the M.A. exercises. In his diary for 1628 Thomas Crosfield records the disputations of five bachelors of Queen's

[51] Clark, *Register*, vol. 2, part 1, pp. 170–1, 177.
[52] Clark, *Register*, vol. 2, part 1, p. 176; *Dudley Carleton to John Chamberlain 1603–1624*, ed. M. Lee Jr (New Jersey, 1972), p. 103.
[53] Hartlib, 'Ephemerides 1640', F–G1, F–G5; *Registrum Annalium Collegii Mertonensis 1567–1603*, ed. Fletcher, pp. 50, 304, 334, 346; Merton College Oxford Register, vol. 2, fol. 310.

College in such subjects as optics, anatomy, chronology and astronomy, without, unfortunately, providing any information on the specific questions to be debated. However, in a diary entry for 1638 Crosfield notes that the topics for debate were related to the issue of tides as well as to the probable habitation of the moon, both of which undoubtedly echoed the recent discoveries of Galileo.[54]

These examples bring us back to the claims of the previous chapters. The university and college officials who were responsible for drawing up the topics of disputation were frequently the very heads of houses and young regent-masters who themselves left behind evidence of their own pursuit and encouragement of scientific enterprise. They neither deemed it the function of the university to transmit only old 'truths' and 'proven authorities' nor did they regard the curriculum as something rigid and incapable of modification. Far from being threatened by the new astronomical and physical ideas, these university members often allowed – and indeed encouraged – a relatively free discussion of the most up-to-date issues even if they themselves were not totally convinced of their truth. Hence, the appearance of frequently provocative issues in the university and college disputations. By forcing students to acquaint themselves with these new ideas, they initiated the first tentative step in the critical dialogue between competing world-views.

Although some eminent, university-trained men of science left little direct evidence of the course of studies they pursued at Oxford or Cambridge, they frequently exhibited a degree of sophistication or gained positions immediately upon taking a B.A. that would suggest that their stay had been devoted in part to mathematical studies. Even allowing for individual ingenuity and incentive, it is extremely rare to find scientific enterprise pursued in a total vacuum.

Thomas Harriot, for example, acquired such repute as an undergraduate that upon obtaining a B.A. from St Mary's Hall, Oxford, in 1580, he was immediately enlisted as a mathematical tutor by Sir Walter Ralegh. It should be added that Ralegh himself had been resident at Oriel College, Oxford, for three years – 1568–71 – without, however, taking a degree.[55] As early as 1603, the year he graduated B.A. from Christ Church, Edmund Gunter had circulated a Latin version of his *New Projection of the Sphere*. (The English version was published only in 1623.) This treatise brought

---

[54] Queen's College Oxford MS 390, fols. 37v, 177. Already mentioned on p. 42 were the injunctions introduced by Samuel Ward at Sidney Sussex College, Cambridge, regulating the disputations of bachelors.

[55] For Harriot, see Wood, *Athenae Oxonienses*, vol. 2, pp. 299–303; *Biog. Brit.*, vol. 4, pp. 2539–43. It was also in 1580 that Gabriel Harvey mentioned Harriot as one of the promising young mathematicians. See Stern, *Gabriel Harvey*, p. 168. For Harriot see also pp. 135–8 below.

the young student to the attention of the Earl of Bridgewater and Henry Briggs as well as Oughtred.[56] Even before he took his B.A. in 1628 from Trinity College, Cambridge, John Pell was steeped in mathematics. In 1627 he received certain 'Tables exactly calculated for the latitude 51°' from Arthur Pollard, the vicar of East Deane; in July 1628 he composed 'Tabulae Directoriae ad praxim Mathematicam nonnichil conferentes. Cum earundem constructione et usu'. In the same year he also wrote 'The Description and Use of the Quadrant' for a friend as well as the 'New Almanacke and Prognostication'. Further to complete these activities, Pell initiated a correspondence with Henry Briggs.[57]

In his autobiography Thomas Hobbes testifies that he devoted his time to astronomy and cosmography during his years at Magdalen Hall, Oxford, for he found logic and other studies dull and tiresome. Nonetheless, Hobbes must have performed well during his four-year stay, for he graduated B.A. in 1606 and received a warm recommendation from the Principal of the hall to the Cavendish family.[58] A student who was a mature astronomer by the time he left university was Jeremiah Horrox, who matriculated at Emmanuel College, Cambridge, in 1632 and left without a degree three years later. Although there is little evidence to suggest that Cambridge contributed directly to Horrox's scientific knowledge, it was nonetheless during his last year at university – if not before – that he embarked upon his astronomical studies. In that year he purchased a copy of Lansberg's *Tabulae Motuum coelestium perpetuae ...* (1632) on the last leaf of which he recorded an impressive list of astronomical books – including some works of Copernicus, Kepler, Longomontanus, Brahe and Gassendi – all of which he had probably consulted by that date.[59]

Thomas Henshaw acquired a considerable degree of mathematical sophistication while a student at University College, Oxford. In 1639 Henshaw left without a degree after a stay of five years in University

---

[56] Wood, *Athenae Oxonienses*, vol. 2, pp. 405–6; *Biog. Brit.*, vol. 3, pp. 2450–4. See p. 69 above and pp. 171–3 below.

[57] BL MS Addit. 4397, fols. 1–5v, 49, 137–9; MS Addit. 4401, fols. 3–14v; MS Addit. 4403, fols. 120–45. The letter to Briggs from MS Addit. 4397, fols. 137–9 is printed in Halliwell, pp. 55–60. For Pell, see Aubrey, *Brief Lives*, vol. 2, pp. 121–31; *Biog. Brit.*, vol. 5, pp. 3312–17; *DNB*.

[58] *The Life of Mr Thomas Hobbes of Malmesbury, Written by himself in a Latine Poem. And Now Translated into English* (London, 1680), pp. 2–4; S. I. Mintz, *The Hunting of Leviathan* (Cambridge, 1962); N. Malcolm, 'Hobbes, Sandys, and the Virginia Company', *Hist. Journ.*, XXIV (1981), 297–321.

[59] *DNB*; J. E. Bailey, 'Jeremiah Horrox and William Crabtree, observers of the Transit of Venus, 24 Nov. 1639', *The Palatine Note-Book*, II (1882), 253–66; although somewhat dated, A. B. Whatton's *Horrocks' Transit of Venus across the Sun, with a Memoir of his Life and Labours* (London, 1859) is still the only full-length biography. See also B. M. Davis, 'The Astronomical Work of Jeremiah Horrox' (Univ. of London M.A. thesis, 1967); W. Applebaum, 'Kepler in England: The Reception of Keplerian Astronomy in England, 1599–1687' (Univ. of New York at Buffalo Ph.D. thesis, 1969), pp. 65–89.

College, during which period Obadiah Walker and Abraham Woodhead, although never his tutors, nonetheless cultivated his mathematical interests. In 1636 Walker and Woodhead sent Henshaw to Oughtred where he remained for nine months to 'complete his education'.[60]

This list of celebrated men of science, all of whom with the exception of Gunter left university either immediately before or after receiving their B.A. degrees, is far from representative. Most continued their education at least until they received their M.A. degrees and, as was shown in chapter II, many held fellowships for some time during their careers. Most significant, there is little in the biographies of the above-mentioned men to indicate that their departure owed itself to the state of science in the universities. In the case of Thomas Harriot and Thomas Hobbes, their leave-taking followed tempting job offers: Harriot was employed by Ralegh, while Hobbes became private tutor to William Cavendish, later 2nd Earl of Devonshire. In the case of Horrox, grave financial difficulties appear to have precipitated his early departure.

Other men of science who left after a short stay were members of a higher social caste that rarely remained as permanent members of the university community. Like many of his class, Thomas Henshaw left for the Inns of Court. In fact, a decade earlier John Twysden, another noted mathematician who had acquired the rudiments of his knowledge while a student at University College, Oxford (1623–5), had also departed for the Inns.[61] Sir Kenelm Digby remained at Gloucester Hall, Oxford, for two years (1618–20) where Thomas Allen, though not his tutor, cultivated those scientific interests that Digby developed more fully later in life.[62] George Clifford, 3rd Earl of Cumberland, remained for three years at Trinity College, Cambridge (1571–4) where, under the tutorship of Whitgift, he was first introduced to mathematics, the study of which continued to preoccupy him after his migration to Oxford.[63] John Blagrave studied for a while at St John's College, Oxford, before retiring to his estate where he devoted himself to mathematics.[64]

Other men afford us a different sort of testimony of their mathematical instruction while undergraduates. Oxford undergraduates include Edward Rishton of Brasenose College (B.A. 1572) who is credited by Wood with 'hav[ing] spent some years in philosophy and mathematics'.[65] John

[60] Wood, *Athenae Oxonienses*, vol. 4, pp. 444–6; S. Pasmore, 'Thomas Henshaw, F.R.S. (1618–1700)', *Notes and Records of The Royal Society*, xxxvi (1982), 177–88.

[61] *DNB*.

[62] R. T. Petersson, *Sir Kenelm Digby, The Ornament of England 1603–1665* (London, 1956), pp. 36–7. See pp. 181–2 below.

[63] Wood, *Athenae Oxonienses*, vol. 3, pp. 80–3; *DNB*; A. Clifford, *Collectanea Cliffordiana* (Paris, 1817), p. 7; G. C. Williamson, *George, Third Earl of Cumberland (1558–1605) His Life and his Voyages* (Cambridge, 1920).

[64] Wood, *Athenae Oxonienses*, vol. 2, pp. 96–7; *Biog. Brit.*, vol. 2, pp. 802–5.

[65] Wood, *Athenae Oxonienses*, vol. 1, p. 511; Clark, *Register*, vol. 3, p. 15.

Elmeston, who matriculated at Lincoln College, Oxford, in December 1579, evidently had arrived at Oxford some months earlier, for Dee's diary contains the following entry: 'Aug. 8th, [1579] John Elmeston, student of Oxford, cam to me for dialling'.[66] Augustine Baker matriculated at Broadgates Hall in 1590 under the tutorship of William Prichard of Christ Church (M.A. 1588). In his autobiography Baker recalls his undergraduate instruction in the classics, Greek, logic and arithmetic, the textbook assigned for the latter being Gemma Frisius.[67] An inventory compiled by Sir Henry Savile of all books missing from his library indicates that Henry Neville, who matriculated at Merton College in 1600 (B.A. 1603), was studying geometry. According to this record Savile made over a copy of Euclid to Christopher Dale (M.A. 1594, Merton College), apparently Neville's tutor, for the youth's instruction.[68] As regards Gilbert Davies, who matriculated at Broadgates Hall in 1601 (B.A. 1604), his biographer informs us that mathematics was one of the subjects he had studied as an undergraduate.[69] Alexander Lower, brother of Sir William Lower, Harriot's close associate, was also engaged in mathematical studies. Having matriculated at Gloucester Hall, Oxford, in 1606 under the tutorship of Thomas Allen, Lower's mathematical interests are suggested by a letter he addressed to Harriot in 1608. From this letter Lower's acquaintance with Thomas Aylesbury – then resident at Oxford – as well as Walter Warner is made apparent.[70]

Francis Potter (B.A. 1613) had been occupied with the practical building of dials during his stay at Trinity College, Oxford. Potter remained in Oxford until 1637 at which time he succeeded into a family living. Highly reputed as a mechanician, later in life Potter published a millenarian tract on the root of the number 666, in the introduction to which he affirmed that his own theory was as true and new as Gilbert's theory of the magnet. Noteworthy is Potter's assertion that he had been developing his ideas since 1625.[71] In 1618 John and Richard Newdigate matriculated at Trinity College, Oxford, where their book purchases during their year-and-a-half stay included Samuel Purchas's *Pilgrimage*, Mercator's *Atlas* and Ortelius's *Theatrum orbis terrarum*. That at least Richard had some additional mathematical instruction is indicated by his intensive study of *De radiis visus et lucis perspectivis et iride tractatus* (1611)

[66] *The Diary of John Dee*, p. 6.
[67] *Memorials of Father Augustine Baker 1575–1641*, ed. J. McCann (London, 1933), p. 41.
[68] Foster, *Alumni Oxonienses*, vol. 3, p. 1058, vol. 1, p. 367; Bodl. MS Arch. F. C.O.*, fol. 92.
[69] W. Miller, *A Sermon Preached at the Funerall of the Worshipfull Gilbert Davies* (London, 1621), sig. C4v.
[70] Clark, *Register*, vol. 2, part 2, p. 288; Bodl. MS Clarendon 1, fol. 54v: A. Lower to T. Harriot, 27 July 1608.
[71] F. Potter, *An Interpretation of the Number 666* (Oxford, 1642), preface sig. **; Wood, *Athenae Oxonienses*, vol. 3, pp. 1151–6; Aubrey, *Brief Lives*, vol. 2, pp. 161–70; DNB.

by Marcantonio de Dominis, Archbishop of Spaleto.[72] The same year Michael Barkley graduated B.A. from Christ Church, on which occasion he presented his college library with a set of globes together with Hues's *Tractatus de globis* 'in gratiam studiosorum mathematicae'.[73]

Mathematical books and instruments were donated to St John's College, Oxford, by other students as well. John Edwards, who was installed as the Sedleian Professor of Natural Philosophy in 1636, had presented his college library with a copy of Kepler's *Astronomia Nova* a year before graduating B.A. in 1621.[74] Morris Williams bestowed upon the library a copy of Bacon's *Novum Organum* in 1621, a year after he took his B.A.,[75] while in 1635, the year of his matriculation, George Barkham gave his college a slide rule; upon leaving the college two years later, he made over a copy of Oughtred's *Description of the Quadrant*.[76]

At Cambridge Henry Blaxton, who graduated B.A. from Trinity College in 1590 and M.A. in 1593, had embarked upon a correspondence with William Camden as early as 1588. In a letter of December 1590 Blaxton informed Camden that he was still pursuing mathematics and asked for his opinion of an edition of Euclid.[77] In his autobiography Thomas Comber, who was installed as Master of Trinity College in 1631, relates that he had received a smattering of mathematics during his first three years in the college (1591–4).[78] Samuel Wright, son of the mathematician, Edward Wright, carried on the family tradition when he matriculated at Gonville and Caius College in 1612. Following his father's death in 1614, Wright edited and supervised the publication of *A Description of the admirable Table of Logarithms* (1616). According to the college annals he was contemplating other works when he died suddenly in 1618.[79] Finally, mention should be made of a copy of Kepler's *Dissertatio cum nuncio sidereo* in the Bodleian Library that was originally purchased by one John Ward in 1619. If Ward's name is too common to allow for positive identification, the identity of the next owner is easier to ascertain; in 1632 the book passed into the

[72] V. M. Larminie, 'The Life Style and Attitudes of the Seventeenth Century Gentleman, with special reference to the Newdigates of Arbury Hall, Warwickshire' (Univ. of Birmingham Ph.D. thesis, 1980), pp. 306ff; Warwickshire County R.O. MS CR 136 B3468, fols. 75–86. I am grateful to Dr Larminie for drawing my attention to this reference.

[73] Christ Church Oxford 'Benefactors' Register', p. 55.

[74] Fuggles, 'A History of the Library of S. John's College', p. 118; *DNB*.

[75] Fuggles, 'A History of the Library of S. John's College', p. 119; Clark, *Register*, vol. 2, part 3, p. 376.

[76] R. T. Gunther, *Early Science in Oxford* (Oxford, 1923), vol. 1, p. 152; Foster, *Alumni Oxonienses*, vol. 1, p. 72.

[77] Cooper, *Athenae Cantabrigienses*, vol. 2, p. 238; Camden, *Epistolae*, p. 45: H. Blaxton to W. Camden, 7 Dec. 1590.

[78] Lloyd, *Memoires of the Lives*, p. 447.

[79] Venn, *Biographical History of Gonville and Caius College*, vol. 1, pp. 218–19.

hands of Daniel Heylett, who had matriculated at Emmanuel College the previous year.[80]

Up until this point I have tried to confine my evidence to the type that would establish the claim that mathematical instruction was offered to undergraduates. Yet, there exists a much larger body of evidence of men who, although proficient in mathematics by the time they proceeded M.A., never made it clear at what stage they had been introduced to the subject. However, since it is my contention that the M.A. course of studies should be viewed as an integral part of the university curriculum, I believe such evidence is valuable for an assessment of the nature of mathematical instruction in the universities.

Some men who became notable divines had earned reputations as competent mathematicians while at university. The prominent preacher, William Whately (M.A. 1604, St Edmund Hall, Oxford), we are told, 'was an hard Student and quickely became a good Logician and Philosopher, a strong disputant, and an excellent Orator. He delighted much in the study of Poetry and the Mathematicks.'[81] A year later in 1605 the 'ever memorable' John Hales was admitted M.A. as a fellow of Merton College. Henry Savile, who initially had been responsible for recruiting Hales to the college in 1603, was only one of many to recognize Hales's abilities, which spanned mathematics and the life sciences. Later testimony of Hales's mathematical interests includes his correspondence with Oughtred and Greaves as well as his encouragement of John Beale's enthusiasm for experimental science while the latter was still a schoolboy at Eton.[82] At Trinity College, Oxford, William Chillingworth (M.A. 1623) is said to have applied himself with great industry and success to mathematics, the knowledge of which aided him some twenty years later when he served as engineer to the King's forces during the siege of Gloucester.[83] In 1631 John Gregory, 'the miracle of his age for critical and curious learning' – as Wood describes him – proceeded M.A. from Christ Church, Oxford, where he distinguished himself as a linguist, a divine and a mathematician. His mathematical abilities, which were commended by Edward Sherburne, are suggested by his *The Description and Use of the Terrestrial Globe*, written c. 1636 but only published posthumously in 1649. The treatise, which probably was composed as a teaching manual for his students, indicates Gregory's familiarity with the most recent astronomical and geographical

[80] Venn, *Alumni Cantabrigienses*, vol. 2, p. 364; Kepler's book is Bodl. sig. Savile 6.18(1).

[81] Henry Scudder's life of Whately, prefaced to W. Whately, *Prototypes or the Primarie Precedent* (London, 1640), sig. A2; Wood, *Athenae Oxonienses*, vol. 2, pp. 638–41; Fuller, *Worthies*, vol. 3, pp. 22–3.

[82] J. Elson, *John Hales of Eton* (New York, 1948); *The Works of the Ever-Memorable Mr John Hales of Eton* (Glasgow, 1765), vol. 1, pp. 196ff; Wood, *Athenae Oxonienses*, vol. 3, pp. 409–16.

[83] Wood, *Athenae Oxonienses*, vol. 3, pp. 86–96.

literature; Clavius, Stevin, Gemma Frisius, Brahe, Copernicus, Wright, Mercator, Ridley, Norman, Carpenter and Kepler are among the authorities cited. In the text Gregory highly praises William Gilbert, discusses in some detail Gellibrand's treatise on the variation of the magnetic needle and accepts the notion of a moving earth.[84]

One of the more prominent Cambridge divines reputed to have been an eager mathematician was William Perkins (M.A. 1584, Christ's College). Although Perkins later became one of the most popular English preachers of the age, as a student he was known to have been so ardent in his pursuit of mathematics that he was considered by many to be a magician.[85] We have already mentioned that the preacher Thomas Gataker (M.A. 1597, St John's College, Cambridge) attended Briggs's mathematical lectures in the college. Gataker, who was tutored by another mathematical enthusiast, Henry Alvey, retained his scientific interests after leaving Cambridge. His writings portray a wide variety of scientific knowledge; he both praises Bacon and shows his familiarity with the work of Kepler. Gataker apparently kept up his friendship with Briggs – when they were both in London in the 1610s – for he occasionally mentions his discussions with the Gresham professor. Also interested in the medical sciences, Gataker both contributed to Theodore Goulston's edition of *Versio, variae lectiones, et annotationes criticae in opuscula variae Galeni* (London, 1640) and published the volume following his close friend's demise. Gataker became an opponent of judicial astrology, as a consequence of which he became embroiled in a bitter controversy with the astrologers William Lilly, John Swan and John Gadbury.[86]

Henry Peacham (B.A. 1595, M.A. 1598), who was largely responsible for the growing emphasis on mathematics, astronomy and mechanical instruments in the courtesy literature of the seventeenth century, records his own scientific pursuits while a Trinity College student. 'Ever naturally addicted to those arts and sciences which consist of proportion and number', Peacham boasted of his ability to draw 'the map of any town according to geometrical proportion, as [he had done] when [he] was of Trinity College and a junior sophister'.[87]

In 1605 John Williams, the future Archbishop of York, was incepted

[84] Wood, *Athenae Oxonienses*, vol. 3, pp. 20–7; E. Sherburne, *The Sphere of Marcus Manilius made an English Poem* (London, 1675), appendix, p. 94; *Gregorii Posthuma*, pp. 257–330.
[85] Cooper, *Athenae Cantabrigienses*, vol. 2, pp. 335–41.
[86] S. Ashe, *Gray Hayres Crowned with Grace, A Sermon Preached ... at the Funerall of ... Mr Thomas Gataker* (London, 1655); Gataker, *Thomas Gataker his Vindication*, p. 87 et passim; idem, *A Discours Apologeticall, wherein Lilies Lewd and Lowd Lies in his Merlin Or Pasquil for the yeer 1654 are cleerly laid open* (London, 1654); DNB.
[87] R. R. Cawley, *Henry Peacham, His Contribution to English Poetry* (University Park, Pa., 1971), p. 4; H. Peacham, *The Complete Gentleman*, ed. V. B. Heltzel (Ithaca, 1962), p. 129. The fullest study still remains M. C. Pitman, 'Studies in the Work of Henry Peacham' (London Univ. Ph.D. thesis, 1933).

M.A. from St John's College and undoubtedly his later patronage of science can be ascribed to his own proclivity towards geometry and the life sciences while a student.[88] At Christ's College William Milbourne (M.A. 1623), who was a pupil of Joseph Mede, earned a reputation for his grasp of the various mathematical sciences which he later disseminated among the young men of his parish; George Wharton and Sir Jonas Moore were two mathematicians who came under Milbourne's influence.[89] The Baptist Henry Jessey (M.A. 1626) was yet another mathematically inclined member of St John's College, and a close friend of John Winthrop. The later correspondence of the two men indicates Jessey's active interest in astronomy, meteorology, medicine and agriculture.[90]

An examination of contemporary accounts reveals a number of university-trained men who, although respected by their contemporaries as highly capable men of science, have not always been given the attention they deserve. John Thornborough, who incepted M.A. from Magdalen College, Oxford, in 1575, was equally known to his contemporaries as bishop and chemist. Throughout his career as Bishop of Limerick, Bristol and then Worcester, he continued to devote himself to chemistry and experimental philosophy and his house was reputed to be a laboratory. Among his friends and dependants he numbered Robert Fludd and Thomas Bushell.[91] Sir John Davies (M.A. 1581), mathematician and chemist, was brought up in the old religion in Gloucester Hall by a Catholic tutor, but was instructed in the sciences by Thomas Allen. After proceeding M.A. Davies moved to London where he continued his scientific studies, especially astrology, under Simon Forman. Davies later turned to navigation, entered the service of the Earl of Essex and just escaped execution for his role in the Earl's rebellion. His remaining days were spent in studious retirement, corresponding with such scientific figures as John Dee and Matthew Gwinne.[92]

After graduating B.A. from Christ Church, Oxford, in 1584, the

[88] J. Hacket, *Scrinia Reserata: A Memorial Offered to the Great Deservings of John Williams D.D. who some time held the Places of Ld Keeper of the Great Seal of England, Ld Bishop of Lincoln and Ld Archbishop of York* (London, 1693), pp. 7–10.

[89] Venn, *Alumni Cantabrigienses*, vol. 3, p. 187; Aubrey, *Brief Lives*, vol. 2, pp. 87, 88; Sherburne, *The Sphere of Manilius*, appendix, pp. 91–2; Wood, *Athenae Oxonienses*, vol. 4, p. 5; C. H. Josten, *Elias Ashmole (1617–1692)* (Oxford, 1966), vol. 2, p. 540; W. Leybourne, *The Line of Proportion, Commonly Called Gunter's Line, Made Easie* (London, 1677), preface; Taylor, *Mathematical Practitioners*, pp. 346–7, 367.

[90] Venn, *Alumni Cantabrigienses*, vol. 2, p. 460; R. C. Black, *The Younger John Winthrop* (New York, 1966), pp. 56, 60–1, 81, 360 and references cited therein; *DNB*.

[91] Wood, *Athenae Oxonienses*, vol. 3, pp. 3–7; A. G. Debus, *The English Paracelsians* (London, 1965), pp. 103–5.

[92] Davies should not be confused with his two namesakes, Sir John Davies, the poet of 'Orchestra', and John Davies, the navigator. Wood, *Athenae Oxonienses*, vol. 2, pp. 373–4.

mathematician and astronomer Nathaniel Torporley set off for France where his mathematical knowledge equipped him to serve as secretary to the famous Vieta. He appears to have returned to Oxford in 1587 or 1588, proceeding M.A. in 1591. Some time afterwards, Torporley settled in London where he enjoyed the patronage of Henry, 9th Earl of Northumberland, and became an associate of Thomas Harriot.[93]

Like his friend Thomas Jackson, Alexander Gill the elder (M.A. 1589, Corpus Christi College) was interested in the mathematical and occult sciences. A scholar until the mid-1590s, Gill appears to have left Oxford on account of his pending marriage. In 1609 Gill applied for a post with the Emperor of Morocco, offering his services in arithmetic, geometry, astronomy, cosmography, gubernatics and gnomics, all subjects he had been instructed in 'from early youth'. By this date Gill was also deeply immersed in alchemy and the Cabala, and included the physicians Peter Turner and Francis Anthony among his friends.[94] Thomas Aylesbury, one of the more prominent patrons of mathematics of his age, acquired his mathematical grounding in Christ Church where he incepted M.A. in 1605. He became first secretary to the Earl of Nottingham, Lord High Admiral of England, and later a favourite of the all-powerful Duke of Buckingham. Among his dependants we find Thomas Harriot, Walter Warner, Thomas Allen and Abraham Woodhead.[95]

Having led a most uneventful career as Dean of Windsor, Christopher Wren is remembered chiefly in connection with his son, the famous architect. Nonetheless, the elder Wren's career might have been altogether different, for immediately after proceeding M.A. from St John's College in 1613 he attempted to channel his love of mathematics and natural philosophy into a career. One of the chief contenders for the lectureship in astronomy at Gresham College vacated following the death of Edward Brerewood, Wren's efforts were to no avail. Upon failing to obtain the post, Wren turned to theology and took his B.D. in 1620, without, however, slackening in his enthusiasm for science.[96]

[93] According to Clark, *Register*, vol. 2, part 2, p. 100, Torporley matriculated in 1581, but Wood dates it as early as 1579; *Athenae Oxonienses*, vol. 2, pp. 524–5. See also J. V. Pepper, 'A letter from Nathaniel Torporley to Thomas Harriot', *Brit. Journ. Hist. Sci.*, III (1967), 285–90.

[94] Wood, *Athenae Oxonienses*, vol. 2, pp. 597–600; A. Gill, *Longonomia Anglica* (1619), ed. B. Danielsson and A. Gabrielson (Stockholm, 1972), vol. I, pp. 9–49; BL MS Addit. 46139; MS Sloane 3722, fols. 24–86.

[95] There is no adequate biography of Aylesbury. See, however, *Biog. Brit.*, vol. I, pp. 318–19; *DNB*. For a sample of Aylesbury's astronomical papers, see BL MS Addit. 4395, fols. 96, 99, 119–29; TCD MS 794, fols. 51–61.

[96] Foster, *Alumni Oxonienses*, vol. 4, p. 1684; Adamson, 'The Foundation and Early History of Gresham College', p. 279; *Parentalia, or Memoirs of the Family of the Wrens*, ed. C. Wren (London, 1750); R. Colie, 'Dean Wren's marginalia and early science at Oxford', *Bodl. Lib. Rec.*, VI (1960), 541–51. His annotation of Sir Thomas Browne's *Religio Medici* is printed in *The Works of Sir Thomas Browne*, ed. Wilkin.

In Trinity College Henry Gellibrand had attained great proficiency in mathematics by the time he received an M.A. in 1623. While still at university Gellibrand constructed a dial in his college as well as formed a close association with Briggs and Bainbridge, both of whom later supported his candidacy for the Gresham chair of astronomy in 1626/27. The testimonial letter given to Gellibrand by his college commended him 'especially [for] his zeale and love for the mathematicks' and for 'his very loving readiness, and also dexterity, and facility, freely to communicate to any one among us his knowledge in those studies'. After moving to London, Gellibrand continued his intensive studies of mathematics and astronomy. The frequent references to Gellibrand in Hartlib's diary suggest his thorough familiarity with recent scientific literature as well as his plans to publish his own astronomical hypothesis which, however, never came to fruit, probably owing to his untimely death in 1637, aged 40.[97]

As regards men of science who departed after obtaining an M.A., the situation at Cambridge was similar to that at Oxford. In 1584 Mark Ridley, one of the fathers of magnetism, took his M.A. from Clare Hall where he had applied himself to the physical sciences and the construction of dials. As noted previously, Ridley's interest in, and conversion to, the new cosmology probably occurred while he was a Cambridge student. His only two publications – both dating from the 1610s while he was practising medicine in London – indicate that he was convinced of the heliocentric theory as well as conversant with the recent work of Kepler and Galileo. Ridley was also one of the first to conduct telescopic observations in England.[98]

William Bedwell, nephew of Thomas Bedwell, proceeded M.A. in 1588 as a scholar of Trinity College. Although he later excelled as an orientalist, Bedwell was nonetheless a highly skilled mathematician whose friends included Henry Briggs and John Greaves. In 1606 he translated Ortelius's *Theatum Orbis Terrarum* and during the following two decades he published a series of his own – as well as his uncle's – mathematical treatises. Bedwell was probably also interested in astrology, for when his library came up for sale following his death in 1632, William Lilly 'bought amongst them [his] choicest Books of Astrology'.[99]

After proceeding M.A. from Emmanuel College in 1607, John Bainbridge stayed on at university without a fellowship until he took his M.D. in 1614.

[97] Wood, *Athenae Oxonienses*, vol. 2, pp. 622–5; *Biog. Brit.*, vol. 3, pp. 2188–91; Ward, *Lives of the Professors*, pp. 81–5; Adamson, 'The Foundation and Early History of Gresham College', pp. 143–5; Hartlib, 'Ephemerides 1634–1637', *passim*.
[98] A short discussion of Ridley's life and work can be found in the *DNB*; Taylor, *Mathematical Practitioners*, p. 183; Waters, *The Art of Navigation*, pp. 333–8.
[99] Although never a fellow, Bedwell probably continued to hold his scholarship for a few years after completing his M.A., for he received his first living only in 1601. *DNB*; *The Last of the Astrologers: Mr. William Lilly's History of his Life and Times*, ed. K. M. Briggs (London, 1974), pp. 22–3.

After practising medicine for a few years, he was installed as the first Savilian Professor of Astronomy at Oxford in 1619. Although Bainbridge was a gifted astronomer, his papers have not received the attention they merit.[100] Two other men of science who proceeded M.A. from Emmanuel College are Samuel Foster and John Sadler. By the time he received his M.A. in 1623, Foster was already deeply involved in his mathematical and astronomical pursuits and the following year his *The Use of a Quadrant* was appended to Gunter's description of the cross-staff. In 1636 Foster was elected Gresham Professor of Astronomy but was forced to vacate the post soon afterwards when Charles I forwarded the appointment of another man. Despite this setback, Foster was reelected professor in 1641 and served in this capacity until his death in 1652. Significantly, Foster's rooms at Gresham College served as one of the meeting places of those men later to found the Royal Society.[101] John Sadler (M.A. 1638) is better known as a lawyer and Master of Magdalene College, Cambridge, from 1650 until 1660. Nonetheless, he published some medical accounts as well as a curious – and strongly Platonic – astronomical/astrological piece entitled *Masquarade du ciel presented to the Great Queene of the Little World. A Celestiall Map representing the True Site and Motions of the Heavenly bodies, through the yeeres 1639, 1640, &c* (1640). Sadler was also one of the men among whom Pell circulated his refutation of Longomontanus.[102]

John Beale (M.A. 1636, King's College, Cambridge) is remembered chiefly for his horticultural publications, but his interests ranged to all aspects of science. As previously mentioned, Beale's interest in science dates back to his school years at Eton where he was encouraged by Sir Henry Wotton and John Hales. Later in life Beale occasionally recalled these pursuits. In 1664, for example, he claimed to have devoted some forty years 'in ye serious study of Experimentall philosophy'. On a different occasion he wrote of the two years he had spent as a college lecturer in natural philosophy, reading to his students 'all sorts of the current philosophy'. Similarly, it was during Beale's abode in Cambridge that he conducted astronomical and meteorological observations, consulted with resident physicians on matters of anatomy and medicine and embarked on his botanical studies. Beale was also deeply interested in all sorts of mathematical instruments and counted Elias Allen and William Oughtred among his friends.[103]

[100] For Bainbridge, see Smith's life in the *Vitae quorundam*; *Biog. Brit.*, vol. 1, pp. 419–21. see pp. 143–8 below.

[101] *Biog. Brit.*, vol. 3, pp. 2009–12; Adamson, 'The Foundation and Early History of Gresham College', pp. 145–6; Ward, *Lives of the Professors*, pp. 85–8.

[102] For Sadler, see *DNB*; Halliwell, p. 89; Webster, *The Great Instauration*, pp. 66 and note 72–7, 80, 84, 145, 183–4.

[103] *DNB*; Sheffield University Library Hartlib Papers 31/1/4; Royal Society Boyle Papers, 7.5; Boyle, *Works*, vol. 6, pp. 331, 336, 344, 355, 394, 421, 432, 435; Christ Church

The year 1640 saw the inceptions of two mathematicians in addition to John Wallis and Seth Ward: Charles Scarburgh of Gonville and Caius College and William Holder of Pembroke Hall. Scarburgh, who later became a celebrated physician, was an extremely able mathematician during his student days. As mentioned earlier, Scarburgh visited Oughtred in order to complete his mathematical education and later taught Oughtred's *Clavis* in Cambridge. He also prepared an English edition of Euclid, which was published by his son following his death.[104] William Holder is remembered chiefly in the context of his controversy with Wallis over their joint instruction of a deaf and dumb person to speak. However, Holder was a mathematician who, upon marrying the daughter of Dean Wren of Windsor in 1643, introduced the young Christopher Wren to mathematics.[105]

Any attempt to assess the scientific interests of the university community must make some mention of libraries. Library probate inventories, which are an important source of information for anyone attempting to determine the interests of their owners, are a particularly invaluable tool for those attempting to gauge the scientific interests of university members. During our period the acquisition of a scientific text tended to indicate more than a minimal interest in the subject. The reason for this is two-fold: first, whereas any library was expected to be well stocked with theological and classical texts, there were seldom the same expectations as regards scientific works. For example, there was even a clause in the 1552 statutes of Trinity College, Cambridge, stipulating that those students 'who did not own private copies of Aristotle, Plato, Demosthenes, the orations and philosophic works of Cicero, a Greek new Testament, and the Bible were to be expelled'.[106] As expected, then, most libraries were heavily stocked with religious books, the classical authorities, histories, aids for language study and perhaps some law and medical guides. The second reason is that although books in general became increasingly less expensive throughout the sixteenth century, most of the professional books remained relatively dear. Consequently, rare was the person who

Oxford Evelyn Letters, fols. 43, 91; BL MS Sloane 427 and MS Sloane 548, fols. 71ff contain some of Beale's astronomical notes. See also Webster, *The Great Instauration*, *passim*, for the wide range of his interests in the 1640s and 1650s. Much more information on Beale's early career has recently become available in M. Stubbs, 'John Beale, philosophical gardener of Herefordshire, part I. Prelude to the Royal Society (1608–1663)', *Annals of Science*, XXXIX (1982), 463–89.

[104] For Scarburgh, see *DNB*; B. Chance, 'Charles Scarburgh, an English educator and physician to three kings: a medical retrospective into the times of the Stuarts', *Bull. Hist. Med.*, XII (1942), 274–303.

[105] Late in life Holder published a treatise on the reformation of the calendar (1694). See *DNB*.

[106] Mullinger, *The University of Cambridge*, vol. 2, p. 616.

did not have second thoughts about purchasing a scientific text, and those who went through with such purchases usually manifested more than a cursory interest in the subject.

Nonetheless, if probate inventories are to be employed as valid evidence, certain of their limitations must be noted. First, most extant inventories specifying individual volumes in the university archives belong to the sixteenth century, when private libraries were relatively small. Once the acquisition of books became a more widespread practice and a private library could contain a few hundred volumes, compilers of inventories merely indicated the sum total of the books. Second, even when an inventory cited individual volumes, they frequently lumped together a number of volumes under such classifications as 'old books' or '20 other books'. One might speculate that in many cases the more common textbooks in philosophy, logic or mathematics were thus designated. Finally, since it appears that students were in the habit of selling off books they no longer required – as is made evident by the example of Mede's students – an inventory which fails to include the basic mathematical texts does not necessarily preclude a student's earlier mathematical instruction.

Despite these limitations, it is significant that over half of the inventories of university men who died while in residence – hence the probate inventories of their goods in the Oxford or Cambridge university archives[107] – included at least one or two of the basic arithmetical and geometrical treatises such as those of Gemma Frisius, Recorde, Tunstall, Ramus, Ryff or Euclid. Of these an additional 25 per cent included cosmographical and astronomical manuals, not to mention the philosophical treatises of a scientific nature, such as those of Aristotle and Plato, and the physical commentaries.

To cite a few examples of Oxford libraries containing scientific texts: the library of Henry Huchenson, who graduated B.A. from St John's College in 1569 and died in 1573, contained the arithmetical treatises of Gemma Frisius and Misilius; Valerius's *Sphaera*; Finé's *De sphaera mundi*; the cosmographical works of Apian and Hunter as well as a 'book of instruments'. Another bachelor, Richard Secol, who graduated in 1574 as a member of New College and died three years later, also possessed the arithmetical treatises of Gemma Frisius and Misilius in addition to an edition of Euclid; Proclus's *Sphaera*; Peucer's *De circulis*; Lemnius's *De astrologica*; Frigius's geometry and Mercator's *Sphaera*.

Thomas Pope, who died two years after proceeding M.A. from St Mary's Hall in 1576, owned the arithmetical treatises of Gemma Frisius and

107 Unless otherwise specified, all quotations from Oxford probate inventories are taken from OUA where transcripts of all inventories containing books are kept. For the Cambridge inventories, I am grateful to Dr E. S. Leedham-Green, Assistant Keeper of the University Archives, who supplied me with the transcripts of Cambridge inventories she is presently preparing for publication.

Recorde as well as Ramus's volume of arithmetic and geometry; Stadius's *Ephemerides*; Leonitus's *De eclipsibus*; Alfonsi's *Tabulae astronomicae*; Stoeffler's *De usu astrolabi* and Dariot's *Astronomia*. Pope also possessed a globe and most probably the 'certain instruments' specified in the inventory were mathematical instruments.

Another Oxford library was that of John Glover, who died shortly after taking his M.A. from St John's College in 1578, which contained three unspecified arithmetical books, Apian's *Cosmographia*; the *De meteoris* of Fritshius as well as the *De meteoris* of Stanhusius; Bartholomeus's *De sphaera*; Cabelius's *Astrolabium*; Mercurius's *De divisione vocabulorum astronomiae*, a dial, maps and a variety of medical books. Upon his death in 1588 Edward Higgins (M.A. 1581, Brasenose College) had in his possession various arithmetical works of Recorde, Clavius, Tunstall and Gemma Frisius as well as Donaeus's *De sphaera*; Fritshius's *De meteoris* and Garcaeius's *Meteorologica*. The inventory drawn up following the death of William Mitchel of Queen's College (M.A. 1584) in 1599 included Baker's *Arithmetic*; Frigius's geometry; Peurbach's *Theoria planetarum*; Sknonburdius's *Computus astronomicus* and Proclus's *Sphaera*.

Thomas Tatham, a fellow of Merton College (M.A. 1573, B.C.L. 1584) who died in 1586, owned the arithmetical works of Peltarius and Tunstall; Lemnius's *De astrologia*; Paracelsus's *De tartaro*; Valerius's *De sphaera*; Gemma Frisius's *Astronomia*; Hunter's *Cosmographia*; Peucer's *De divinatione*; Peurbach's *Theoria planetarum* and Porta's *Magiae naturalis*. In 1599 Robert Barnes, a much longer-standing fellow of Merton College (M.A. 1541, M.D. 1561), bequeathed to his alma mater some forty-eight volumes which, in addition to medical and anatomical works, included various works of Ptolemy, Stoeffler, Euclid, Agricola, Regiomontanus and Copernicus.[108] In 1599 William Hendley (M.A. 1593) bequeathed to his college, All Souls, a volume which included the works of Euclid and the *Perspectiva* of Peacham; Stoeffler's *Astrolabi* and Peurbach's *Theoricarum novarum textus*.[109]

Of the libraries of Cambridge men mention should be made of that of Edward Lively, Regius Professor of Hebrew from 1575 to 1605 and a noted chronologer whose chronology of the world Archbishop Ussher attempted to publish following his death. Lively's chronological interests are reflected in the range of astronomical books in his library, including the Prutenic Tables; Peucer's *De sphaera*; Peurbach's *Theoria planetarum*; *Tabula Johannis de Monte Regio* and Piccolomini's *De sphaera*.

The library of Thomas Lorkin, the Regius Professor of Medicine who died in 1591, included the medical and anatomical works of such authors as

[108] A. B. Emden, *A Biographical Register of the University of Oxford A.D. 1501 to 1540* (Oxford, 1974), pp. 714–15.
[109] N. Ker, *Records of All Souls College Library 1437–1600* (Oxford, 1971), p. 104.

Vesalius, Columbus, Paracelsus and Severinus, while the works of Gemma
Frisius, Euclid, Finé, Peucer, Peurbach, Mizauld, Stadius, Digges and
Erasmus Reinhold were among the mathematical and astronomical
treatises.[110] The inventory of William Ball, a fellow of Trinity College (M.A.
1598) who died in 1601, included the arithmetical and geometrical works
of Ramus, Recorde and Frigius as well as Lemnius's *De miraculi*; Bourne's
Regiment for the Sea; Digges's *Alae seu scalae mathematicae*; Dryander's
Astronomia; Valerius's *Sphaera* and Copernicus's *De revolutionibus*. It is
noteworthy that the small library of Richard Fletcher, who died shortly
after incepting M.A. at St John's College in 1611, contained a copy of
Kepler's *Optics*.

Brief mention should also be made of some libraries which suggest their
owners' interest in Platonic and occultist works in addition to an interest
in the more common astrological works. Robert Hart, who died two years
after graduating M.A. at St John's College, Oxford, in 1570, possessed three
works of Lull as well as three arithmetical treatises, the *Sphaera* of
Sacrobosco, the *Sphaera* of Proclus and Hunter's *Cosmographia*. Robert
Hooper, Master of Balliol College, who died in 1572, possessed the works
of Nicholas of Cusa, while John Hornsley, a fellow of Magdalen College
(M.A. 1577) who died in 1578, owned two works of Lull. The inventory
drawn up following the death of Philip Johnston, a fellow of Queen's
College (M.A. 1568), in 1570 recorded his possession of Ficino's *De vita*.
Finally, the library of John Hayne (M.A. 1585, St Mary's Hall) included
the works of Pico della Mirandola as did the library of Robert Singleton,
a member of St John's College (M.A. 1574) who died in 1578.

The way a library can occasionally provide virtually the only evidence
of the scientific interests of its owner is well illustrated by the following
examples. William Gent (a member of Gloucester Hall from the 1580s until
his death in 1613) was a close friend of Thomas Allen, John Chamberlain
and Dudley Carleton, and like them he belonged to a circle that included
William Gilbert and Mark Ridley. Gent actively participated in the
foundation of the Bodleian Library, donating to it some 400 works from
his own personal library, almost all of them mathematical, astronomical
and medical volumes. The donation of 1600 included the works of
Apollonius Pergaeus, Diophantus, Pappus, Archimedes, Regiomontanus,
Clavius, Commandino, Schoner, Tartaglia, Durer, Finé and Copernicus as
well as the Alphonsian tables. Among the medical authors were numbered
Columbus, Fernel, Vesalius, Valverde, Paracelsus, Fuchs, Gesner, Agricola
and Cardan. Most significant, the donation was clearly part of Gent's own
working library, for when he first requested permission to use the Bodleian

[110] The medical books in the library are specified in C. Sayle, 'The library of Thomas Lorkyn',
Annals of Medical History, III (1921), 310–23.

Library on 20 July 1604, he cited as his reason his wish to consult the volumes he had donated as well as certain others.[111]

John Harrison was Headmaster of Eton from 1630 until his death in 1642. He left us no clues to his origins and the name is too common to be identified positively with any one of the many John Harrisons who studied at Oxford and Cambridge in the first three decades of the seventeenth century. He might have been the Mr Harrison who in January 1627 was an unsuccessful candidate for the post of Gresham Professor of Astronomy – a post awarded to Gellibrand. The first positive mention of Harrison is made by Sir Henry Wotton only in 1629. In 1640 Hartlib commends Harrison in his diary as 'an excellent astronomer and other parts of Mathematics'. Such a judgement is corroborated by the books Harrison bequeathed to Eton. Although some books appear to be missing – as are his instruments – even the 120 or so scientific books attributed to him by Robert Birley make an impressive list. Harrison owned the 1543 edition of Copernicus, the works of Tycho Brahe, Gilbert's *De magnete*, two works by Kepler, three by Scheiner, seven by Lansberg, six by Campanella, two by Gassendi as well as works by Regiomontanus, Rheticus, Paracelsus, Napier, Snell, Briggs, Dominis, Bacon, Oughtred, Sennert, Mersenne and Boulliau.[112]

Assuming that at least some of these scientific works had been acquired in Oxford or Cambridge during a student's or a fellow's residence there, it might be argued that the probate inventories of bookshops should correlate to some extent with probate inventories of private libraries. Before this issue is discussed, however, it should be noted that the university booksellers were not the sole suppliers of scholarly works; students often brought books along with them to university as well as journeyed to London at some point during the year.

As with the probate inventories of private libraries, the probate inventories of booksellers discontinued the previous practice of listing books according to titles as a result of the steep increase in the number of volumes from the end of the sixteenth century onward. Hence, an examination of the inventories of booksellers and printers in Cambridge between 1504 and 1699 reveals only two inventories citing individual volumes; the remainder provide only an estimate of the entire stock. These two inventories nonetheless offer an interesting commentary on the developing

---

[111] *The Letters of John Chamberlain*, ed. N. E. McClure (Philadelphia, 1939), *passim*; Bodl. Benefactors' Book, vol. I, pp. 14–21; Clark, *Register*, vol. 2, part 2, p. 264; *Letters of Sir Thomas Bodley to Thomas James*, ed. G. W. W. Wheeler (Oxford, 1926), pp. 182–3, *et passim*.

[112] R. Birley, 'Robert Boyle's headmaster at Eton', *Notes and Records of The Royal Society*, XIII (1958), 104–14; Adamson, 'The Foundation and Early History of Gresham College', p. 279; Hartlib, 'Ephemerides 1640', A–B2.

interests of Cambridge scholars and bear out the evidence of probate inventories of private libraries.

The probate inventory initiated following the death of Nicholas Pilgrim in 1545 cited 382 books, most of which reflect the prevailing humanism. Nonetheless, among the mathematical and astronomical books stocked by Pilgrim were Gemma Frisius's *Arithmetic* (3); Proclus's *Sphaera* (7); Gyraldus's *De annis & mensibus* and Valerius's *De mathematicarum disciplinarum*.[113] A generation later, the variety of mathematical works was greatly increased. John Denys's probate inventory of 1578, which included 488 books, specified Ramus's *Geometry and Mathematics*; Baker's *Arithmetic*; Sacrobosco's *Sphaera*; Peucer's *De divinatione*; Digges's *Pantometria*; Psellus's *Arithmetic* and *Geometry*; Mizauld's *De planetarum*; Clemendes's *Meteorum libri duo*; Offusius's *De divina astrorum*; Munster's *Cosmographia*; Frobisher's *Voyages* in addition to a variety of almanacs, maps and compasses.[114] This increase in the number and range of scientific works suggests that mathematics, astronomy and astrology, although in no way rivalling the classics, nonetheless occupied a respectable position in the libraries of a significant number of scholars.

The evidence of the previous two chapters suggests the existence of a significant number of scientifically oriented lecturers and tutors in Oxford and Cambridge as well as a significant number of university students who left testimony of their mathematical instruction and interest. Most important for our purposes, a large part of the evidence relates to the 'average', anonymous student about whom so little has been written concerning his instruction in mathematics. The evidence of these students suggests that, in addition to the traditional mathematical textbooks, they were assigned the more recent scientific texts as well. Unfortunately, it is virtually impossible to establish the beliefs of the majority of tutors and students as regards the contemporary modes of thought circulating during the period under review. However, even if the intention of such exposure to new concepts was to convince the student of their erroneousness, the fact remains that some students did formulate their own opinions, often assisted by mathematicians and astronomers at both Oxford and Cambridge.

Now that my case concerning the function of the universities as institutions inculcating new generations with a mixture of ancient and contemporary scientific knowledge has been presented, it is time to assess the extent to which Oxford and Cambridge fulfilled the other essential function of a university, namely, served as institutions conducive to a critical dialogue between the scientifically oriented members among themselves as well as with non-university members of the scientific

[113] Gray and Palmer, *Abstracts from the Wills*, pp. 10–26.
[114] Gray and Palmer, *Abstracts from the Wills*, pp. 35–61.

community. Curtis, who was inclined to argue for the existence of mathematics in the universities, nonetheless claimed that 'to add to the inherited store of knowledge and wisdom by providing facilities and leisure for research into the unknown' was a function not deemed essential for either Oxford or Cambridge.[115] The aim of the following chapter, therefore, will be to examine the available evidence concerning the scientific pursuits and scientific associations of certain university members in order to ascertain the extent to which university members took part in the scientific exchange of the period.

[115] Curtis, *Oxford and Cambridge in Transition*, p. 227.

IV

The scientific community and its connections with Oxford and Cambridge

In spite of a tremendous increase in the university population during the second half of the sixteenth and first half of the seventeenth centuries, as academic communities the universities retained their closely knit networks of association. Such networks were not limited to members of the individual colleges, but for the most part extended well beyond the college gates to include members of other colleges as well as scholars unaffiliated with the universities. The process of initiation into such networks of association usually began with the matriculation of the newly enrolled undergraduate and his introduction to other college members. His familiarity with the university community increased as the identity of university lecturers, masters of the street and proctors were made known to him. As soon as the student began to attend public disputations, he was brought into direct contact with students of other colleges as well as the various moderators. The additional three years allotted to the M.A. course of studies allowed the student to nurture friendships begun earlier as well as to initiate new friendships, often with those who revealed similar scholarly inclinations. Thus, by the time a student had completed the course of studies leading to an M.A. degree, the number of university members with whom he was familiar must have been large indeed.

As soon as the newly elected fellow embarked upon a more specialized course of studies, his relations with academics of similar interests undoubtedly strengthened and intensified. Dining at high table at his own as well as other colleges, the young fellow came to know the more senior members more intimately. This network of association proved crucial to every aspect of the young academic's career. Whereas on one level academic pursuits were fertilized by a cooperative exchange of information, on a more elementary level hearsay often provided an indispensable flow of information on fellowships or appointments for one's own, or one's friends', advancement.

Friendships often continued to flourish long after a member's departure from Oxford or Cambridge. The evidence of the following pages suggests that the various networks of association not only survived this uprooting from the university, but usually continued to evolve; former fellows were introduced to fellows elected long after their departure and, conversely, acquainted their former colleagues with coworkers with whom they later formed an association.

In the course of this chapter it will be argued that there were a number of scientific and intellectual networks which, while sometimes centred upon a particular college or university, neither restricted themselves to college or university members nor worked in ignorance of, or isolation from, each other. Indeed, the evidence of the following two chapters suggests that as these networks radiated out from the various colleges – or for that matter from other scientific centres such as London – in ever-widening circles, they usually intersected at a number of crucial points, so that the men pivotal to one network often reappear in others as well. It is believed that the effect of this increasingly complex configuration of scientific associations will be to establish the existence of a single scientific community which, with its extensive network of connections stretching as far as the Continent, contributed to the scrutiny of scientific issues in England between the years 1560 and 1640.

The following reconstruction of the scientific community in Renaissance England relies upon two fundamental types of evidence. The primary source of evidence is the extant correspondence between men with intellectual affinities. It is often through the more personal, and for the most part less polished, form of communication that the nature of the day-to-day work in a particular discipline is best revealed. Not only are the on-going projects disclosed, but in the richest correspondence the books consulted, the manner in which they had been acquired, and, most important for our purposes, the identity of those men who assisted in the labours, are all indicated. Even letters that offer no direct insight into the scholarly pursuits of the correspondents or relate to non-scientific subjects can be useful. Allusions to social engagements or mutual acquaintances often provide circumstantial evidence upon which a working association may be conjectured. A second type of evidence for determining the composition and pursuits of the scientific community includes such ephemera as notebooks, diaries, laudatory verses or funeral orations. However fragmentary such evidence at first may appear, if used cautiously in conjunction with the correspondence, it can prove an invaluable aid in deciphering the working associations of men of science and scholars alike.

Given the importance of such evidence in the reconstruction of a scientific community, it is unfortunate that so few significant collections of correspondence or papers of English intellectuals prior to the middle of the seventeenth century have survived. Pitted against the corpus of Tycho Brahe, Kepler or Galileo, the thirty-odd letters of Thomas Harriot appear meagre indeed, while in comparison with the correspondence of such scholars as Casaubon or Peiresc, even the approximately 350 unpublished letters of John Selden seem unexceptional. Nonetheless, once the sporadic correspondence of English scientists is supplemented by the larger, but by no means comprehensive, correspondence of English general scholars – men for whom science signified only one aspect of a many-faceted intellectual activity – the underlying configuration of the English scientific community in the years between 1560 and 1640 becomes increasingly manifest. In the following pages I make no pretence of completeness. More often than not the evidence at our disposal is haphazard, dictated by the simple fact of its survival. To interpret the surviving evidence and say that this is what existed is not to say that this is all that existed. Thus, the fact that certain men figure prominently in the following account does not necessarily mean that I am passing qualitative judgement on their importance in the overall scientific community. This brings us to my second point. As stressed in the introduction, my aim is not to discuss the English scientific community in its entirety, but to concentrate on those men who maintained contact with the universities. By so doing I hope to suggest that even the fragmentary evidence at our disposal illustrates the active role played by university members within the English scientific community.

To return to one of the assumptions of this book, in the period under review science had not as yet evolved into a professionalized activity confined to fully committed scientists; hence an examination of the scientific community must, by definition, take into account scientifically inclined scholars and intellectuals who, with varying degrees of expertise and commitment, contributed to the scientific dialogue. The purpose of the concluding section of this chapter, therefore, will be to present one case study in support of this claim. By demonstrating the way in which devout astronomers, general scholars and interested students eagerly observed such celestial phenomena as eclipses and comets, I shall argue for the participation of many university-based scholars in astronomical observations.

Since the order in which the material is presented inevitably influences its interpretation, I thought it best to organize this chapter according to the seniority of the men involved rather than their alleged importance in the scientific community. Such an organization will also best suggest the evolving networks of association.

Sir Henry Savile's contribution to scientific studies in Oxford has been a recurrent theme in this book, and there is much to suggest that Savile was one of the most influential intellectual figures at Oxford in the period after 1570. At this time I propose to examine in detail what is known of the scholarly network that Savile helped develop in an attempt to gauge the extent to which he became an authority among English intellectuals and acted as an intermediary between English scholars and their Continental counterparts.

By the time Savile had applied to Merton College, Oxford, for leave to travel abroad in 1578,[1] his reputation as both a mathematician and a general scholar was well established. In 1575 Savile, together with John Underhill (M.A. 1568, New College),[2] was elected proctor and the term of office of both men was extended for an additional year at the insistence of the then Chancellor, the Earl of Leicester.[3] Savile's life-long friendship with William Camden, which dates back to the 1570s, has already been mentioned. Sir Philip Sidney was another celebrated intellectual to have heard of Savile's early reputation. Although direct evidence is wanting, it is quite likely that Sidney and Savile became acquainted while the former was a student at Christ Church between 1568 and 1570,[4] and Savile was a young bachelor. During his stay at Oxford, Sidney revealed an inclination for mathematics in which he was instructed by Thomas Allen.[5] During this period Sidney also made the acquaintance of William Camden, whose patron, Thomas Thornton, had also served as Sidney's tutor.[6] Regardless of whether Sidney knew Savile personally, writing to his brother, then on a tour of the Continent, in 1580, Sidney was clearly gratified by his brother's impending encounter with Savile. 'I have written to Mr. Savile, I wish you kept still together, he is an excellent man; ... Mr. Savile will with ease help you to set down such a table or remembrance to yourself, and for your sake I perceive he will do much, and if ever I be able I will deserve it of him ... Now (dear brother), take delight likewise in the mathematicals; Mr. Savile is excellent in them.'[7] Although Robert Sidney and Savile remained travelling companions for the next year or so, there is little to indicate the extent of Savile's influence.[8]

[1] *Registrum Annalium Collegii Mertonensis 1567–1603*, ed. Fletcher, p. 107.

[2] Underhill, like Savile, was a protégé of Leicester and as a result of the pressure exerted by Leicester was installed as Rector of Lincoln College, Oxford, in 1577, much to the chagrin of the fellows. See V. H. Green, *The Commonwealth of Lincoln College 1427–1977* (Oxford, 1979), pp. 139–42. In 1583 Underhill gained notoriety as the 'reactionary' doctor of divinity who disputed with Giordano Bruno at Oxford. See Stern, *Gabriel Harvey*, p. 74.

[3] OUA NEP/Supra Register KK (1564–82), fols. 189v, 209v, 212.

[4] See p. 101 above. J. M. Osborn, *Young Philip Sidney 1572–1577* (New Haven, 1972), p. 16.

[5] Bodl. MS Ashmole 356(5) contains a horoscope of Sidney, almost certainly cast by Thomas Allen, which includes a testimonial to Sidney's studiousness as well as to the relations between them. See Osborn, *Young Philip Sidney*, pp. 18–19 and appendix 1.

[6] Thornton took Camden from Broadgates Hall to Christ Church and provided for all his needs. See M. W. Wallace, *The Life of Sir Philip Sidney* (Cambridge, 1915), pp. 101–2, 108.

[7] *The Correspondence of Sir Philip Sidney and Hubert Languet*, ed. S. Pears (London, 1845), pp. 199–201: P. Sidney to R. Sidney, 18 Oct. 1580.

[8] The two already had met more than a year earlier in Strasbourg, for Robert's father, Sir Henry Sidney, had written to his son: 'I here you are fallen into consort and Felloshyp wyth Sir *Harry Nevellys* soon and Ayer, and one Mr. *Savell*. I here of syngular Vertues

As regards this same foreign tour, it is highly likely that Philip Sidney furnished Savile with letters of introduction to many of the most prominent European intellectuals. Sidney himself had made a similar tour of the Continent between 1572 and 1575, during which time he had become acquainted with many of the leading scholars in France, the Habsburg Empire and Italy, mainly through the offices of Hubert Languet. Among the scholars to whom Sidney might have recommended Savile was Thadeus Hajec, a prominent astronomer residing in Prague. Hajec's son, Johannes, had been entrusted to Sidney for his education, and both Johannes and Robert Sidney matriculated at Christ Church, Oxford, in June 1575.[9] Thus a meeting between Johannes and Savile at Oxford was not unlikely. Although no letters between Henry Savile and Thadeus Hajec are known to have survived, the two apparently had met in Prague, for a letter from Hajec to Henry's younger brother Thomas a decade later makes it clear that he was well affected to the elder Savile.[10]

In contrast to the initial period of Savile's Continental tour about which very little is known, from the time Savile came into the orbit of the great Hungarian humanist André Dudith in Breslau a year and a half after he left England, his movements and activities begin to be more clearly documented.[11] Having arrived in Breslau early in 1581 in the company of Robert Sidney and Henry Neville – a mathematically oriented student of Merton College, who was to become highly esteemed by Dudith[12] – the entire company remained for six months.[13] Once again it is very likely that Sidney, who himself had been recommended to Dudith by Languet in 1574,[14] furnished Savile with this introduction. The bonds of friendship that were forged between Savile and Dudith, and which included Hajec, are made clear by the following event. When Hajec dedicated to Dudith his *Apodixis physica et mathematica de cometis* in 1581, the latter responded with an epistle to the work in which he referred to the opinion of 'Dn.

of them both.' A. Collins, *Letters and Memorials of State in the Reign of Queen Mary, Queen Elizabeth, King James, King Charles the First, Part of the Reign of King Charles the Second, and Oliver's Usurpations* (London, 1746), vol. 1, p. 246: H. Sidney to R. Sidney, 25 March 1578/79.

9 Osborn, *Young Philip Sidney*, pp. 242, 312–13. Johannes proved a failure at Oxford, and his wish was to become a courtier. See ibid., pp. 415–16, 428–9, 435.

10 BL MS Harl. 7011, fols. 1–2.

11 Various sources suggest that during this period Savile was engaged in some diplomatic missions. In October 1569 Arthur Ayte, secretary to Leicester, thought he was with Thomas Bodley in Paris, but R. Lloyd reported that only Bodley was to be found. A. G. H. Bachrach claims that Savile was the 'resident of Queen Elizabeth in the Low Countries' where he befriended Constantine Huygens the elder, but no evidence for it is to be found in the state papers. See *Cal. Stat. Pap. For. 1579–80*, p. 79; A. G. H. Bachrach, *Sir Constantine Huyggens and Britain* (Leiden, 1962), p. 79; *DNB*.

12 For Neville, see Foster, *Alumni Oxonienses*, vol. 3, p. 1057; *DNB*.

13 P. Costil, *André Dudith, Humaniste Hongrois* (Paris, 1935), p. 34.

14 BN MS Dupuy 797, fols. 321ff. Quoted by Costil, p. 147.

Henrici Savile Angli ... praestantissimi iuvenis' as well as to the opinions of Tycho Brahe, Maestlin and Wittich. Dudith continued: 'nobiles & doctrina ac moribus praestantes adolescentes, Anglos, Dn. Robertum Sidnaeium ac Dn. Henricum Nevellum, officiose ex me ut salutes, valde et rogo.'[15] During his sojourn Savile also appears to have availed himself of Dudith's library and proved himself an indefatigable collector of manuscripts. After Savile's departure, he forwarded to Dudith copies of manuscripts sought by the Hungarian.

In this task of collecting manuscripts for Dudith's benefit, Savile collaborated with Dudith's close friend, the German astronomer Johannes Praetorius, who lived in Altdorf where he occupied the first chair of mathematics in the academy. Savile and Praetorius had corresponded as early as August 1580,[16] and if not before, then most probably by October of that year the two became acquainted when Savile and his friends stayed briefly in Altdorf on their way to Prague. Savile's party had been joined some time previously by Arthur Throckmorton who, according to his own diary, received some mathematical instruction from Praetorius in Altdorf at this time.[17] The correspondence between Savile and Praetorius, which continued during the subsequent years of Savile's tour as well as after his return home, suggests an intimate friendship as well as a sharing of ideas in mathematics and astronomy.[18]

In 1581 the party set off in the direction of Italy, their first destination being Vienna, where Dudith had furnished them with introductions to another Hungarian humanist, Johannes Sambuc.[19] In Vienna Savile was also befriended by Hugo Blotius, court librarian and general scholar, who was interested in natural philosophy and numbered Camerarius and Kepler among his friends and correspondents.[20] Another member originally of Sidney's entourage to share in Savile's labours in Vienna was George Carew, brother to Richard Carew of Anthony, and later a noted diplomat. An exact contemporary of Philip Sidney and William Camden, Carew – who matriculated at Christ Church in 1566 but resided at Broadgates Hall – probably had encountered Savile at Oxford.[21] Carew transcribed

---

[15] Quoted by W. P. D. Wightman, *Science and the Renaissance* (Aberdeen, 1962), vol. 2, p. 123.

[16] Bodl. MS Savile 108, fols. 104, 105: J. Praetorius to H. Savile, 2 and 22 Aug. 1580, respectively.

[17] A. L. Rowse, *Ralegh and the Throckmortons* (London, 1962), p. 85.

[18] Costil, *passim*. Bodl. MS Savile 108, fols. 106–114v; OUA, SP Pyx F. fol. 1; Bodl. MS Top. Oxon. c. 326, fol. 65. They include five letters written by Praetorius during Savile's tour and three letters written subsequent to Savile's return to England, the last of which is dated 8 Nov. 1597. Bodl. MS Savile 24, a Latin translation of Ptolemy's optics, was given to Savile by Praetorius. See fol. 170v.

[19] Costil, pp. 441–2: A. Dudith to J. Sambuc, 22 June 1581.

[20] For Blotius, see R. J. W. Evans, *The Making of the Habsburg Monarchy 1550–1700* (Oxford, 1979), pp. 23–5.   [21] For George Carew, see *DNB*.

Ptolemy's *De hypothesibus planetarum* which is now included in one of Savile's manuscripts in the Bodleian Library.[22] The transcription of Geminus's *Elementa astronomicae* was a joint effort, the fruits of which were sent to Dudith for his projected edition of the work (1590) as well as carried home to England.[23]

After a short stay in Vienna the group continued on to Italy where they spent the summer and autumn of 1581. Again it was probably Dudith who was instrumental in introducing Savile to Wolfgang Zündelin in Venice and Giovanni Vincenzo Pinelli in Padua. It is noteworthy that much of Savile's collection of manuscripts was assembled during the Italian years and traces of Savile's industriousness still can be found among Pinelli's papers now housed in Milan. MS 227 supra (fols. 57–67v) contains 'ad definitiones V libri Elementor Euclidis annotationes Henrici Savilii'[24] while MS D. 243 inf. is a collection of mathematical transcriptions including some Euclid, Eutocius and Papus.[25]

Some time after Savile's departure from Breslau, another Mertonian, John Chamber, had been due to arrive there, and apparently Dudith had been asked by Savile to look after his friend. From Dudith's letters to Savile in Venice, however, it appears that Chamber's visit never materialized.[26]

Early in 1582 Savile began his return journey home, stopping briefly on the way in many of the places he had visited previously. Hence, in March of that year he found himself in Breslau once again. It appears highly likely that if not before, then at this time, Savile encountered the young and talented astronomer Paul Wittich. Wittich, who had studied for a short while under Tycho Brahe, taught mathematics in Breslau between 1582 and 1584[27] and it would have been odd indeed if Dudith had failed to acquaint his two friends. Indeed, Dudith's previously cited preface to Hajec's *Apodixis*, which refers to the opinion of Savile and

[22] Bodl. MS Savile 10, fols. 43–9, 'ex antiquo manuscripto bibliothecae Caesareae'.
[23] MS Savile 10, fols. 51–77v (Carew's transcripts), fols. 80–117v, his and Savile's hand together with an anonymous scribe 'Explicit opus feliciter 1581 18 Julii George Karew' on fol. 117v; Costil, p. 305.
[24] Fols. 51–4v of the same manuscript contain the notes of Henry's younger brother Thomas on Geminus made a decade later. See *Catalogus Codicum Graecorum Bibliothecae Ambrosianae*, ed. A. Martini and D. Bassi (Milan, 1906), vol. 2, p. 727, n. 652.
[25] *Catalogus Codicum Graecorum*, ed. Martini and Bassi, vol. 2, p. 1042, n. 944. See also MS D.246 inf. (ibid., vol. 2, p. 1042, n. 945), fols. 33–7, 'observazioni di certe cose militari per miglior intelligenza dell'historia Romana'. See also MS Savile 108, fol. 3, 'ex ms. Joannis Vincensii Pinelli'; M. Grendler, 'A Greek collection in Padua: the library of Gian Vincenzo Pinelli (1535–1601)', *Renaissance Quarterly*, XXXIII (1980), 386–416.
[26] Costil, pp. 442, 446–7: A. Dudith to H. Savile, 19 July 1581 and two letters of September 1581. There is no record in the Merton College Register of a leave of absence granted to Chamber. This could mean that Chamber cancelled the tour he had planned and concerning which he had communicated with Savile. For Savile's letter, see Bodl. MS Savile 6, fols. 110–13v.
[27] Costil, p. 202. For Wittich's career, see *DSB*.

Wittich, as well as a letter of Dudith to Henry Neville in Italy – relating a discussion he had had with Wittich on the Copernican system – might indicate an even earlier association.[28]

Wittich's name crops up yet again, this time in connection with another friend of Savile in Breslau: Johann Matthias Wacker, politician and future adviser to the Emperor Rudolf II. Wacker, who was a friend and correspondent of Sir Philip Sidney,[29] was a close friend of Kepler as well as an admirer and patron of Giordano Bruno.[30] In a letter to Savile written shortly after his departure, Wacker asked his friend to cast his son's horoscope, to which purpose he also enclosed Wittich's judgement.[31]

Savile returned to Oxford late in 1582[32] and within three years he was to be installed as the Warden of Merton College. Savile's interests turned increasingly towards antiquarian and patristic subjects, and for this reason what little correspondence has survived is devoted to such issues.[33] Nonetheless, John Dee's diary records a visit made by Savile – in the company of Jean Hotman, the son of the French humanist, Francis Hotman – to his home in Mortlake not long after Savile's return to England.[34] Shortly after this visit Savile was to be cast as an arbitrator in a dispute involving the new calendar introduced by Pope Gregory XIII. In March 1582/83 Sir Francis Walsingham asked Dee for his learned opinion on this new calendar. Dee responded with a tract in which he admitted the validity of the calculations carried out by the Pope's

[28] Costil, p. 444: A. Dudith to H. Neville, 7 Aug. 1581.
[29] Osborn, *Young Philip Sidney*, pp. 160–1 *et passim*; Westman, 'The astronomer's role in the sixteenth century', 130.
[30] For Wacker, see R. J. W. Evans, *Rudolf II and his World* (Oxford, 1973), pp. 154–6, 232.
[31] BL MS Harl. 6993, fols. 22–3v: J. M. Wacker to H. Savile, 13 May 1582. Occasional references to Wittich are also to be found in the correspondence between Savile and Praetorius cited above. Owen Gingerich and Robert Westman are currently preparing a study of Wittich to be published in *Centaurus*.
[32] By January 1582/83 Savile had requested Merton College to rebate him for his fourth year abroad. *Registrum Annalium Collegii Mertonensis*, ed. Fletcher, p. 156.
[33] By 1591 Savile had published his *The Ende of Nero and Beginning of Galba, Fower books of the Histories of C. Tacitus, etc* followed by *Rerum Anglicarum Scriptores post Bedam praecipui ... primum in lucem editi* (1596) as well as his magnificent eight-volume edition of Chrysostom's *Opera* (1610–13). His surviving letters attest to this shift in interests. He corresponded with Casaubon before the latter's arrival in England in 1610 (M. Pattison, *Isaac Casaubon 1559–1614*, 2nd edn (London, 1892), pp. 183, 231); he kept up a lively exchange with Jacques Auguste De Thou in Paris (BN MS Dupuy 836, fols. 137–43; MS Dupuy 632, fols. 105–7; MS Dupuy 706, fols. 39, 45, 48). Perhaps Savile also corresponded with Peiresc whom he had met in 1605 while the French scholar was in London (P. Gassendi, *The Mirrour of True Nobility & Gentility. Being the Life of the Renowned Nicolaus Claudius Fabricius Lord of Peiresk*, trans. W. Rand (London, 1657), p. 100). Various other scholars on the Continent also assisted Savile in collecting notes and manuscripts for his edition of *Chrysostom*; hence, his name is frequently cited, for example, in Camden's correspondence.
[34] 'Feb. 3rd [1582/83], Mr. Savile, Mr. Powil the younger, travaylors, Mr. Ottomeen his sonne, cam to be acquaynted with me'. *The Private Diary of Dr. John Dee*, p. 18.

mathematician, yet nonetheless disputed their basis, preferring instead to rectify the calendar on the basis of 'the actual position of the earth in relation to the sun at the birth of Christ ... and not on that of the assumed accuracy of the Council of Nice'. The matter was brought before a committee which included Thomas Digges, Henry Savile and John Chamber, but despite their favourable report, the devout Protestant bishops refused to adhere to 'Popish' innovations and the matter was dismissed for 150 years.[35]

In 1595 Savile was involved in an altogether different type of controversy, this time involving Joseph Scaliger's fresh attempt to prove the possibility of squaring the circle. Scaliger published his 'proof' in his *Cyclometrica elementa* of 1594 and forwarded a copy to Savile, as well as to other mathematicians, requesting their support. Savile's annotated copy of the *Cyclometrica* makes it evident that he was far from convinced by Scaliger's proof. In fact, so sure was he of Scaliger's misjudgement in the matter that he jotted down 'Insanis Iosephe', adding, 'This man had a good meaning but speakes like a foole'. In the covering letter Scaliger had asked Savile to employ his influence in order to dissuade Thomas Oliver from writing a refutation of the *Cyclometrica*. Glucker speculates that Scaliger's source of information concerning Oliver's intention – his *De circuli quadratura thesis logica* was written only in 1597 and published in 1601 – was Oliver's fellow Cantabrigian, Richard Thomson, with whom Scaliger corresponded frequently during these years.[36]

Savile's death in 1621 was mourned by the Oxford community. The funeral oration was delivered by Thomas Goffe (M.A. 1616, Christ Church), who was both a protégé of Savile and a talented mathematician. The volume commemorating Savile's death contained contributions from over forty members of the university, including Henry Briggs, John Bainbridge, Robert Pink and Robert Burton.[37]

In many respects Thomas Savile followed in the footsteps of his elder brother. By the time he graduated B.A. in 1580 from Merton College, the younger Savile was widely reputed for his proficiency in mathematics and history, and almost immediately thereafter was elected a fellow of his college. It is highly likely that during his student years Savile had made the acquaintance of Robert Hues, Thomas Harriot and Walter Warner – all of whom were his exact contemporaries – and it was only owing to

---

[35] Dee's proposal can be found in Bodl. MS Ashmole 1789, no. 3 (MS Ashmole 179, no. 7 is a copy). Other relevant documents are printed in *The Gentleman's Magazine*, xxxvi (1851), 451–9.

[36] The incident is related by J. Glucker, 'An autograph letter of Joseph Scaliger to Sir Henry Savile', *Scientiarum Historia*, viii (1966), 214–24 where the letter is also published. For Thomson, see *DNB*.

[37] *Ultima linea Savilii* (Oxford, 1622).

Savile's untimely death in 1593 that his acquaintance with them went unrecorded.

There is, however, direct evidence attesting to Thomas Savile's close friendship with William Camden. Thomas was one of the most important collaborators in Camden's *Britannia*,[38] while their extant correspondence relates to a wide gamut of subjects, including philology, history and geography.[39] The correspondence also contains useful allusions to some of Savile's Oxford friends. In this way we learn that by 1580 Thomas was an intimate friend of Richard Hakluyt of Christ Church[40] and had befriended Alberico Gentili, the Italian jurist with mathematical interests, almost immediately upon the latter's arrival. In fact, it was Savile who introduced Gentili to Camden at the time of Gentili's very first visit to London.[41] Other colleagues included Stephen Parmenius, the young Hungarian scholar, who in 1581 arrived at Christ Church where he was befriended by both Hakluyt and Savile. Parmenius was later to lose his life in a voyage to Newfoundland.[42] Another friend mentioned in the correspondence is Jean Hotman, who resided in Oxford from 1581 until 1583 where he served as tutor to the children of Amias Paulet.[43] The correspondence between Thomas Savile and Camden also makes it apparent that both men shared the friendship of Thomas Allen.

By 1588 Thomas Savile was ready to embark upon a Continental tour and only awaited leave from Merton College, which was granted in June of that year.[44] His first destination appears to have been Vienna where many of his brother's friends resided. Already in March 1588 Henry had written a letter to Hugo Blotius, recommending his brother as well as conveying greetings from young Sidney and Neville.[45] From the few extant

[38] F. Levy, 'The making of Camden's *Britannia*', *Bibl. d'Hum. Ren.*, XXVI (1964), 85.

[39] Fifteen letters from Savile to Camden are to be found in Camden's *Epistolae*, pp. 3–51, *passim*. Two additional letters are in Bodl. MS Smith 74, fols. 5–6 and six more in BL MS Addit. 36299, fols. 1–13.

[40] See, for example, Camden, *Epistolae*, pp. 4–5: T. Savile to W. Camden, 2 June [1580]. Since Hakluyt was a close friend of Walter Warner, it would not be rash to assume an additional avenue for acquaintance between Warner and Savile. See *The Original Writings and Correspondence of the Two Richard Hakluyts*, ed. E. G. R. Taylor, Hakluyt Soc., 2nd Ser. (London, 1935), vol. I, p. 198.

[41] BL MS Addit. 36299, fol. 3: T. Savile to W. Camden.

[42] For Parmenius, see D. B. Quinn and N. M. Cheshire, *The New Found Land of Stephen Parmenius* (Toronto, 1972). In February 1582/83 Parmenius stayed with Savile and presented him with his *Paean ... ad Psalmun Davidis CIV* (1582).

[43] For Hotman's stay in Oxford, see the rich body of letters surviving for the period as well as the letters with people he subsequently met in England in *Francisci et Joannis Hotmanorum Epistolae*, ed. J. G. Meelii (Amsterdam, 1700), pp. 259–421 *et passim*. Among his correspondents we find Isaac Wake, Henry Cuffe, Richard Hakluyt and John Underhill.

[44] *Registrum Annalium Collegii Mertonensis*, ed. Fletcher, p. 237.

[45] ÖNB MS 9737²¹⁷, fol. 22: H. Savile to H. Blotius, 12 March 1588.

letters that were written subsequent to Savile's departure from Vienna, it appears that Blotius and Thomas Savile struck up a warm friendship.[46] Another of Henry's close friends to befriend Thomas during his foreign tour was André Dudith. By the time of Thomas's arrival in Breslau, Dudith had only a few months to live, and Thomas remained with the great humanist up until his death.[47] There remains an interesting letter from Thomas to Praetorius in which he renders an account of Dudith's last days.[48] In addition to widening his scholarly acquaintance, like his brother before him, Thomas spent much of his time collecting and transcribing manuscripts. Thus in November 1588, for example, he was occupied in the translation of yet another manuscript of Geminus in Dudith's possession.[49]

Almost immediately following Dudith's death, Thomas continued on his journey, setting off for Italy where he remained for almost two years. Residing mainly in Venice and Padua, Savile participated in the network of scholars originally encountered by his brother a decade earlier. Hence, the Pinelli circle was also made available to Thomas. During this time he also engaged in extensive literary work, transcribing manuscripts[50] and collecting books and manuscripts for himself[51] as well as for the Merton College library.[52]

From Italy Thomas continued to correspond with his newly formed associates. In addition to the previously mentioned correspondence with Blotius, Savile also corresponded with the Silesian Jakob Monav, Wolfgang Zündelin and Georges Dietrich.[53] It was also from the time of Savile's stay in Italy that we learn of his correspondence with Tycho Brahe. The letter of the Danish astronomer was a reply to an earlier letter of Savile – now lost – and indicates that Brahe had enclosed two copies of his *De mundi aetherei recentioribus phaenomenis* (1588), requesting Savile to obtain the opinions of Dee and Digges on his work. At the same time he enclosed some copies of an engraving of himself, this time requesting Savile to find

[46] In December 1590, for example, Blotius was discussing with Savile an intended translation of Ptolemy, a project he had also discussed with Henry Wotton who at that time was lodging at his house in Vienna. BL MS Harl. 6995, fol. 23: H. Blotius to T. Savile, 27 Dec. 1590. For other letters, see ÖNB MS 9737²¹⁷, fols. 55, 85, 95: T. Savile to H. Blotius, 30 July 1589, 20 March 1589/90, 11 July 1590, respectively.
[47] Costil, p. 36.
[48] BN MS Dupuy 348, fols. 154v ff: T. Savile to J. Praetorius, March 1589, quoted by Costil, *passim*.
[49] Costil, pp. 218, 306.
[50] See, for example, Codex Ambr. P-227 Supra, fols. 51–4v, 'Thomas Savilii Angli notae in Geminum cuius loci nonnulli adferuntur'.
[51] Some of Thomas's books can be found in Eton College. See R. Birley, 'The history of Eton College Library', *The Library*, 5th Ser., XI (1956), 244.
[52] *Registrum Annalium Collegii Mertonensis*, ed. Fletcher, pp. 248, 273–4.
[53] ÖNB Vienna MS 9737²¹⁷, fols. 48, 68, 69: 6 April, 2 Aug., 7 Oct. 1590, respectively.

someone who might compose a suitable epigram in praise of himself and his work.[54]

In England, William Camden fulfilled a function similar to that of Peiresc in France. An extremely able general scholar, highly respected both at home and abroad, Camden carried on a wide-ranging correspondence with most of the leading English and Continental intellectuals and in this way acted as a conduit for a flow of ideas and books. The Continental scholars with whom Camden corresponded on geographical and astronomical subjects include Ortelius, Merula, Peucer, Peiresc, Gruter, Scaliger and Sweertius. These letters suggest the manner in which these men had first been introduced to each other as well as the way they obtained information from each other. Thus, a letter of 1606 from Johannes Jonston, the Scottish scholar living in Heidelberg, indicates that he was acquainted with the Cambridge men Lancelot Browne and John Overall, to both of whom he conveyed greetings. A name that recurs in many of the letters of Gruter, Sweertius and Peiresc is that of Henry Savile.[55]

Camden's association with the Saviles as well as with Richard Hakluyt has already been mentioned, but other men of science also numbered among his close friends. Camden was well-acquainted with both John Dee and Sir Christopher Heydon. In July 1610, for example, Heydon addressed to Camden a letter in which he discussed Galileo's recent telescopic discoveries, at the same time disclosing that he himself had used 'one of our ordinary Trunkes'.[56] Camden, we may remember, was a keen observer and his *Annales* indicate the diligence with which he observed the star of 1572 and the comet of 1618. It is sometimes the case that the odd letters that have survived rarely relate to scientific subjects, but since the bond between such men existed, it would not be rash to expect that occasionally scientific subjects were discussed as well. Thus, we find two letters from Thomas Allen, one of them recommending Degory Whear as the first incumbent of the chair of history newly founded by Camden in Oxford;[57] a correspondence with Brian Twyne and John Budden on antiquarian

---

[54] BL MS Harl. 6995, fol. 21: T. Brahe to T. Savile, Dec. 1590, printed in Halliwell, pp. 32–3.

[55] Many letters of Merula, Peiresc, Ortelius, Sweertius and Gruterus are contained in Camden's *Epistolae*. For Peucer and Scaliger, see BL MS Cott. Julius c.v., fols. 29–30: C. Peucer to W. Camden, Dec. 1588; fols. 58–58v: J. Scaliger to W. Camden, 1594.

[56] Camden, *Epistolae*, pp. 128–30: C. Heydon to W. Camden, 6 July 1610. For other letters from Heydon, see *Epistolae*, pp. 130–1, 165–7, 27 July 1610 and 16 June 1616, respectively.

[57] Camden, *Epistolae*, pp. 315–16: T. Allen to W. Camden, 19 Nov. 1621. An earlier and more familiar letter of Allen is in BL MS Cott. Julius c.v., fol. 295: T. Allen to W. Camden, 1 March 1619/20. Camden may also have known Harriot for he recorded the latter's death in his *Annales*: 'Th. Hariotus, Mathematicus insignis, moritur: bona legavit Vicecomiti Isulae & Thomas Ailsburio', *Epistolae*, appendix, p. 72.

subjects; and a correspondence with John Case on the latter's poor state of health.[58] Among Camden's Cambridge correspondents we find Richard Thomson, whose letter of 1594 indicates Camden's acquaintance with William Alabaster.[59]

Illustrative of the role Camden played as a channel for the flow of information between England and the Continent is the way in which he was asked in 1618 to assist Caspar Gevartius in obtaining manuscripts for the latter's projected edition of Manilius. Having received Gevartius's letter,[60] Camden communicated his request to Thomas James who, in turn, was asked to assist the Frenchman. Camden went on to write:

I have beene informed that there is one, and that a learned student of your Universitie hath conferred it with Scaligers Edition. Yf this be true, I most earnestley request you to communicate thus much with him and to understand whether he be purposed to sett it out himself: yf not, whether he wilbe content to impart *Variantes Lectiones* with Gevartius, who (I presume so much of his candor) will not defraud him of the honour due to his labour and learning, yf not, I will send you a copie of Scaligers Edition, and desire you to get some student to conferre it with the MS.[61]

Camden had to disappoint Gevartius, informing him that none of Manilius's manuscripts was to be found in the Bodleian. However, Patric Young, who was also mobilized in the effort, did manage to acquire the needed manuscript from the library of Corpus Christi College, the authenticity of which Camden left it to Gevartius to judge.[62]

Patric Young, son of Sir Peter Young and a celebrated Greek scholar, was another London-based general scholar to maintain contact with the university in which he was educated. Having matriculated at New College in 1605 under the patronage of Henry Savile, Young served as chaplain of All Souls College until 1608, at which time he migrated to London where he became librarian to Prince Henry. Subsequently, he served as librarian both to James I and Charles I.[63] Young visited Paris in 1618, apparently carrying with him letters of introduction from William Camden, and became acquainted with Peiresc, Gevartius and other French scholars. That Young had gained some repute as one interested in mathematics may be inferred from the following incident. When Young's position as a

---

[58] Camden, *Epistolae*, pp. 335–7 for Twyne; pp. 228, 239–40 for Budden; pp. 49–50 for Case. Another letter to Case is contained in Bodl. MS Smith 74, fols. 17–18.

[59] Camden, *Epistolae*, p. 54: R. Thomson to W. Camden, July 1594.

[60] Camden, *Epistolae*, pp. 259–60: J. C. Gevartius to W. Camden, 5 Nov. 1618.

[61] Bodl. MS Ballard 44, fol. 193: W. Camden to T. James, 22 Jan. 1618/19, printed in *Letters Addressed to Thomas James*, ed. G. W. W. Wheeler (Oxford, 1933), pp. 20–1. I was unable to identify this Oxford student.

[62] Bodl. MS Smith 74, fol. 57: W. Camden to J. C. Gevartius, [January] 1618/19. The manuscript located by Young, 'Marci Manilii astronomicorum libri quinque', is Bodl. MS Corpus Christi 66, fols. 1–62.

[63] For Young, see A. J. Kemke, *Patricius Junius* (Leipzig, 1898), introduction.

librarian became tenuous in 1631, Vossius considered procuring for him the post of professor of mathematics at the newly founded college in Amsterdam, a post Sir William Boswell tried to procure for John Pell, also through the offices of Vossius, eight years later.[64]

Again, although very little of Young's surviving correspondence relates specifically to scientific subjects, it nonetheless provides an insight into the well developed network of communications in which he participated. Apart from the assistance Young provided in the Manilius project of 1618,[65] he furnished Isaac Casaubon with information on Thomas Lydiat. In a similar manner, in 1618, when Peiresc wished to establish an avenue to Lydiat, he turned to Young.[66] Young was also a close friend of Lucas Holsten with whom he had formed especially warm relations during the latter's stay in England from 1622 until 1624, and their correspondence is a valuable source of information on their common acquaintances, including Briggs, Bainbridge and John Rous, Bodley's librarian.[67]

Young's Oxford correspondents included William Burton, the Greek scholar of Gloucester Hall, whose letters indicate that Young was also a friend of Thomas Allen.[68] Young was also familiar with John Greaves, for the astronomer forwarded to Young a detailed description of his intended observations of the 1638 eclipse to be carried out in the Near East.[69] Cambridge scholars with whom Young corresponded included John Bois, Samuel Collins, Samuel Ward and James Duport; the surviving evidence, however, relates almost exclusively to Greek and antiquarian studies.[70]

Thomas Harriot has been singled out as a genius far outranking his contemporaries of the first half of the seventeenth century in both depth and breadth of knowledge, and with good reason. His extant manuscripts dispersed between Petworth House and the British Library attest to his sophisticated treatment of algebra, optics, astronomy, ballistics, mechanics and cartography. Unfortunately, the richness of these manuscripts is unmatched by a rich correspondence, and the thirty-odd letters comprising the Harriot correspondence link him almost exclusively with the circle of

[64] G. J. *Vossii et clarorum virorum ad eum epistolae* (London, 1690), p. 178: G. J. Vossius to P. Young, 6 Aug. 1631; Bodl. MS Rawl. Lett. 83, fol. 172: W. Boswell to G. J. Vossius, 23 Aug. 1639.
[65] Kemke, pp. 30, 35: J. C. Gevartius to P. Young, 20 March 1618 and P. Young to P. Dupuy, mid-1619, respectively.
[66] Kemke, p. 15: P. Young to I. Casaubon, 8 Oct. 1612; pp. 32–3: N. F. Peiresc to P. Young, 4 July 1618.
[67] For the exchange between Young and Holsten, see Kemke, pp. 54–64, 106–7, 109–10.
[68] Kemke, pp. 64–5: W. Burton to P. Young, 23 March and 1 June 1631, respectively.
[69] Kemke, pp. 83–4: J. Greaves to P. Young [1638]. See also pp. 85–6: J. Greaves to P. Young, 2 Aug. 1638.
[70] Kemke, pp. 67–9 for Bois; pp. 66–7 for Collins; pp. 17–18 for Ward; pp. 103–4 for Duport.

Henry Percy, 9th Earl of Northumberland. For this reason Harriot has been viewed as a scientist almost entirely cut off from his colleagues in both England and abroad. There does exist, however, some indirect evidence to suggest that Harriot was better acquainted with scientific members of the universities and they, in turn, had greater knowledge of the research conducted by his circle than is often allowed. It appears that Thomas Allen had been one of Harriot's earliest scientific acquaintances and, according to Wood, had acted as Harriot's scientific teacher during the latter's stay at Oxford.[71] Whatever their relations, it is clear that their association did not terminate with Harriot's departure from Oxford in 1580. As early as 1601 we find Allen soliciting books from Harriot for the newly founded Bodleian Library; it was Sir Thomas Bodley's belief that the benefaction '[would] be greater for the qualitie then quantity'. Twenty years later, in 1621, Harriot's will contains additional evidence for their continuing exchange.

I doe acknowledge that I have some written Coppies to the number of twelve or fowerteene (more or lesse) lent unto me by Thomas Allen of Gloster Hall in Oxford ... Unto whom I desire my Executors ... to restore them safely according to the Noate that hee shall deliv[er] of them.[72]

Stevens also suggests that Allen as well as one Standish of Oxford communicated with Harriot about the comet of 1618.[73] Both Allen and Standish are also on record as having communicated to Harriot their observations of an earlier comet, that of 1607.[74]

Other associations which might have originated in Harriot's undergraduate years at Oxford include friendships with Walter Warner (B.A. 1578/79) and Robert Hues, both of whom were close contemporaries.[75] Evidence suggests that Harriot's association with Dee dates back to a period just prior or subsequent to Harriot's departure from Oxford, for when Dee returned from his extended stay on the Continent (1583–90), he was given a book by Harriot as a token of friendship.[76] Ralegh is most likely to have

[71] Wood, *Athenae Oxonienses*, vol. 2, p. 543. Previously (p. 107) we mentioned a letter of Alexander Lower to Thomas Harriot from 1608 in which the former conveyed greetings from his tutor Allen to Harriot. Bodl. MS Clarendon 1, fol. 54.

[72] *The Letters of Sir Thomas Bodley to Thomas James*, ed. Wheeler, p. 3. If indeed Bodley received the benefaction the following day – as he had expected – it must have remained anonymous, for Harriot's name does not appear in the Benefactors' Register. H. Stevens, *Thomas Hariot the Mathematician, the Philosopher and the Scholar* (London, 1900), p. 199.

[73] Stevens, p. 138. The man Standish, whom we shall encounter later in the chapter, p. 144, is probably the Nicholas Standish who took his M.A. from Brasenose College in 1602. Clark, *Register*, vol. 2, part 3, p. 175.

[74] Petworth House HMC 241/VII, fol. 7; *Miscellaneous Works and Correspondence of the Rev. James Bradley, D.D. F.R.S.*, ed. S. P. Rigaud (Oxford, 1832), pp. 511, 514.

[75] Clark, *Register*, vol. 2, part 3, pp. 78, 76, 88.

[76] The book, *El Viaie Que Hizo Antonio de Espeio in el Anno de Ochenta y Tres* ... (Paris, 1586), can be found in BL sig. c.32.a.32.

brought these men together. Dee's diary also records two visits by Harriot in the early 1590s,[77] while the association between the two must have extended into the new century. In 1602 Harriot gave Dee's son, Arthur, an alchemical manuscript.[78] It is also likely that Harriot was in contact with one of the Saviles, probably Sir Henry, for there is mention of 'Mr. Savill' in one of Harriot's papers.[79]

While Harriot might not have been eager to communicate with his fellow scientists, his collaborators might have been of a different mind, for the Oxford scientific and intellectual community appears to have had knowledge of Harriot's work. Significantly, most members of the Northumberland circle – including Sir William Lower (resident of Exeter College, 1586–93), Nathaniel Torporley, Robert Hues, Sir Thomas Aylesbury and Sir Walter Ralegh – had studied at Oxford at some time and might very well have acted as channels for information between the two centres. For example, the verses Dr Richard Corbet of Christ Church, Oxford (M.A. 1605) addressed to Sir Thomas Aylesbury in 1618 attest to his awareness of Harriot's scientific repute.

> Now, for the peace of God and men, advise,
> Thou; who has wherewithall to make us wise,
> By thy rich Studeys, and deep Harriots Minde,
> In which there is noe drosse, but all's refin'd.[80]

Francis Bacon[81] and Henry Briggs[82] also took a continuing interest in Harriot's work, although the extent of their knowledge and the manner in which it was acquired remain open to conjecture.

An intriguing document which suggests first-hand information of Harriot by a member of the Oxford community is a reference to Harriot's observation of sunspots in a notebook of Robert Burton. It is significant that Burton, who himself was a keen astronomer and astrologer, recorded

---

[77] *The Private Diary of Dr. John Dee*, p. 41: 26 Aug. 1592; p. 48: 18 March 1594.

[78] Bodl. MS Ashmole 1507, fols. 158–81 contains 'Benjamin Lock his Picklock to Riply his Castle' with a preface by Arthur Dee who wrote on the original copy, as recorded by Ashmole: 'This booke I received from Mʳ Heriot, at Sion-house, who for many yeares instructed the Earle of Northumberland in the Mathematicks when he lived in the towre. Anº 1602: June 6.' This is a copy made by Ashmole, of which the original is in the Welcome Library, London, MS 436.

[79] BL MS Addit. 6787, fol. 200.

[80] *The Poems of Richard Corbet*, ed. J. W. A. Bennett and H. R. Trevor-Roper (Oxford, 1955), p. 64, ll. 47–50.

[81] By 1608 Bacon considered Harriot, in addition to Ralegh and the Earl of Northumberland, as the men most appropriate to support the Great Instauration, 'themselves being already inclined to experiments'. Bacon, *Works*, vol. ll, p. 63.

[82] Although there is no evidence that the two ever met, both were resident in London and corresponded with Kepler. The only direct evidence of Briggs's knowledge of Harriot is to be found in his short discussion of the new inventions in mathematics and astronomy published by Hakewill in his *Apologie*.

the only instance in which Harriot observed thirty-three sunspots in a single day.[83] The channel for Burton's information has not been identified, but it is noteworthy that Burton was a contemporary of Sir Thomas Aylesbury and Richard Corbet, both of whom were Christ Church alumni. Burton was also a contemporary of Edmund Gunter with whom he corresponded. Corbet's previously cited verses occasioned by the 1618 comet also attest to an on-going association between Burton and Gunter, who in 1618 was resident in Gresham College where, within a year, he was to succeed Thomas Williams as Gresham Professor of Astronomy.[84]

> Burton to *Gunter* writes, and *Burton* heares
> From *Gunter*, and th' Exchange both tongue and eares
> By carriage.[85]

Gunter's presentation copy of *The Description and Use of the Sector* inscribed to Burton can be found in the Christ Church Library. Other scientifically minded associates of Burton who might have acted as channels for scientific information include Sir Thomas Smith (M.A. 1582, Christ Church, Oxford), a mathematician whose son was committed to Burton's care in 1620, and George, Lord Berkeley, who matriculated in 1618 and had been placed under Burton's charge in Christ Church. Berkeley, who was created M.A. in 1623, later bestowed upon his former tutor the living at Segrave.[86]

The correspondence of Henry Briggs, although modest in size, suggests that he shared with his fellow Savilian professor, John Bainbridge, an extensive network of association, which included members of the university intellectual community as well as men of science and intellectuals in other parts of England and abroad. Although Briggs is remembered today chiefly as a geometrician who advanced our knowledge of logarithms, in his youth he had gravitated towards the study of astronomy. In August 1610, for example, he was occupied in the study of eclipses, for which reason he had immersed himself in Kepler's work. Writing to James Ussher, Briggs confided his opinion of Kepler '[who] hath troubled all, and erected a new

[83] Burton recorded in the back of a volume of astronomical and astrological treatises (now Bodl. Lib. 4° R9 Art) that on 12 Sept. 1612 Harriot had seen 33 sunspots. Burton appears to have erred in the month, for the cross reference in the Harriot papers reads 12 July. Petworth House 241/VIII, fol. 43.

[84] In fact, already in 1618 Oughtred had mistaken him for a lecturer. See Oughtred, *To the English Gentrie*, sig. B3v–B4.

[85] *The Poems of Richard Corbet*, p. 64, ll. 41–3. Another acquaintance of Corbet is William Whately – the preacher of Banbury and an avid mathematician – who is mentioned in 'Iter Boreale'. See p. 57, l. 467.

[86] See P. Jordan-Smith, *Burton's Anatomy of Melancholy and Burtoniana* (Oxford, 1959), p. x. For Berkeley, who also served as a patron of John Wilkins, see Wood, *Athenae Oxonienses*, vol. 4, p. 625; *DNB*; Shapiro, *John Wilkins*, pp. 20–1.

frame for the Motions of all the Seven upon a new foundation, making scarce any use of the former Hypotheses; yet dare I not much blame him, save that he is tedious and obscure'.[87] Five years later Briggs was still engaged in his study of eclipses when, having heard of Napier's invention, he rechannelled his energies into work on logarithms.[88]

Of Briggs's closest associates, mention should be made of Samuel Ward, Master of Sidney Sussex College, Cambridge, from 1610 until 1643, whose friendship with Briggs extended from the time they shared scientific interests as young fellows at Cambridge in the 1590s until Briggs's death in 1631. Even in their comparative youth the two appear well informed of mathematicians outside the university, for in early 1595/96 they discussed the former Oxford mathematician Ralph Latham (M.A. 1565/66, Merton College) who had just died.[89] In 1610 Ward requested Briggs to transcribe certain manuscripts housed in Lambeth Palace,[90] while in 1627–8 the two actively campaigned in aid of the destitute Protestant professors of Heidelberg.[91] Another person active in this campaign was Briggs's friend, the German-born orientalist and mathematician Mathias Pasor. Given their shared interests, it is not at all surprising that Briggs was instrumental in bringing together Pasor and Ward. In a letter to Ward in 1628 Briggs voiced the conviction that Pasor's Arabic lectures 'which findethe diverse constante hearers ... shall have some here able to interprete our Arabicke Euclide or any ordinarie booke written withe pointes'. In fact, it had been an ambition of Briggs to persuade the then Chancellor of Cambridge, the Duke of Buckingham, to endow Cambridge with similar facilities.[92] Briggs's concern with the advancement of scientific studies in the universities had been formulated in even stronger terms seven years earlier when he wrote to Ward concerning the newly founded scientific chairs in Oxford. Briggs proposed to devote much of his summer vacation 'in survayinge and plottinge the grounde, for the love [he] owe[d] to [his] mother Cambridge' if such people were to be found who could bestow similar chairs there.[93]

Friendships initially formed at Cambridge were maintained during Briggs's London residence. Edward Wright was an exact contemporary of

[87] Parr, p. 12: H. Briggs to J. Ussher, Aug. 1610.
[88] Parr, pp. 35–6: H. Briggs to J. Ussher, 10 March 1615/16. Thomas Smith provides a colourful description of Briggs's attempt to achieve through the study of eclipses an accurate representation of the celestial motions, a project which greatly frustrated him. See 'The Life and Works of Mr. Henry Briggs', trans. J. T. Foxwell in appendix I of Briggs's *Logarithmetica Britannica*, ed. A. J. Thompson (Cambridge, 1952), vol. 2, pp. lxix–lxx.
[89] 'Feb. 19 1595/6 ... My ovir rash iudgment of Mr. Latham his death to Mr. Brigs'. Knappen, *Two Elizabethan Puritan Diaries*, p. 112.
[90] Bodl. MS Tanner 75, fol. 350: H. Briggs to S. Ward, 8 June 1610.
[91] Bodl. MS Tanner 72, fols. 211, 228, 308.
[92] Bodl. MS Tanner 72, fol. 211: H. Briggs to S. Ward, 1627/28.
[93] Bodl. MS Tanner 73, fol. 68: H. Briggs to S. Ward, 6 Aug. 1621.

Briggs at Cambridge and, as will be later shown, collaborated with him on certain astronomical observations during their stay at university. By 1598 both Briggs and Wright had moved to London where they continued their association up until Wright's death in 1614. Briggs contributed various astronomical tables to the second edition of Wright's *Certaine Errors in Navigation* (1610) and the two collaborated closely in order to advance their knowledge of logarithms.[94] William Bedwell, who was slightly junior to Briggs, moved to London about 1600 and remained a close friend of Briggs until the latter's death in 1631. In an undated letter to Briggs, Ambrose Ussher, brother of the Archbishop, requested the Gresham professor to forward a letter and an Arabic book to Bedwell.[95] In 1606, we find Briggs forwarding one Ralph Clarke of Gravesend a description of – and directions for – the use of 'Bedwell's rule', a measuring instrument invented by William's uncle, Thomas Bedwell, but perfected by William.[96]

Sir Christopher Heydon was still another contemporary of Briggs and Wright at Cambridge, where the three enjoyed an especially close friendship. Wright's notebooks, for example, contain numerous allusions to astronomical observations he had conducted at Heydon's house at Baconsthorpe.[97] Also preserved are eight letters from Heydon to Briggs written between 1603 and 1619. The earlier letters indicate Heydon's preoccupation with astrology and his repeated attempts to convince Briggs of its mathematical and astronomical basis.[98] The later letters suggest an increasing concern with 'purer' astronomy, and Heydon frequently discusses the application of geometry and mathematics to astronomy. In a letter of 1609 devoted to a discussion of Kepler's research on the theory of Mars, Heydon criticizes Kepler as one 'utterly destitute of any helpe from Geometry & as well as of ye reason of either of nature or Arte'.[99] The last four letters of the correspondence, all of which were written in 1619, refer

---

[94] For Briggs's and Wright's early association, see p. 161. Briggs assisted Wright's son, Edward, in his efforts to publish posthumously *A Description of the Admirable Table of Logarithms* (London, 1616).

[95] Bodl. MS Rawl. c. 849, fol. 5: A. Ussher to H. Briggs, undated.

[96] Rigaud, *Correspondence of Scientific Men*, pp. 1–2: H. Briggs to R. Clarke, 25 Feb. 1606/07. In the preface to his *Via Regia ad Geometriam* (1636), Bedwell mentioned his friendship with Briggs, who had encouraged him to publish the work.

[97] See, for example, TCD MS 387, fol. 52 for a letter from Heydon to Wright dated 15 March 1602/03; fol. 53v, 'observatio eclipseos lunaris Mart. 24 1605'; fol. 54, 'The use of the prostaphaeretical instrument of the moone for Sir Christopher Heydon'.

[98] See, for example, Bodl. MS Ashmole 242, fols. 164–6v: C. Heydon to H. Briggs, 5 Nov. 1633. We already had occasion to discuss Heydon's astrological correspondence with John Fletcher, a fellow of Caius College, Cambridge, and yet another contemporary of Briggs and Wright. See ch. II, p. 79.

[99] Bodl. MS Ashmole 242, fol. 168v: C. Heydon to H. Briggs, 14 Dec. 1609. The discussion of the most recent astronomical topics can also be seen in Heydon's immediate response to Galileo's lunar observations in the letter to Camden already mentioned.

to the comet of the previous year. The focus of these exchanges is Heydon's disagreement with certain of Bainbridge's conclusions concerning the orbit of the comet.[100]

Briggs's relations with his contemporary mathematicians were little affected by his move to Oxford in 1619. Significantly, his major works on logarithms, the *Arithmetica Logarithmica* (1624) and the *Trigonometria Britannica* (1633), were, to a large extent, the products of work carried out at Oxford. Briggs's correspondence with the Oxford-based mathematician Thomas Lydiat on chronological and astronomical subjects will be treated shortly, and it is sufficient to note that Archbishop Ussher was their common friend. Although no letters exchanged between Briggs and Ussher for the period after 1615 have survived, there are other indications of their continuing association. Hence, in 1625 when Thomas James supplied Ussher with chronological information for a project on which the two were collaborating, he added that by its very nature the project necessitated the assistance of both Briggs and Bainbridge.[101] Briggs also offered assistance to Young as well as to the promising mathematician John Pell, who was still a student at Cambridge. Pell had sought Briggs's guidance in solving certain logarithmic problems.[102] Briggs's relations with contemporaries, albeit in a slightly different context, are made evident by his contribution to George Hakewill's *Apologie*. As one of an impressive gallery of contributors, including John Bainbridge, Thomas Clayton (Regius Professor of Medicine), Edward Lapworth (Sedleian Professor of Natural Philosophy), Thomas Allen and Sir Kenelm Digby, Briggs narrated the recent mathematical and astronomical discoveries that had expanded the body of knowledge possessed by the ancients.[103]

Briggs's scientific interests were not confined solely to the mathematical sciences. In 1621, for example, Briggs – together with such scientifically oriented university members as Ralph Kettle (President of Trinity College), Thomas Clayton and Robert Burton – sat on a committee appointed to superintend the newly founded Botanical Gardens.[104]

Briggs was also one of the more celebrated Englishmen to act as a conduit between England and the Continent. On at least one occasion he corresponded with Kepler on logarithms and their application to astronomical computations.[105] Another foreign correspondent was the German chronologer and geographer Lucas Holsten, who from 1627 served as Keeper of the Vatican Library. Holsten was in England from 1622 until

---

[100] Bodl. MS Ashmole 242, fols. 168, 169–70v.
[101] Parr, p. 320: T. James to J. Ussher, 15 Feb. 1624/25.
[102] Halliwell, pp. 55–7: H. Briggs to J. Pell, 25 Oct. 1628.
[103] Hakewill, *Apologie*, pp. 301–2.
[104] OUA NEP/Supra Register N, fol. 106v quoted in S. H. Vines and G. C. Druce, *An Account of the Morisonian Herbarium* (Oxford, 1914), p. xii.
[105] J. Kepler, *Gesammelte Werke*, ed. W. Von Dyck and M. Caspar (Munich, 1937–59), vol. 18, pp. 220–9: H. Briggs to J. Kepler, 10 March 1625.

1624, most of which time he spent at Oxford.[106] Henry Bourgchier, in a letter to Ussher early in 1625, mentions his having met Holsten in London.[107] Almost certainly Briggs was introduced to Holsten at the same time. From Briggs's letter to Holsten, it is evident that Holsten had shown a treatise of Briggs to the chronologer Petavius, while for his part Briggs expressed the hope that Petavius would produce still a more accurate revision of Scaliger. Holsten also appears to have commended Briggs's edition of *Euclid* (1620) to Morellus, an act for which Briggs thanked him, adding that he hoped to be able to complete the task. At this time Briggs was also forwarding notes intended to assist Frobenius with his intended edition of Ptolemy's *Almagest*.[108] Although this is the only surviving letter documenting the association between Briggs and Holsten, the correspondence appears to have been more extensive. As previously noted, a year and a half earlier Holsten had written a letter to Patric Young in which he referred to a letter containing notes on Geminus he had received from Briggs.[109] In his subsequent letters to Young, Holsten continued to convey greetings to Briggs.[110]

A nice illustration of the impoverished state of Briggs's present correspondence is to be found in Thomas Smith's biography of Briggs. At one point Smith claimed to possess two letters from Briggs to the Danish mathematician Christian Severin (Longomontanus), which he intended for publication. Unfortunately, Smith's plan never materialized and the letters have been lost. However, Smith's biography does offer an account of these letters. Apparently in 1627 Severin forwarded to Briggs a copy of his *Cyclometrica ex lunulis reciproce demonstrata* (first published in 1612) asking for comments. According to Smith, Briggs's first letter of September 1627 was polite 'but he clearly and frankly pointed out the errors and fallacies of which [Severin] had been guilty in his presuppositions and his calculations'. After receiving a rebuke, Briggs responded in June 1630, 'counter[ing] the charges brought against him ... that he and other analysts ... had degraded and defiled geometry by trying to express irrational lines in numerical form'. In Briggs's opinion 'unless geometry were linked up with arithmetic, it was all but dead'.[111]

Briggs's funeral service in 1630 was attended by several heads of college as well as by many members of the Oxford scientific community. The

---

[106] John Milton, writing to Holsten years later, depicts the entire period of Holsten's abode in England as years of study at Oxford. See *Milton: Private Correspondence and Academic Exercises*, trans. P. B. Tillyard (Cambridge, 1932), pp. 19–22. Holsten was registered as a reader in the Bodleian Library on 28 June 1622. See Clark, *Register*, vol. 2, part 1, p. 282.

[107] Parr, p. 311: H. Bourgchier to J. Ussher, 17 Jan. 1624/25.

[108] Bodl. MS d'Orville 52, fol. 134: H. Briggs to L. Holsten, 4 Oct. 1626.

[109] Kemke, pp. 55–6: L. Holsten to P. Young, May 1625.

[110] Kemke, p. 62: L. Holsten to P. Young, 28 May 1628.

[111] Smith, 'The Life and Works of Henry Briggs', pp. lxxv–vi.

funeral orations were delivered by William Sellar (M.A. 1615, Merton College) and Hugh Cressey (M.A. 1629), a young Mertonian already praised as a promising mathematician. The orientalist, Henry Jacob, composed a Greek epitaph as well as 'Panegyricon in logarithmorum inventionem et trigonometriae Britanicae editionem'.[112]

While the paucity of Briggs's surviving correspondence is balanced somewhat by the many references of contemporaries to him and his work, the situation of his fellow Savilian professor, John Bainbridge, is just the opposite; it is only by way of his letters and notebooks that the merits of his work and the identity of the men with whom he associated can begin to be appreciated. Furthermore, unlike Briggs, Bainbridge's name is associated neither with an invention nor a major publication; his first book was a discussion of the then fashionable comet of 1618,[113] while his subsequent publications were oriented towards ancient astronomy and mathematics.[114] Yet to judge Bainbridge's contribution to the scientific community solely on the basis of his publications would do him a great disservice. The Bainbridge papers housed in Trinity College, Dublin, suggest an indefatigable astronomer familiar with the most recent observations and speculations, who both applied such contemporary accounts to his own research and integrated them into his teaching. Even if Bainbridge was not a particularly 'original' thinker – and again such a verdict must await a more intensive examination of his papers – his correspondence indicates that his advice was often sought by contemporaries and his observations communicated to interested parties, in both England and abroad.

The very first letter of the Bainbridge papers suggests that Wood's claim concerning the reasons for Bainbridge's appointment as the first Savilian Professor of Astronomy is somewhat inaccurate. While Wood credits Sir Henry Savile with having nominated Bainbridge on the basis of his publication of the *Astronomicall Description*, the evidence suggests that these observations had been communicated to Savile immediately after the comet's appearance on 18 November 1618. Indeed, in a reply to Bainbridge dated 2 December 1618 Savile thanked the astronomer for his letter and observations, expressing the hope that their discussion might be continued at their impending meeting.[115] Bainbridge, who had arrived in London just a few months earlier (he had been licensed to practise

---

[112] *Biog. Brit.*, vol. 3, p. 981; Jacob, a fellow of Merton College (1629–48), owed his fellowship to Archbishop Laud, a fact which caused difficulties with the college following Laud's imprisonment. See p. 156 below. Jacob was also a close associate of Selden, for whose *De diis Syris* he supplied much of the material.

[113] *An Astronomicall Description of the Comet from the 18. of Novemb. 1618 to the 16. of December following* (London, 1619).

[114] *Procli sphaera et Ptolomaei de hypothesibus planetarum* (London, 1620).

[115] TCD MS 382, fol. 57: H. Savile to J. Bainbridge, 2 Dec. 1618.

medicine on 6 November 1618 by the College of Physicians of London),[116] attached himself to Henry Briggs at Gresham College, and most probably Briggs introduced his colleague to Savile.

Bainbridge's publication of the *Astronomicall Description* indeed did lay the foundations for his correspondence with Sir Christopher Heydon. Heydon, who was not entirely satisfied with certain of Bainbridge's conclusions concerning the path and inclination ('nod') of the comet, initiated an intensive correspondence which included detailed computations as well as comparisons with earlier comets and references to the conclusions drawn by such astronomers as Tycho Brahe, Kepler and Willebrord Snell.[117] Echoes of this exchange can be found in Heydon's contemporaneous correspondence with Henry Briggs mentioned previously.

As might be expected from Bainbridge's subsequent publications, his twenty-four-year service as Savilian Professor of Astronomy bore witness to an interesting mixture of 'modern' and 'ancient' scientific activity. His notebooks indicate an unflagging concern with celestial phenomena, and his observations of eclipses and the moon as well as an attempt to observe the transit of Venus in 1631 are all carefully recorded. Bainbridge's astronomical computations were facilitated by a rich collection of astronomical instruments which included everything from traditional quadrants and sextants to the most sophisticated telescope of his day.[118]

Motivated by the desire to improve upon his results, Bainbridge actively sought the data collected by his contemporaries. Hence, copies of observations conducted at Heydon's house in Baconsthorpe in 1605, most probably by Edward Wright, as well as Standish's observations of eclipses, came into his possession.[119] Bainbridge showed himself equally eager to communicate his own observations. In 1635, for example, when Wilhelm Schickard requested Bainbridge's observations of lunar eclipses carried out in Oxford, Bainbridge responded with a compilation of his data from a series of observations made in 1621. Ismael Boulliau and Pierre Gassendi also benefited – directly or indirectly – from Bainbridge's observations.[120]

Much of Bainbridge's efforts were directed at promoting information-

[116] W. Munk, *The Roll of the Royal College of Physicians of London* (London, 1878), vol. 1, p. 175.

[117] TCD MS 382, fols. 59–70v contain three letters of Heydon and two draft replies of Bainbridge. Bainbridge himself corresponded with Snell in 1622. See TCD MS 382, fols. 82–3v: J. Bainbridge to W. Snell, 24 Sept. 1622.

[118] The list of instruments used by Bainbridge is to be found in TCD MS 383, fols. 142–3v. Apparently Bainbridge also corresponded with Kepler, although no letters documenting the exchange have survived. See Kepler, *Gesammelte Werke*, vol. 18, p. 516.

[119] See, for example, TCD MS 386/6, fols. 155, 159, 164v.

[120] TCD MS 382, fols. 122v–3: J. Bainbridge to W. Schickard, 5/15 Feb. 1634/35, followed by the observations in fols. 123v–5; Ismael Bulliadus, *Astronomia philolaica* (Paris, 1645), p. 467; P. Gassendi, *Opera Omnia* (Lyons, 1658), vol. 6, pp. 424–5.

gathering expeditions to various parts of the world. The seaman Roger Fry, who set sail for Guiana in 1631, had stayed intermittently with Bainbridge in Merton College from 1626. As Tyacke has already noted, Fry later recorded his measurements of star altitudes and observed sunspots 'using the same method as recommended by Bainbridge in order to observe the transit of Venus'.[121] Unfortunately, the vessel was attacked by the Portuguese before it could reach its destination and Fry was taken prisoner. Despite this misfortune, however, Fry did not abandon his astronomical observations – in the cause of which he even enlisted the aid of his guard – and regularly dispatched his results.[122] As regards the same ill-fated expedition, Bainbridge arranged for simultaneous observations of a solar eclipse to be carried out in England, the purpose of which was to elucidate the problem of longitudes. Henry Gellibrand was one of those who was to carry out such observations.[123]

Gellibrand, it should be noted, had been Bainbridge's pupil and colleague at Oxford and the two maintained contact following Gellibrand's departure for London. Of the four surviving letters comprising their correspondence, two were devoted to a technical discussion of what proved to be a constant preoccupation of astronomers in the 1630s, namely the correction of the Lansberg tables. Also recorded are Gellibrand's efforts to procure through Bainbridge certain books that the Dutch mathematician Adrian Vlaq was supposed to deposit with him following Vlaq's arrival in England in 1634.[124]

A much more ambitious project involved Bainbridge's long-term efforts to launch an expedition to the Middle East. Having obtained the assistance of William Hakewill, Bainbridge was informed by him that both Sir Thomas Roe and Sir Kenelm Digby were enthusiastic about the project and even ready to contribute funds in order to bring it to fruit. However, the expenses proved greater than originally envisaged and necessitated more broad-based support; hence, it was not until 1637 that John Greaves finally set sail from England.[125]

Although Bainbridge showed himself interested in 'modern' astronomical ventures, he was not any less interested in ancient astronomy or chronology. Bainbridge's research into eclipses which helped to solve problems of longitudes was equally important for chronological research. Bainbridge's notebooks indicate that chronology ranked high among his priorities and numerous excerpts from modern authors such as Scaliger and Petavius are dispersed among ancient historical treatises important

[121] Tyacke, 'Science and religion at Oxford before the Civil War', pp. 82–3.
[122] TCD MS 382, fols. 105–105v: R. Fry to J. Bainbridge, 10 May 1633.
[123] TCD MS 382, fol. 119: H. Gellibrand to J. Bainbridge, 6 Dec. 1634.
[124] TCD MS 382, fols. 107–112, 119. The letters are for the years 1633–4.
[125] TCD MS 382, fol. 98: W. Hakewill to J. Bainbridge, 5 April 1631; Tyacke, 'Science and religion at Oxford before the Civil War', p. 84.

to chronology.[126] He also seems to have lectured on chronologically related topics, for in 1625 Thomas Lydiat found himself deeply offended by one of Bainbridge's lectures on the reformation of the calendar.[127] Given Bainbridge's predisposition to chronology, it is not surprising that he was hastily mobilized into Archbishop Ussher's extensive network of scholars. In 1626 Bainbridge was already hard at work seeking 'an expedite and resolute method of calculating Eclipses' for Ussher's benefit.[128] Despite the antagonism generated by the above-mentioned lecture, especially on the part of Lydiat, ironically both Bainbridge and Lydiat were the main sources of information for Ussher's chronological studies. Some of the chronological data communicated to Ussher derived from Bainbridge's collaboration with Henry Briggs and Thomas James discussed earlier.[129]

Bainbridge's publication of *Proclus and Ptolemy* in 1620 heralded his interest in ancient Greek astronomers, but thereafter his interests gravitated more towards Arabic which was an invaluable aid to the deciphering of certain mathematical, astronomical and chronological treatises. As early as 1624 Bainbridge was engaged in a correspondence with the celebrated Dutch orientalist Erphenius,[130] while at home he had befriended the grand old man of Arabic studies in England, William Bedwell. Indeed, so immersed in the study of Arabic was Bainbridge in 1626 that in the above-quoted letter to Ussher he delighted in the many fruits that were to be born of its study.[131]

The two letters of 1627 documenting Bainbridge's associations with John Selden suggest their common spheres of interest. The first letter indicates that Selden had wanted to consult an Arabic astronomical manuscript, but Bainbridge had already returned it to his 'good frende' William Bedwell. Nonetheless, for Selden's benefit he related its contents, adding that he had asked Bedwell to translate this 'precious treasure'. Two months later Selden wrote to Bainbridge thanking him for some notes on Ptolemy and divulging certain chronological issues with which he was then occupied.[132]

Bainbridge's associates at Oxford were as diverse as were his interests, and included men of some intellectual stature as well as men about whom next to nothing is known. Shortly after his arrival in Oxford as Savilian

---

[126] Bainbridge's notes on chronology are dispersed throughout almost all the notebooks.
[127] Bodl. MS Bodley 313, fol. 37: T. Lydiat to T. Man, 12 May 1625, reprinted in Halliwell, p. 53.
[128] Parr, p. 370: J. Bainbridge to J. Ussher, 3 Oct. 1626. See also p. 390: J. Bainbridge to J. Ussher, 7 April 1628.
[129] See p. 141 above. See Parr, p. 320: T. James to J. Ussher, 15 Feb. 1624/25.
[130] TCD MS 382, fols. 86–7: J. Bainbridge to Erphenius, 1 Sept. 1624.
[131] Parr, pp. 370–1: J. Bainbridge to J. Ussher, 3 Oct. 1626.
[132] Bodl. MS Selden Supra 108, fol. 230: J. Bainbridge to J. Selden, 22 Aug. 1627; TCD MS 382, fol. 92: J. Selden to J. Bainbridge, 5 Oct. 1627. MS 382, fol. 91 contains Bainbridge's draft of the former letter.

professor, Bainbridge was asked by a Richard Harris to comment on Regiomontanus's *De triangulis* (1561).[133] Thomas Man, whom we shall encounter in greater detail in connection with Lydiat, appears to have been in the habit of conferring with both Savilian professors on various scientific subjects.[134] John Greaves, like Gellibrand, had been both a pupil and colleague of Bainbridge, as is made evident by the testimony provided by Bainbridge following Greaves's application to the Gresham post.[135] When Vincent Goddard, a fellow of Magdalen College, travelled to Spain as part of the entourage of Prince Charles to negotiate the latter's marriage, Bainbridge asked him to search for various works in the Spanish libraries.[136] In 1632 Bainbridge sought an introduction from Griffin Higgs (M.A. 1615, Merton College) to the renowned orientalist Jacob Golius,[137] while in 1639 a Richard Haydock consulted Bainbridge following his encounter with a theological treatise on the diminution of the magnetic needle.[138]

A most interesting associate was Sampson Johnson (M.A. 1625), a fellow of Magdalen College who shared Bainbridge's interests in astronomy and Oriental languages. Johnson is first mentioned in 1629 when Bainbridge requested Archbishop Ussher to employ his offices to procure for Johnson the post of chaplain to the merchants of Aleppo in order that he might perfect his knowledge of Arabic and conduct some 'other Observations as may tend to the advancement of Learning'.[139] Johnson obtained a year's leave from his college on 14 March 1630/31, but there is no evidence suggesting one way or the other the outcome of the matter.[140] If Johnson did take up the post, he must have returned before April 1632, for at that time he departed from England in the entourage of Lord Anstruther. In an extremely interesting letter of March 1632/33 Johnson offers Bainbridge an account of his journey up until his arrival in Vienna. Johnson relates that in Hamburg he had visited Frobenius. While narrating the episode, Johnson recalls Frobenius's request to

---

[133] TCD MS 382, fols. 72–5v: R. Harris to J. Bainbridge, undated, with Bainbridge's draft reply of 14 Oct. 1619. I was unable to identify positively Harris.

[134] Bodl. MS Bodley 313, fol. 36: T. Man to T. Lydiat, 19 April 1625, reprinted in Halliwell, pp. 49–50.

[135] BL MS Addit. 6196, fol. 88 includes a copy of Bainbridge's testimonial on Greaves's behalf to the Gresham committee.

[136] TCD MS 382, fol. 84: V. Goddard to J. Bainbridge, 5 Sept. 1623.

[137] TCD MS 382, fol. 102: J. Bainbridge to G. Higgs, 17 Dec. 1632: fol. 102v contains a draft letter from Bainbridge to Sampson Johnson to the same effect. Higgs was one of the mourners of Sir Henry Savile.

[138] TCD MS 382, fols. 128–9: R. Haydock to J. Bainbridge, 15 Oct. 1639 with Bainbridge's draft reply of 2 Nov. 1639. I was unable to identify Haydock positively but he might have been the same Haydock who corresponded during the same period with Joseph Mede on theological issues. See Mede, *Works*, ed. Worthington, pp. 789–91.

[139] Parr, p. 411: J. Bainbridge to J. Ussher, 20 July 1629.

[140] Macray, *A Register of Magdalen College*, pp. 164–5.

Bainbridge in 1626 for assistance in his projected edition of Ptolemy's *Almagest* and the latter's rejection of what he considered a useless and irritating labour.[141] While abroad Johnson also pursued Tycho Brahe's astronomical instruments, only to find that they had been dispersed in the Thirty Years War, and attended Kepler's funeral.[142]

Miscellaneous sources often afford additional clues to Bainbridge's network of association. Mention has already been made of the short account of modern astronomical developments composed by Bainbridge for Hakewill's *Apologie*.[143] Bainbridge also contributed laudatory verses to an edition of *Hippocratis magni aphorismi* (1633) brought out by the Cambridge physician and mathematician Ralph Winterton as well as to the *Theatrum botanicum* (1635) of the apothecary John Parkinson. Bainbridge's occasional references to the location of certain of the manuscripts he had consulted also allow us to reconstruct the men with whom he associated. Thus, we find Bainbridge utilizing the collection of his friend Thomas Allen – who, it appears, had been instrumental in making him a member of Gloucester Hall[144] – as well as the libraries of Sir Robert Cotton, Sir Henry Spelman, and Patric Young.[145] Additional mention should be made of Bainbridge's attendance at the undergraduate disputation of Seth Ward at Cambridge, an incident that might suggest the interest shown in promising young mathematicians by certain senior members of the scientific community.[146]

The correspondence of Thomas Lydiat is particularly valuable in the reconstruction of an often ignored scientific and intellectual network at Oxford. As mentioned previously, Lydiat's main interests were mathematics and astronomy, both of which he pursued either as ends in themselves or as the fundamental tools for his sophisticated chronological studies. Although a significant number of letters deal specifically with Lydiat's imprisonment from 1627 until 1632 owing to his brother's debts, they are still useful in identifying his colleagues.

As the network of Lydiat's associates unfolds, it becomes increasingly clear that in many respects he did not conform with the 'ideal' model of

---

[141] See TCD MS 382, fols. 88–9v: G. Frobenius to J. Bainbridge, 1626. It is possible that Bainbridge was the colleague alluded to by Briggs as having sent notes on Ptolemy to Frobenius. Bodl. MS d'Orville 52, fol. 134: H. Briggs to L. Holsten, 4 Oct. 1626.

[142] TCD MS 382, fols. 103–4v: S. Johnson to J. Bainbridge, 28 Feb./9 March 1632/33. Johnson, who probably knew William Boswell in England, met the diplomat in The Hague as he was making his way to Germany. In a letter to Joseph Mede, Boswell mentioned his having entrusted Johnson with a book intended for someone in Germany. See Mede, *Works*, ed. Worthington, p. 789: W. Boswell to J. Mede, 21/31 May 1633.

[143] Hakewill, *Apologie*, pp. 107–8.

[144] TCD MS 384/1, fol. 129v; C. H. Daniel and W. R. Barker, *Worcester College* (London, 1900), p. 126.

[145] TCD MS 384/2, fol. 87 for Cotton; TCD MS 386/1, fol. 38 for Spelman; TCD MS 384/1, fol. 139, MS 386/1, fol. 36 for Young.   [146] Pope, *Life of Seth*, p. 10.

cooperative exchange. A scrutiny of Lydiat's surviving letters suggests that his somewhat eccentric and quarrelsome nature alienated many colleagues and no doubt dissuaded some potential colleagues from cooperating with him. Although Lydiat actively sought the opinion and confirmation of his colleagues, his strong and uncompromising beliefs – especially in chronological matters – made him unusually sensitive to any criticism whatsoever, whether solicited or not.

Such an ambivalence towards a critical exchange of ideas characterizes Lydiat's relations with John Bainbridge. Since both men were capable astronomers and chronologers as well as intimate friends of James Ussher, it was only natural that Lydiat should have sought out Bainbridge's opinion. Nonetheless, once criticism was forthcoming, Lydiat found himself offended by the result. Thus, as the following excerpt from a reply of Robert Pink to a request by Lydiat for potential commentators on his geometrical treatise makes clear, in the past Lydiat had been highly offended by Bainbridge's comments. 'And as for Dr Bainbridge, I know not howe hee stands affected to you, somewhat there was, wch I remember not well now, that relished not well wth you nor wth us that love you, in giving his opinion of your Calender.'[147] Pink appears to be referring to an incident surrounding a lecture, attended by Lydiat, in which Bainbridge discoursed on the reformation of the calendar. In the words of Lydiat as set down in a letter to Thomas Man, during this lecture Bainbridge 'sharply and bitterly inveighed against certain absurd periods', a remark which Lydiat interpreted as directed against his own work on the calendar.[148] Years later in a letter to John Rous, Bodley's librarian from 1620 until 1652, Lydiat again alluded to Bainbridge's criticism of one of his chronological treatises.[149] Such an apparently unfavourable attitude on the part of Bainbridge, however, did not deter Lydiat from continuing either to seek Bainbridge's opinion or to enlist his aid, and there is evidence that on at least one occasion Bainbridge acted as an intermediary for Lydiat, delivering a letter and some treatises to Sir William Boswell.[150]

Such sensitivity to criticism never made Lydiat any less vocal in expressing disdain for the work of some of his colleagues. Thus, the single recorded instance of an ungenerous act on the part of John Selden is *vis-à-vis* Lydiat. At the time it was rumoured that Selden had refused to assist in the overall effort to procure Lydiat's release from prison. The reason for such meanness on Selden's part appears to have been the disrespect expressed by Lydiat for Selden's *Marmora Arundelliana* (1628).[151]

[147] Bodl. MS Bodley 313, fol. 75: R. Pink to T. Lydiat, 30 April 1636.
[148] MS Bodley 313, fols. 36v–7: T. Lydiat to T. Man, 12 May 1625, printed in Halliwell, pp. 50–3.
[149] MS Bodley 313, fol. 15: T. Lydiat to J. Rous, 2 Aug. 1638, printed in Halliwell, p. 70.
[150] MS Bodley 313, fol. 79: T. Lydiat to W. Boswell, 9 Jan. 1631/32.
[151] Wood, *Athenae Oxonienses*, vol. 3, p. 186.

Lydiat's relations with Henry Briggs appear to have been somewhat less fractious than those with either Bainbridge or Selden. Yet they were not entirely free from tension. Although the six letters documenting this association date from the 1620s, the two men appear to have been acquainted for years, as a 1610 letter from Briggs to Ussher in Dublin, conveying respects to Lydiat, suggests.[152] The overall impression of friendship suggested by the correspondence is somewhat contradicted by the 1635 diary of Samuel Hartlib in which he writes: 'Mr Brigges a judicious et godly man did not esteeme so highly of Lydiat as commonly they doe.'[153] For his part, Lydiat occasionally complained of Briggs's negligence in responding to his requests for information and answering his letters.[154] A long and undated letter of Lydiat offers an interesting rendition of his early relations with Briggs. According to this account, Lydiat communicated to Briggs his detailed observations and faithfully forwarded his draft treatises on astronomy and chronology. The treatises in question appear to have been Lydiat's animadversions on the astronomical work of Longomontanus, Kepler, Lansberg as well as Edward Wright. Since Briggs's interest in eclipses corresponded with Lydiat's own, he requested comparative observations which, it might be added, he never received.[155] Lydiat also appears to have solicited Briggs's opinion of his chronological work on the parallax of the sun as part of his attempt to refute the basis of the Gregorian calendar and determine the age of the world.[156]

Apart from its scholarly value, Lydiat's correspondence is an invaluable source of information on his associates in Oxford, many of whom were members of New College, Lydiat's alma mater. One such member was Thomas Crane (M.A. 1617/18). Although Crane – an associate of Henry Briggs who referred to him as 'my very good friend'[157] – was not on familiar terms with Lydiat, he was nonetheless requested to transcribe for him a manuscript of Ptolemy housed in the New College Library.[158]

[152] Parr, p. 12: H. Briggs to J. Ussher, Aug. 1610.

[153] Hartlib, 'Ephemerides 1635', fol. A. 5.

[154] 'After a full year gone and past, from the time I delivered you the two little notes in August (was twelve months) which you say you lost': T. Lydiat to H. Briggs, 31 Oct. 1628. Bodl. MS Bodley 313, fol. 65, printed in Halliwell, p. 58. See following note.

[155] MS Bodley 313, fols. 73–73v: T. Lydiat to H. Briggs, undated: 'you may remember I verie earnestlie intreated you to calculate mee an Eclipse ... but could never obteine so much of you. Neither did you, when I wrote to you two years agone, to get mee what moderne observations you could ... make any mention at al of Mr Wrights Observations.'

[156] MS Bodley 313, fols. 85–85v: T. Lydiat to H. Briggs, 4 April 1623, printed in Halliwell, pp. 47–9; MS Bodley 313, fol. 65v: T. Lydiat to H. Briggs, June 1626, printed in *Remarks and Collections of Thomas Hearne*, ed. C. E. Doble and others (Oxford, 1885), vol. I, p. 147.

[157] MS Bodley 313, fol. 85: H. Briggs to T. Lydiat, 11 July 1623, printed in Halliwell, pp. 46–7.

[158] This letter has not survived.

Although the reasons are unclear, the requested transcription was not forthcoming. When the transcription was finally completed some two years later by Thomas Man (M.A. 1620/21), in a letter thanking the New College fellow, Lydiat insisted that 'some sinister surmise arising upon the impairing of my credit amongst you was the cause of the differing of it so long'.[159] As one of Lydiat's more conscientious transcribers, Man usually took the pains to comment upon the manuscript as well. Thus, he compared the Ptolemy manuscript both to a related manuscript in All Souls College as well as to a printed version, discussing with John Bainbridge the probable identity of the translator and the antiquity of the manuscript.[160]

From Lydiat's reply to Man other facts become apparent as well. First, another member of the team of transcribers, Thomas Miller (M.A. 1622/23), then the New College mathematical lecturer, is identified. Apart from assisting in the transcription, Miller also provided some appended notes 'about the confounding or dividing of two of Hipparchus his vernal observations'. Miller, it might be added, was also a friend of Henry Briggs, and it was Lydiat's hope that this association might enable Miller to consult a related manuscript in the mathematics library bequeathed by Sir Henry Savile.[161]

The moving force behind the New College circle appears to have been the Warden, Robert Pink. Pink actively endeavoured to effect Lydiat's release from prison, and later suggested that rooms in college be made available to Lydiat for as long as he wished to keep them. On a more scholarly level, Pink coordinated the transcription and collation of manuscripts among the New College fellows as well as contributed to the effort.[162] Pink was also occasionally asked to comment upon Lydiat's various tracts. For example, when Lydiat was writing and revising his *Mesolabium geometricum et circuli dimensio* in 1635–6, he appealed to Pink for comments. The latter declined, however, judging himself incapable of passing judgement upon such 'an abstruse mysterie'. Pink nonetheless suggested Sir Henry Spelman and Sir Kenelm Digby as potential commentators.[163] At least as regards Spelman, we know that Lydiat

---

[159] MS Bodley 313, fols. 36v–7: T. Lydiat to T. Man, 12 May 1625, printed in Halliwell, pp. 50–3. The quotation is on pp. 50–1.

[160] The manuscripts involved, 'Claudii Ptolemaei liber Almagesti in distinctiones tredecim distributus, ex Arabico in Latinum versus a Magistro Gerardo Cremonensi, tabulis glossulisque marginalibus penitus instructus', are New College MS 281 and Bodl. MS All Souls College 95. [161] Halliwell, p. 52.

[162] Wood, *Athenae Oxonienses*, vol. 3, p. 186; MS Bodley 313, fol. 19: R. Pink to T. Lydiat, 13 Nov. 1641, printed in Halliwell, p. 75. Four other letters exchanged between them from 1643 until 1644 are in MS Bodley 313, fols. 16–16v.

[163] MS Bodley 313, fol. 75: R. Pink to T. Lydiat, 30 April 1636. Many draft copies of the *Mesolabium*, which, like so many of Lydiat's tracts, were written in an attempt to gain patronage and favour, can be found in MS Bodley 664.

followed the Warden's advice, for in August 1636 Lydiat wrote to Spelman requesting him to return the manuscript, as he had discovered an error in it.[164]

Other associates of Lydiat to emerge from the correspondence are Mathias Pasor, John Rous, Sir Henry Savile and Sir William Boswell. Pasor visited Lydiat frequently during the latter's term in prison where, amongst other things, they conversed on astronomy.[165] John Rous often served as an intermediary between Lydiat and other scholars. Thus, in 1638 he was requested to pass on some of Lydiat's astronomical papers to Hugh Morrison, a former member of New College (M.A. 1611) and at the time Archdeacon of Gloucester, as well as to apologize to Peter Turner for Lydiat's having missed him during the former's visit to Oxford.[166] It is also evident that Lydiat had had some contact with Sir Henry Savile, for in 1620 he addressed to him *De anni solaris mensura epistola astronomica ad Hen. Savilium.*

Lydiat's close friend, Sir William Boswell, had been – together with Pink – most instrumental in effecting Lydiat's release from prison, and to this end he had enlisted the support of Sir Thomas Aylesbury. Boswell also occasionally commented on Lydiat's treatises. In fact, in 1632 Boswell bluntly advised Lydiat against publishing some of his astronomical observations, cautioning 'if my leisure before my departure as I hope make it, I shall give you infallible reasons ag^t excentr^{ty} of ye sun & shew y^t your observations conclude not'.[167]

Finally, mention should be made of Lydiat's life-long association with James Ussher which dates back to the opening years of the seventeenth century. From 1609 until 1611 Lydiat resided with the Archbishop in Ireland, and subsequently they maintained an active correspondence and met occasionally during Ussher's visits to London or Oxford. As previously noted, Lydiat's astronomical and chronological studies – together with those of Bainbridge – provided the backbone of Ussher's writings on chronology.

The relatively extensive correspondence of Archbishop Ussher enables us to reconstruct a larger intellectual network than is possible with Lydiat.

[164] CUL MS Dd III.64, fol. 3: T. Lydiat to H. Spelman, 16 Aug. 1636.
[165] MS Bodley 313, fol. 65: T. Lydiat to H. Briggs, 31 Oct. 1628, printed in Halliwell, p. 58.
[166] MS Bodley 313, fol. 15: T. Lydiat to J. Rous, 2 Aug. 1638, printed in Halliwell, p. 70. Two years earlier Pink refrained from submitting the *Mesolabium* for Turner's judgement, since the latter was 'soe imployed howerly in my Lord our Chancellors businesses heere that I might not interrupt him wth such difficulties'. MS Bodley 313, fol. 75: R. Pink to T. Lydiat, 30 April 1636.
[167] Sixteen letters in the collection are between Boswell and Lydiat, relating mainly to the latter's imprisonment. The quotation is in fols. 26–7: W. Boswell to T. Lydiat, 16 April 1632.

In addition to colleagues common to the two scholars – including Sir William Boswell and Robert Pink[168] – Ussher was also well acquainted with the three scientifically minded fellows of Exeter College: John Prideaux, George Hakewill and Nathaniel Carpenter. On at least one occasion Prideaux and Hakewill took charge of a student referred by Ussher to Exeter;[169] the Archbishop wrote a laudatory letter in praise of Hakewill's *Apologie* which was appended to the third edition of 1635 and in 1626 Carpenter had been installed as his chaplain.[170]

Ussher also mobilized the efforts of Thomas James, who contributed his extensive knowledge of patristics to Ussher's chronological studies. Writing to Ussher in February 1624, James discussed one project on which the two collaborated. James proposed to commence collating the chronology of Marianus Scotus – which had been printed from a mutilated copy in 1569 – with other manuscript versions, both in the Bodleian and in Corpus Christi College libraries.[171]

A letter from Brian Twyne to Thomas James indicates that the former also assisted Ussher in his studies, while the single extant letter of Edward Brouncker (M.A. 1609), of Wadham College, reveals that he, too, was involved in the collation and transcription of manuscripts for the Archbishop's benefit.[172] Previous mention has been made in chapter II of the only extant letter of William Gilbert, formerly a member of Gloucester Hall, which treated certain recent astronomical discoveries. It might be added that the single remaining letter of John Greaves to Ussher relates to issues of Arabic astronomy and suggests the extent of Greaves's responsibility for William Harvey's election to the wardenship of Merton College.[173]

Ussher's associates in Cambridge also formed an impressive group. Ussher was on especially good terms with Samuel Ward, their extensive correspondence being devoted mainly to theological subjects. Occasionally, however, their letters turned towards chronology. Mentioned in the course of their correspondence are two major projects that were executed by

---

[168] Parr, p. 77: W. Boswell to J. Ussher, 17 March 1621/22 and references to Boswell in various other letters. Ussher resided with Pink during a visit to Oxford. See Bodl. MS Bodley 313, fol. 19: R. Pink to T. Lydiat, 13 Nov. 1641, printed in Halliwell, p. 75.

[169] Parr, pp. 398–400: G. Hakewill to J. Ussher, 16 July 1628; J. Prideaux to J. Ussher, 27 Aug. 1628.

[170] One of Carpenter's notebooks later passed into Ussher's possession. See TCD MS 150.

[171] Parr, pp. 318–20: T. James to J. Ussher, 15 Feb. 1624/25. The manuscripts in question are Bodl. MS Corpus Christi College 157, fols. 77–199: 'Mariani Scoti chronicon ab initis mundi usuque ad annum post Christi Incarnationem 1082, per Florentium Wigorniensem adauctum et ad annum 1118 deductum, unde interum ad annum 1141 continuantum est' and Bodl. MS Bodley 521. The latter, which was given to the library in 1620 by Sir Henry Savile, is a chronicle wrongly attributed to Scotus.

[172] See p. 73 above. *Letters Addressed to Thomas James*, ed. Wheeler, pp. 59–60: B. Twyne to T. James; Parr, p. 72: E. Brouncker to J. Ussher, 11 Sept. 1620.

[173] Parr, pp. 492–4: W. Gilbert to J. Ussher, 11 Dec. 1638; ibid., pp. 509–10: J. Greaves to J. Ussher, 19 Sept. 1644.

Cambridge men. The first involved an attempt to complete and prepare for publication Edward Lively's 'Chronologia à Mundo Conditio ad annum 3498'.[174] In July 1626 Ward wrote to Ussher informing him that Thomas Whalley had asked him 'above a month ago to write to your Lordship to leave Mr. *Lively* his Chronology with him and me, and we would take care for the publishing thereof'.[175] Ussher appears not to have forwarded the chronology in question, for seven months later Ward repeated his request.[176] Not long afterwards, however, Ussher must have complied with Ward's request, for a series of four letters were exchanged between Whalley and Ussher documenting the progress of the project. Much of this exchange was devoted to a comparison between Lively's computations and those of Erasmus Reinhold and Copernicus.[177]

The second project involved a request on the part of Ussher for cooperation in rendering Ignatius's 'Epistolae' for use in his own chronological studies.[178] Again Ward informed Ussher that Whalley had volunteered his assistance in the project. Ward furthermore pledged the Archbishop the assistance of Walter Foster of Emmanuel College – brother to Samuel Foster, later Gresham Professor of Astronomy – 'who it seemeth hath taken some pains already in it'.[179]

Another Cambridge fellow cited in the correspondence is Joseph Mede of Christ College with whom Ussher recollected he had dined in the company of Samuel Ward, their conversation centring on Scaliger's chronological studies.[180] Abraham Wheelock (M.A. 1618), who corresponded with Ussher on various Greek manuscripts, also alluded to Ward and John Bois (M.A. 1582), whose aid he had availed himself in the course of this project.[181]

Finally, mention should be made of some men who might have known Ussher while they were still at university, but whose letters belong to a later period. Around 1650, for example, Henry Hammond (M.A. 1625, Magdalen College, Oxford) exchanged four letters with Ussher on various chronological subjects[182] and in 1646/47 Edward Davenant, formerly a

174 The work remained unpublished and is to be found in TCD MSS 125–6.
175 Parr, p. 369: S. Ward to J. Ussher, 5 July 1626.
176 Parr, p. 378: S. Ward to J. Ussher, 13 Feb. 1626/27.
177 Parr, pp. 599–604. The letters lack the year in which they were written, but from the subject matter it is clear that they were composed in 1627.
178 The required manuscript is Gonville and Caius College MS 395, fols. 164–81. The transcript made for him is Gonville and Caius College MS 445.
179 Parr, pp. 437–8: S. Ward to J. Ussher, 25 May 1630.
180 Parr, p. 469: J. Ussher to S. Ward, 30 April 1634. From a letter of 1628 we learn that Mede sent Ussher a copy of his *Clavis apocalyptica* (1627) and discussed with him some chronological aspects of Selden's treatise on the Arundelian Marbles. Elrington, *The Whole Works of Ussher*, vol. 15, pp. 406–8: J. Mede to J. Ussher, 22 May 1628.
181 Parr, pp. 329, 545–6: A. Wheelock to J. Ussher, 12 July 1625 and another undated letter *c.* 1650, respectively.
182 Parr, pp. 542–3: H. Hammond to J. Ussher, 16 May, 21 July, 10 Dec. 1650 and 14 Jan. 1650/51, respectively.

fellow of Queens' College, Cambridge, corresponded with Ussher on eclipses and the application of geometry to astronomical problems.[183]

Still another man to have corresponded with Ussher was John Selden. At least twelve letters documenting the association, spanning from 1621 until Selden's death in 1654, have survived. The wide-ranging interests of the two men are well reflected in their correspondence, which includes antiquarian and philological exchanges as well as patristic discussions with particular reference to chronology.[184]

Like Lydiat and Ussher, Selden was a man unaffiliated with a university who, nonetheless, was able to mobilize a significant number of academics to assist in the transcription and collation of manuscripts as well as to advise and comment on scholarly matters. Although most of the Selden correspondence belongs to a period after 1630, it often sheds light on an earlier period as well.

Thomas Allen seems to have been Selden's very dear friend. Only one letter of Allen to Selden – a short letter dealing with a manuscript of Fortescue[185] – is known to have survived, but then again only three letters of Allen have been preserved. On the other hand, Selden possessed a unique manuscript containing extracts relevant to Allen from the Trinity College, Oxford, Register, together with nine unpublished elegiac verses to Allen. Included among the contributors were William Burton, Edward Bathurst, Lawrence Humphrey, Josiah How and Thomas Dudley. Selden also acquired at least three manuscripts that had previously belonged to Allen.[186]

A similar disparity between the relations suggested by the correspondence and those suggested by more circumstantial evidence exists with regard to Brian Twyne. Although there are only two extant letters from Twyne to Selden, both of which are concerned with transcriptions from some Arabic manuscripts that Twyne was in the process of preparing for Selden in 1641, Selden's library contained certain of Twyne's manuscripts.[187] It is also worthy of note that in the above-mentioned project Twyne was

[183] Elrington, *The Whole Works of Ussher*, vol. 16, pp. 75–7: E. Davenant to J. Ussher, 29 Jan. 1646/47; pp. 114–15: J. Ussher to E. Davenant, 14 Feb. 1646/47.
[184] For the Ussher–Selden correspondence, see Parr, pp. 78–9, 81, 332, 338, 383–6, 591–4; Bodl. MS Selden Supra 108, fols. 93, 174–5v, 184, 217.
[185] Bodl. MS Selden Supra 108, fol. 163: T. Allen to J. Selden, 9 July 1616. Allen, who greatly assisted Selden in his research, was described by the latter as 'A person of the most extensive learning and consummate judgement, the brightest ornament of the famous university of Oxford', *Eadmer* (1623), p. 200, translated in *Biog. Brit.*, vol. I, p. 106.
[186] For the elegies to Allen, see Bodl. MS Selden Supra 120, fols. 9–23v. The Allen manuscripts that came into Selden's hands are Bodl. MS Arch. Selden B. 8, fols. 303–13; MS Arch. Selden B.26, fols. 34, 35–94; MS Selden Supra 45. See Watson, 'Thomas Allen of Oxford and his manuscripts', p. 312.
[187] MS Selden Supra 79 is one of Twyne's manuscripts and it contains numerous notes taken from various manuscripts which had belonged to John Dee and Thomas Allen.

assisted by yet another of Selden's correspondents, John Gregory of Christ Church (M.A. 1631).[188] Apart from this assistance, it appears that Gregory had applied to Selden for astrological, astronomical and chronological works, at which time he also discussed related matters.[189]

Peter Turner (a fellow of Merton College, Gresham Professor of Geometry 1620–31 and Savilian Professor of Geometry 1631–48) corresponded with Selden as early as 1627, at which time the latter was searching for copies of Gaudentius's *Harmonica* – both of which were given by Sir Henry Savile – in the Merton College and Bodleian libraries. At Selden's request, Turner compared these copies with Alypius's *Introductio musica* as well as with the Magdalen College copy of Aristides Quintilian's *Liber de arte musica.*[190]

We next encounter Turner in 1641 during his efforts to enlist Selden's support for the orientalist Henry Jacob. Jacob, who owed his Merton College fellowship to Archbishop Laud, found himself in trouble following his patron's disgrace, and in a long letter to Selden, Turner attempted to justify the lawfulness of Jacob's fellowship.[191]

In Cambridge Selden maintained an active correspondence with Ralph Cudworth whom he consulted chiefly on Talmudic and chronological subjects. In a letter dated 15 November 1643, for example, Cudworth discoursed on the chronology of a Karaite manuscript that had been supplied to him by Selden, and promised to look further into its astronomical data. Cudworth fulfilled his promise almost immediately, and two weeks later he commented upon its astronomical aspect, comparing its data with

---

[188] Bodl. MS Selden Supra 109, fols. 278a, 278c: B. Twyne to J. Selden, 7 Feb. and 16 March 1641/42, respectively. Ibid., fol. 243: J. Gregory to J. Selden, 21 March 1641/42.

[189] MS Selden Supra 108, fols. 52, 74: J. Gregory to J. Selden, 27 Jan. 1633 and 2 April, respectively.

[190] MS Selden Supra 108, fols. 228, 180: P. Turner to J. Selden, 19 and 28 August 1627, respectively. Turner's transcripts are in MS Selden Supra 121, fols. 5–8. The Bodleian copy of Gaudentius and Alypius is MS Auct. F. 1.3, fols. 116–27 and 128–44, respectively and the Magdalen copy of Quintilian is Bodl. MS Magdalen College Gr.12, fols. 35–96. I was unable to trace the Merton College copy of Gaudentius and Alypius, but oddly enough these two treatises comprise St John's College, Oxford MS 168, which was given to the College by Archbishop Laud in 1638. It appears likely that Turner, a close friend of the Archbishop, 'pinched' the manuscript and gave it to Laud who, in turn, bestowed it upon the mathematical library he was building at St John's. Turner also provided Selden with a catalogue of the Barocci Collection of Greek manuscripts shortly after its donation by Sir Thomas Roe in 1629. The catalogue is to be found in the back of some treatises on chirurgy and medicine (Bodl. sig. AA.1.Med.Seld.). In 1651 at the request of Marcus Meibomius, Selden again asked for the collation of the Magdalen copy of Quintilian and the Bodleian copy (MS Auct. F. 1.2). This time the transcriptions were made by Edward Sylvester and corrected by Gerard Langbaine. They were sent to Meibomius in April 1651 and were included in his *Antiqui musici scriptores* (1652). The transcripts are to be found in MS Selden Supra 122 and the covering letters from Langbaine and Meibomius are in MS Selden Supra 109, fols. 384, 325, 291, 283.

[191] MS Selden Supra 108, fol. 17: P. Turner to J. Selden, 30 Oct. 1641.

the computation of Kepler's Rudolphine Tables.[192] Selden also corresponded with Herbert Thorndike, but the only extant letter documenting the association is devoted to Talmudic issues. However, on 15 October 1642 Selden sent both Thorndike and Cudworth a copy of his *Eutychius* as a token of affection and gratitude.[193]

Although Thomas Allen is one of the more senior members of the scientific community in the period between 1560 and 1640, it has been my decision to discuss the network of association that formed around him only after some of his more well-known students and friends have been discussed. This is because astonishingly little evidence of his papers or his correspondence has survived. Of his extant writings there remain only a transcript of his commentary on Ptolemy's astrology,[194] some notes on John Beale's 'Illustrium maioris Britanniae scriptorum' (1559)[195] as well as a few random horoscopes and alchemical notes.[196] Only three of Allen's letters are known to have survived, two to Camden and one to Selden, all of which have been previously noted. However, some additional fragments of information on his associations may be pieced together.

One of Allen's earliest friends appears to have been John Dee, although there is no record to document conclusively a meeting between them. There is, however, sufficient evidence of a circumstantial nature to connect the two. Both were employed in the service of the Earl of Leicester as well as charged specifically by the author of *Leicester's Ghost* as conjurors of the Earl. Another common acquaintance was the Polish prince, Alberto Laski, who visited England in 1583. Indeed, Laski attempted to persuade Allen to return to the Continent with him, an invitation later extended to Dee. Allen also appears to have engaged the alchemist Edward Kelly some time before the latter became the famous medium of John Dee.[197] Most significant is Dee's gift to Allen of certain of his manuscripts as well as his curious mirror which had the property of casting and inverting images.[198]

[192] MS Selden Supra 109, fols. 266, 258–58v: R. Cudworth to J. Selden, 14 Nov. and 2 Dec. 1643, respectively.
[193] MS Selden Supra 108, fols. 247–47v: H. Thorndike to J. Selden, 1642; MS Selden Supra 109, fol. 262: R. Cudworth to J. Selden, 25 Oct. 1642.
[194] 'Claudii Ptolomaei Pelusiensis de Astrorum Judiciis, aut ut vulgo vocant Quadripartitae Constructionis.' Bodl. MS Ashmole 388.
[195] The notes were printed by Thomas Hearne in his edition of Leland's *Itinerary* (London, 1712), vol. 9, pp. 206–8.
[196] Bodl. MSS Ashmole 350(4); MS Ashmole 394, fols. 113–14v; MS Ashmole 1441, fols. 369–70.
[197] Wood, *Athenae Oxonienses*, vol. 1, p. 639; T. Rogers, *Leicester's Ghost*, ed. F. B. Williams (Chicago, 1972), p. 14; I. R. F. Calder, 'John Dee Studied as an English Neo-Platonist' (London Univ. Ph.D. thesis, 1952), pp. 621–3.
[198] For a description of the mirror, see Bodl. MS Selden Supra 79, fol. 150c.

Unfortunately, only a few of the many students nurtured by Allen at Oxford left some testimonial of their continuing relationship with their mentor. Brian Twyne's manuscripts attest to his frequent and extensive consultation of Allen's manuscripts. Moreover, when Twyne describes Allen's concave glass – the gift of Dee – he relates that occasionally he had borrowed it from Allen. Twyne also serves as Wood's source of information on another of Allen's Oxford associates, Robert Barnes, whom we encountered previously as the donor of an interesting mathematical and medical library. According to Twyne, Barnes related to Allen the story concerning the way Sir Henry Billingsley obtained the papers of Friar Whitehead which Billingsley subsequently used for his translation of Euclid.[199] Another Oxford man to make extensive use of Allen's manuscripts was Thomas Payne of Christ Church who, it appears, also consulted the manuscripts of Brian Twyne and John Prideaux.[200]

Some additional associations can be ascertained from Allen's will. Although the largest share of Allen's library was bequeathed to Sir Kenelm Digby, there were other beneficiaries as well. Sir Thomas Aylesbury, who most probably met Allen while a student at Christ Church, Oxford, in the first years of the seventeenth century, received 'the great concave glasse', the original copy of Allen's commentary on Ptolemy – copies of which also reached William Lilly and Johannes Banfi Hunyades – and, according to Wood, certain other manuscripts.[201] Other friends mentioned in Allen's will include Ralph Kettle, President of Trinity College, and John Tolson, Provost of Oriel College.[202]

When Allen died in 1632 the funeral oration was delivered by two former pupils and friends: William Burton of Gloucester Hall (D.C.L. 1630) and George Bathurst of Trinity College (M.A. 1632).[203] Bathurst was also the recipient of at least one Allen manuscript, as was John Newton of Brasenose College (M.A. 1629).[204] A third mourner was Richard James (M.A. 1615, Corpus Christi College) who appended verses commemorating the death of both Allen and Robert Cotton (who died in 1631) to his *Epistola ... Thomas Mori ad Academiam Oxon.* (1633). Nine additional elegies by members of Oxford were noted previously.

---

[199] See, for example, Bodl. MS Corpus Christi College 260, fols. 82–4v; Bodl. MS Wood F.26; Bodl. MS Corpus Christi College 160 was given to Twyne by Allen in 1624; Bodl. MS Selden Supra 79, fols. 150[a–c]; Wood, *City of Oxford*, vol. 2, pp. 471–2.

[200] Bodl. MSS University College 47–9 contain the transcripts made by Payne in 1616–17 of various treatises of Roger Bacon in the possession of Allen, Twyne and Prideaux.

[201] Watson, 'Thomas Allen of Oxford and his manuscripts', p. 301; Bodl. MS Ashmole 388, facing p. 1; Wood, *Athenae Oxonienses*, vol. 2, p. 544.

[202] Allen's will is in PRO, PCC 110 Audley.

[203] W. Burton and G. Bathurst, *In viri doctissimi, clarissimi, optimi, Thomae Alleni ... orationes binae* (London, 1632).

[204] Bodl. MS Bodley 680 came into Bathurst's hands and Bodl. MS e mus. 224 into Newton's.

In direct contrast to the personages we have been discussing stands Richard Madox. Having graduated M.A. in 1576 as a fellow of All Souls College, Oxford, Madox was elected a university lecturer in 1580 and became a proctor the following year. Almost immediately upon completion of this tenure, Madox set sail for Cathay in the famous voyage of Edward Fenton. Madox, who was neither an important man of science nor a major intellectual, is nonetheless important for a diary he left behind in which he recorded his preparations for the journey and the few months of the voyage leading up to his death.[205]

The activities cited and people alluded to in Madox's diary suggest that he had shown at least some inclination towards astronomy and mathematics before his departure from university. Madox's network of association at Oxford appears to have included a significant number of scientifically oriented fellows. On 6 February 1582 Madox dined at the table of Dr Tobie Matthew, Dean of Christ Church, the other guests including Dr Martin Culpepper, Warden of New College, and Thomas Allen.[206] A week later he had supper with the future Bishop of Worcester, John Thornborough, who was then a fellow of Magdalen College and an ardent chemist. Also present on this occasion was James Bissle, another Magdalen fellow and the college lecturer in natural philosophy.[207]

Madox's scientific associations also stretched beyond the university gates. On 19 February, for example, we find him visiting Robert Norman in Ratcliff where he was shown 'how the strength of his lodestone was increased'.[208] Madox was also a close friend of the scientific writer Cyprian Lucar.[209] On 9 March he was a dinner guest of Gabriel Goodman, Dean of Westminster, together with Thomas Wagstaffe, a former fellow of All Souls College. Their conversation on that occasion centred upon 'the great and bluddy meteor which was seen at 9 overnyght from the northwest to the sowtheast, dreading the betokenings thereof'.[210]

Shortly before leaving Madox recorded the purchase of a 'mappa mundi and other pamphlets' together with a dial, and immediately after having set sail, he recorded a discussion of a method for finding out a perfect

---

[205] The diary was already consulted to some extent by Curtis while it was still in manuscript form. It has recently been published by the Hakluyt Society under the title *An Elizabethan in 1582: The Diary of Richard Madox Fellow of All Souls*, ed. E. S. Donno, Hakluyt Soc., 2nd Ser., vol. 147 (London, 1976).

[206] *Diary of Richard Madox*, pp. 81–2.

[207] *Diary of Richard Madox*, p. 84.

[208] *Diary of Richard Madox*, p. 87.

[209] *Diary of Richard Madox*, pp. 95, 96, 98. For Lucar, see Aubrey, *Brief Lives*, vol. 2, pp. 38–41; DNB.

[210] *Diary of Richard Madox*, p. 92.

longitude and began correcting Erasmus Reinhold's tables.[211] By the time
of Madox's death he had recorded observations of comets and eclipses, and
on one occasion he discussed the nature and qualities of the loadstone.[212]

This record of the scientific activities of this otherwise obscure university
member has been included in order to suggest the existence of other men
like Madox; although interested in the new scientific frontiers being
constantly opened up, these men never became consequential figures in
the scientific community.

The absence of an observatory in England comparable to Tycho Brahe's
observatory in Denmark prior to the foundation of Greenwich Observatory
in 1675 did not negate the possibility of serious astronomical observations.
By the early years of the seventeenth century, even before the founding
of the Savilian chairs of astronomy and geometry in 1619, Oxford had
come to recognize the importance of astronomical observations. Hence,
when the schools were rebuilt and reorganized at the bottom of the
Bodleian Library in 1613, a 'room on the east side of the Schools
quadrangle' was appropriated for the improvement of scientific teaching
facilities, while the top room of the tower was converted to an observatory.[213]
Most likely this tower room served as a base from which the future Savilian
professors Briggs and Bainbridge carried out some of their astronomical
observations.[214]

Even in the sixteenth century, however, observations appear to have
been carried out at Oxford and Cambridge with some regularity. Although
certain places lent themselves to observations more than others, in the
years before the invention of the telescope observations could be carried
out almost anywhere. One favoured spot might have been Folly Bridge
in Oxford which, according to Wood, served as the site of Roger Bacon's
observations.[215] The bridge, which in any case was a popular attraction
for visitors, probably served as a suitable site for subsequent observations
as well.

Unfortunately, the extent to which men applied their instruments to the
sky to observe phenomena unrelated to comets, new stars or eclipses is
unclear. Although the little surviving evidence directly relevant to the
period before 1640 tends to document the more exceptional phenomena,
this might well be because observations that lacked the exceptional
dimension for the most part went unappreciated by contemporaries.

---

[211] *Diary of Richard Madox*, pp. 79, 92–3, 122.
[212] *Diary of Richard Madox*, pp. 113, 134, 146, 222, 227, 246, 260.
[213] Gunther, *Early Science in Oxford*, vol. 2, p. 78.
[214] TCD MS 385, fol. 144 contains a statement by Bainbridge in 1629 to the effect that
Savile had intended to erect a 'musaeum mathematicum', including an observatory, but
died before he could implement such a plan.
[215] Wood, *City of Oxford*, vol. 1, p. 425.

Hence, weeks and months could be spent in the daily notation of meteorological data or data relating to the sun's declination, only to disappear for ever with the dispersal of the observer's papers.

Noteworthy, however, are the diligent observations of winds, rainbows and related meteorological phenomena recorded by a young Cambridge fellow by the name of William Gilbert. At least as far back as the late 1560s until his departure for London in 1573 Gilbert investigated the celestial spheres, paying particular attention to the comet of 1569 and the new star of 1572. The results of these observations were later incorporated into his posthumous *De Mundo* (1651).[216]

Edward Wright commenced his astronomical observations shortly after he graduated B.A. in 1581, if not earlier.[217] Thus, the systematic observations he carried out in 1589 when he accompanied George Clifford, Earl of Cumberland, on his voyage to the Azores were only the culmination of a long apprenticeship. According to Wright's extant notebooks – which reveal him as a diligent and methodological observer – he resumed his comparative observations following his return to Cambridge in 1590. This time Wright embarked upon a series of solar observations which culminated in the investigation of the solar eclipse of 21 July 1592. Similar observations were carried out throughout the 1590s, both at Cambridge and in London, and at least on one occasion there is information of a fellow observer. In the course of his solar observations at Cambridge in 1594, Wright mentions Henry Briggs whose observations were recorded alongside his own.[218] Although this is the single instance in which Wright referred specifically to a fellow observer, given Wright's eagerness to communicate his observations and compare his results with those of his colleagues, it is likely that there had been others as well. In 1601, for example, Wright and Sir Christopher Heydon exchanged information on still another set of solar observations.[219]

When John Bainbridge was installed as Savilian Professor of Astronomy in 1619, observations in Oxford took a leap forward. In planning and carrying out the previously noted observations, Bainbridge proved himself a dedicated observer who possessed not only endless zeal but sophisticated apparatus capable of precise measurement. Significantly, many of Bainbridge's observations found their way into the papers of contemporaries. As mentioned earlier, Boulliau and Gassendi received certain of Bainbridge's observations during the 1630s, perhaps via Schickard; they appeared in

---

[216] G. Gilberti, *De mundo nostro sublunari philosophia nova* (Amsterdam, 1651), pp. 227–37, 268–9, 275.

[217] TCD MS 387, fol. 40.

[218] TCD MS 387, fol. 45.

[219] TCD MS 396, fols. 8v, 40 include observations conducted by Wright and Heydon in Baconsthorpe, Heydon's home, in 1598. See also TCD MS 387, fol. 52: C. Heydon to E. Wright, 15 March 1602/03.

Vincent Wing's *Astronomia Britannica*, and even John Locke recorded one set of his lunar observations of 1634.[220] For his part Bainbridge appears to have made use of earlier observations as well. Among the Bainbridge papers are some of Edward Wright's astronomical observations,[221] and quite possibly all of the Wright manuscripts now housed in Trinity College, Dublin had originally been purchased by Bainbridge following Wright's death.[222]

If a reconstruction of the astronomical observations of many men must remain a matter of conjecture, the appearance of a comet turned almost everyone into an astronomer. The comet of 1618 – which was especially bright and long-lasting – is a case in point. To understand the impression this comet made on both the scholarly community and the uneducated majority, it should be borne in mind that comets were the last of the extraordinary celestial occurrences to be ascribed to natural causes, and their regularity ascertained. Thus, for example, when the comet of 1577 appeared on the horizon, Elizabeth I gained a reputation for boldness when, ignoring the warnings of her courtiers against viewing the comet, she responded: 'Iacta est alea'.[223]

Owing to the aura of the extraordinary surrounding comets and new stars, Englishmen – like their Continental counterparts – carefully recorded such phenomena. We have already mentioned the detailed observations of the 1572 star by William Camden and its disappearance sixteen months later.[224] Eight years later during his Continental tour, Arthur Throckmorton made almost daily entries of the position of the 1580 comet,[225] and Sir Henry Wotton managed to catch cold in Venice when he too avidly observed the comet of 1618.[226]

As might be expected, such phenomena brought in their wake a significant amount of exploratory literature. Much of it – unfortunately for the most part lost – was intended to calm the anxiety of the uneducated majority. More scholarly treatises as well as requests for explanations were nonetheless evident among educated men. John Dee, who frequently attended Elizabeth I, also acted as her authority on comets. It would be

---

[220] Gassendi, *Opera Omnia*, vol. 6, pp. 424–5; V. Wing, *Astronomia Britannica* (London, 1669), p. 343; Bodl. MS Locke c. 31, fol. 2.

[221] TCD MS 386/6, fols. 155, 164v.

[222] Wright's surviving notebooks are TCD MSS 387, 396. The former (fol. 55rv) contains a letter from S. Wright, probably to Bainbridge, dated 29 Aug. 1634, informing him that 'Booke of Observations in 4° which I formerly lent you is now in ye hands of Mr. Gelibrand'. MS 396 is entitled 'Edwardi Wrighti Observationes' and thus is probably the manuscript quoted.

[223] Thomas, *Religion and the Decline of Magic*, p. 299.

[224] Camden, *The True and Royall History of the Famous Empresse Elizabeth*, p. 319. For his observations of the 1618 comet, see Camden, *Epistolae*, appendix, pp. 38–9.

[225] Rowse, *Ralegh and the Throckmortons*, p. 85.

[226] *The Life and Letters of Sir Henry Wotton*, ed. L. P. Smith (Oxford, 1907), vol. 2, p. 160.

interesting to speculate the extent to which his sober explanations of certain celestial phenomena were responsible for Elizabeth's disdain for the advice of her courtiers.[227]

Elizabeth's successor, James I, became preoccupied with the comet of 1618, and appears to have consulted a battery of mathematicians in order to satisfy his curiosity. On 1 December 1618 Sir Thomas Lorkin wrote to William Pickering that 'concerning the blazing star, his majesty they say, swears it is nothing but Venus with a firebrand in her –'.[228] In this instance it is possible to identify the person who so convinced James. Writing to Thomas Harriot, Thomas Aylesbury reported: 'The comet being spent, the talke of it still runnes current here. The King's Majesty before my comming spake with one of Cambridg called Olarentia (a name able to beget beleefe of some extraordinarie qualities), but what satisfaction he gave I cannot yet learne.'[229] Fortunately, a third source provides us with a first-hand account of the views of the above-mentioned Olarentia. Simonds D'Ewes, then an undergraduate at Emmanuel College, Cambridge, witnessed the comet for the first time in the company of his tutor, Richard Holdsworth, the latter immediately recognizing the 'very coruscant and unusual star' as a comet. Desirous of a second opinion in this matter, however, D'Ewes consulted a fellow of St John's College by the name of Ollerenshaw who had a reputation as a mathematician. His opinion was that 'it was only Venus at the full'.[230]

Ollerenshaw was not the only Cambridge scholar to advise the King on astronomical matters. John Gostlin, Master of Gonville and Caius College from 1619 until 1626, wrote 'a short treatise on Comets, which he dedicated to his most serene Highness King James, who was curious about that one which appeared in the year 1618; and he gained no small favour from his Majesty on account of it'.[231]

Another treatise on the 1618 comet to be dedicated to King James was that of John Bainbridge, and it was later rumoured that Bainbridge owed his appointment to the Savilian chair of astronomy to this treatise.[232] The interest in the comet, however, was much wider, and in the previously quoted letter about the blazing star Lorkin continued: 'Mr. Briggs conceive it to be a perfect comet and therefore above the moon (so mathematicians have demonstrated Aristotle's tenet in this point to be false), and thinks the comet to be a hundred thousand miles in length – I say, thinks because,

[227] *Autobiographical Tracts of Dr. John Dee*, p. 21.
[228] T. Birch (ed.), *The Court and Times of James I* (London, 1848), vol. 2, p. 110: T. Lorkin to W. Pickering, 1 Dec. 1612.
[229] Halliwell, p. 44: T. Aylesbury to T. Harriot, 19 Jan. 1618/19.
[230] *College Life in the Time of James the First as Illustrated by an Unpublished Diary of Sir Symonds D'Ewes*, ed. J. H. Marsden (London, 1851), p. 54.
[231] Venn, *Biographical History of Gonville and Caius College*, vol. 3, p. 78.
[232] Bainbridge, *An Astronomicall Description*; *Biog. Brit.*, vol. 1, p. 419.

as yet, his observations hath found no ground for geometrical demonstrations.'[233] Finally, Joseph Mede also seems to have articulated his opinion on the comet in response to the request of his good friend William Boswell.[234]

In the process of collecting the material for his *Athenae Oxonienses*, Wood was seeking information on the whereabouts of Peter Turner's papers. In 1690 information was forthcoming from one William Watts with whose aunt Turner had resided during the years leading up to his death in 1659. Watts informed Wood that the aunt, not wishing to be troubled, simply burned all the papers of the deceased. Watts himself visited Turner's rooms in London after the Restoration, at which time he caught sight of one of Turner's chemical manuscripts as well as many letters addressed to Turner by eminent scholars; needless to add, even these fragments have been lost.[235] This episode, I believe, best illustrates the arbitrary conditions that determined the fate of most personal papers of contemporary mathematicians and astronomers as well as of other intellectuals. Only if such personal papers were bequeathed to, or immediately came into the possession of, some noted scholar whose personal library, in turn, was kept intact and deposited with some institution did the papers stand much chance of survival. Thus, Camden's papers passed first into Cotton's library and then into the possession of the British Museum. As for Bainbridge's papers, they were made over to Ussher whose library was later bequeathed to Trinity College, Dublin.

The scarcity of surviving scientific papers has served as the rationale for the organization and content of this chapter. Having provided information on the scientifically inclined members of the universities in chapters II and III, I have attempted to utilize whatever fragmentary evidence exists in order to suggest the various scientific networks of university men that evolved during the period between 1560 and 1640 and the manner in which they stretched far beyond the walls of the university. As much as possible the projects on which these men communicated and often collaborated have been indicated, as have been the scientific topics that most absorbed them. As stressed previously, the evidence at our disposal is not always strictly pertinent to scientific pursuits. However, if the fragmentary state of our evidence as well as the importance of the general scholar for scientific enterprise are borne in mind, the association indicated by this evidence is itself important; it

[233] *The Court and Times of James I*, ed. Birch, vol. 2, p. 110.
[234] Mede, *Works*, ed. Worthington, page facing sig.**.
[235] Bodl. MS Wood F.45, fol. 187: W. Watts to S. Hamer (for A. Wood), 25 June 1690. See also M. Hunter, *John Aubrey and the Realm of Learning* (London, 1975), pp. 90–2 for a similar – if somewhat less disastrous – episode determining the fate of Aubrey's own manuscripts.

establishes a link upon which a working relationship may be conjectured. The cumulative effect of this chapter is to suggest that a reassessment of the function of the universities as scientific centres is in order. However, the way in which the universities differed from London as teaching centres is a subject to be explored in chapters V and VI.

V

Gresham College and its role in the genesis of 'London science'

In contrast to the university-based scholars whose contribution to the genesis of science in pre-Civil War England has been highly disputed, the mathematical practitioners of London have been singled out as the vanguard of the new, utilitarian science embraced by such forward-looking men as merchants and Puritans. 'The science of Elizabeth's reign', pronounced Hill, 'was the work of merchants and craftsmen, not of dons; carried on in London, not in Oxford and Cambridge'.[1] The reason for this alleged shift was that science, in Mason's words, was 'closely connected with mercantile enterprise throughout the sixteenth century', when much of the activity was directly towards solving problems of navigation, accounting, surveying or military engineering.[2] In their studies Hill and Mason both depended heavily on the data compiled by Taylor in her study of Tudor and Stuart science. For her part Taylor presents a gallery of humble practitioners whose initial commitment to naval and military occupations was responsible for their later initiation into the sciences and their attempts to use astronomical and mathematical data to advance the general body of knowledge of their respective professions.[3] It is in this context that Gresham College in the heart of the City of London has been accorded a significant role in stimulating interest in the capital's practitioners. The inherent novelty of the institution was manifold. Gresham College was intended to provide instruction in the seven liberal arts – in English as well as in Latin – free of charge to whomsoever wished to attend. Most important for our purposes, the first endowed chairs of geometry and astronomy in England were established here and their incumbents were directed to expound on practical issues relevant to the

---

[1] Hill, *Intellectual Origins*, p. 15.
[2] S. F. Mason, 'Science and religion in seventeenth-century England', *Past & Present*, III (1953), reprinted in *The Intellectual Revolution of the Seventeenth Century*, ed. C. Webster (London, 1974), p. 198.
[3] E. G. R. Taylor, *Tudor Geography* (London, 1930); *Late Tudor and Early Stuart Geography* (London, 1935) and especially *Mathematical Practitioners*. Unfortunately, for the most part Professor Taylor did not document her books, and no doubt as a result of the extensive nature of her studies, her statements and illustrations have often been accepted by historians without further questioning.

needs of London's inhabitants. All of these factors have contributed to the view of Gresham College as a mirror of the progressive forces animating London's population and the antithesis of the reactionary forces dictating scientific enterprise in the universities.

The purpose of the following chapter will be to examine Gresham College and 'London science' *vis-à-vis* scientific enterprise in the universities. The extent to which Gresham College served as a successful teaching institution benefiting significant numbers of London's mathematical practitioners will be assessed as part of an overall attempt to determine the role played by the College in the genesis of 'London science'. Such an assessment of Gresham College as a teaching institution, however, entails a critical assessment of the degree of sophistication attained by the vast majority of London's practitioners who were supposedly the beneficiaries of the College's up-to-date scientific instruction. Only after the above questions have been answered will it be possible to discuss the way in which the science pursued by the segment of London's scientific community allied with Gresham College differed from that pursued by the university-based and non-urban members of the scientific community.

It should be stressed at the outset that in no way does this chapter purport to be a comprehensive study of either 'London science' or Gresham College; an overall reconsideration of the subject is beyond the scope of this book. The studies of Taylor and Waters remain the bases of our information on 'London science',[4] while the work of Adamson, which incorporates virtually every surviving document relevant to Gresham College, remains the most detailed and best account of its history.[5] One of the central premises accepted by historians concerns the educational qualifications of those committed to 'London science'; it is believed that the vast majority of practitioners lacked a formal education. As for the few eminent men of science who were university trained, it is generally argued that their early education had little bearing on the course of their future scientific pursuits; only after they settled in London were their scientific inclinations allowed to ripen. Such a claim is implicit in Hill's argument that

all the greatest scientists and scientific writers of the pre-revolutionary period (though sometimes educated at Oxford and Cambridge – where else could they

---

[4] Waters, *The Art of Navigation.*

[5] The comprehensiveness and accuracy of Adamson's 'The Foundation and Early History of Gresham College' as well as his 'The administration of Gresham College and its fluctuating fortunes as a scientific institution in the seventeenth century', *History of Education*, IX (1980), 13–25, have made it possible for me to rely on his quotations and transcriptions without reference to the original documents. Despite my sometimes critical remarks and different interpretation of the situation, I remain indebted to Adamson for much of the data.

have been educated?) were not at the universities when they did their most important work – Recorde, Dee, the Diggeses, Gilbert, Bacon, Wright, Hariot, Briggs, Gunter, Gellibrand, Foster, Napier, Oughtred, Harvey, Digby, Horrocks, Wilkins, Pell, to name only those in the first rank.[6]

This is a serious criticism. It is also an exaggerated criticism. While at university, Dee, Gilbert, Gunter, Wright, Gellibrand and Oughtred embarked on research which later was to be incorporated in their publications. As for Briggs, Digby, Horrox and Pell, the level of competence they attained while at university undoubtedly had some bearing on their mature work. Nevertheless, Hill's assertion remains provocative. Why, indeed, did most scientists leave the universities, quite often for London? Was their departure due to their refusal to tolerate science as it was practised in the universities? Or were there contributory factors which had little relation to the state of university science? Finally, what was the effect of London upon their scientific work?

There are many reasons why scientifically oriented graduates and fellows frequently left the universities, an important one being the scarcity of scientific appointments at both Oxford and Cambridge. As previously mentioned, before the endowment of the scientific chairs at Oxford in 1619 and at Cambridge in 1663, mathematical lecturers were invariably young regent-masters who were expected to teach for a year or two before proceeding to their proper callings; the stipend associated with such a post, it should be noted, was minimal. The endowment of the scientific chairs at Oxford and Cambridge did not improve the employment situation appreciably, for the long-term occupancy of their incumbents necessitated a long wait for future contenders. In this context the foundation of Gresham College in 1597 proved a temporary boon to prospective scientists, and it should come as no surprise that all of the candidates for the Gresham scientific posts – which carried with them the generous remuneration of £50 p.a. – were university men. The long-term incumbency of the Gresham professors, however, did little to relieve the employment prospects of those aspiring men of science who graduated at a time when no vacancy in either institution was forthcoming. There was little choice for such a man but to bide his time, confident of some future appointment – as did Edmund Gunter – or seek his fortune elsewhere.

Although scientific posts undoubtedly remained the goal of many aspiring men of science, even lacking such a post many scientifically oriented

[6] C. Hill, 'Puritanism, capitalism, and the scientific revolution', *Past & Present*, XXIX (1969), reprinted in *The Intellectual Revolution*, p. 248. For similar views, see also Johnson, 'Thomas Hood's inaugural address', p. 96; Boas, *The Scientific Renaissance*, p. 239; J. Simon, *Education and Society in Tudor England* (Cambridge, 1966), p. 387.

graduates would have stayed on at Oxford and Cambridge if only this had been within their power. However, there were certain peculiarities of the English university system which sometimes made this difficult. Anyone who wished to remain at Oxford and Cambridge on a permanent basis and was not already in possession of a profession capable of sustaining him there, was dependent upon obtaining a college scholarship or fellowship. While scholarships were awarded only for very limited periods, there was not always a surplus of fellowships; moreover, a multiplicity of factors were brought to bear upon the allocation of fellowships. It sometimes happened that no vacancies in one's college were imminent, or that those available were open only to students of particular counties, in this way keeping in check the quotas often designated for the various regions. For the above reasons graduates sometimes had to leave university shortly after proceeding M.A. or at least migrate to another college. Hence Samuel Ward had to leave Christ's College, Cambridge, for Sidney Sussex College, while John Wallis departed from Emmanuel College for Queens' College, Cambridge. Some others were not as fortunate. John Milton and John Pell had little choice but to seek their fortunes elsewhere.[7]

It might also be noted that the system of election employed by the colleges also took its toll of talented young men. Owing to some peculiarity of character or belief, some men found themselves with too many enemies when their candidacy was announced. The annals of most colleges are full of such cases of controversy, one of the most frequently cited being that of Gabriel Harvey.

An additional factor influencing the steady trickle of graduates away from the universities was the duration of most fellowships and the restrictions attached to them. Many colleges restricted the duration of their fellowships to twenty-one years or less.[8] If it is borne in mind that election usually occurred by the time a man had reached his early twenties, by the time he reached his late thirties or early forties he faced the prospect of enforced resignation.[9] The requirement of celibacy also affected the choices of fellows. Given the prohibition against marriage as well as the early age of resignation, then, it is not surprising that many chose to vacate their fellowships as soon as a suitable preferment was forthcoming. To this bleak employment situation must be added the modest remuneration attached to the fellowships. Although many fellows could – and did –

[7] Scriba, 'The autobiography of John Wallis', p. 30. (Wallis later vacated his new fellowship in order to marry.) Knappen, *Two Elizabethan Puritan Diaries*, pp. 128–9; W. R. Parker, *Milton, A Biography* (Oxford, 1968), vol. 1, p. 85.

[8] Sidney Sussex College and Emmanuel College, Cambridge, as well as Wadham College, Oxford, are just some that did so. See Mullinger, *The University of Cambridge*, vol. 3, pp. 315–19.

[9] Walter Foster, whom we encountered earlier, was one fellow forced to leave his college following the completion of his term of fellowship. See Parr, pp. 437–8: S. Ward to J. Ussher, 24 May 1630. See p. 80 above.

supplement their stipends by offering tutorials and lectures, their total income remained modest. Moreover, a fellow was forbidden, on pain of forfeiting his fellowship, to accept any preferment or living which carried with it remuneration above a specified sum, again usually quite modest. Therefore apart from the few livings attached to each college – which, in turn, were usually allocated to the more senior or needy members – most preferments in the church or state necessitated a fellow's resignation.

The requirement that every college fellow embark upon the study of divinity – and in due course take orders – no doubt also caused a significant number of fellows to leave university. Temporary exemptions were awarded to college and university lecturers as well as to recipients of fellowships designated for students of medicine, law and astronomy. But even such fellows were eventually required to take orders. Reluctance to pursue a clerical career, however, should not be interpreted as proof of Puritan beliefs. In an age in which religious beliefs – regardless of their orientation – were accepted as the highest of man's priorities, it was taken for granted that once a man had assumed orders his religious concerns would take precedence over his secular interests. Those unwilling to commit themselves to a clerical profession – and the most devoted students of science were doubtless among them – often took the first opportunity to leave the universities.

This evidence brought to explain the steady flow of scientifically oriented members away from the universities should not be interpreted wrongly. Whereas in retrospect the clerical requirement might be viewed as an obstruction to intellectual inquiry, before 1640 the function of the universities as seminaries of the church was never questioned. In contradistinction to law and medicine which had emerged as distinct professions affiliated with separate institutions, mathematical studies had not as yet become fully professionalized. Hence, their most committed students remained more dependent upon, and experienced more fully, the requirements and contingencies of the university system. Nevertheless, none of these contributory factors leading to a fellow's departure should be taken out of its context and interpreted as an intellectual bias of the universities against scientific inquiry.

The idealization of Gresham College as a microcosm of the progressive forces that animated London and attracted the most gifted university men has already been discussed. It is worthy of note, however, that Gresham College was initially projected as a teaching institution by Sir Thomas Gresham in his will of 1575, and it is on the merits of its alleged early success as a flourishing teaching institution benefiting the multitude of London's laymen that its reputation survives. As Adamson reminds us: 'the College was envisaged by the trustees as primarily a teaching institution, where the professors would be constantly in residence for personal consultation, not just by other academics but by mariners, boat builders and the general public'.[10] For this reason the College has been assigned a special place in the history of adult education in England.[11] It was supposedly here that the most talented astronomy and geometry professors of the age inculcated into a generation of mariners and instrument-makers the scientific knowledge that previously had been denied them. The fact that both Gresham's will and the ordinances governing Gresham College single out the citizens of the capital as the beneficiaries of the lectures together with the fact that no records of attendance have survived have contributed to the widespread assumption that the auditors of the lectures were drawn from the multitude of London's inhabitants. Thus, implicit in the remarks of Wright, Taylor and Waters is the view that the lectures were comprehensible to the ordinary Londoner. Johnson claims that since 'the lecturers at the college were widely patronized by the skilled artisans, expert mechanics, and navigators for whose instruction they had been founded, the Gresham professors were always in close touch with the practical workers in many fields of applied science'. It is not within the sphere of this chapter to assess the ideal behind Sir Thomas's proposed institution: only to determine the extent to which Gresham College deserves the reputation it has been accorded as a teaching institution generating scientific sophistication among significant numbers of London's practitioners.[12]

In the light of the role the College has been assigned as a teaching institution, it is of utmost significance that there remains virtually no evidence regarding the lectures delivered in Gresham College.[13] Admittedly, on one or two occasions a Gresham professor reflected retrospectively on his college lectures, as did Briggs when he mentioned his having lectured on logarithms at the College.[14] However, on closer examination the few examples brought forward as proof of Gresham College as a teaching institution are exposed as biased elucidations of the evidence.

An often cited example is provided by Edmund Wingate. Relating the way in which Wingate introduced Gunter's 'rule of proportion' into

[10] Adamson, 'The administration of Gresham College', 19.

[11] Hill, *Intellectual Origins*, pp. 37, 45. See also T. Kelly, *A History of Adult Education in Great Britain* (Liverpool, 1970), pp. 26–7, 52.

[12] L. B. Wright, *Middle-Class Culture in Elizabethan England* (Chapel Hill, 1935), p. 599; Taylor, *Mathematical Practitioners*, p. 50; Waters, *The Art of Navigation*, p. 244; Johnson, *Astronomical Thought*, p. 264. See also Simon, *Education and Society in Tudor England*, p. 388.

[13] The lectures in divinity were probably best attended, although even here the evidence is negligible. However, attendance at sermons was popular among all classes and Gresham College had some skilful and controversial divines such as Anthony Wotton and Richard Holdsworth. See P. S. Seaver, *The Puritan Lectureships* (Stanford, 1970).

[14] H. Briggs, *Arithmetica Logarithmica* (London, 1624), sig. A3.

France, Taylor explained that 'as a young man [Wingate] followed the lectures at Gresham College'. Hill, deriving his information from Taylor, took the Gresham connection one step further. Wingate, Hill informs us, 'taught himself mathematics by attending Gresham lectures as a young man'. A relevant fact, recorded by Taylor but omitted by Hill, was that Wingate had studied at Queen's College, Oxford, where he graduated B.A. in 1614. More significant still, neither Taylor nor Hill recorded the testimony of Wood to the effect that Wingate's mathematical studies had begun during the latter's stay at Oxford. From an examination of the evidence it appears that Taylor's initial claim derived from Wingate's allegation that Briggs 'highly extolled' logarithms 'in his ordinary *Lectures at Gresham Colledge*'. There is little evidence to suggest, however, that Wingate ever attended these lectures, still less to suggest that he educated himself at Gresham College. It will be argued later that Wingate associated with certain of the Gresham professors, not as a student, but as a colleague.[15]

A similar misrepresentation of the evidence occurs with Richard Delamain. According to Taylor's account Delamain 'by attending the Gresham lectures and mixing with learned men, acquired enough knowledge to become a *teacher of practical mathematics*'. Again Taylor, who provided no references for her claims, was followed by Hill as well as by Adamson.[16] An examination of the evidence once again reveals a disparity between what Delamain said and what he has been quoted as saying. The episode which caused Delamain to mention Gresham College centres around his controversy with William Oughtred over the originator of the 'circles of proportion'; while the invention was claimed as Oughtred's own, Delamain attributed it to Gunter. Initially, Delamain had been a friend of Oughtred, perhaps even his student. In the midst of the controversy, however, Delamain contested Oughtred's claim for the invention as it had been formulated by Oughtred's student William Forster.[17] Delamain instead claimed that the instrument had been first invented by Edmund Gunter who then communicated it to Oughtred. To this effect he quoted a letter of 1618 from Briggs to Oughtred in which Briggs intimated that he had forwarded notes to Oughtred by way of Gunter. Delamain then went on to praise Gunter's generosity: 'Gunter, satisfying many of his friends ... by *Transcripts* in that of more solid matter, but such of vulgar *Practices*

[15] Taylor, *Mathematical Practitioners*, p. 205; Hill, *Intellectual Origins*, p. 72; Wood, *Athenae Oxonienses*, vol. 3, p. 423; E. Wingate, *Arithmetique Made Easie, the Second Book* (London, 1652), sig. A3v.

[16] Taylor, *Mathematical Practitioners*, p. 50; Hill, *Intellectual Origins*, p. 45; Adamson, 'The administration of Gresham College', p. 20.

[17] W. Oughtred, *The Circles of Proportion and the Horizontall Instrument*, trans. W. Forster (London, 1632), dedicatory epistle. For the controversy, see A. J. Turner, 'Mathematical instruments and the education of gentlemen', *Annals of Science*, xxx (1973), 58–61.

he hath publikely made manifest for the use of all such as affect those *Studies.*' While a liberal reading of Delamain's testimony might suggest that Delamain, too, had been a recipient of Gunter's transcripts, the passage cannot be construed as evidence of Gunter's lectures in Gresham College. The 'vulgar *Practices* he hath publikely made manifest' refers to Gunter's publications, as is made evident by Delamain's subsequent reference to Gunter's treatise on the sector published in 1623 but written as early as 1607 and circulated in manuscript form.[18]

Ralph Handson was described as a 'pupil' of Briggs by Taylor and Hill and, according to Adamson, 'attended the Gresham lectures'. Handson, who was a teacher of mathematics in London, was well versed in mathematical and astronomical literature, including the works of Copernicus, Regiomontanus and Clavius. In 1614 at the instigation of Richard Hakluyt, Handson published his translation of Pitiscus's *Trigonometry* which had been circulated earlier for the use of his students. Apart from Handson's testimony that he 'had from Mr. Henry Briggs' a certain method of calculation, there is nothing in Handson's translation of the *Trigonometry* to suggest that he ever attended lectures at Gresham College.[19]

The two other examples sometimes cited in support of the function of Gresham College as a teaching institution are equally unacceptable. From Richard More's casual mention of the Thursday geometry lectures at Gresham College when he cited the possible ways in which carpenters might learn geometry,[20] it has been inferred that London's carpenters attended Briggs's lectures. Indeed, More's reference to such lectures is brought by Hill to substantiate the claim that 'under Briggs ... Gresham College was a centre of advanced science as well as of adult education'. In addition to Wingate and Delamain, Hill includes Captain Luke Foxe among 'many of those whom Briggs helped'. Hill, however, refrains from informing the reader that this last episode occurred in 1629–30, over a decade after Briggs had resigned from Gresham College and had been installed as Savilian professor at Oxford. On the basis of the above-

---

[18] R. Delamain, *The Making, Description and Use of a Small Portable Instrument for the Pocket ... in form of a Mixt Trapezia, thus called a Horizontall Quadrant* (London, 1632), 'To the Reader'; E. Gunter, *The Description and Use of the Sector, the Cross-staffe and other Instruments* (London, 1624), p. 143. In the preface Gunter admits that one of the incentives for publication was his dislike of the tiresome task of transcribing the manuscript whenever someone asked for a copy.

[19] Taylor, *Mathematical Practitioners*, p. 203; Hill, *Intellectual Origins*, p. 42; Adamson, 'The administration of Gresham College', p. 20; *Trigonometry: Or the Doctrine of Triangles. First Written in Latine by Bartholmew Pitiscus of Grunberg in Silesia, and now Translated into English by Ra: Handson* (London, 1614), appendix, 'Questions of Navigation', p. 33.

[20] Taylor, *Mathematical Practitioners*, p. 50; Hill, *Intellectual Origins*, p. 45; Adamson, 'The administration of Gresham College', p. 20; R. More, *The Carpenters Rule* (London, 1602), 'To the Reader'.

mentioned examples Hill goes on to conclude that 'there can be no doubt
that Gresham College helped greatly to raise the level of mathematics
teaching in this period as well as to increase the number of teachers'.[21]
Such a questionable elucidation of the evidence might cause us to cast
doubt on the conclusions concerning the teaching function of Gresham
College.[22] This is not to claim that no lectures ever took place or that some
of London's mathematical practitioners might not on occasion have
attended them. It is simply to state that the evidence presented thus far
is insufficient to warrant the place the College has been accorded as a
teaching institution.

There is evidence of a very different sort to suggest that Gresham College
was a failure as a teaching institution. The responsibility for this failure,
it will be argued, should be shared equally between the Gresham professors
and trustees on the one hand, and the vast majority of mathematical
practitioners whom the college was intended to benefit on the other.
Adamson has already demonstrated that although Gresham College
officially opened in 1597, apart from the Inaugural Lectures that were
delivered the following year, any teaching that took place before 1600
was negligible.[23] Such a situation, unknown to historians before Adamson,
arose from a fierce power struggle between the College trustees – the
Company of Mercers and the City of London – and five of the seven
professors, including Henry Briggs.[24] The outcome of the conflict spelled
virtual defeat for the trustees; the lecturers managed to reduce significantly
the number of hours they were required to teach from three hours a week
spread over three days, to two hours a week concentrated on one day.
Moreover, the lectures were confined to term rather than continued
throughout the year as originally stipulated.

Athough Adamson painstakingly records the stages of this conflict, he
misinterprets the significance of its outcome for the future of Gresham
College. Since the hour abolished was the weekly hour in Latin, Adamson
assumes that 'the second set of Ordinances ... provides for vastly more
vernacular lecturing than the first set' and 'must be regarded as a
significant victory for educational progress in Gresham College'. It should
be noted, however, that such a revision did not provide for quantitively
more instruction in English, as both the first and second set of ordinances

---

21 Hill, *Intellectual Origins*, pp. 45–6; cf. *The Voyages of Captain Luke Foxe of Hull, and Captain Thomas James of Bristol*, ed. M. Christy, Hakluyt Soc., vols. 88–9 (London, 1893), pp. lxii–iv.

22 Adamson has concluded that More, Wells, Hopton, Handson, Wingate and Delamain were 'definitely known to have attended lectures at Gresham College'. 'The Foundation and Early History of Gresham College', p. 41.

23 Adamson, 'The Foundation and Early History of Gresham College', pp. 49, 54.

24 This and subsequent struggles are treated at some length in Adamson, 'The Foundation and Early History of Gresham College', pp. 47–61.

stipulate only a single hour. As for the lectures in geometry and astronomy, the second set of ordinances might actually have reduced the instruction in English, since the first set provided for equal instruction in Latin and English: 'The first reading of the said lectures [Geometry and Astronomy] is to be in Latin, the next in English, and so following the same order.'[25] Moreover, the revision did not involve any modification of the curriculum; the content of the lectures as stipulated in the first set of ordinances is carried over almost verbatim into the second set. Significantly, neither was this second set ever endorsed by the professors and consequently their views concerning the 'practical' nature of their instruction must remain a matter of speculation.[26] From a comparison of the two sets of ordinances it should be clear that the significance of the revisions lies not in the changes they introduced in teaching content or teaching method, but in the reduction of the teaching load of the professors. For this reason it is difficult to interpret the outcome of the struggle as a 'significant victory for educational progress' as suggested by Adamson.

More thought, however, should be paid to the crippling effects of this power struggle upon the authority of the Gresham trustees. Having failed to impose their will on the manner in which the College was to be governed – apart from the election of the professors and the payment of their fees – the trustees subsequently relinquished their function as agents for future initiative or reform. The subsequent power struggles which sporadically broke out between the trustees and the professors were on increasingly smaller scales as the confidence of the professors increased inversely with the diminishing force of the trustees. No doubt this situation did irrevocable damage to the reputation of the College as well as contributing to the widespread nepotism, absenteeism and neglect of duties that we hear about from 1600 onward.

Implicit in a unique document drawn up by the Gresham trustees following the death of Edmund Gunter in 1626 and presented to his successor, Henry Gellibrand, for his signature is their disapproval of certain of Gunter's occupations while he was Gresham professor. Upon his appointment Gunter never relinquished his position as parson of St George's, Southwark, and apparently his clerical activities continued to absorb much of his attention. In any case, it is instructive to note that Mede, describing a dinner party given by Gunter in 1626, referred to him first as the parson of St George's and only afterwards as a mathematical professor.[27] It is almost certainly for this reason that Gellibrand had to promise that 'he [would] not hereafter take any calling or course upon

---

[25] Adamson, 'The Foundation and Early History of Gresham College', p. 261. Adamson provides full transcripts of both sets of ordinances.

[26] Adamson, 'The Foundation and Early History of Gresham College', p. 55.

[27] For Mede's letter, see *The Court and Times of Charles*, ed. Birch, vol. 1, p. 182.

him but apply himself wholly to this, or else wholly leave the place. Likewise he promised to rest in the house as well in term as out of term, whereby the more commodiously to give help to gents and mariners by private conference.'[28] Despite this effort the trustees were never able to regain their grip upon the obstinate professors and the reputation of the Gresham College as a teaching institution continued to deteriorate. The flagrant disregard of professors for their teaching duties might even have contributed to what appears to have been the poor attendance at the lectures. Such a situation is suggested by Thomas Winston, Professor of Medicine from 1615 until 1655, who complained of the scarcity of auditors in his lectures as well as by Sir William Boswell, who in 1639 complained of the Gresham professors 'who excepting few have beene very idle ... Only Brigs, Gelebrand and some other few have beene doing any thing there'.[29]

Although the early power struggle between the Gresham professors and the Gresham trustees disrupted the academic routine of the College, it is not entirely clear how far this struggle was responsible for the failure of the institution. The question, which remains to be answered, is whether the vast majority of the practitioners of London and the Gresham science professors had enough common ground between them to warrant a teaching institution. Was the disregard shown by the Gresham professors the sole cause of the deterioration of the College? Or was their disregard for their duties at least in part a result of the lack of enthusiasm shown by the London population for the fledgling institution? Although the institution remains unnamed, it appears that the complaint voiced in 1613 by John Tapp, one of the most influential teachers of navigation in the period, is directed at London's mariners who failed to take advantage of the Gresham lectures as well as other lectures in the capital: 'what good doth these publique readings which hath now beene a reasonable time continued in this Cittie, with great charge, to good purpose, but little profit and may be guessed, by the little Audience which doe commonly frequent them'. The reason for such an attitude towards lectures on the part of the mariners is suggested by Henry Philippes half a century later:

For what *knowledge* can be *gained* in *this* or any *other Art*, by the *hearing* a *Lecture* there of *now and then*, wherein onely some *one point* of the Art is treated of; though it be never so *well demonstrated*, if the *hearer* cannot have *time* or *opportunity* to hear out the *whole*, or *liberty* to *ask* such *questions*, as may be *most useful* for his

---

[28] Quoted by Adamson, 'The administration of Gresham College', p. 19.
[29] Adamson, 'The Foundation and Early History of Gresham College', p. 164, n. 108. Owing to the political upheaval, Winston's term as Gresham Professor of Medicine was interrupted from 1643 until 1652, during which time he resided on the Continent. Hartlib, 'Ephemerides 1639', H–J2.

present purpose, or *most tending* to his *instruction* in those things he doth not fully know.[30]

The underlying assumption of those historians who have documented the history of Gresham College and its role in the genesis of 'London science' is that London's mathematical practitioners were both capable of, and eager to understand, the lectures and publications of the Gresham professors as well as other 'scholars' interested in applied mathematics. This simply was not the case. While the scientific sophistication of the professors has been played down and the audience for whom they wrote misrepresented, the capability and interests of the vast majority of common practitioners have been exaggerated out of all proportion.

The evidence of chastising scientists and suspicious practitioners suggests that although they might have dealt with similar problems, they often remained sceptical of each other's basic orientation. Convinced of the superiority of practical, over theoretical, knowledge, many practitioners remained highly critical of the advice and tone of superiority of their more learned brethren.[31] Such an attitude is made clear in the following comments of Arthur Hopton in 1611: 'I know divers great Scholers, deeply seene in the Theoreticall Part, though in the active meere novices: which is a cause that such so learned, were never able to correct and amend many defects.'[32] Already aware of such a bias, in 1579 Thomas Digges chastised the practitioners of the military arts for refusing to learn new methods. He continued:

In like sort by *Masters*, *Pilotes* and *Mariners*, I have bene answered, that my *Demonstrations* were pretie devises: but if I had bene in any Sea services, I should find all these my *Inventions* meere toyes, & their Rules onely praiseable: Adding further, that whatsoever I could in *Paper* by *Demonstrations* perswade, by *Experience* on *Seas* they found their *Charts* and *Instruments* true and infaliable.[33]

Two decades later William Barlow found it necessary to justify why a divine who had never been on a ship could yet think himself capable of advising mariners on their art.[34] Barlow's contemporary, Edward Wright, expressed the feelings prevalent among most mathematicians:

if any shall thinke it to be beyond a landmans skill, to finde faults in matters belonging to the seamans profession; they must know, if they be yet to learne,

---

[30] J. Tapp, *The Pathway to Knowledge* (London, 1613), sig. A2v; H. Philippes, *The Advancement of the Art of Navigation, in Two Parts* (London, 1657), 'An Apologetical Preface for the Advancement of the Art of Navigation'.

[31] A common phrase used by the more learned mathematicians when referring to the multitude of day-to-day practices of mariners was 'vulgar errors'.

[32] A. Hopton, *Speculum Topographicum, or the Topographicall Glasse* (London, 1611).

[33] T. Digges, *An Arithmeticall Militare Treatise, named Stratioticos: compendiously Teaching the Science of Numbers, as well in Fractions as Integers and so much of the Rules and Aequations Algebraicall, and Arte of Numbers Cossicall, as are requisite for the Profession of a Soldier* (London, 1579), 'The Preface to the Reader'.

[34] W. Barlow, *The Navigators Supply* (London, 1597), sig. A4v.

that one that is but reasonably well acquainted with Geometricall conceits, may as well, if not better then most seamen, know the nature properties of the sphaericall forme of the earth and sea, with all consequents and dependances thereof.[35]

There has emerged an historical view that the proliferation of books treating the application of mathematics to navigation, surveying, building and fortifications – many of them in the vernacular – bridged the gap between practice and theory and made such information available to the run-of-the-mill carpenter, mariner or gunner. Even leaving aside the highly charged debate concerning the degree of literacy in the period, contemporary witnesses suggest that the most important works went unappreciated by the vast majority of practitioners. In 1582 Edward Worsop, a land surveyor from London, wrote of:

Sundry learned workes of the Mathematicals ... are extant in our vulgar tongue: as Euclide, the workes of Doctor Record, of Master Leonard Digges, of Master Thomas Digges, and of some others. But because these learned bookes can not bee understoode of the common sorte, and that they be as juels, and riches, shadowed or wrapped up from their sight: I have thought good by a plaine and popular discourse to laie open unto the understanding of every reasonable man the necessities and commodities of those singular workes and knowledges.

Highly significant is Worsop's reference to Billingsley's translation of Euclid – with a preface by Dee – Recorde's mathematical books and the Diggeses' treatises on applied mathematics, for it has been precisely these books and their authors who have been credited with having brought the 'new science' to the door-steps of London's practitioners as well as its scholars. A different set of books was singled out for criticism by Henry Philippes when he discussed existing 'sea-books', all of which were 'very defective and erroneous'. 'And though Mr *Wrights*, Mr *Gunter*, and Mr *Norwood* have done very well in those parts thereof, which they have undertaken, yet they have not gone through with the whole Art, neither have they made those things they write about so plain and practical as they might be.'[36] While other authors of scientific treatises are rarely as explicit in

[35] E. Wright, *Certaine Errors in Navigation Detected and Corrected by Edw: Wright* (London, 1599), 'The Preface to the Reader'. Wright again voiced the feeling of distrust that characterized relations between mariners and scholars in his 'The convenience of a lecture of navigation', *The Naval Tracts of Sir William Monson*, ed. M. Oppenheim, Navy Rec. Soc. (London, 1913), vol. 4, p. 393. Interestingly, a learned practitioner could reverse the criticism. Robert Norman, one of the earliest Englishmen to learn magnetism, accused the scholars of wishing the 'mechanics' to remain ignorant and of refusing to believe that they were capable of understanding their sciences. See *The Newe Attractive, containyng a Short Discourse of the Magnes or Lodestone* (London, 1581).

[36] E. Worsop, *A Discoverie of Sundrie Errours and Faults Daily Committed by Landemeaters Ignorant of Arithmetike and Geometrie* (London, 1582), sig. A2v; Philippes, *The Advancement of the Art of Navigation*. 'An Apologetical Preface'.

their references as either Worsop or Philippes, their attempt to simplify and elaborate upon existing books were animated by the same motive; all shared the view that the original scientific treatises were either too complicated for, or not sufficiently applicable to, the needs of the vast majority of their fellow practitioners. Thus, for example, when the London publisher William Fischer decided to reissue Henry Gellibrand's *Institution Trigonometricall* in 1674, he nonetheless opted for a more simplified edition: 'understanding that Mr. *Gellibrand's Institution* was somewhat obscure, and besides contained nothing of the Use and Application of Triangles in the three kinds of *Sailing*, and for this reason not so proper for sea men'.[37] A most illuminating reference to the degree of competence needed by mathematical practitioners to appreciate scientific treatises is made by Edmund Wingate in his preface to his *The Use of the Rule of Proportion in Arithmetick and Geometry* (1658). Wingate cautioned:

it is desired that he, who intends to read this book with profit, should have a proper *Genius* and Phansie for the Mathematicks, not onely ready to conceive *Mathematical* notions; but likewise able to wrestle with them, and apt to take pleasure in them; ... Again, it is expected he shall be aforehand furnished with competent knowledge in those Sciences, viz. [Arithmetic, Geometry, Astronomy and Dialling].[38]

No doubt fearful that his words of caution might frighten off some potential buyers, Wingate nonetheless assures his audience of surveyors, merchants, gunners, miners, goldsmiths, etc., that even their limited knowledge would not necessarily prevent them from applying the instrument to their respective professions: 'but here I would not bee mistaken, as if I did totally excluded all others, who are not prepared with such an universal knowledge in the Mathematicks, from having any capacity at all of understanding this book'.[39] More interesting still is Wingate's explanation why he and not Gunter – who was naturally more competent in the matter – had written the treatise:

Yet this I can aver upon mine own knowledge, that he did forbear to explain that use thereof, because he took it for granted none would meddle with it, but such onely as were already well able to understand how to number upon it, having beforehand acquainted themselves with the manner of *numbering* upon *Scales*, and with the nature of *Logarithmes*: For, when after my return out of *France*, I importuned him to make a fuller explanation how to number upon it, to the end the use thereof might by that means be made more publick, his answer was, *That it could not be expected the Rule should speak*: Intimating thereby, that the Practitioner should (in that point) rely much upon discretion, and not altogether depend upon precepts and examples.[40]

[37] H. Gellibrand, *An Epitome of Navigation with a Table of Logarithms*, ed. E. Speidell (London, 1674), sig. A2. The first edition of the *Institution* appeared in 1638.
[38] Sig. A3v. The book was originally published in France in 1624, and the English edition appeared in 1645. [39] Sig. A.4. [40] Sig. A.5.

It is little wonder, then, that Taylor concluded: 'Gunter's writings had only an indirect influence on navigation ... surveying, dialling and mensuration of solids, for they were too mathematical for most people and needed the interpretation of a teacher as intermediary.'[41] If Gunter's *De Sectore* consisted of the lectures he provided at Gresham College – as Waters claims – then we are provided with an important indication of the calibre of the auditors needed to appreciate such lectures.[42] It might be noted at this point that Richard More admitted that some grounding in geometry was needed if one were to follow the Gresham lectures in geometry.[43]

My last example is drawn from the work of John Newton, a prolific writer whose wide-ranging books, especially in mathematics, were for the most part directed at laymen and youth. In 1654 he published a book intended to provide 'the first principles and foundation of these studies (which until now were not to be known, but by being acquainted with many Books) might in due method and a perspicuous manner, be as it were at once, presented to thy view'.[44]

Edward Wright, sceptical of the willingness of seamen to read the scientific treatises on the market, concluded that the only way to bring home such knowledge to mariners and encourage them to adopt new methods was by frontal confrontation and demonstration. Hence, he attempted to persuade William Monson to establish a lectureship in navigation. One can only wonder whether, had this foundation occurred, it would have had as little success as the Gresham lectures, or whether its more specialized subject matter would have made it more readily acceptable to the city's mariners.[45]

The myth of the vernacular which arose as the result of the increasing number of scientific tracts in English towards the end of the sixteenth and the beginning of the seventeenth centuries has contributed to the view that the most recent discoveries in the 'new science' were immediately and readily apprehended by the common practitioners. It simply is not true that either the Gresham professors or other scholars involved in the applied aspects of mathematics wrote in English in defiance of scholarly standards and in anticipation of the interest their work would engender in the common practitioner. Henry Briggs, who contributed some short pieces in English to the volumes published by such friends as Blundeville and Wright, nevertheless wrote his major works in Latin. None of these, it should be noted, was translated into English before his death in 1631. Even

[41] Taylor, *Mathematical Practitioners*, p. 64.
[42] Waters, *The Art of Navigation*, p. 416. Part of the work had been completed by 1607 and even if Waters's claim is correct, the fact remains that the book was somewhat beyond the capabilities of the common artisan.
[43] More, *The Carpenters Rule*, 'The Preface to the Reader'.
[44] Newton, *Institutio Mathematica* (London, 1654), sig. A2v.
[45] In *The Naval Tracts of Sir William Monson*, vol. 4, p. 392.

Briggs's unfinished masterpiece, the *Trigonometria Britannica*, was composed in Latin; Henry Gellibrand, who undertook its completion and publication, preserved the original Latin. Like Briggs, Gunter wrote some of his important tracts in Latin, but in his case the translations were more rapidly forthcoming. Also noteworthy, the important 'practical' works of Robert Hues and William Oughtred were written in Latin, to be translated only a generation later.

The evidence presented thus far will caution us against forming hasty conclusions concerning the scientific sophistication of the mathematical practitioners of London. This is not to deny that some practitioners were capable of appreciating the scientific works that were making their appearance from the end of the sixteenth century onward as well as of benefiting directly from the scientific lectures at Gresham College. My contention is only that such pursuits were beyond the capabilities of the vast majority of common practitioners who were insufficiently grounded in mathematics to appreciate such works without the mediation of teachers and writers whose task it was to simplify and elaborate upon them. The proliferation of popular treatises is the best proof of the necessity of their services as intermediaries. However, even as regards these popularizing scientific manuals very little speculation has been carried out concerning the audience to whom they were directed. It seems just as likely that they were directed at the upper classes or members of the Inns of Court as at London's humble citizens. Not only were the former better able to afford such manuals, but they, too, showed some interest in acquiring the rudiments of mathematics and astronomy. As for the more gifted mathematical practitioners who kept pace with the rapidly changing body of knowledge – many of whom have already been cited in this chapter – it will be argued that they forged a very different type of relationship with the Gresham professors; they approached them not as pupils in a lecture hall, but as colleagues who worked together and were dependent upon each other's services in order to advance their common body of scientific knowledge.

Although Gresham College proved itself unsuccessful as a teaching institution, it became the most important research centre in England in the first half of the seventeenth century, providing a meeting place for those committed to the advancement of science. Among the more celebrated researchers to associate with Gresham College was Sir Kenelm Digby who was resident there from 1633 until 1635, most probably without the knowledge of the Gresham trustees. Following the death of his beloved Venetia, Digby retired to Gresham College where, having adorned himself with 'a long mourning cloake, a high crowned hatt, his beard unshorne', he 'look't like a hermite'. During his stay 'he diverted himselfe with his

chymistry, and the professors' good conversation'.[46] Digby occupied five
or six rooms under the lodgings of the Professor of Divinity which in the
College's plan of 1740 are designated as the 'Physic prof. elaboratory'.[47]
Four of these rooms were converted to Digby's laboratory and furnished
with ovens, furnaces, glasses, trivets, etc., and it was here that Digby's
research into palingenesis, his attempts to 'revivify or resurrect plants
and animals from their calcined ashes', was carried out.[48] Before Digby's
alchemical studies are further elaborated upon, it is worth noting that his
seclusion in the College did not prevent him from communicating with
colleagues. It was during his residence in Gresham College that Digby
negotiated his donation of manuscripts to the Bodleian Library[49] and
towards the end of his stay that he addressed to Hakewill a long letter
commending the latter's *Apologie*.[50]

Although Dobbs was unable to trace any record of Digby's alchemical
work conducted during the latter's Gresham period, it remains most likely
that such work was carried on. When Digby 'retired' to Gresham College,
he engaged the service of the Hungarian alchemist Johannes Banfi
Hunyades to serve as his operator there.[51] Hunyades had been in England
from 1608, but virtually nothing is known of his activities before his move
to Gresham College. In 1619 he met Joachim Morsius in London, for his
signature appears in the 'Album Amicorum' of the German.[52] It is also
likely that by this time he had gained some repute by his chemical work
and had formed ties with such men as Thomas Allen and William
Oughtred. After Digby left Gresham College in 1635, Hunyades remained
at least until 1642, for in a letter of that year to a Hungarian friend,
Hunyades reported that he was resident in Gresham College where he
served as a master of chemistry.[53] This allusion to scientific instruction
suggests certain of Hunyades's activities during his Gresham years.

[46] Aubrey, *Brief Lives*, vol. I, p. 226.
[47] Ward, *The Lives of the Professors*, facing p. 33.
[48] The inventory of the laboratory is among the Hartlib papers at Sheffield. It was printed
by B. J. Dobbs, 'Studies in the natural philosophy of Sir Kenelm Digby, part II: Digby
and alchemy', *Ambix*, xx (1973), 146–7.
[49] Macray, *Annals of the Bodleian Library*, pp. 74–81.
[50] The letter dated 13 May 1635 was printed by V. Gabrieli, *Sir Kenelm Digby: un Inglese
Italianto Nell'eta Della Controriforma* (Rome, 1957), pp. 278–83.
[51] K. Digby, *A Discourse concerning the Vegetation of Plants* (London, 1661), p. 77. Digby
also invited the famous Theodore de Mayerne to comment upon some of his experiments.
See ibid., p. 78.
[52] See H. Schneider, *Joachim Morsius und sien kreis* (Lubeck, 1929), p. 79.
[53] J. von Magyary-Kossa, *Ungarische Medizinische Erinnerungen* (Budapest, 1935), p. 91: J.
Hunyades to P. Medgyesi, 1642. For Hunyades, see also F. S. Taylor and C. H. Josten,
'Johannes Banfi Hunyades 1576–1650', *Ambix*, v (1953), 44–52; J. H. Appleby, 'Arthur
Dee and Johannes Banfi Hunyades: further information on their alchemical and
professional activities', *Ambix*, xxiv (1977), 96–109; G. Gomori, 'New information of
Janos Banfihunyadi's life', *Ambix*, xxiv (1977), 170–3.

Hunyades apparently supplemented his research with instruction, probably in a manner similar to that carried on by Stähl in Oxford two decades later. One man about whom evidence of instruction by Hunyades has survived is the future critic of the universities, John Webster, who received his instruction from him *c.* 1635.[54] Hunyades's position as an instructor in Gresham College is corroborated by two additional sources. In a letter to his friend William Oughtred in 1637, Hunyades referred to the enforced resignation from the College of 'Our lecturer in astronomy' for having failed to kneel down before the communion table.[55] Finally, the following two inscriptions inserted in Hunyades's engravings suggest his service as an instructor in the College: 'Effig. Johan: Banfi Huniades Riuuliensis Ungari: Olim Anglo-Londini in Illustri Collegio Greshamensi Hermeticae Disciplinae Sectatoris & Philo–Mathematici'; and 'Hermeticae philosophiae scrutatoris, et artis spagyricae Anglo-Londini professoris'.[56] As a result of the activities of the Hungarian alchemist, Gresham College appears to have acquired a reputation as a centre for chemical studies in addition to its reputation as a centre of mathematical and astronomical studies.[57]

In deciphering the role of Gresham College in the genesis of 'London science' it is highly significant that the close association of men unaffiliated to the College with the Gresham professors caused them to be mistaken for 'official' professors in the institution. Robert Hues, one of the members of the Northumberland circle, resided in London during the first two decades of the seventeenth century. The fact that Sherburne was under the impression that Hues was a Gresham professor of mathematics suggests the nature of Hues's association with the College.[58] Indeed, as one closely in touch with Gresham College, Hues might have served as an additional link between Henry Briggs and Thomas Harriot.

Edmund Gunter, who replaced Thomas Williams as Professor of Astronomy in 1619, had been associated with the College for some years previously, perhaps as early as 1613 when he had made an unsuccessful bid for the same post. Regardless of the duration of this association, by the summer of 1618 Gunter was already resident in the College, a fact

---

[54] J. Webster, *Metallographia: Or an History of Metals, Wherein is Declared the Signs of Ores and Minerals both before and after Digging* (London, 1671), p. 161.

[55] Rigaud, *Correspondence of Scientific Men*, vol. 1, p. 30: J. Hunyades to W. Oughtred, 15 Dec. 1637. Hunyades's son, John, was a student of Oughtred. See Aubrey, *Brief Lives*, vol. 2, p. 106.

[56] Taylor and Josten, 'Johannes Banfi Hunyades', 44, 46.

[57] It is noteworthy that Hunyades apparently was not the only assistant installed by Digby in Gresham College, for as late as 1652, when Digby was in some trouble with the authorities, the Gresham committee ordered a search of the rooms of one 'John Lee, a servant or agent of Sr Kenelm Digby' who had been lodging in the College without the committee's authorization. See BL MS Addit. 6195, fol. 59v.

[58] Sherburne, *The Sphere of Manilius*, appendix, p. 86.

which caused William Oughtred to mistake him for a reader during the latter's visit there.[59] John Bainbridge was still another astronomer to frequent the College in 1618 and to be mistaken for a lecturer. As mentioned in the previous chapter, Bainbridge appears to have contacted Briggs almost immediately upon his arrival in London, and the two recorded observations of the comet of that year on an almost daily basis.[60]

This evidence concerning cases of prolonged residence in, and frequent visits to, the College and, most especially, mistaken identity suggests that the role played by Gresham College in the genesis of ' London science' is different from the one attributed to it by historians. It was primarily as a research, rather than as a teaching, institution that Gresham College bore fruit. Whatever instruction did occur appears to have been the result of a more informal exchange of information between colleagues, some of whom, no doubt, were the more educated mathematical practitioners and instrument-makers of the capital. But these practitioners were certainly not the only ones to associate with the Gresham scientists, and Gresham College was as much a national, as a local, scientific centre. In fact, there is more similarity between the role the College and its scientific professors played in the meetings leading to the foundation of the Royal Society in 1660 and the early function of the College as a meeting place for mathematicians and astronomers than is usually assumed. In this context the discussion of Rooke and Wren on the most recent astronomical observations are comparable to the earlier lectures and discussions of Briggs on logarithms; in both cases, the professors conveyed the most advanced and provocative problems in their related fields to interested colleagues. The fact that logarithms could be directly applied to problems of navigation is irrelevant in this respect, and surely Briggs did not occupy himself with logarithms solely for the benefit of merchants and navigators. The difference between the period preceding the founding of the Royal Society and the earlier period is limited to the more informal and, one might add, less adequately chronicled associations of the earlier period. For the early history of Gresham College there is no chronologer comparable to John Wallis who recorded the activities of the later professors. Although John Ward provided us with the biographical sketches of the early Gresham professors, unlike Wallis, he showed little interest in recording the network of associations that grew up around them. Similarly, during the earlier period there was not as yet the need for a well-defined membership body with rules of protocol that arose with the coming of the Civil War followed by the Interregnum. Nonetheless, despite the looser and

---

[59] Oughtred, *To the English Gentrie* (London, 1632), sigs. B3v–B4. Oughtred visited the college in the summer of 1618 and Gunter was not elected professor until March 1619/20.

[60] BL Addit. MS 6209, fol. 339.

less formal relations of the early period, its function as a centre for scientific exchange remained the same.

Furthermore, the fact that Londoners were in a better position to benefit from the lectures originally envisaged by its founder should not lead us to assume that they necessarily did so. Neither should the fact that the Gresham professors left the universities lead us to conclude that they severed all connections with their former colleagues. Not only did there occur a continual process of exchange between London and the universities – as suggested by the exchange of information that occurred between Gunter and Burton, and Ward and Briggs – but when the Gresham professors were able to return to the universities, they invariably did so; hence, Briggs, Turner and Greaves opted for scientific posts at Oxford, while Isaac Barrow was installed as first Lucasian Professor at Cambridge. Unfortunately, almost no personal papers of Brerewood, Gunter, Williams and Gellibrand have been preserved and the nature of their association with the universities must remain a matter of speculation only.

As regards the association of the mathematical practitioners of London with the Gresham professors, it should come as no surprise that, as members of a single scientific community, men like John Tapp, Arthur Hopton and Elias Allen – all of whom referred to their association with the Gresham professors in their published tracts – should come together. However different their orientation, both groups participated in the imperialist fervour that gripped England from the middle of the sixteenth century onward as navigation and its related studies increasingly absorbed the imagination – and pocket – of many Englishmen.[61] If the English were to compete successfully with the Spanish, Portuguese or the Dutch, then navigation had to be revolutionized. There should be little wonder, then, that so-called 'scholars' found themselves increasingly drawn into this national effort.[62] Apart from a genuine interest in the way mathematics might be applied towards solving problems of navigation or a possible fascination with such routes as the Northwest Passage, more often than is readily discernible their frequent dependence on patronage necessitated their attention to such problems as occupied every English peer. Edward Wright, for example, admitted that the patronage of the Earl of Cumberland had necessitated his shift to issues preoccupying the Earl: 'by whom [he] was first moved, and received maintenance to divert by mathematicall studies, from a theoretical speculation in the Universitie, to the practical

---

[61] As early as 1587 Camden could write to a colleague that in England navigation was a national craze. Bodl. MS Smith 74, fol. 2: W. Camden to A. Ortelius, 3 Feb. 1586/87.

[62] A few mathematicians no doubt were full participants in the colonizing ventures. Briggs's will, for example, makes it clear that he held shares in some Lincolnshire mines. It also stipulated that £10 of his legacy be invested in the efforts to discover the Northwest Passage. For Briggs's will, see his *Logarithmetica Britannica*, ed. Thompson, vol. 2, unpaginated.

demonstration of the use thereof in Navigation'.[63] In a similar manner Thomas Digges virtually abandoned his theoretical studies once he entered the service of the Earl of Leicester, while Thomas Harriot was probably fortunate in having the Earl of Northumberland replace Sir Walter Ralegh as his patron, for the latter had been responsible for his earlier absorption in problems of navigation and colonial enterprise.

By its very nature, the study of magnetism, comets, and eclipses not only necessitated more accurate and sustained observations, but required comparative observations from various places on the globe. Hence, one of the most important features of the astronomical and physical sciences was the growing need for cooperative research and a continual exchange of information. One way of obtaining observations was by correspondence between English men of science and their Continental counterparts; more efficient and productive would be to enlist the aid of seamen. The exact time and place of the simultaneous observations as well as the method to be employed could be determined beforehand. The close collaboration between men of science and seamen on the technical aspects did not mean, however, that the seamen necessarily had much concept of the theory underlying their observations. As Taylor has aptly commented: 'Thomas Digges had believed long since that reliable observations could be collected from untrained, uneducated observers and had been disappointed. The early Fellows and Officers of the Royal Society after distributing instructions and questionnaires without number must be presumed eventually to have learned the same lesson.'[64] Here, in fact, lies the rationale for the increasing cooperation and informal instruction between London's foremost men of science and its practitioners; as long as the seamen enlisted to gather observations lacked the necessary mathematical grounding, the chances of success were limited indeed. Moreover, the fact that London's practitioners provided the more complex instruments with which observations were to be performed also necessitated close collaboration. We have already noted the care and diligence taken by John Bainbridge in preparing Roger Fry for his voyage to the Americas. A similar success was met by Captain Thomas James in his simultaneous observations of a moon eclipse, 'with the result that they determined the longitude of James's position to within 15''.[65] It should be noted, however, that these men were better educated than most seamen. James was a barrister who turned to the sea, while Fry spent some time in Merton College where his notebook attests to the eagerness with which he embraced scientific studies.[66]

Simultaneous astronomical observations remained the goal of others as

[63] Wright, *Certaine Errors in Navigation*, 'Dedicatory Epistle'.
[64] Taylor, *Mathematical Practitioners*, p. 101.
[65] Waters, *The Art of Navigation*, pp. 499–500.
[66] For Fry's notebook, see TCD MS 443.

well. John Greaves set up no less than four posts in the Middle East in 1638 in order to observe the eclipse of the moon due to occur in December of that year. Greaves also expressed the hope that the eclipse would be observed in England as well as in the Azores.[67] One Englishman whose attempts to observe this eclipse were frustrated by clouds was William Gilbert who at the time was in Ireland.[68] In a similar manner, Jeremiah Horrox urged William Crabtree to find observers for the transit of Venus which he predicted would be seen on 24 November 1639; one of the men whom he had in mind was Samuel Foster in London.[69]

This preoccupation with simultaneous observations was not limited to celestial phenomena; the variation of the magnetic needle was a comparable earthly project. Edmund Gunter and Henry Gellibrand, together with John Marr, John Wells, and a few others all carried out such observations. Significantly, it was this project that was so instrumental in bringing about the discovery of the diminution of the variation of the magnetic needle.[70]

Contacts with mathematical practitioners and instrument-makers, however, were not the private domain of the Gresham professors. Many other 'scholars' invented, constructed or described scientific instruments either as students or as fellows at Oxford or Cambridge. This impressive list includes: Mark Ridley, Thomas Hood, Thomas Oliver, Thomas and William Bedwell, Charles Turnbull, Robert Hues, William Oughtred, Thomas Harriot, Robert Hegge, Edmund Gunter, Samuel Foster, Francis Potter, John Pell and Brian Twyne. The mathematical and astronomical pursuits of such 'scholars' as Gabriel Harvey, John Selden, Robert Payne, Thomas Harriot, John Bainbridge and Thomas Hobbes led them, as a matter of course, to associate with certain instrument-makers. In fact, the universities themselves were not devoid of mathematical practitioners. John Hulett at Oxford and George Atwell at Cambridge, both of whom we have had occasion to mention earlier, served as teachers and instrument-makers in their respective institutions.

The difference of roles played by university-trained men of science and the London mathematical practitioners in the greater scientific community involved the more limited participation of the practitioners. While both groups were usually committed to applied aspects of science – in which their collaboration proved critical – most seamen, gunners, merchants and artisans were either unable or unwilling to appreciate the theoretical considerations that lay behind such preoccupations. Although the dissociation between practice and theory is not always readily discernible in the

---

[67] Kemke, p. 86: J. Greaves to P. Young, 2 Aug. 1638.
[68] Parr, p. 492: W. Gilbert to J. Ussher, 11 Dec. 1638.
[69] Whatton, *Memoir of the Life of Horrox*, p. 43.
[70] Gellibrand, *A Discourse Mathematicall, passim.*

late sixteenth and early seventeenth centuries when the major astronomical and physical as well as mathematical research was at least marginally connected with navigation, ballistics, surveying, magnetism, mechanics, logarithms or astronomical precision, scholars and practitioners alike commented upon its existence. In 1611 Robert Peake voiced the opinion of many architectural technicians who did not believe geometry and perspective were worth their time. In a similar manner, the controversy between Oughtred and Delamain revolved around whether or not teachers of mathematics should convey the principles underlying the instruments they made and sold. Samuel Pepys's enthusiasm for telescopes, microscopes and other instruments caused him to form a close association with the celebrated instrument-maker Richard Reeves. Reeves, who began his career by offering assistance to the circle that formed around Sir Charles Cavendish, was later hired by such men as Hooke. Nonetheless, Pepys could only lament how 'it vexed [him] to understand no more from Reeves and his glasses touching the nature and reason of the several refractions of the several figured glasses, he understanding the acting part, but not one bit of the theory, nor can make any body understand it, which is a strange dullness, methinks'. In a similar manner, Wood commented on John Graunt's 'Excellent working head' which 'was much commended, and the rather for this reason, that it was for the public good of learning, which is very rare in a trader or mechanic'. Finally, when the compass-maker, John Seller, communicated some magnetical observations to the Royal Society, he limited his remarks to comments upon what came 'within the Cognizance & sphere of [his] profession and practice', neither theorizing nor thinking it necessary to expand upon the experimental data.[71]

To conclude: my argument is not with the massive data collected by Taylor or Waters, but with their biased elucidation. My purpose is not to deny the role played by the London community in the evolution of modern science, but only to view the mathematical practitioners of London as well as the Gresham professors within the context of an even larger scientific community. To say that Gresham College was the most important scientific centre in England in the seventeenth century does not mean that the universities were reactionary. Conversely, it does not mean that every merchant or artisan had much conception of sophisticated theories or that

[71] S. Serlio, *The First Booke of Architecture*, trans. R. Peake (London, 1611), 'To the Lovers of Architecture'; Delamain, *The Making of a Horizontall Quadrant, passim*; Oughtred, *To the English Gentrie, passim*; M. H. Nicolson, *Pepys' Diary and the New Science* (Charlottesville, 1965), p. 27; Wood, *Athenae Oxonienses*, vol. 1, p. 712. For the Seller episode I am indebted to Michael Hunter who also drew my attention to the Pepys and Graunt episodes, all of which are included in his *Science and Society in Restoration England* (Cambridge, 1981), pp. 75–6.

Gresham College was a successful teaching institution. Only as a research centre – a place in which interested members of the scientific community from London, the universities and abroad could exchange information and advance the general body of scientific knowledge – did Gresham College prove a success.

VI

The mechanism of patronage

'The clientage system', Stone reminds us, 'dominated scholarship and letters as well as elections to the House of Commons; both were aspects of the new structure of politics and the new role played in it by the Court aristocracy'.[1] Indeed, it is all but inconceivable to discuss scientific enterprise in the sixteenth and seventeenth centuries without some reference to the system of patronage that, on the most basic level, provided employment for numerous practitioners, but more significantly, by so doing brought pressure to bear upon the scientific problems to be investigated and the over-all orientation of the inquiry. In view of the importance of patronage for all intellectual activity in the sixteenth and seventeenth centuries, it is surprising how little sustained attention has been given to the subject. Apart from some studies of political patronage under the Tudors and Stuarts, the few treatments of patronage have focussed upon the subject of literary patronage. What little mention has been made of scientific patronage has been in the context of such general studies of scientific activity as those of Taylor, Waters and Hill. Without in any way pretending to do justice to a subject that merits a full-length study, the following chapter will be devoted to an examination of certain aspects of patronage in an attempt to determine how far the 'clientage system' influenced scientific enterprise in the period between 1560 and 1640. However, before the scientific implications of the prevailing system of patronage can be assessed, it is first necessary to discuss the ideal of education that first prompted young gentlemen to turn their attention towards scientific studies and the preoccupations that accounted for their sustained appreciation of the sciences and caused them to patronize a new generation of scientific practitioners.

The evidence of the previous chapters suggests that during their stay at university the upper classes received some instruction in the mathematical sciences, as did all undergraduates. However, as already noted in chapter I, while the study of mathematics was accepted as an integral part of a young gentleman's studies, the dangers of overindulgence in mathematics,

[1] L. Stone, *The Crisis of the Aristocracy 1558–1641* (Oxford, 1965), p. 708.

especially in its more theoretical aspects, were always stressed. Moderation and, most important of all, attention only to those aspects relevant to practical everyday pursuits were the seminal concepts underlying mathematical instruction. The numerous letters of advice – a few of which have been cited previously – all contain similar warnings against a too eager pursuit of mathematics. For example, in reply to Hubert Languet's cautionary words of advice concerning his enthusiasm for astronomy and geometry – studies difficult, time-consuming and not befitting the rank of gentleman – Sidney reassured his tutor that he had not allowed his predisposition towards these subjects a free rein.

I am glad you approve of my intention of giving up the study of astronomy, but about geometry I hardly know what to determine. I long so greatly to be acquainted with it, and the more so because I have always felt sure that it is of the greatest service in the art of war; nevertheless I shall pay but sparing attention to it, and only peep through the bars, so to speak, into the rudiments of the science.[2]

It is worth noting that when Sidney was placed in a position of counsel in 1580, he maintained the basic position he had first adopted with Languet, recommending only the practical and, one might add, less demanding aspects of mathematics to Edward Denny.

it shall be necessary for you to exercise your hande in setting downe what you reed, as in descriptions of battaillons, camps, and marches, with some practise of Arithmetike, which sportingly you may exercise ... For historical maters, I woold wish you before you began to reed a litle of Sacroboscus Sphaere & the Geography of some moderne writer, whereof there are many & is a very easy and delightfull studdy.[3]

In the same year Sidney also penned a letter of advice to his brother Robert – previously quoted in chapter IV – wherein he recommended Henry Savile as the person most capable of providing Robert with the necessary grounding in arithmetic, geometry and mechanical instruments.[4]

The conviction that members of the upper classes should confine their studies only to those elements of the mathematical sciences directly relevant to practical affairs was a notion continually reiterated throughout the latter part of the sixteenth, and the first part of the seventeenth, centuries. Sir Francis Walsingham advised his nephew to 'take some taste of the mathematics, especially of that part which concerneth cosmography, that in traveling ... [he] may observe the countries themselves ... [as well

[2] Pears, *The Correspondence of Sir Philip Sidney*, p. 28; P. Sidney to H. Languet, 4 Feb. 1573/74.

[3] J. Buxton, 'An Elizabethan Reading List', *TLS*, 24 March 1972: P. Sidney to Edward Denny, 1580.

[4] Pears, *The Correspondence of Sir Philip Sidney*, p. 201: P. Sidney to R. Sidney, 18 Oct. 1580.

as to] learn matters ... of fortifications and leading armies'.[5] Cosmography, which necessitated some grounding in mathematics, astronomy and geography as well as some knowledge of the use of instruments, was also recommended to Edward de Vere, 17th Earl of Oxford, by William Cecil.[6] When James I contemplated the education of his son, Prince Henry, he justified a grounding in mathematics in a similar manner:

As for the studie of other liberall artes and sciences [apart from history and religion], I would have you reasonablie versed in them, but not preassing to be a passe-maister in any of them ... I graunt it is meete ye have some entrance, speciallie in the Mathematickes; for the knowledge of the arte militarie in situation of Campes, ordering the battels, making Fortifications, placing of batteries, or such like.[7]

The scientific instruction that would have been implemented had the many schemes for academies for gentlemen bore fruit suggests the same educational bias away from the theoretical. In his proposals for an academy for noblemen, Nicholas Bacon resolved upon a lecturer to teach 'de disciplina militari'. The mathematical lecturers stipulated by Sir Humphrey Gilbert were directed to emphasize only such scientific subjects as were pertinent to the art of war and navigation. Such a tradition was carried well into the seventeenth century and may be detected in the projected institutions of Sir Francis Kynaston and Sir Balthazar Gerbier, both of which were intended to include basic mathematical instruction as part of the education of a gentleman.[8]

The cumulative effect of this evidence is to suggest that the vast majority of the upper classes pursued the mathematical sciences as one more accomplishment in a many-faceted, but by no means profound, education. Indeed, the language often employed to describe mathematical pursuits in these letters of advice affords an additional insight into the nature of a young nobleman's contact with mathematics. The repeated recommendation of the 'pleasing', 'delightful' and 'pretty' aspects of the mathematical sciences suggests that for many, even as part of the official curriculum, the study of mathematics was purged of the disciplined, often

[5] C. Read, *Mr Secretary Walsingham and the Policy of Queen Elizabeth* (Oxford, 1925), vol. I, p. 19.
[6] B. M. Ward, *The Seventeenth Earl of Oxford 1550–1604* (London, 1928, repr., 1979), p. 20.
[7] *The Basilicon Doron of King James VI*, ed. J. Craigie, Scottish Text Soc., 3rd Ser. (Edinburgh, 1944–50), vol. I, pp. 151–3.
[8] J. Conway Davies, 'Elizabethan plans and proposals for education', *Durham Research Review*, II (1954), 4; Sir H. Gilbert, 'Queene Elizabethes Achademy', ed. F. J. Furnivall, Early English Text Soc., Extra Ser., vol. 8 (London, 1869), pp. 4–5; Sir F. Kynaston, *The Constitutions of the Musaeum Minervae* (London, 1636), p. 5; Sir B. Gerbier, *The Interpreter of the Academie for Forrain Languages and All Noble Sciences and Exercises. The First Part* (London, 1648), sig. A2–A2v.

tedious, pursuit of abstract principles in favour of a relaxed pursuit of its more superficial attributes. One of the most widely recommended of these attributes was the use of the globe. In chapter III we mentioned a concerned father's request to Richard Holdsworth that his son acquire such gentlemanlike accomplishments as the study of the globe.[9] A similar concern with the rudiments of mathematics and the use of the globe as the instruction befitting a gentleman is expressed by Sackvile Crow's tutor in a letter to his pupil's father: 'For the Mathematiques I never invite any of my Pupils to engage farther in them than the plaine & necessary Doctrines of Arithmetique & Geometry, and ye use of the Globes. If theyr owne Genius delights to wade deeper, I assist them what I can.'[10] As in the case of Sidney, the language connotes an immense and somewhat intractable expanse into which the young gentleman is allowed only the briefest glimpse. Once again it must be stressed that any attempt to define an ideal of education necessitates the majority of students – in this case aristocratic students – as one's frame of reference; those gentlemen who wished to pursue the sciences in greater depth – some of whom have been discussed previously in earlier chapters – could be assisted by their tutors, and almost certainly by the scientifically oriented fellows of the universities.

For other gentlemen the visible phenomena which increasingly came to characterize the sciences accounted for their sustained interest in mathematics. The dedicatory epistle to Leurechon's *Mathematicall Recreations* suggests that a facility with such visible phenomena became one more accomplishment befitting a gentleman: 'the *Nobilitie*, and *Gentrie* rather studie the *Mathematicall* Arts, to content and satisfie their affections, in the speculation of such admirable experiments as are extracted from them, than in the hope of gaine to fill their *Purses*'.[11] The insistence on delight rather than profit as the incentive for scientific enthusiasm on the part of the upper classes does not necessarily contradict what was said earlier about utility; however, the author exaggerates somewhat to make his point and a concern with the practical uses of the 'mathematical arts', especially as far as they were relevant to the interests of the state, were as important as a delight in their visible phenomena. Commenting on a similar situation a generation later, Robert Boyle remarked that among those enamoured with the 'corpuscularian' philosophy:

there are many ingenious persons, especially among the nobility and gentry, who, having been first drawn to like this new way of philosophy by the sight of some experiments, which for their novelty or prettiness they were much pleased with, or for their strangeness they admired, have afterwards delighted themselves to

[9] Cary, *Memorials*, vol. I, p. 14: R. Holdsworth to W. Sancroft, 30 April 1646.
[10] BL MS Addit. 27606, fol. 9v.
[11] J. Leurechon, *Mathematicall Recreations*, trans. W. Oughtred (London, 1633), sig. A3v.

make or see variety of experiments, without having ever had the opportunity to be instructed in the rudiments of fundamental notions of that philosophy whose pleasing or amazing productions have enamoured them of it.[12]

Such a view of science as an 'accomplishment' will culminate in the phenomenon of the virtuoso later in the century. However, in the period under review the beginnings of this tendency are already evident. As Houghton has pointed out, in the period before 1640 the important element of natural history for the mid- and later part of the seventeenth century 'made little appeal in comparison with alchemy or mechanics, and especially the latter. It is safe to say that before 1640 practical or "mixed" mathematics was the major field of virtuoso science, partly because it was here that the most startling advances had been made.'[13]

It is not surprising, then, that the numerous mechanical devices that were becoming increasingly evident in England in the period before 1640 appealed to the upper classes, and frequently accounted for their patronage of science. As the author of a treatise on mathematical instruments reminds us, it is by instruments that the mathematical sciences 'are rendered useful in the Affairs of Life. By their assistance it is that subtile and abstract Speculation is reduced into Act ... the knowledge of these is the knowledge of Practical Mathematicks.'[14] The numerous astronomical instruments donated to colleges during our period are just one manifestation of this fascination with instruments and curious mechanical devices on the part of the English nobility. Although a few may have grasped the principles underlying the construction of such instruments and mechanisms, the majority delighted in their novelty and visible attributes with little concept of their theoretical basis. To quote Turner, being 'concerned with immediate practical matters, to be able to use the necessary instruments seemed enough'.[15] This fascination with mathematical instruments also supports what was suggested earlier about the increasing numbers of practical tracts containing directions for the use of these instruments, namely that they were directed as much to the upper classes as to the humble mathematical practitioners of London.

Concomitant with this growing delight in instruments and mechanical

[12] R. Boyle, 'The origin of forms and qualities according to the corpuscular philosophy', *Selected Philosophical Papers of Robert Boyle*, ed. M. A. Stewart (Manchester, 1979), p. 4. The tract was composed in the 1650s.

[13] Houghton, 'The English virtuoso in the seventeenth century', 69. The most recent study of the movement is by R. L-W. Caudill, 'Some Literary Evidence of the Development of English Virtuoso Interests in the Seventeenth Century, with Particular Reference to the Literature of Travel' (Oxford Univ. D.Phil. thesis, 1975).

[14] *The Construction and Principal Uses of Mathematical Instruments Translated from the French of M. Bion, Chief Instrument-maker to the French King* (London, 1723), trans. E. Stone, preface, quoted in Turner, 'Mathematical instruments and the education of gentlemen', 51.

[15] Turner, 'Mathematical instruments and the education of gentlemen', 58.

devices was an ever-increasing interest in 'artificial miracles', which were little more than mechanical devices on a grand scale, their purpose being to delight all who witnessed them. As the English nobility increasingly encountered – or heard talk of – those artificial miracles installed in Italian and French palaces, they sought to acquire similar commodities for their own pleasure. Water-works, artificial rainbows and musical instruments are just a few of the curiosities that became increasingly popular in England from the latter part of the sixteenth century.

In the previous chapter the inhibiting effect of patronage upon the theoretical aspects of the mathematical sciences was already suggested. Indeed, if the educational ideal animating the encounter of the upper classes with science and the preoccupations that accounted for their interest in science are borne in mind, it is only natural that patrons invariably encouraged those aspects of mathematics that ranged from the delightful to the practical, quite often both. While the element of delight was rooted in a fascination with visible scientific phenomena, the conviction that applied mathematics could advance one's own interests as well as the glory of England appealed to many patrons. This is not to deny that theoretical issues were sometimes pursued: only that the mechanism of patronage facilitated advances in the practical, and sometimes curious, aspects of science for the reason that mathematicians were influenced by the preoccupations of their patrons.

On the simplest level this attempt to appeal to the preoccupations of the upper classes is reflected in the practice of presenting a potential patron with an invention or a mechanical device, or alternatively, of dedicating to him a treatise of a practical nature. A mechanical device could be explained in simple terms and both delight and flatter its recipient as much as the offering of verse. The appeal of a dedication of a treatise lay in the assumption that the applied sciences were the key to a patron's or England's future. It is not surprising, then, that the royal family as well as the influential courtiers – especially William Cecil, Lord Burghley, and Robert Dudley, Earl of Leicester – were the recipients of numerous inventions and dedications. Treatises of a practical nature frequently contained dedications to such peers of the realm as were identified with the causes addressed by the books. The Lord High Admiral, for example, was a natural patron for books pertinent to matters of navigation and applied mathematics. Thus, we find that both Diggeses, Bourne and Norman dedicated their works to Edward Fiennes, Earl of Lincoln – Lord High Admiral from 1558 until 1585 – while his successor, Charles Howard, Earl of Nottingham – Lord High Admiral from 1586 until 1618 – received the dedications of Hakluyt, Norman, Hood, Davis, Blagrave and Wright. Other natural candidates included those noblemen closely associated with the colonizing enterprise, especially George Clifford, Earl of Cumberland, and Sir Walter Ralegh. Although these men did not commission the works dedicated to them, they were regarded as the peers who would most appreciate them and reward their authors accordingly.

The following pages will discuss in some detail the two manifestations of the patronage of science on the part of the upper classes: an abundance of mechanical devices to cater to their amusement and the proliferation of practical devices and projects to ensure the place of England among the powers.

The appreciation of mathematical instruments may be traced back to Henry VIII, who greatly delighted in such instruments and supported various mathematicians and instrument-makers, the most celebrated of whom was Nicholas Kratzer. Kratzer arrived in England around 1517 and shortly thereafter was engaged as the King's astronomer and horologer.[16] Among other things, he presented Henry with a beautiful manuscript containing instructions for the use 'of an instrument which he called his *horoptrum*', probably as a new year's gift of 1528/29.[17] Henry's delight in clocks is corroborated by other facts. In 1531 Kratzer was paid 40s for mending a clock;[18] in 1540 a sophisticated clock was constructed for Henry in Hampton Court, probably by Nicholas Oursian,[19] while the household accounts contain frequent references to dials and clocks.[20] No doubt Henry's delight in mechanisms made him the recipient of many such presents. Sir Anthony Denny commissioned Holbein to design a clock, the result of which was one 'driven by wheel-work, below which are 'fore and after noon dials shewing time by shadows, and beneath them is a clepsydra indicating by means of a fluid the quarter of an hour'.[21] In a similar manner John Poynet, the future Bishop of Winchester, deemed it advantageous to give

unto King Henry the eight a diall of his owne devise, shewing not onely the hower of the day, but also the day of the moneth, the signe of the sun, the planetary hower; yea the change of the moone, the ebbing and flowing of the sea; with divers other things as strange, to the great woonder of the King and his owne no lesse commendation.[22]

[16] The most recent account of Kratzer is by J. D. North, 'Nicholaus Kratzer – the King's astronomer', *Studia Copernicana*, XVI (1978), 205–34.

[17] Bodl. MS Bodley 504. The quote is from North, 'Nicholaus Kratzer', 225. Kratzer also lectured on mathematics at Corpus Christi College, Oxford.

[18] *Letters and Papers Foreign and Domestic of the Reign of Henry VIII*, vol. 5, p. 754.

[19] E. Law, *The New Guide to the Royal Palace of Hampton Court* (London, 1882), pp. 102–6.

[20] E. J. Wood, *Curiosities of Clocks and Watches from the Earliest Times* (London, 1886), p. 57.

[21] W. H. Smyth, 'Description of an astrological clock, belonging to the Society of Antiquaries of London', *Archaeologia*, XXXIII (1849), 16.

[22] F. Godwin, *A Catalogue of the Bishops of England, since the First Planting of Christian Religion in this Island, together with a Briefe History of their Lives and Memorable Actions*, 2nd edn (London, 1615), p. 249. Poynet was educated under Sir Thomas Smith at Queens' College, Cambridge, in the 1530s.

Henry's son and heir, Edward VI, revealed himself no less interested in mechanical devices than his father. His accounts also contain numerous references to the purchase of clocks and watches,[23] and he was the recipient of various gifts of instruments. Thus, Thomas Gemini engraved a fine astrolabe bearing the arms and initials of Edward as well as those of the Earl of Northumberland and Sir John Cheke, both of whom served as the Prince's tutors.[24] Edward also attracted Ottiwel Hollinshed, brother of the chronologer, who presented him with a treatise on the construction and use of the ring-dial, probably as a new year's gift of 1551/52.[25]

This tradition was continued and cultivated by Elizabeth. While still a princess, Elizabeth commissioned William Buckley, a fellow of King's College, Cambridge, to construct a ring-dial. The dial, together with directions for its use, was presented to her in 1546.[26] As previously noted, John Dee was engaged as Elizabeth's 'adviser' on scientific matters during much of her reign. As early as 1555 Dee was requested to calculate the then Princess's nativity, while five years later his advice was sought when the date most appropriate for Elizabeth's coronation was being contemplated.[27] It is worthy of note that Dee was probably the designer of the astrological astrolabe presented to Elizabeth by Thomas Gemini in 1559,[28] and that Humphrey Cole presented Elizabeth with a circular astrological calendar.[29]

Like her father and half-brother, Elizabeth also delighted in watch pieces and clocks, many of which were bestowed upon her as new years' gifts by the great peers of the realm. The Earl of Leicester and Lord Russell presented their royal mistress with richly decorated watches and clocks.[30] Indeed, an inventory of the Queen's watches included no less than twenty-four items.[31] A clockmaker and clock-keeper were also engaged by the palace with annual stipends of £18 and £13, respectively.[32] As with all mechanisms, innovations in the field were constantly being sought. In 1582, for example, Thomas Bedwell was preoccupied with

[23] Wood, *Curiosities of Clocks*, p. 235.

[24] Taylor, *Mathematical Practitioners*, p. 165.

[25] BL MS Royal 17A.XXXIII. Hollinshed (M.A. 1544) became a founding fellow of Trinity College, Cambridge, in 1546. See Cooper, *Athenae Cantabrigienses*, vol. I, p. 431.

[26] BL MS Royal 12A.XXV. For Buckley, see Cooper, *Athenae Cantabrigienses*, vol. I, p. 292; Taylor, *Mathematical Practitioners*, p. 169; P. Rose, 'Erasmians and mathematicians at Cambridge in the early sixteenth century', *Sixteenth Century Journal*, VIII (supplement 1977), 47–59.

[27] *Cal. Stat. Pap. Dom. 1547–1580*, p. 67.

[28] R. T. Gunther, 'The astrolabe of Queen Elizabeth', *Archaeologia*, LXXXVI (1936), 65–72; G. H. Gabb, 'The astrological astrolabe of Queen Elizabeth', ibid., 101–3.

[29] R. T. Gunther, 'The great astrolabe and other scientific instruments of Humphrey Cole', *Archaeologia*, LXXVI (1926/27), 302.

[30] J. Nichols, *The Progresses and Public Processions of Queen Elizabeth* (London, 1823), vol. I, p. 294, vol. 2, pp. 249, 300.

[31] Wood, *Curiosities of Clocks*, pp. 252–5.

[32] Wood, *Curiosities of Clocks*, p. 74.

the problem how 'to make a clock to go by water continually without setting'.[33]

Elizabeth's greatest delight, however, was music, and here, too, new instruments were constructed at her request. Having been commissioned by the Queen c. 1587 to construct some sophisticated musical chimes, the subdean of her chapel, one Mr Tirwitt, wrote to Burghley shortly thereafter, assuring the Lord Treasurer that, providing that funds were forthcoming, he would 'with all expedition devise her that worcke by geometrie, arithmeticke, and musicke, that I suppose was never devised sins Christes assention: which shallbe an everlasting memori of her so longe as Englande remayneth'.[34] Mention should also be made of curiosities in Whitehall recorded by a German traveller, Paul Hentzner, during his visit in 1598: 'a jet-d'eau, with a sun-dial, which while strangers are looking at, a quantity of water, forced by a wheel, which the gardener turns at a distance, through a number of little pipes plentifully sprinkles those that are standing around'.[35]

Under the Stuarts the pursuit of the mechanically curious reached new heights. It is regrettable that there is no study of James's interest in, and patronage of, science, for there are many allusions to his involvement in scientific enterprise. We have already had occasion to remark upon his fascination with the comet of 1618. However, James showed himself no less interested in astronomical instruments and mechanical devices. Like many of his contemporaries, he became fascinated with the numerous inventions tendered by Cornelis Drebbel who arrived in England c. 1607, especially by his *perpetuum mobile*. James rewarded Drebbel with a place in Eltham Palace where the invention was also displayed.[36] Other of Drebbel's inventions that fascinated the King included a *camera obscura*, a magic lantern, a mechanism that produced optical illusions and another that promoted artificial freezing. Drebbel was also employed to produce spectacular effects for the various palace masques.[37]

James's enthusiasm for mechanical devices was apparently recognized beyond England. In 1609 the Emperor Rudolph II presented the English monarch with a celestial globe and a clock.[38] The same year we find a

[33] *Cal. Stat. Pap. Dom. 1581–1590*, p. 52.
[34] H. Ellis (ed.), *Original Letters, Illustrative of English History* (London, 1846), vol. 4, p. 65.
[35] Hentzner also recorded 'a piece of clock work, an Ethiop riding upon a Rhinoceros, with four attendants, who all make their obeisance, when it strikes the hour; these are all put into motion by winding up the machine'. P. Hentzner, *Travels in England During the Reign of Queen Elizabeth*, trans. Horace, Earl of Oxford (London, 1797), pp. 23–4.
[36] W. B. Rye, *England as Seen by Foreigners* (London, 1865), p. 61. For Drebbel, see G. Tierrie, *Cornelis Drebbel* (Amsterdam, 1932); R. L. Colie, 'Cornelis Drebbel and Salomon de Caus: two Jacobean models for Solomon's House', *Huntington Library Quarterly*, XVIII (1954–5), 245–60; L. E. Harris, *The Two Netherlanders, Humphrey Bradley and Cornelis Drebbel* (Cambridge, 1961).
[37] Tierrie, *Cornelis Drebbel*, pp. 5, 45, 49–52.
[38] Evans, *Rudolph II and his World*, p. 81, n. 1.

letter from the Chancellor of the Exchequer, Sir Julius Caesar, to the clerks of the signet ordering the payment of £300 to one Hans Niloe for a clock, complete with music and motion, constructed by him for the King.[39] James, whose passion for clocks and watches rivalled that of Elizabeth, also 'discovered' the talents of David Ramsey, who already in 1613 had been granted a pension of £50 and in 1618 had been promoted to chief clockmaker. The occasional surviving bills indicate that James's taste for clocks caused him considerable expense. In 1616, for example, Ramsey was paid £234 for repairing the King's clocks and in 1622 a total of £232 was paid for the maintenance of clocks at Theobalds, Oatlands and Westminster as well as for the construction of a set of chimes to adjoin a clock at Theobalds.[40] There were also other clockmakers favoured by James; Uldrich Hench, Humphrey Flood and Randolph Bull all were generously remunerated by the King for clocks they either constructed or mended.[41]

Apart from his pursuit of instrument-makers and clockmakers, James showed himself interested in certain prominent men of science. Even before his accession to the English throne, he expressed admiration for Tycho Brahe, and at the request of the Danish astronomer James composed some verses commending him and his work. These verses appeared in Tycho's *Astronomica Progymnasmata* (1593). James also granted Tycho a thirty-year patent for the sole distribution of his books.[42] Years later James extended his favours to Kepler. Already in 1607 the great astronomer forwarded to the King a presentation copy of his *De stella nova*, while in 1619 he dedicated to James his *Harmonices mundi libri V*. The book was delivered by John Donne who had accompanied James Hay, Earl of Carlisle, in his embassy to the Emperor Ferdinand II. Apparently James invited Kepler to settle in England, but despite the persuasive arguments of Sir Henry Wotton, Kepler declined this invitation.[43] Also noteworthy is that Edmund Gunter composed his 'Description of the Dialls at Whitehall' (*c.* 1623) for James's benefit.[44]

More ample evidence has survived to document James's patronage of Robert Fludd. Fludd dedicated his *Utriusque cosmi historici* of 1617 to James as well as his unpublished treatise 'Philosophical Key'. Following the accusation made against Fludd for his alleged 'innovation in religion and

---

[39] *Cal. Stat. Pap. Dom. 1601–1603*, p. 534.

[40] *Cal. Stat. Pap. Dom. 1611–1618*, pp. 211, 419, 598; *Cal. Stat. Pap. Dom. 1619–1623*, pp. 365, 451.

[41] F. Devon, *Issues of the Exchequer being Payments made out of His Majesty's Revenues During the Reign of King James I* (London, 1836), pp. 27, 67, 196.

[42] A. Gill, *The New Starr of the North* (London, 1632), pp. 3–6.

[43] Kepler, *Gesammelte Werke*, vol. 16, pp. 103, 215; vol. 6, pp. 9–12; W. Applebaum, 'Donne's meeting with Kepler: a previously unknown episode', *Philological Quarterly*, 1 (1971), 132–4; *The Life and Letters of Sir Henry Wotton*, vol. 1, p. 171, vol. 2, p. 205, n. 4.

[44] BL MS Royal 17A.XVIII. The tract was published in 1624.

heresy', Fludd was apparently summoned before the King who suggested that he vindicate himself of the allegation. Fludd's 'Declaratio brevis', written shortly afterwards and dedicated to James, did exactly this.[45]

One of the best documented examples of royal interest in, and patronage of, science is provided by Henry Frederick, Prince of Wales. The admiration that Henry engendered in his contemporaries together with his untimely death in 1612 at the age of 18 combined to generate a myth about the heroic virtues of the young Prince.[46] While this combination of events doubtlessly resulted in an idealization of the young Prince's character, it was also responsible for the documentation of many biographical details of his early life which otherwise might have gone unrecorded. For our purposes it is important to emphasize that from the time of Henry's arrival in England following his father's accession to the throne in 1603, his time was given over almost entirely to his education. Young, charming and as yet free of public responsibility, Henry cultivated the cultural and scientific attractions of his time as an integral part of his education.

The ideal of education that informed the course of studies pursued by Henry was similar to that discussed previously, and no doubt the example set by the young Prince helped to reinforce such an ideal for the next generation as well. James's advice to his son concerning the advisability of a broad, but by no means intense, education has already been noted, and from the account of Birch, this advice was apparently followed. '[Prince Henry] studies two hours a day, and employs the rest of his time in tossing the pike, or leaping, or shooting with the bow, or vaulting or some other exercise of that kind; and he is never idle.'[47] It might be noted that Bacon's characterization of Henry as one who 'was fond of antiquity and arts: and a favourer of learning, although rather in the honour he paid it than in the time he spent upon it' confirms this lenient ideal of education.[48]

Some of the most talented men of the age were introduced into the household for Henry's benefit. Sir Thomas Chaloner served as Henry's governor, while the scientifically minded 2nd Baron Exton, John Harrington, was his close companion.[49] Previous mention has been made of

[45] For Fludd's relation with James, see C. H. Josten, 'Robert Fludd's "Philosophical Key" and his alchemical experiment on wheat', *Ambix*, XI (1963), 1–23; W. H. Huffman and R. A. Seelinger, 'Robert Fludd's "Declaratio Brevis" to James I', *Ambix*, XXV (1978), 69–92; A. G. Debus, *Robert Fludd and his Philosophical Key* (New York, 1979).

[46] The major sources of Prince Henry's life are Sir C. Cornwallis, *The Life and Death of our late most Incomparable and Heroique Prince, Henry Prince of Wales* (London, 1641); T. Birch, *The Life of Henry Prince of Wales, Eldest Son of King James I* (London, 1760); E. C. Wilson, *Prince Henry and English Literature* (Ithaca, 1946). For an example of the mythical element, see F. A. Yates, *Shakespeare's Last Plays: A New Approach* (London, 1975).

[47] Birch, *The Life of Henry Prince of Wales*, p. 75.   [48] Bacon, *Works*, vol. 6, p. 328.

[49] Birch, *The Life of Henry Prince of Wales*, p. 117; Wilson, *Prince Henry and English Literature*, pp. 57–9.

Thomas Williams who served as one of Henry's tutors, translating Sacrobosco's *Sphaera* into English for his royal charge.[50] Henry's grounding in astronomy is indicated by a copy of Sacrobosco, together with other astronomical tracts, bearing the Prince's initials and once housed in the Lumleian Library.[51] Williams, however, was not the only tutor in the mathematical sciences. Cosmography, wherein Henry was 'very studious',[52] was taught by Edward Wright who, assisted by a German, constructed at great expense

a large *Sphere* with curious Movements, which by the help of Spring-Work, not only represented the Motion of the Whole *Celestial Sphere*, but shewed likewise the Particular *Systems* of the *Sun* and *Moon*, and their Circular Motions, together with their Places, and possibilities of eclipsing each other. There is in it a Work by Wheel and Pinion for a Motion of 17100 years, certainly affected, if the Sphere should be so long kept in Motion.[53]

Henry's scientific inclinations were also nurtured by other mathematicians who sought to obtain his patronage. Thomas Lydiat dedicated his *Emendatio Temporum* to the Prince, with the result that the latter 'took so much notice of him, as to receive him into His service, and to have him reade to him'.[54] Henry's scientific discussions were not limited to his tutors. William Barlow, who served as the Prince's chaplain, recalled how Henry loved Sir Dudley Digges 'singularlie well for [his] vertues, and delighted no lesse to conferre with [him] for [his] knowledge in matters appertaining unto Discoveries and Cosmographicall learnings, in the which his highnes was more than vulgarly skilful'.[55]

As the Prince's predisposition towards the sciences became increasingly known, various men of science sought to procure his patronage. Some, like Lydiat, were favourably received. William Gilbert – younger half-brother of the author of *De Magnete* – dedicated and presented to the Prince his compilation from his half-brother's papers of *De Mundo c.* 1610.[56] Harriot's manuscripts also contain some references to the Prince suggestive of an association. One such reference gives 'the solution of a cubic equation', while 'the other is an exercise in combinatories with the phrase

[50] See p. 69 above.
[51] S. Jayne and F. R. Johnson (eds.), *The Lumley Library: The Catalogue of 1609* (London, 1956), p. 222, item 1917.
[52] Peacham, *The Complete Gentleman*, p. 69.
[53] Sherburne, *The Sphere of Manilius*, appendix, p. 86. An astrolabe constructed by Humphrey Cole in 1574 came into the hands of Henry at some stage. Gunther, 'The great astrolabe and other scientific instruments of Humphrey Cole', 278–80.
[54] Mede, *Works*, ed. Worthington, 'An Appendix to ... the Authour's Life', p. xliv. In 1611 we also find Lydiat forwarding to Prince Henry his opinion of Kepler's *Astronomia Nova*. Bodl. MS Bodl. 313, fols. 83–4: T. Lydiat to A. Newton, 26 July 1611.
[55] Barlow, *Magneticall Advertisements*, sig. A3v.
[56] The manuscript is in BL MS Royal 12 F.XI.

Henricus princeps fecit which could have been used in devising a cypher'.[57] Another who sought to procure Henry's patronage was Francis Bacon, who turned to the Prince of Wales after having failed to persuade James I to support his schemes.[58] Bacon dedicated the 1612 edition of his essays to the Prince and probably some scientific discussions occurred between them, for Thomas Bushell quotes an otherwise unknown letter from Bacon to Henry treating magnetical properties and magic.[59]

As one who 'greatly delighted in all rare inventions and arts, and military engines both at land and sea', as he is described by Birch,[60] Henry was the natural patron for Cornelis Drebbel and Salomon de Caus. As previously mentioned, upon arrival in England Drebbel was engaged by James I. However, it appears that Drebbel was transferred to Henry's service, for in 1609 and 1610 Drebbel was paid £40 out of the purse of the Prince.[61] It was also to Henry that in 1612 Drebbel petitioned for permission to raise a lottery on behalf of his impoverished state following his return from Bohemia.[62] On the other hand Salomon de Caus, the engineer, was probably mobilized directly into the Prince's service. In his dedication of *La Perspective avec la Raison des Ombres et Miroirs* (1612) to the Prince, de Caus attests to their association as early as 1608. During this time de Caus occupied himself in constructing various inventions for the Prince's entertainment as well as in supervising the erection of the palace gardens.[63] De Caus was well rewarded for his efforts, for apart from the usual payments for services rendered, he received an additional £50 following Henry's death.[64]

The practical orientation to knowledge recommended by King James for his son also characterized the education of the future Charles I: 'there were few Gentlemen in the world, that knew more of useful or necessary learning, than this Prince did: and yet his proportion of books was but small, having like Francis of France, learnt more by ear, than by study'.[65] Charles proved as willing as his brother and his father to extend his royal patronage, and even a hostile biographer had to concede that he was 'a

---

[57] BL MS Addit. 6782, fol. 27; BL MS Addit. 6783, fol. 75; R. C. H. Tanner, 'Henry Stevens and the associates of Thomas Harriot', *Thomas Harriot Renaissance Scientist*, ed. J. W. Shirley (Oxford, 1974), p. 96.

[58] Bacon, *Works*, vol. 11, pp. 63, 340.

[59] J. W. Gough, *The Superlative Prodigall, a Life of Thomas Bushell* (Bristol, 1932), p. 147.

[60] Birch, *The Life of Henry Prince of Wales*, p. 389.

[61] Tierrie, *Cornelis Drebbel*, p. 5.

[62] *Cal. Stat. Pap. Dom. 1611–1618*, p. 130.

[63] In his dedication of the second part of his *Institution Harmonique* (1615) to Queen Anne, de Caus mentions that his experiments in the mechanical powers of water had begun while he was in Henry's service. Similarly, in his *Les Raisons des Forces Mouvantes* (1615) we find a great deal that de Caus had contrived while in Henry's service.

[64] *Cal. Stat. Pap. Dom. 1611–1618*, p. 195.

[65] Sir P. Warwick, *Memoires of the Reigne of King Charles I*, 2nd edn (London, 1702), p. 65.

good Mathematician [and] not unskilful in Musick'.[66] Both fields, it should be noted, were supported generously by Charles. He continued the patronage of Robert Fludd begun by his father, and in 1629 he bestowed upon Fludd and his heirs the rents from a 'messuage and lands in Kirton, co. Suffolk'.[67] In a similar manner he continued to support Cornelis Drebbel and David Ramsey, the latter of whom was appointed the first Master of the Clockmaker's Company in 1631. John Evelyn provides a description of one of the more extraordinary clocks in the King's collection, a gift valued at £200 from a German prince:

I was shew'd a Table Clock whose balance was onely a Chrystall ball, sliding on parallel Wyers, without being at all fixed, but rolling from stage to stage, till falling on a Spring concealed from sight, it was throwne up to the upmost chanell againe made with an imperceptible declivity, in this continual vicissitude of motion prettily entertaining the eye every halfe minute, and the next halfe minute giving progresse to the hand that shew'd the houre, & giving notice by a small bell; so as in 120 halfe minuts or periods of the bullets falling on the ejaculatorie Spring the Clock-part struck.[68]

Charles equally appreciated astronomical instruments. In 1627 William Oughtred was summoned to London when, in his words:

Elias Allen having been sworne his Majestie's servant, had a purpose to present his Majestie with some New-yeares gift, and requested me to devise some pretty instrument for him. I answered, that I have heard his Majesty delighted much in the great concave diall at White-hall: and what fitter instrument could hee have than my horizontall [dial].

Oughtred, it might be noted, instructed Allen in the construction of his horizontal instrument.[69] John Marr served as compass-maker and diallist to Charles as he had served previously to James, and in 1632 he presented the King with a treatise on 'The Description and Use of such lines and circles as are drawn uppon ye Stone-Dialls in ... Hampton Courte'.[70] Charles was also the patron of Richard Delamain. Among the various mathematical instruments made by the instrument-maker for the King was a mathematical ring 'of Silver, a Jewel his Majesty much value'd'. Presented to Charles in 1630, the ring was bestowed by him upon his son on the day of his execution.[71]

[66] W. Lilly, *Several Observations upon the Life and Death of Charles late King of England* (London, 1651), p. 75.
[67] *Cal. Stat. Pap. Dom. 1628–1629*, p. 570.
[68] *The Diary of John Evelyn*, ed. E. S. de Beer (Oxford, 1955), vol. 3, pp. 147–8.
[69] *Biog. Brit.*, vol. 5, p. 3279.
[70] BL MS Royal 17 A.V.
[71] Sir T. Herbert, *Memoirs of the Two Last Years of the Reign of that Unparallel'd Prince, of ever blessed memory King Charles I* (London, 1702), p. 130; *Cal. Stat. Pap. Dom. 1637–1638*, pp. 121, 282; Taylor, *Mathematical Practitioners*, p. 201.

In their pursuit of curious mechanical commodities the English aristo-cracy followed in the footsteps of the monarchs. Kratzer, for example, was also employed by English peers, while the household accounts of the Earl of Northumberland between 1512 and 1525 record the purchases of clocks.[72] By the time Elizabeth ascended the throne in 1558, the trend was well established. The man who most vigorously sought to acquire such mechanisms and consequently became one of the most important patrons of science in the second half of the sixteenth century was William Cecil, Lord Burghley. Despite the reputation the Earl of Leicester has acquired as a patron of science, in quantitative terms Burghley certainly supported many more mathematicians and astronomers than did Leicester. In fact many of those who dedicated their works to Leicester had been maintained, to some extent, by Burghley who by all accounts was a most benevolent supporter of the sciences. It should be noted that Burghley had begun his interest in science while a gifted student in St John's College, Cambridge, under the tutorship of John Cheke. John Dee, Thomas Digges, William Bourne, John Blagrave and Thomas Hood all were numbered among those helped by Burghley. As regards Burghley's pursuit of mechanical curiosities, Theobalds, the magnificent house commissioned by him, was the best testament to his taste. When Frederick, Duke of Wirtemberg, visited the Palace in 1592, he noted some of these wonders: 'the ceiling or upper floor is very artistically constructed: it contains the twelve signs of the zodiac, so that at night you can see distinctly the stars proper to each; on the same stage the sun performs its course, which is without doubt contrived by some concealed ingenious mechanism'.[73] So magnificent and so unusual was Theobalds that in 1605 James I persuaded Burghley's heir, Sir Robert Cecil, to exchange it for Hatfield House. The younger Cecil, it should be noted, went on to embellish his new residence with similar wonders, spending some £40,000 between 1607 and 1612 in doing so. Among the engineers employed by Cecil was the ingenious Frenchman, Salomon de Caus, who was responsible for the construction of the hydraulic system in the East Garden's set of waterworks.[74]

The Cecils were not alone in their pursuit of the mechanical and strange. When Mr Tirwitt depicted his scheme for the construction of a set of musical chimes for Elizabeth, he alluded to one such instrument already in the possession of the Earl of Leicester.[75] Leicester, as already noted, enjoyed the taste of his times. In 1581 he received a gift of a clock and

[72] Wood, *Curiosities of Clocks*, p. 55.
[73] Rye, *England as Seen by Foreigners*, p. 44.
[74] L. Stone, *Family and Fortune. Studies in Aristocratic Finance in the Sixteenth and Seventeenth Centuries* (Oxford, 1973), pp. 62–91.
[75] Ellis, *Original Letters*, vol. 4, p. 66.

a dial from Lord North,[76] while at his house in Kenilworth he installed a striking clock with two large dials.[77] In 1594 we find the instrument-maker, James Kynuyn, constructing a pocket-dial for the Earl of Essex, while a letter from William Barlow to the Earl seven years later indicates Essex's preoccupation with astronomical instruments and magnetism, both of which he pursued with the assistance of Barlow and Edward Wright.[78] Mark Ridley recorded how the stir brought about by the discovery of magnetism caused Lord Arundel to purchase a huge loadstone 'which took up an Anchore weighing about twenty foure pounds in weight'.[79] When Philip Herbert, 4th Earl of Pembroke, sought to install certain 'artificial miracles' in Wilton House, he engaged the services of John de Caus, son of Salomon, to build his waterworks. These, recorded Aubrey, 'had ... a contrivance, by the turning of a cock, to shew three rainbowes, the secret whereof [de Caus] did keep to himself'. An earlier visitor recorded his having seen in this 'House of Pleasure' a 'hydraulic device for mechanical singing birds, based, presumably, on that at Tivoli'.[80]

Such interests were not confined to the great peers of the realm but instead rapidly percolated down to the gentry, many of whom delighted in instruments and mathematical problems. In his dedication of his *A New Handling of the Plenisphere* (1601) to Sir John Peter, for example, Thomas Oliver mentioned his having previously sent Peter some easy problems that required only the aid of a ruler and a compass.[81] Certain other young and promising mathematicians were supported by the lesser members of the aristocracy. John Blagrave recalled how Sir Francis Knollys provided him with a stipend and Sir Thomas Parry allowed him access to his library containing mathematical books.[82] Magnetism ranked high among the scientific interests of the gentry, and William Barlow records that a workman from Winchester shaped loadstones for the amusement of

---

[76] Nichols, *Progresses of Queen Elizabeth*, vol. 2, p. 248. In 1629 the Countess of Arundel gave a watch and a dial to her son, William Howard. See Wood, *Curiosities of Clocks*, p. 265.

[77] Wood, *Curiosities of Clocks*, pp. 68–9.

[78] J. Bruce, 'Description of a pocket-dial made in 1593 for Robert Devereaux, Earl of Essex', *Archaeologia*, XL (1866), 343–60; *Hist. MSS Comm. Salisbury MSS*, vol. 11, p. 4: W. Barlow to the Earl of Essex, 5 Jan. 1600/01.

[79] Ridley, *Magneticall Animadversions*, p. 2.

[80] J. Aubrey, *Natural History of Wiltshire*, ed. J. Britton (London, 1847), p. 87; 'A relation of a short survey of the western counties', *Camden Miscellany*, XVI (1936), 66; H. M. Colvin, 'The south front of Wilton House', *Archaeological Journal*, CXI (1954), 181–90; Stone, *The Crisis of the Aristocracy*, p. 717.

[81] Sig. A2.

[82] J. Blagrave, *Baculum Familliare Catholicon sive Generale, A Book of the Making and Use of a Staffe* (London, 1590), sig. A2–A2v; idem, *The Art of Dyalling* (London, 1609), sig. A2v.

gentlemen.[83] After 1610 telescopes were frequently sought. In 1619 Sir Robert Killigrew sent Sir Dudley Carleton a telescope,[84] while twenty years later John Hutchinson forwarded a similar instrument along with a set of detailed instructions for its use to his father.[85] Mention should also be made of the pursuit of mechanical curiosities which, by the end of our period, had become prevalent among all the upper classes. The extent of this interest is suggested by John Evelyn in his account of a visit to a relative who 'shewed [him] such a lock for a doore, that for its filing, & rare {contrivances}, was a masterpiece, yet made by a Country Black-Smith: But we have seen Watches made by another, with as much curositie, as the best of the Profession can brag off.'[86]

In contrast to the more grandiose European courts, the English court never engaged court scientists to cater solely to its taste for mechanical devices. Although mathematicians, astronomers and instrument-makers were encouraged and commissioned to produce mechanical curiosities for the monarchs, almost without exception these men were expected to contribute at least equal energy to advancing the practical interests of the nation. The fields requiring their scientific expertise were numerous. The need for innovations and increased efficiency in navigation, ballistics, mining, surveying and coinage during the sixteenth and seventeenth centuries necessitated the participation of all qualified men. In cases in which men did not volunteer their knowledge and services, they were called upon to do so whenever specific difficulties arose. Such a phenomenon was particularly evident during Elizabeth's reign. Owing to pressing economic problems, the increasing Spanish threat and the explosion of colonizing ventures, all men deemed qualified were asked to contribute to the national effort. Thus, in 1577 George Thorneton petitioned the Council for permission to utilize the mathematical talents of Thomas Digges, whose services were required for a survey to be carried out on the vital harbour at Winchelsea.[87] Thereafter, Digges's interests shifted entirely into the practical sphere. From 1582 until 1584 Digges was absorbed almost exclusively with the pressing problems arising from the repairs being

[83] Barlow, *Magneticall Advertisements*, p. 29. This workman is presumably the one who presented Prince Henry with a rare instrument. Ibid., p. 86.
[84] *Cal. Stat. Pap. Dom. 1619–1623*, p. 77: R. Killigrew to D. Carleton, 14 Sept. 1619.
[85] L. Hutchinson, *Memoirs of the Life of Colonel Hutchinson*, ed. C. H. Firth (London, 1906), pp. 388–9: J. Hutchinson to T. Hutchinson, 20 Aug. 1638.
[86] *The Diary of John Evelyn*, vol. 3, pp. 111–12.
[87] *Cal. Stat. Pap. Dom. 1547–1580*, p. 577. Even earlier, in 1572, Digges responded to the request of William Cecil, Lord Burghley, providing him with his learned opinion of the new star of 1572 together with an astrological prediction of its consequences. PRO SP 12/90/12.

carried out at Dover Harbour.[88] Subsequently, he attached himself to the
Earl of Leicester whom he advised on a wide range of military matters
and was appointed chief muster-master in Leicester's expeditionary force
to the Low Countries.[89]

Digges was not the only practitioner whose services were required in
the rehabilitation of Dover Harbour. Thomas Bedwell was also mobilized
in the effort, precisely at the time, it might be noted, he was occupied in
constructing a clock activated by water.[90] As the Spanish threat intensified,
Bedwell was drawn increasingly into military affairs. Early in 1587 the
Earl of Essex instructed Burghley to send Bedwell on an inspection tour
of fortifications, while the following year Bedwell's services were required
in the Gravesend fortifications.[91] John Dee's talents were also widely
exploited; he advised on such diverse matters as navigation, the instruction
of sailors, problems of fortifications and drainage.[92]

The somewhat young mathematicians Harriot, Wright and Briggs were
also drawn into the national effort. Harriot, as we mentioned earlier, found
his first employment in the service of Walter Ralegh, providing instruction
to sailors and harnessing his energy to various aspects of the colonizing
enterprise.[93] Harriot was also required to provide similar services to other
peers. In 1596, for example, following the request of Sir Robert Cecil,
Harriot brought up to date certain of Ralegh's charts for Cecil's use.[94]
Wright, who was first employed by the Earl of Cumberland, later served
Prince Henry and the Lord High Admiral. He also advised and assisted the
East India and Virginia companies.[95] Around 1600 he obtained a licence
to construct mathematical instruments,[96] and he could very well have

[88] *Cal. Stat. Pap. Dom. 1581–1590*, pp. 44, 49–51, 110–11, 173, 180, 184, 214. See also
W. Minet, 'Some unpublished plans of Dover Harbour', *Archaeologia*, LXXII (1921),
184–224.

[89] *Hist. MSS Comm. Salisbury MSS*, vol. 5, p. 240. Digges dedicated his *An Arithmeticall
Militare Treatise, named Stratioticos* (1579) to the Earl of Leicester. For his military
writings, see H. J. Webb, 'The mathematical and military works of Thomas Digges, with
an account of his life', *Modern Language Quarterly*, VI (1945), 389–400.

[90] *Cal. Stat. Pap. Dom. 1547–1580*, pp. 52, 55, 78–80, 94, 100.

[91] *Cal. Stat. Pap. Dom. 1547–1580*, pp. 394, 550.

[92] French, *John Dee*, ch. 7; Bodl. MS Ashmole 242, art. 45, 'Questions and observations
about draining and imbanking the Fens'.

[93] E. G. R. Taylor, 'Hariot's instructions for Ralegh's voyage to Guiana, 1595', *Journal of
the Institute of Navigation*, V (1952), 345–50; E. G. R. Taylor and D. H. Sadler, 'The
doctrine of nauticall triangles compendious', *Journal of the Institute of Navigation*, VI
(1953), 131–47; J. W. Shirley, 'Sir Walter Ralegh and Thomas Harriot', *Thomas Harriot
Renaissance Scientist*, ed. Shirley, pp. 16–35; D. B. Quinn, 'Thomas Harriot and the New
World', ibid., pp. 36–53; J. V. Pepper, 'Harriot's earlier work on mathematical
navigation: theory and practice', ibid., pp. 54–90.

[94] *Hist. MSS. Comm. Salisbury MSS* vol. 6, pp. 256–7: T. Harriot to R. Cecil, 11 July 1596.

[95] See Taylor, *Mathematical Practitioners*, passim; Waters, *The Art of Navigation*, passim.

[96] *Sotheby Sale Catalogue*, 22 June 1976, lot 89.

been the Mr Wright who was employed by the Earl of Salisbury to construct a set of waterworks.[97]

Like his friend Wright, Henry Briggs was closely associated with navigation as well as with the colonizing enterprise.[98] Briggs, however, provided other services as well. In 1608 Briggs, together with Sir Thomas Chaloner, was cast as an arbitrator in the debate concerning the construction of a large ship for the Prince of Wales proposed by Phineas Pett.[99] In 1625 Briggs's advice was sought by the commissioners in charge of repairing the sea breaches between Great Yarmouth and Happisburgh in Norfolk,[100] while from 1629 until his death in 1631 he was preoccupied with problems of drainage. Hence, in 1629 Briggs served on a committee that petitioned Charles I for a scheme to drain the fens within 'counties Norfolk, Suffolk, Cambridge, Isle of Ely, Huntingdon, Northampton, and Lincoln on the south side of the Gleane', while the following year he collaborated with Cornelis Drebbel on a similar project.[101]

Other Gresham professors also volunteered their services. In 1626 Sir William Heydon, John Wells, Phineas Pett and Edmund Gunter presented their formulation of a rule for measuring the tonnage of ships,[102] while a decade later Henry Gellibrand served on a committee – together with Sir John Galloway, John Selden and William Oughtred – charged with considering the method for determining longitudes proposed by Captain Marmaduke Nelson.[103]

Many of the professional instrument-makers we had occasion to mention in connection with the luxurious commodities commissioned by monarchs and peers were involved in more useful schemes as well. In 1578, for example, Humphrey Cole sat on a committee – together with John Dee and Sir Edward Dyer – commissioned to analyse the content of an ore brought back by Frobisher and determine its commercial value. Cole also was engaged as Sinker of the Stamps at the Mint.[104] In addition to being a successful clockmaker, David Ramsey was an inventor who was granted a licence to make engines for ploughing without horses, dyeing cloths without cochineal, etc.[105] Drebbel was another whose time was divided between satisfying the ornamental taste of his masters and devising more useful inventions. He served as a military engineer, designing and

[97] *Hist. MSS Comm. Salisbury MSS*, vol. 12, pp. 370, 407.
[98] Taylor, *Mathematical Practitioners, passim*; Waters, *The Art of Navigation, passim*.
[99] *The Autobiography of Phineas Pett*, ed. W. G. Perrin, Navy Rec. Soc., vol. 51 (London, 1918), p. 59.
[100] *Cal. Stat. Pap. Dom. 1625–1626*, p. 168.
[101] *Cal. Stat. Pap. Dom. 1628–1629*, p. 579; *Cal. Stat. Pap. Dom. 1629–1631*, pp. 111, 163.
[102] *Cal. Stat. Pap. Dom. 1625–1626*, pp. 341, 346, 460, 475.
[103] *Cal. Stat. Pap. Dom. 1635–1636*, p. 445.
[104] Gunther, 'The great astrolabe and other scientific instruments of Humphrey Cole', pp. 310–14.
[105] *Cal. Stat. Pap. Dom. 1619–1623*, pp. 5, 525.

constructing engines for fireworks, fireships, torpedoes and submarines, the last of which was envisaged as the secret weapon of the English enabling them to lift the siege of the French army on the Huguenot city of La Rochelle. Although the scheme failed, Drebbel was rewarded handsomely for his efforts,[106] as he was to be again rewarded in 1627 when some water engines of his design rendered him £100.[107]

Richard Delamain provides yet another interesting example. Having recently obtained the patronage of Charles I, Delamain was granted permission to travel abroad in 1637 – presumably in search of inventions that might prove of some use – as well as an allowance of £30 and a servant.[108] The following year Delamain petitioned for an appointment as King's Engineer, which was almost certainly granted, for shortly afterwards he was busy engaging workers to carry out Charles's request for mathematical instruments.[109] By 1643 Delamain's attention appears to have shifted towards military matters, for in that year he received permission to publish a book on fortifications, in the writing of which he took great pains.[110] By the outbreak of the Civil War mathematical expertise was applied as a matter of course in fortifications, as was already noted in the work carried out by Chillingworth as the Engineer of the King's forces.[111]

A topic which has been approached only tangentially, yet lies at the heart of the 'clientage system', involves the question of rewards – both short-term and long-term – of those mathematicians, instrument-makers and engineers engaged by the upper classes. Although a reward was usually forthcoming upon the presentation of a book – Prince Henry was in the habit of giving between £3 and £5 for each dedication[112] – the authors could not expect to subsist on such a haphazard basis. In terms of remuneration, the immediate reward was less important than a long-term settlement. Those who sought patronage hoped either to be employed directly by the patron, often in his household, or to acquire employment through the latter's intervention. For the most part employment in the patron's household entailed service either as his chaplain or as the tutor of his children. But even this employment was regarded as temporary by most clients; while a patron's death usually signalled an end to a chaplain's services, his children would require the services of a tutor for

[106] *Cal. Stat. Pap. Dom. 1629–1631*, pp. 212, 215.
[107] *Cal. Stat. Pap. Dom. 1627–1628*, p. 206.
[108] *Cal. Stat. Pap. Dom. 1636–1637*, pp. 289, 392.
[109] *Cal. Stat. Pap. Dom. 1637–1638*, p. 121.
[110] *Journal of the House of Lords*, vol. 6, p. 171.
[111] See p. 109 above.
[112] Quoted by E. H. Miller, *The Professional Writer in Elizabethan England* (Cambridge, Mass., 1959), p. 126.

no more than a few years. The uncertain future faced by almost all clients ensured that the search for an assured income remained paramount in their minds. For their part, however, most patrons were reluctant either to be drawn into a long-term commitment or to assume the entire burden of financial support. Thus, while many patrons would go so far as to employ their clients in their households on a temporary basis or to procure for them a church living or a state office, only a few would commit themselves further. Indeed, from the second half of the sixteenth century there occurred a sharp increase in the number of cases in which peers employed their offices to ensure that university fellowships and church or state offices were allocated to the candidates of their choice.[113] Having once acquired some long-term means of employment for their clients, these men considered their obligations fulfilled.

Occasionally, however, the installation of a client in the first available position was intended to satisfy his immediate needs, while ensuring that he remained available for future employment. Such was the case when John Whitgift, Archbishop of Canterbury, was urged by the Privy Council to bestow on Richard Hakluyt the London living of Great All Hallowes in 1599. Although Hakluyt may have admirably fulfilled his duties while serving the English embassy in France in the late 1580s, the rationale for his later appointment was his usefulness in applied science. Hakluyt, it was said,

hath bestowed his tyme and taken very great paynes in matters of navigacion and dyscoveryes, a labor of great desert and use, wherein there maie be often occacion to imploie him, and therefore our desire ys for the good of her Majesty's service that he might be provided of some competent living to reside in these partes.[114]

What is made strikingly clear in all these examples of patronage – both private and public – is that the client was expected to attune his talents and energies to those of his employer. At certain times his sole task was to construct curious mechanical devices for the patron's amusement, while at other times the immediate needs of the nation took precedence.

In view of the mechanism of patronage, it is not surprising that the employment of men solely for research purposes was almost unprecedented. Not that various mathematicians and astronomers did not strive to procure such patronage. Such remained the life-long ambition of John Dee. In 1563, for example, he asked Sir William Cecil to procure for him the learned leisure of which his country and the republic of letters would reap the fruit.[115] This was also the ambition of Thomas Lydiat in the following generation. Both tried to convince those in power that it would prove to

[113] See Stone, *The Crisis of the Aristocracy*, pp. 446–7.
[114] *Acts of the Privy Council*, 1599–1600, pp. 330–1.
[115] J. E. Bailey, 'Dee and Trithemius's "Steganography"', *Notes & Queries*, 5th Ser., XI (1879), 402.

their benefit to support 'pure' research as well as applied mathematics. Most such attempts at persuasion did not bear fruit. Sir Hugh Platt, writing in 1594, predicted the bright future that might be England's if only the needed support was forthcoming: 'and were it the good will and pleasure of [Queen Elizabeth] ... to propound some liberall stipende for all such of her ingenious Subjects as should bring forth any profitable or rare particulars ... I would hope to see a new revolution of the first golden age.' Owing to the lack of such patronage, the forecast for many men remained gloomy indeed.

there remaine a secret number of choice wits, who being full fraught of more necessarie, yea more invaluable commoditie, then either the East or West Indies are able to afford, are nonetheless forced to consume their daies in melancholie, & (almost to the hazard of their soules) to burie their talents in the bottomles pit of oblivion.[116]

There were certain exceptions to the situation we have been describing, and these exceptions are as instructive for what they suggest about patronage in our period as the rule. In those cases in which the theoretical, as well as the practical, aspects of the mathematical sciences were encouraged, the patron was invariably an active participant in the scientific process as well as an admirer who found them delightful and useful. The Earl of Northumberland both supported and participated in the scientific work of Harriot, Torporley and Warner, while in the next generation Sir Charles Cavendish carried on the tradition of patron and contributor to the theoretical sciences. Unlike most patrons whose active involvement in government ruled out all but the most elementary contact with the work being carried out, these men were in retirement from public life – Northumberland in the Tower – and consequently able to devote all their energy to science. For all intents and purposes they were men of science as well as patrons of science. Although certain other aristocratic patrons might have appreciated and delighted in the mathematical bases of navigation, ballistics or surveying, their appreciation was confined to the visible mathematical phenomena. More often than not these men of affairs expected those supported by them to harness their theoretical knowledge to the practical problems at hand. Fortunately, before 1640 the distinction between theory and practice was far less rigid than it was to become later in the century and research into magnetism, longitudes, mechanics or logarithms could be either theoretical or practical, depending upon the demands of the situation.

An additional avenue of patronage was the church. However, as previously mentioned, the choice of a career in the church was a problematic one for many men of science; the taking of holy orders and

[116] H. Platt, *The Jewell House of Art and Nature* (London, 1594), sig. B2–B2v.

the devotion to pastoral duties tended to conflict with their dedication to scientific pursuits. Nevertheless, we still encounter many prominent mathematicians and astronomers who held church livings at some time, including William Bedwell, William Oughtred, Jeremiah Horrox, Thomas Lydiat and William Barlow. This apparent contradiction may be explained, at least in part, by the very system of patronage we have been examining. First, owing to the scarcity of suitable employment, some men settled for a career in the church. A few others – including Hakluyt – were installed in church livings by patrons as a means of reward. In this respect these livings served as sinecures. Since the number of positions was limited, patrons did not always distinguish greatly between a college fellowship, preferment in the church, or an appointment to an ambassadorial staff. All such employments were allocated as rewards for services rendered.

Occasionally, however, continued employment in the church, or for that matter the refusal to surrender a university fellowship, were in defiance of the patronage system. Having acquired such appointments at the outset of their careers, some men enjoyed the ability to devote themselves to scientific pursuits, free from the demands of patrons. Again and again we encounter this phenomenon. Thomas Allen repeatedly refused to leave his beloved Oxford for any dignity of office, a bishopric included. Joseph Mede was another not to be lured away from his university. William Oughtred was content with his living at Albury, as were presumably Lancelot Morehouse, Edward Davenant and many other divines. For these men the conflict between their commitment to science and their duties as churchmen was resolved in an original manner. Although they all fulfilled the pastoral duties required of them, unlike most divines, they did not pursue their theological studies into publications. Either they published nothing at all, or their publications consisted of works of a scientific nature only. Those few who did publish in both fields – including William Fulke and, later, Seth Ward and Isaac Barrow – published their theological works only after they ceased publishing their scientific works.

Another advantage of church preferment was that the bishops who extracted much of the patronage were themselves frequently scholars who were in a position to reward intellectuals without, however, directing their talents to specific ends. Lancelot Andrewes, George Abbot, John Williams and William Laud are the most important of these patrons. This is not to deny that divines were sometimes called upon to apply themselves to the needs of the state, the colonizing enterprise or the instruction of the upper classes: only that the pressures brought to bear upon them were measurably less than those brought to bear upon men whose very livelihood depended upon the monarchs or the great peers of the realm.

Ironically, such freedom from the pressures of public life resulted in the neglect of their scientific work after their death. On the other hand those men who chose to attach themselves to the great patrons – and consequently left behind more visible evidence of their scientific pursuits – are the men of science remembered today.

Conclusion

The purpose of this book has been to suggest the continuity of scientific activity in England from the middle of the sixteenth until the middle of the seventeenth century, exposing the often-made differentiation between the pre-1640 and the post-1640 generation as both arbitrary and unjustified. Admittedly, the generation after 1640 witnessed the establishment of England as a major scientific centre for the first time since the Middle Ages. However, the fact that England lagged behind the Continent in terms of scientific creativity during the previous century does not mean that scientific enterprise was lacking. Although before 1640 England produced few scientists and philosophers of the first rank – William Gilbert, Francis Bacon, Thomas Harriot, Henry Briggs and William Harvey being virtually the only men that merit the distinction – it has been my aim to demonstrate that the scientific community in the eighty years leading up to 1640 was receptive to ideas infiltrating from the Continent, and so laying the foundation for the rapid fermentation that characterized the latter half of the seventeenth century.

As regards the 'worth' of the scientific activity carried on in the period between 1560 and 1640, it is anachronistic to isolate for study only those men who allegedly advocated modern cosmologies or only those aspects of their corpus that subsequently came to be regarded as consequential for the genesis of modern science. Especially before, but even after, 1640 elements of the old and the new, the rational and the irrational, the scientifically productive and the scientific dead-end were almost always present to some extent in the scientific pursuits of English men of science. In this context the contribution of the general scholar, the man for whom science was only one component of a many-faceted intellectual activity, has been stressed. Although these men, many of whom were university-educated, varied widely in talent, devotion to science, originality and eagerness to accept new cosmologies, they collaborated on scientific projects and commented upon the new modes of thought – both among themselves as well as with contemporaries in London, elsewhere in England and, most significantly, on the Continent – thereby contributing to scientific enterprise. Moreover, it has been demonstrated that the networks of association that evolved around some of the most active men of science in our period intersected at a number of points to form one, elaborate, interlocking scientific community. Indicative of the cohesion of this community are the absence of any attitude of disrespect or superiority on the part of London-based men of science towards their counterparts in the universities and the readiness with which they returned to Oxford and Cambridge as soon as long-term scientific employment was forthcoming.

Indeed, seminal to this book is the belief that the universities played a vital role in this incubatory period of English science, helping to foster a generation of men able to turn to account the implications of the scientific modes of thought that were becoming increasingly apparent during the second quarter of the seventeenth century. There is little justification for the frequently made allegation that mathematics was not included in the undergraduate curriculum. Not only does an examination of the university and college statutes in effect for the period fail to confirm a bias against mathematics; there is a significant body of evidence to suggest that students were exposed to mathematical instruction with regularity as undergraduates, and that this instruction was elaborated upon during the M.A. course of studies. Whatever evidence shedding light on the identity of the mathematical lecturers or the content of their mathematical instruction has survived suggests the adequacy of mathematical instruction. Although instructors were not always 'progressive' and the knowledge they conveyed was sometimes 'conservative', students were exposed to the recent scientific findings and competing modes of thought circulating at the time. Those students who were stimulated to interpret differently the material presented to them and to seek further scientific knowledge could always avail themselves of a significant number of scientifically oriented members of the university available for consultation. Thus, evidence relevant to the mathematical education of men of science suggests that they embarked upon their scientific studies at a very early stage in their education, and almost always were assisted in their endeavours by members of the university community.

Although the framework of mathematical instruction at both Oxford and Cambridge remained fairly constant throughout the period 1560–1640, there were significant developments. By the beginning of the seventeenth century the elementary textbooks of Recorde, Gemma Frisius and Valerius were being increasingly replaced by the more comprehensive and elaborate expositions of Clavius, Maestlin, Blundeville and Keckermann. A growing awareness of the need for endowed mathematical posts is also evident. Thus, in the period under review there occurred the creation of many college lectureships in mathematics as well as the foundation of the two Savilian chairs of geometry and astronomy. The effect of these endowments was twofold: they provided encouragement for more sustained mathematical activity and contributed towards the growing professionalization of the mathematical sciences.

Although London's importance as a scientific centre remains undisputed, this book has sought to reinterpret certain of the social forces that contributed to the peculiar character of 'London science'. Owing to the concentration of wealth, patronage and employment opportunities in London on the one hand, and the scarcity of scientific posts and the restrictions on fellowships at the universities on the other, the capital attracted many scientifically oriented graduates and fellows. This steady trickle of university men into London, however, should not be extrapolated out of its context and interpreted as an intellectual bias of the universities against scientific inquiry. Neither should the concentration of scientifically minded men in the capital lead us to conclude that developments in adult education followed as a matter of course. There is virtually no evidence to indicate that Gresham College ever fulfilled an important educational function among the multitude of London's mathematical practitioners. In fact, the evidence suggests that the vast majority of these practitioners had little conception of, or concern for, the sophisticated scientific theories that remained the domain of the Gresham professors and only the most talented scientific practitioners.

Most significant, it was precisely the social forces that caused many university men to seek their fortune in London that brought about a reorientation of their talents. Scientific activity that previously had been dispersed between many fields came increasingly to be channelled into avenues that, to a large extent, were determined by the preoccupations of their patrons. A proliferation of practical projects to ensure England's place among the powers and the advancement of their patrons' fortunes as well as mechanical devices for the amusement of the upper classes was the immediate result of this redirection of energy. Undoubtedly, some of these men continued to pursue the 'purer' aspects of science, but for the most part our evidence is limited to those projects they undertook while in the service of their patrons, the evidence of other pursuits most probably disappearing with their death. These London-based men of science, however, continued to share with their contemporaries in the universities a similar intellectual framework as well as common scholarly interests, the main difference being that the former earned their livelihood by exploiting the possibilities opened up by the widespread interest in applied science.

Bibliography

A. MANUSCRIPT SOURCES

BODLEIAN LIBRARY, OXFORD

Benefactors' Book, vol. 1
MS Arch B.C.O.* A list of books missing from Henry Savile's library
MSS Auct.
    F.L.2 Collation of Greek musical manuscripts made for Selden
    F.I.3 Gaudentius's *Harmonica* and Alypius's *Introductio musica*
MSS Ashmole
    209 Richard Foster Adversaria
    242 Letters from Christopher Heydon to Henry Briggs
    350, 394, 1441 Fragments of Thomas Allen's writings
    356(5) Philip Sidney's horoscope cast by Thomas Allen
    388 Thomas Allen's commentary on Ptolemy's astrology
    1057 Commonplace book of Arthur Dee
    1789 John Dee's proposal for the reformation of the calendar
MS Ballard
    44 Correspondence of Thomas James
MSS Bodley
    313 Correspondence of Thomas Lydiat
    504 Nicholas Kratzer's description of his 'horoptrum'
    664 Thomas Lydiat's 'Mesolabium geometricum'
MS Clarendon
    l Letter of Alexander Lower to Thomas Harriot
MS d'Orville
    52 Letter of Henry Briggs to Lucas Holsten
MS Locke
    c.31 Commonplace book of John Locke
Oxford University Archives
    Box of transcripts of all inventories mentioning books
    NEP/Supra Register I Register of Convocation & Congregation, 1535–63
    NEP/Supra Register KK Register of Convocation & Congregation, 1564–82
    NEP/Supra Register N Register of Convocation, 1611–22
MS Don.
    D. 152 Commonplace book of John Mansell, 1601

MSS Rawlinson
  Rawl. Lett. 83 Correspondence of G. J. Vossius
  c. 849 Letter of Ambrose Ussher to Henry Briggs
  D. 47 Notebook of Daniel Featley, c. 1605
  D. 188 Guide of study, c. 1675
  D. 233 Commonplace book of Benjamin Gostlet c. 1650
  D. 746 Commonplace book of Nicholas Tufton, 1649
  D. 1147 Anonymous commonplace book of an Oxford student, c. 1630
MS Sancroft
  122 Catalogue of Sancroft's library
MSS Savile
  6 Notebook of Henry Savile
  10 Transcripts of scientific manuscripts made by Henry Savile and George Carew
  26–32 Henry Savile's lecture notes
  108 Henry Savile's commonplace book and correspondence
MSS Selden Supra
  79 Notes of Brian Twyne
  108–9 Correspondence of John Selden
  120 Elegies for Thomas Allen
  121–2 Astronomical and musical transcripts made for John Selden
MS Smith
  74 Letters addressed to William Camden
MSS Tanner
  72–5 Correspondence of Samuel Ward
  204 Edmund Chilmead's treatise on sounds
MS Top. Oxon
  c. 326 Letter of Johannes Praetorius to Henry Savile
MS Wood
  D.10 Library Catalogue of John Rainolds
  F.45 Correspondence of Anthony Wood
Sig.AA.1. Med. Seld. Printed book at the back of which is a catalogue of the Barocci
    Collection of Greek manuscripts

ALL SOULS COLLEGE, OXFORD (DEPOSITED AT THE BODLEIAN LIBRARY)

95 Ptolemy's 'Almagest'

BRASENOSE COLLEGE, OXFORD

80 Notebook of Thomas Sixsmith

CHRIST CHURCH, OXFORD

Benefactors' Register
'Dean and Chapter Book' Lists of college officials

CORPUS CHRISTI COLLEGE, OXFORD (DEPOSITED AT THE BODLEIAN
LIBRARY UNLESS OTHERWISE INDICATED)

40 Robert Hegge's treatise on dials (in the college library)
66 Manilius's treatise on astronomy
157 The 'Chronology' of Marianus Scotus
254–65, 279–80 Brian Twyne's notebooks (MS 280 in the college library)
430 Robert Hegge's commonplace book (in the college library)

EXETER COLLEGE, OXFORD

73–5 Notebooks of Edward Davenant
A.I(2) 1560 statutes of Exeter College

JESUS COLLEGE, OXFORD (DEPOSITED AT THE BODLEIAN LIBRARY)

87 Anonymous commonplace book of early seventeenth century
92 Commonplace book of Samuel Brown, *c.* 1600

LINCOLN COLLEGE, OXFORD (DEPOSITED AT THE BODLEIAN LIBRARY)

124 Commonplace book of a Cambridge student, *c.* 1610

MAGDALEN COLLEGE, OXFORD (DEPOSITED AT THE BODLEIAN LIBRARY)

Gr 12 Quintilian's *Liber de arte musica*

NEW COLLEGE, OXFORD

281 Ptolemy's 'Almagest'

QUEEN'S COLLEGE, OXFORD

196, 224 Natural philosophy commentaries by Richard Crakanthorpe
241 John Rainolds's oration 'In Praise of Astronomy'
390 Diary of Thomas Crosfield

ST JOHN'S COLLEGE, OXFORD

168 Gaudentius's *Harmonica* and Alypius's *Introductio musica*

UNIVERSITY COLLEGE, OXFORD (DEPOSITED AT THE BODLEIAN LIBRARY)

47–9 Notebooks of Robert Payne, 1616–17
153 Nathaniel Carpenter's treatise on optics
175 Thomas Chasey's commonplace book, *c.* 1640

WADHAM COLLEGE, OXFORD

A4/24 Astronomical treatise of John Goodridge, *c.* 1600

WORCESTER COLLEGE, OXFORD

5.5 Edward Davenant's notebook

CAMBRIDGE UNIVERSITY LIBRARY

Dd.III.17 Notebook of John Stay
Dd.III.24 Commonplace book of Henry Ford, 1640
Dd.III.64 Letter of Thomas Lydiat to Henry Spelman
Dd.IV.5 Library catalogue of William Moore
Dd.IV.81 Medical notebook of William Moore
Dd.IX.44 Commonplace book of John Smith
Additional MSS
    102 Commonplace book of Edmund Lee, 1607
Cambridge University Archives
    Registry 51 Proctors' accounts
    Univ. Acct. 1(1–4) Vice-Chancellors' vouchers to the accounts
    2 Cambridge University Audit Book

CHRIST'S COLLEGE, CAMBRIDGE

'Account Books of Joseph Mede', 4 vols.

GONVILLE AND CAIUS COLLEGE, CAMBRIDGE

73 Letters of Sir Christopher Heydon to John Fletcher

BRITISH LIBRARY, LONDON

Additional MSS
    4387, 4394–4404 Notebooks of John Pell, *c.* 1625–80
    4395 Astronomical notes of Thomas Aylesbury
    6193–6209 Notebooks of John Ward relating to Gresham College
    6782–89 Harriot Papers
    27606 Letters of Sackvile Crow and his tutor to his father
    36299 Correspondence of William Camden
    36674 Magical tracts belonging to Gabriel Harvey
    46139 Alchemical notebook of Alexander Gill, the elder
MSS Cotton
    Julius C.V. Correspondence of William Camden
    Julius F.XI Commonplace book of William Camden, *c.* 1570
MSS Harleian
    191 Commonplace book of Simonds D'Ewes, *c.* 1618

374 Letters of William Boswell

3230 Commonplace book of an anonymous Cambridge student, late 16th century

4048 Commonplace book of an anonymous student at Christ Church, Oxford, *c.* 1581

6360 Henry Spelman's notebook, *c.* 1581

6796 The Cambridge lectures of Henry Briggs and Robert Payne's translation of Galileo's *Le Meccaniche*

6993, 6995, 7011 Letters to Henry and Thomas Savile

MSS Lansdowne

  20 List of students attending university lectures at Cambridge in 1575

  57 List of students attending university lectures at Cambridge in 1588

  93 Letter from Robert Payne to Gilbert Sheldon

  107 John Gerard's petition for a botanic garden at Cambridge

  841 Letters from Robert Payne to Gilbert Sheldon

MSS Royal

  12A.XXV William Buckley's treatise on the ring-dial

  12B.XI Astrological treatise by Richard Forster

  12E.II Astrological treatise by Richard Forster

  17A.V John Marr's treatise on the construction of a ring-dial

  17A.XXXIII Hollinshed's treatise on the construction of a ring-dial

  17A.XXVIII Edmund Gunter's treatise on the dials of White-hall

MSS Sloane

  427, 548 Notebooks of John Beale, *c.* 1635–70

  651 Description of Edward Wright's mechanical sphere

  1472 Commonplace book of John Hearne, *c.* 1660

  1838 Thomas Lushington's commentary on Proclus

  2563 John Fletcher's treatise on urines

  3722 Commonplace book of Alexander Gill, the elder

ÖSTERREICHISCHE NATIONALBIBLIOTHEK, VIENNA

9737[217] Letters of the Saviles and Henry Wotton

BIBLIOTHÈQUE NATIONALE, PARIS

Dupuy MSS

  348, 632, 706, 797, 836 Letters of Henry and Thomas Savile

TRINITY COLLEGE, DUBLIN

125–6 Edward Lively's 'Chronologia seu notitia temporum'

150 Commonplace book of Nathaniel Carpenter

382–6 Notebooks of John Bainbridge

387, 396 Notebooks of Edward Wright

443 Commonplace book of Roger Fry

794 Thomas Aylesbury's astronomical notes

SHEFFIELD UNIVERSITY LIBRARY

Hartlib Papers

PETWORTH HOUSE

HMC 241/1–x Thomas Harriot's papers

PUBLIC RECORD OFFICE, LONDON

P.C.C. 110 Audley Thomas Allen's will
SP 46/15 Notebook of the Carnsew brothers

WARWICKSHIRE COUNTY RECORD OFFICE

CR 136 B3468 Commonplace book of the Newdigate brothers, *c.* 1618

B. PRIMARY SOURCES

Abbot, G. *A Briefe Description of the Whole Worlde*, London, 1599.
Acts of the Privy Council, 1599–1600.
The Sonnets of William Alabaster, ed. G. M. Story and H. Gardner, Oxford, 1959.
Ascham, R. *English Works*, ed. W. A. Wright, Cambridge, 1904, repr. 1970.
   The Whole Works of Roger Ascham, ed. J. A. Giles, 3 vols., London, 1864–5.
Ashe, S. *Gray Hayres Crowned with Grace, A Sermon Preached at Redrith, near London,*
   Aug. 1 1654, at the Funeral of that Reverend, Eminently Learned and Faithfull
   Minister of Jesus Christ Mr Thomas Gataker, London, 1655.
Atwell, G. *An Apology, or, Defence of the Divine Art of Natural Astrologie*, London,
   1660.
   The Faithfull Surveyour Discovering Divers Errours in Land-measuring, Cambridge,
   1658.
Aubrey, J. *Brief Lives*, ed. A. Clark, 2 vols., Oxford, 1898.
   Natural History of Wiltshire, ed. J. Britton, London, 1847.
Bacon, F. *Resuscitatio, or, Bringing into Publick Light Severall Pieces, of the Works,*
   Civil, Historical, Philosophical, & Theological, hitherto Sleeping, ed. W. Rawley,
   London, 1657.
   The Works of Francis Bacon, ed. J. Spedding, R. L. Ellis and D. D. Heath, 14 vols.,
   London, 1857–74.
Bailey, J. 'Dee and Thrithemius's "Steganography"', *Notes & Queries*, 5th Ser.,
   XI (1879), 401–2, 422–3.
Bainbridge, J. *An Astronomicall Description of the late Comet from the 18. of Novemb.*
   1618 to the 16. of December following, London, 1619.
Baker, A. *Memorials of Father Augustine Baker 1575–1641*, ed. J. McCann, London,
   1933.
Ball, T. *Life of the Renowned Doctor Preston Writ by his Pupil Master Thomas Ball*
   in the year 1628, ed. E. W. Harcourt, Oxford and London, 1885.

Barksdale, C. *An Oxford Conference of Philomathes and Polymathes*, London, 1660.

Barlow, T. *The Genuine Remains of that Learned Prelate Dr Thomas Barlow late Lord Bishop of Lincoln*, London, 1693.

Barlow, W. *Magneticall Advertisements: or Divers Pertinent Observations, and Approved Experiments concerning the Nature and Properties of the Load-Stone: very Pleasant for Knowledge, and most Needful for Practise of Travelling, or Framing of Instruments fit for Travellers both by Sea and Land*, London, 1616.

The Navigators Supply, London, 1597.

Barnard, J. *Theologo-Historicus, or the True Life of the most Reverend Divine, and Excellent Historian Peter Heylin*, London, 1683.

Barrow, I. *The Geometrical Lectures*, trans. E. Stone, London, 1735.

Bedwell, W. *Via Regia ad Geometriam: the Way to Geometry, being Necessary and Useful for Astronomers, Geographers, Land-Meters, Seamen, Engineers, Architecks, Paynters, Gravers etc.*, London, 1636.

Biographia Britannica, ed. A. Kippis, 6 vols., 1747–66.

Bion, N. *The Construction and Principal Uses of Mathematical Instruments Translated from the French of M. Bion, Chief Instrument-maker to the French King*, trans. E. Stone, London, 1723.

Birch, T. (ed.) *The Court and Times of Charles the First*, 2 vols., London, 1848.

The Court and Times of James the First, 2 vols., London, 1848.

The Life of Henry Prince of Wales, Eldest Son of King James I, London, 1760.

Blagrave, J. *The Art of Dyalling*, London, 1609.

Baculum Familliare Catholicon sive Generale, A Book of the Making and Use of a Staffe, London, 1590.

Blundeville, M. *His Exercises, containing Sixe Treatises the Titles wherof are set down in the next printed page: which Treatises are verie Necessarie to be Read and Learned of all young Gentlemen that have not bene Exercised in such Disciplines, and yet are Desirous to have Knowledge as well in Cosmographie, Astronomie*, London, 1594.

Boas, F. S. *The Diary of Thomas Crosfield*, London, 1935.

Boase, C. W. *Registrum Collegii Exoniensis*, Oxford, 1894.

Bodley, T. *Letters of Sir Thomas Bodley to the University of Oxford 1598–1611*, ed. G. W. W. Wheeler, Oxford, 1927.

Letters of Sir Thomas Bodley to Thomas James, ed. G. W. W. Wheeler, Oxford, 1926.

Boyle, R. *Selected Philosophical Papers of Robert Boyle*, ed. M. A. Stewart, Manchester, 1979.

The Works of the Honourable Robert Boyle, ed. T. Birch, 6 vols., London, 1772.

Bradley, J. *Miscellaneous Works and Correspondence of the Rev. James Bradley, D.D. F.R.S.*, ed. S. P. Rigaud, Oxford, 1832.

Briggs, H. *Arithmetica Logarithmica*, London, 1624.

Logarithmetica Britannica, ed. A. J. Thompson, 2 vols., Cambridge, 1952.

Trigonometria Britannica: sive de doctrina triangulorum, ed. Henry Gellibrand, Goudae, 1633.

Browne, Sir T. *The Works of Sir Thomas Browne*, ed. G. Keynes, 4 vols., London, 1964.

The Works of Sir Thomas Browne, ed. S. Wilkin, 3 vols., London, 1852.

Bruno, G. *La Cena de le Ceneri*, ed. G. Aquilecchia, Turin, 1955.

Bullialdus, I. *Astronomia philolaica*, Paris, 1645.

Burton, W. and Bathurst, G. *In viri doctissimi, clarissimi, optimi, Thomae Alleni ... orationes binae*, London, 1632.

Buxton, J. 'An Elizabethan reading list', *TLS*, 24 March 1972, pp. 343–4.

Camden, W. *Annales. The True and Royall History of the Famous Empresse Elizabeth*, London, 1625.

    V. Cl. Gulielmi Camdeni et illustrium virorum ad G. Camdenum epistolae. cum appendice varii argumenti accesserunt annalium regni Regis Jacobi I. Apparatus, ed. Thomas Smith, London, 1691.

Carleton, D. *Dudley Carleton to John Chamberlain 1603–1624*, ed. M. Lee Jr, New Jersey, 1972.

Carpenter, N. *Geography Delineated Forth in Two Bookes*, Oxford, 1625.

    Philosophia libera triplici exercitationum decade proposita, Frankfurt, 1621.

Cary, H. (ed.) *Memorials of the Great Civil War in England from 1646 to 1652*, 2 vols., London, 1842.

Caus, S. de *Institution Harmonique*, Frankfurt, 1615.

    La Perspective, avec la Raison des Ombres et Miroirs, London, 1612.

Cavendish, Margaret, Duchess of Newcastle *The Life of William Cavendish Duke of Newcastle*, ed. C. H. Firth, London, n.d.

Chamberlain, J. *The Letters of John Chamberlain*, ed. N. E. McClure, 2 vols., Philadelphia, 1939.

Clark, A. and Boase, C. W. *The Register of the University of Oxford*, 2 vols. in 5, Oxf. Hist. Soc., Oxford, 1885–9.

Clark, S. *The Lives of Sundry Eminent Persons in this Later Age, in Two Parts*, London, 1683.

Collins, A. *Letters and Memorials of State in the Reign of Queen Mary, Queen Elizabeth, King James, King Charles the First, Part of the Reign of King Charles the Second, and Oliver's Usurpations*, 2 vols., London, 1746.

Corbet, R. *The Poems of Richard Corbet*, ed. J. W. A. Bennett and H. R. Trevor-Roper, Oxford, 1955.

Cornwallis, Sir C. *The Life and Death of our late most Incomparable and Heroique Prince, Henry Prince of Wales*, London, 1641.

Culverwell, N. *An Elegant and Learned Discourse of the Light of Nature*, ed. R. A. Greene and H. MacCallum, Toronto, 1971.

Debus, A. G. *Robert Fludd and his Philosophical Key*, New York, 1979.

Dee, J. *The Private Diary of Dr. John Dee and the Catalogue of his Library of Manuscripts*, ed. J. O. Halliwell, Camden Soc., vol. 19, London, 1842.

De Jordy, A. and Fletcher, H. F. '*A Library for Younger Schollers*' Compiled by an English Scholar Priest about 1655, Urbana, 1961.

Delamain, R. *The Making, Description and Use of a Small Portable Instrument for the Pocket ... in form of a Mixt Trapezia, thus called a Horizontall Quadrant*, London, 1632.

Devon, F. *Issues of the Exchequer being Payments made out of His Majesty's Revenues During the Reign of King James I*, London, 1836.

D'Ewes, S. *The Autobiography and Correspondence of Sir Simonds D'Ewes*, ed. J. O. Halliwell, 2 vols., London, 1845.

Digby, K. *A Discourse concerning the Vegetation of Plants*, London, 1661.

Digges, L. *A Geometrical Practise named Pantometria ... with Sundray Straunge Conclusions, both by Instrument and without, and also by Perspective Glasses ... lately finished by Thomas Digges*, London, 1571.

Digges, T. *An Arithmeticall Militare Treatise, named Stratioticos: compendiously Teaching the Science of Numbers, as well in Fractions as Integers and so much of the Rules and Aequations Algebraicall, and Arte of Numbers Cossicall, as are requisite for the Profession of a Soldier*, London, 1579.

Documents relating to the University and Colleges of Cambridge, 3 vols., London, 1852.

Duport, J. *Musae subsecivae, seu poetica stromata*, Cambridge, 1676.

Duppa, B. *The Correspondence of Bishop Brian Duppa and Sir Justinian Isham, 1650–1660*, ed. G. Isham, Northamptonshire Rec. Soc., vol. 17, Lamport Hall, Northamptonshire, 1955.

Ellis, H. (ed.) *Original Letters, Illustrative of English History*, 11 vols., London, 1824–46.

Evelyn, J. *The Diary of John Evelyn*, ed. E. S. de Beer, 6 vols., Oxford, 1955.

Favaro, Antonio (ed.) *Carteggio inedito di Ticone Brahe, Giovanni Keplero e di altri celebri astronomi e mathematici dei secoli xvi. e xvii. con Giovanni Antonio Magini*, Bologna, 1886.

Fletcher, J. M. (ed.) *Registrum Annalium Collegii Mertonensis 1567–1603*, Oxf. Hist. Soc., New Ser., vol. 24, Oxford, 1976.

Fludd, R. *Integrum morborum mysterium: sive medicinae catholicae*, Frankfurt, 1631.

Foster, S. *Miscellanies, or, Mathematical Lucubrations*, ed. J. Twysden, London, 1659.
The Use of a Quadrant, London, 1627.

Foxe, L. *The Voyages of Captain Luke Foxe of Hull, and Thomas James of Bristol*, ed. M. Christy, Hakluyt Soc., 1st Ser., vols. 88–9, London, 1893.

Fuller, T. *The History of the Worthies of England*, ed. P. A. Nuttall, 3 vols., London, 1840.

Furnivall, F. J. (ed.) *Harrison's Description of England in Shakespeare's Youth*, New Shakespeare Soc., 6th Ser., vols. 1, 5, 8, London, 1877–81.

Gassendi, P. *The Mirrour of True Nobility & Gentility. Being the Life of the Renowned Nicolaus Claudius Fabricius Lord of Peiresk*, trans. W. Rand, London, 1657.
Opera Omnia, 6 vols., Lyons, 1658.

Gataker, T. *A Discours Apologeticall, wherein Lilies Lewd and Lowd Lies in his Merlin or Pasquil for the yeer 1654 are cleerly laid open*, London, 1654.
Thomas Gataker D.D. his Vindication of the Annotations by him published upon ... Jer. 10.2 against Mr William Lillie ... and Mr John Swan, London, 1653.

Gellibrand, H. *A Discourse Mathematicall on the Variation of the Magneticall Needle, together with its admirable Diminution lately Discovered*, London, 1635.
An Epitome of Navigation with a Table of Logarithms, ed. E. Speidell, London, 1674.
An Institution Trigonometricall, London, 1635.

Gerbier, Sir B. *The Interpreter of the Academie for Forrain Languages and All Noble Sciences and Exercises. The First Part*, London, 1648.

Gibson, S. (ed.) *Statuta Antiqua Universitatis Oxoniensis*, Oxford, 1931.

Gilbert, Sir H. 'Queene Elizabethes Achademy', ed. F. J. Furnivall, Early English Text Soc., Extra Ser., vol. 8, London, 1869, pp. 1–12.

Gilbert, William *De Magnete*, London, 1600.
De mundo nostro sublunari philosophia nova, Amsterdam, 1651.

Gill, A. *Longonomia Anglica* (1619), ed. B. Danielsson and A. Gabrielson, 2 vols., Stockholm, 1972.

Gill, A. the younger *The New Starr of the North*, London, 1632.

Glucker, J. 'An autograph letter of Joseph Scaliger to Sir Henry Savile', *Scientiarum Historia*, VIII (1966), 214–24, where the letter is also published.

Godwin, F. *A Catalogue of the Bishops of England, since the First Planting of Christian Religion in this Island, together with a Briefe History of their Lives and Memorable Actions*, 2nd edn, London, 1615.

Gray, G. J. and Palmer, W. M. *Abstracts from the Wills and Testamentary Documents of Printers, Binders, and Stationers of Cambridge, from 1504 to 1699*, London, 1915.

Greaves, J. *The Miscellaneous Works of John Greaves*, ed. T. Birch, 2 vols., London, 1737.

Greaves, T. *De linguae Arabicae utilitate et praestantia: oratio Oxonii habita Iul. 19 1637*, Oxford, 1639.

Gregory, J. *Gregorii Posthuma: or Certain Learned Tracts Written by John Gregorie M.A. and Chaplain of Christ-Church in Oxford*, London, 1650.

Griffiths, J. (ed.) *Statutes of the University of Oxford Codified in the Year 1636*, Oxford, 1888.

Gunter, E. *The Description and Use of his Maiesties Dials in White-Hall Garden*, London, 1624.

The Description and Use of the Sector, the Crosse-staffe and other Instruments, London, 1624.

Hacket, J. *Scrinia Reserata: A Memorial Offered to the Great Deservings of John Williams D.D. who some time held the Places of Ld Keeper of the Great Seal of England, Ld Bishop of Lincoln, and Ld Archbishop of York*, London, 1693.

Hackett, M. B. *The Original Statutes of Cambridge University. The Text and its History*, Cambridge, 1970.

Hajec, T. *Apodixis physica et mathematica de cometis*, Gorlitz, 1581.

Hakewill, G. *An Apologie or Declaration of the Power and Providence of God in the Government of the World*, 3rd edn, Oxford, 1635.

Hakluyt, R. *The Original Writings and Correspondence of the Two Richard Hakluyts*, ed. E. G. R. Taylor, 2 vols., Hakluyt Soc., 2nd Ser., vols. 76–7, London, 1935.

Hales, J. *The Works of the Ever-Memorable Mr. John Hales of Eton*, 3 vols., Glasgow, 1765.

Halliwell, J. O. *A Collection of Letters Illustrative of the Progress of Science in England*, London, 1841.

Handson, R. *Trigonometry: Or the Doctrine of Triangles. First Written in Latine by Bartholmew Pitiscus of Grunberg in Silesia, and now Translated into English by Ra: Handson*, London, 1614.

Harvey, G. *Gabriel Harvey's Marginalia*, ed. G. C. Moore Smith, Stratford-upon-Avon, 1913.

Hearne, T. *Remarks and Collections of Thomas Hearne*, ed. C. E. Doble and others, 11 vols., Oxford, 1885–1925.

Hentzner, P. *Travels in England During the Reign of Queen Elizabeth*, trans. Horace, Earl of Oxford, London, 1797.

Herbert, Sir T. *Memoirs of the Two Last Years of the Reign of that Unparallel'd Prince, of ever blessed memory King Charles I*, London, 1702.

Heth, T. *A Manifest and Apparent Confutation of an Astrologicall Discourse ... with a Briefe Prognostication, or Astrologicall Prediction, of the Conjunction, of the Two Superiour Planets, Saturn and Iupiter*, London, 1583.

Hewlett, J. *The Description and Use of a Quadrant*, London, 1672.

Heydon, C. *An Astrological Discourse with Mathematical Demonstrations proving the Powerful and Harmonical Influence of the Planets and Fixed Stars upon Elementary Bodies, in Justification of the Validity of Astrology*, London, 1650.

Heylin, P. *Memorial of Bishop Waynflete*, ed. J. R. Bloxam, London, 1851.

Microcosmus: or a Little Description of the Great World, Oxford, 1621.

Heywood, J. (trans.) *Collection of Statutes for the University and Colleges of Cambridge*, London, 1840.

Hobbes, T. *The Life of Mr Thomas Hobbes of Malmesbury, Written by himself in a Latine Poem. And now Translated into English*, London, 1680.

Hood, T. *The Use of Both the Globes, Celestiall and Terrestriall*, London, 1590.

The Use of the Celestial Globe in Plano, London, 1590.

The Use of Two Mathematicall Instruments, the Crosse Staffe, (differing from that in Common Use with the Mariners:) and the Jacob's Staffe, London, 1595.

Hopton, A. *Speculum Topographicum, or the Topographicall Glasse*, London, 1611.

Hotman, F. and Hotman, J. *Francisci et Joannis Hotmanorum Epistolae*, ed. J. G. Meelii, Amsterdam, 1700.

Hues, R. *Tractatus de globis*, London, 1594.

Hutchinson, L. *Memoirs of the Life of Colonel Hutchinson*, ed. C. H. Firth, London, 1906.

Isaacson, H. *An Exact Narration of the Life and Death of the Reverend and Learned Prelate, and most Painfull Divine Lancelot Andrewes late Bishop of Winchester*, London, 1650.

James I *The Basilicon Doron of King James VI*, ed. J. Craigie, 2 vols., Scottish Text Soc., 3rd Ser., Edinburgh, 1944–50.

James, M. R. *A Descriptive Catalogue of the Manuscripts in the Library of Gonville and Caius College*, Cambridge, 1907–8.

James, R. (ed.) *Epistola ... Thomae Mori ad Academiam Oxon.*, Oxford, 1633.

The Poems of Richard James, ed. A. B. Grosart, London, 1880.

James, T. *Letters Addressed to Thomas James*, ed. G. W. Wheeler, Oxford, 1933.

Josten, C. H. *Elias Ashmole (1617–92)*, 5 vols., Oxford, 1966.

Journals of the House of Lords.

Justa Funebria Ptolemaei Oxoniensis, Oxford, 1613.

Kempe, A. J. (ed.) *The Loseley Manuscripts*, London, 1836.

Kepler, J. *Gesammelte Werke*, ed. W. Von Dyck and M. Caspar, 18 vols., Munich, 1937–59.

Ker, N. B. (ed.) *Records of All Souls College Library 1437–1600*, Oxford, 1971.

Knappen, M. M. (ed.) *Two Elizabethan Puritan Diaries by Richard Rogers and Samuel Ward*, Chicago and London, 1933.

Kynaston, Sir F. *The Constitutions of the Musaeum Minervae*, London, 1636.

Lake, A. *Sermons [with some Religious and Divine Meditations]*, London, 1629.

Lamb, J. (ed.) *A Collection of Letters, Statutes, and other Documents from the MS Library of Corp. Christ. Coll. illustrative of the History of the University of Cambridge during the period of the Reformation from 1500 to 1572*, London, 1838.

Laud, W. *The Works of the most Reverend Father in God William Laud D.D. sometime Lord Archbishop of Canterbury*, ed. W. Scott and J. Bliss, 7 vols., Oxford, 1847–60.

Leland, J. *The Itinerary of John Leland the Antiquary*, ed. Thomas Hearne, 9 vols., London, 1710–12.

Letters and Papers Foreign and Domestic of the Reign of Henry VIII.

Leurechon, J. *Mathematicall Recreations*, trans. W. Oughtred, London, 1633.

Leybourne, W. *The Line of Proportion, Commonly Called Gunter's Line, Made Easie*, London, 1677.

Lilly, W. *The Last of the Astrologers: Mr William Lilly's History of his Life and Times*, ed. K. M. Briggs, London, 1974.

   Several Observations upon the Life and Death of Charles late King of England, London, 1651.

Lloyd, D. *Memoires of the Lives, Actions, Sufferings & Deaths of those Noble, Revered and Excellent Personages, that Suffered by Death, Sequestration, Decimation, or otherwise, for the Protestant Religion and the Great Principle thereof, Allegiance to their Soveraigne, in our late Intestine Wars, from the year 1637, to the year 1660*, London, 1668.

Locke, J. *The Educational Writings of John Locke*, ed. J. L. Axtell, Cambridge, 1968.

The Lumley Library; The Catalogue of 1609, ed. S. Jayne and F. R. Johnson, London, 1956.

Madox, R. *An Elizabethan in 1582: The Diary of Richard Madox Fellow of All Souls*, ed. E. S. Donno, Hakluyt Soc., 2nd Ser., vol. 147, London, 1976.

Martini, A. and Bassi, D. (eds.) *Catalogus Codicum Graecorum Bibliothecae Ambrosianae*, 2 vols., Milan, 1906.

Mayor, J. E. B. (ed.) *Early Statutes of the College of St John the Evangelist in the University of Cambridge*, Cambridge, 1859.

Mede, J. *The Works of the Pious and Profoundly Learned Joseph Mede*, ed. J. Worthington, London, 1677.

Miller, W. *A Sermon Preached at the Funerall of the Worshipfull Gilbert Davies*, London, 1621.

Millington, E. *Bibliotheca Cudworthiana*, London, 1691.

   Bibliotheca Oweniana, London, 1684.

Milton, J. *Milton: Private Correspondence and Academic Exercises*, trans. P. B. Tillyard, Cambridge, 1932.

Minet, W. 'Some unpublished plans of Dover Harbour', *Archaeologia*, LXXII (1921), 184–224.

Monson, Sir W. *The Naval Tracts of Sir William Monson*, ed. M. Oppenheim, 5 vols., Navy Rec. Soc., vols. 22, 23, 43, 45, 47, London, 1902–14.

More, R. *The Carpenters Rule*, London, 1602.

Newton, J. *Institutio Mathematica*, London, 1654.

Nichols, J. *The Progresses and Public Processions of Queen Elizabeth*, 3 vols., London, 1823.

Norman, R. *The Newe Attractive, containyng a Short Discourse of the Magnes or Lodestone*, London, 1581.

Osborn, F. *The Miscellaneous Works*, 2 vols., London, 1722.

Oughtred, W. *The Circles of Proportion and the Horizontall Instrument*, trans. W. Forster, London, 1632.

    Clavis Mathematicae, London, 1631.

    To the English Gentrie, and all others Studious of the Mathematicks which shall be Readers hereof. The just Apologie of Wil: Oughtred, against the Slaunderous Insinuations of Richard Delamain, in a Pamphlet called Grammelogia, London, 1632.

Oxinden, H. *The Oxinden Letters, 1607–1642*, ed. D. Gardiner, London, 1933.

Parkinson, J. *Theatrum botanicum*, London, 1635.

Parr, R. *The Life of the Most Reverend Father in God, James Ussher Late Lord Arch-Bishop of Armagh, Primate and Metropolitan of all Ireland with a Collection of 300 Letters*, London, 1686.

Peacham, H. *The Complete Gentleman*, ed. V. B. Heltzel, Ithaca, 1962.

Pears, S. A. (ed.) *The Correspondence of Sir Philip Sidney and Hubert Languet*, London, 1845.

Pemble, W. *A Briefe Introduction to Geography*, Oxford, 1630.

    The Workes of that Late Learned Minister of God's Holy Word Mr William Pemble, 4th edn, Oxford, 1659.

Pett, P. *The Autobiography of Phineas Pett*, ed. W. G. Perrin, Navy Rec. Soc., vol. 51, London, 1918.

Philippes, H. *The Advancement of the Art of Navigation, in Two Parts*, London, 1657.

Platt, H. *The Jewell House of Art and Nature*, London, 1594.

Plot, R. *Natural History of Oxford-Shire*, Oxford, 1677.

Pocock, E. *The Theological Works of the Learned Dr. Pocock*, ed. L. Twells, 2 vols., London, 1740.

Pope, W. *The Life of the Right Reverend Father of God, Seth, Lord Bishop of Salisbury*, ed. J. B. Bamborough, Oxford, 1961.

Potter, F. *An Interpretation of the Number 666*, Oxford, 1642.

Powell, T. *Elementa opticae: nova, facili & compendiosa methodo explicata*, London, 1651.

    Humane Industry, or a History of the Most Curious Manual Arts etc., London, 1661.

A Projecte, Conteyninge the State, Order, and Manner of Governmente of the University of Cambridge: As Now it is to be Seene in the Three and Fortieth Yeare of the Raigne of our most Gracious and Sovereigne Lady Queen Elizabeth, Cambridge, 1769.

The Responsa Scholarum of the English College, Rome, ed. A. Kenny, 2 vols., Catholic Rec. Soc., vols. 54, 55, Newport, Mon., 1962.

Ridley, M. *Magneticall Animadversions. Made by Marke Ridley, Doctor in Physicke Upon Certaine Magneticall Advertisements, lately Published, From Maister William Barlow*, London, 1617.

    A Short Treatise of Magneticall Bodies and Motions, London, 1613.

Rigaud, S. P. and Rigaud, S. J. (eds.) *Correspondence of Scientific Men of the Seventeenth Century*, 2 vols., Oxford, 1841–62.

Rogers, T. *Leicester's Ghost*, ed. F. B. Williams, Chicago, 1972.

Rye, W. B. *England as Seen by Foreigners*, London, 1865.

Sadler, R. *Masquarade du Ciel Presented to the Great Queene of the Little World. A Celestiall Map representing the True Site and Motions of the Heavenly Bodies, through the yeeres 1639, 1640, &c.*, London, 1640.

Scriba, C. J. 'The autobiography of John Wallis, F.R.S.', *Notes and Records of The Royal Society*, xxv (1970), 17–46.

Serlio, S. *The First Booke of Architecture*, trans. R. Peake, London, 1611.

Sherburne, E. *The Sphere of Marcus Manilius made an English Poem*, London, 1675.

Simpson, N. *Arithmeticae Compendium*, London, 1623.

Smith, T. *The Life and Death of Mr William Moore, Late Fellow of Caius Colledge, and Keeper of the University Library*, Cambridge, 1660.

Vitae quorundam eruditissimorum et illustrium virorum, London, 1707.

Stafford, R. *A Geographicall and Anthologicall Description of all the Empires and Kingdomes, both of Continent and Islands in the Terrestriall Globe, etc.*, London, 1608.

Statutes of the Colleges of Oxford, 4 vols., London, 1853.

Tapp, J. *The Pathway to Knowledge*, London, 1613.

Turnbull, C. *A Perfect and Very Easie Treatise of the Use of the Celestiall Globe*, London, 1585.

Ultima linea Savilii, Oxford, 1622.

Ussher, J. *The Whole Works of the Most Rev. James Ussher*, ed. C. R. Elrington, 17 vols., Dublin, 1847–64.

Venn, J. (ed.) *Annals of Gonville and Caius College*, Camb. Antiq. Soc. Octavo Publ., vol. 40, Cambridge, 1904.

Grace Book Δ, Cambridge, 1910.

The Verney Papers, ed. J. Bruce, Camden Soc., 1st Ser., vol. 56, London, 1853.

Vernon, G. *Life of the Learned and Reverend Dr. Peter Heylin*, London, 1682.

Vives, J. L. *On Education*, ed. F. Watson, Totowa, New Jersey, repr. 1971.

Voss, G. J. G. J. *Vossii et clarorum virorum ad eum epistolae*, London, 1690.

Walton, I. *The Lives of John Donne, Sir Henry Wotton, Richard Hooker, George Herbert and Robert Sanderson*, London, repr. 1973.

Ward, G. R. M. (trans.) *The Foundation Statutes of Bishop Fox for Corpus Christi College in the University of Oxford A.D. 1517*, London, 1843.

Oxford University Statutes, 2 vols., London, 1845.

The Statutes of Magdalen College Oxford, Oxford, 1840.

Ward, J. *The Lives of the Professors of Gresham College*, London, 1740.

Ward, S. *Opera nonnulla*, ed. Seth Ward, London, 1658.

Warwick, Sir P. *Memoires of the Reigne of King Charles I*, 2nd edn, London, 1702.

Waterland, D. *Advice to a Young Student*, London, 1730.

Webster, J. *Metallographia: Or An History of Metals, Wherein is Declared the Signs of Ores and Minerals both before and after Digging*, London, 1671.

Whately, W. *Prototypes or the Primarie Precedent*, London, 1640.

Wheeler, H. A. (ed.) *A Short Catalogue of Books Printed in England, and British Books Printed Abroad before 1641 in the Library of Wadham College Oxford*, London, 1929.

Wilson, A. *The Inconstant Lady*, Oxford, 1814.

Wing, V. *Astronomia Britannica*, London, 1669.

Wingate, E. *Arithmetique Made Easie, the Second Book*, London, 1652.
  The Use of the Rule of Proportion in Arithmetick and Geometry, London, 1658.
Winterton, R. (trans.) *The Considerations of Drexelius*, Cambridge, 1636.
  Hippocratis magni aphorismi soluta et metrici, Cambridge, 1633.
Wood, Anthony à *Athenae Oxonienses*, ed. P. Bliss, 4 vols., Oxford, 1813–20.
  The History and Antiquities of the University of Oxford, ed. J. Gutch, 2 vols. in 3, Oxford, 1796.
  Survey of the Antiquities of the City of Oxford, ed. A. Clark, 3 vols., Oxford, 1889–99.
Worsop, E. *A Discoverie of Sundrie Errours and Faults Daily Committed by Landemeaters Ignorant of Arithmetike and Geometrie*, London, 1582.
Wotton, H. *The Life and Letters of Sir Henry Wotton*, ed. L. P. Smith, 2 vols., Oxford, 1907.
Wren, C. (ed.) *Parentalia, or Memoirs of the Family of the Wrens*, London, 1750.
Wright, E. *Certaine Errors in Navigation Detected and Corrected by Edw: Wright*, London, 1599.
  A Description of the Admirable Table of Logarithms, London, 1616.

C. SECONDARY SOURCES

Abromitis, L. I. 'William Gilbert as Scientist: The Portrait of a Renaissance Amateur', Brown Univ. Ph.D. thesis, 1977.
Adamson, I. 'The administration of Gresham College and its fluctuating fortunes as a scientific institution in the seventeenth century', *History of Education*, IX (1980), 13–25.
  'The Foundation and Early History of Gresham College, London, 1596–1704', Cambridge Univ. Ph.D. thesis, 1975.
Applebaum, W. 'Donne's meeting with Kepler: a previously unknown episode', *Philological Quarterly*, L (1971), 132–4.
  'Kepler in England: The Reception of Keplerian Astronomy in England, 1599–1687', Univ. of New York at Buffalo, Ph.D. thesis, 1969.
Appleby, J. H. 'Arthur Dee and Johannes Banfi Hunyades: further information on their alchemical and professional activities', *Ambix*, XXIV (1977), 96–109.
Aston, M. 'The fiery trigon conjunction: an Elizabethan astrological prediction', *Isis*, LXI (1970), 159–87.
Bachrach, A. G. H. *Sir Constantine Huygens and Britain 1596–1687: A Pattern of Cultural Exchange*, Leiden, 1962.
Bailey, J. E. 'Jeremiah Horrox and William Crabtree, observers of the Transit of Venus, 24 Nov. 1639', *The Palatine Note-Book*, II (1882), 253–66.
Bamborough, J. B. 'Robert Burton's Astrological Notebook', *Rev. Eng. Stud.*, New Ser., XXXII (1981), 267–85.
Barnett, P. R. *Theodore Haak F.R.S., 1605–1690*, The Hague, 1962.
Bauckham, R. 'The Career and Thought of Dr William Fulke 1537–89', Cambridge Univ. Ph.D. thesis, 1973.
  'Science and religion in the writings of Dr William Fulke', *Brit. Journ. Hist. Science*, VIII (1975), 17–31.
Ben-David, J. 'Scientific growth: a sociological view', *Minerva*, II (1963–4), 455–76.
  The Scientist's Role in Society: A Comparative Study, New Jersey, 1971.

Bill, G. 'Lambeth Palace Library', *The Library*, 5th Ser., XXI (1966), 192–206.

Birley, R. 'The history of Eton College Library', *The Library*, 5th Ser., XI (1956), 231–61.

'Robert Boyle's headmaster at Eton', *Notes and Records of The Royal Society*, XIII (1958), 104–14.

Black, R. C. *The Younger John Winthrop*, New York, 1966.

Boas, M. *The Scientific Renaissance 1450–1630*, London, 1962.

Bowden, M. A. 'The Scientific Revolution in Astrology: The English Reformers 1558–1686', Yale Univ. Ph.D. thesis, 1974.

Brown, H. *Scientific Organizations in Seventeenth-Century France (1620–1680)*, New York, 1934, reissue 1967.

Bruce, J. 'Description of a pocket-dial made in 1593 for Robert Devereaux, Earl of Essex', *Archaeologia*, XL (1866), 343–60.

Cajori, F. *William Oughtred, A Great Seventeenth-Century Teacher of Mathematics*, Chicago and London, 1916.

Calder, I. R. F. 'John Dee Studied as an English Neo-Platonist', London Univ. Ph.D. thesis, 1952.

Capp, B. *Astrology and the Popular Press*, London and Boston, 1979.

Caudill, R. L-W. 'Some Literary Evidence of the Development of English Virtuoso Interests in the Seventeenth Century, With Particular Reference to the Literature of Travel', Oxford Univ. D.Phil. thesis, 1975.

Cawley, R. R. *Henry Peacham, His Contribution to English Poetry*, University Park, Pa., 1971.

Chambers, D. D. C. 'A catalogue of the library of Bishop Lancelot Andrewes 1555–1626', *Trans. Camb. Bibl. Soc.*, V (1969–71), 99–121.

Chance, B. 'Charles Scarburgh, an English educator and physician to three kings: a medical retrospective into the times of the Stuarts', *Bull. Hist. Med.*, XII (1942), 274–303.

Clifford, A. *Collectanea Cliffordiana*, Paris, 1817.

Colie, R. 'Cornelis Drebbel and Salomon de Caus: two Jacobean models for Solomon's house', *Huntington Library Quarterly*, XVIII (1954–5), 245–60.

'Dean Wren's marginalia and early science at Oxford', *Bodl. Lib. Rec.*, VI (1960), 541–51.

Colvin, H. M. 'The south front of Wilton House', *Archaeological Journal*, CXI (1954), 181–90.

Conway Davies, J. 'Elizabethan plans and proposals for education', *Durham Research Review*, II (1954), 1–8.

Cooper, C. H. *Annals of Cambridge*, 5 vols., Cambridge, 1842–53.

'An early autograph of Sir Henry Spelman', *Camb. Antiq. Soc. Communications*, II (1860–4), 101–12.

and Cooper, T. *Athenae Cantabrigienses*, 3 vols., Cambridge, 1858–1913.

Costello, W. T. *The Scholastic Curriculum at Early Seventeenth-Century Cambridge*, Cambridge, Mass., 1958.

Costil, P. *André Dudith, Humaniste Hongrois*, Paris, 1935.

Cox-Johnson, A. 'Lambeth Palace Library, 1610–1669', *Trans. Camb. Bibl. Soc.*, II (1955), 105–26.

Crino, A. M. 'Il Duca di Northumbria in Toscana', *English Miscellany*, XXVIII–XXIX (1978–80), 19–59.

Curtis, M. *Oxford and Cambridge in Transition, 1558–1642*, Oxford, 1959.

Daniel, C. H. and Barker, W. R. *Worcester College*, London, 1900.

Davies, G. *Autobiography of Thomas Raymond and Memoirs of the Family of Guise*, Camden Soc., 3rd Ser., vol. 28, London, 1917.

Davis, B. M. 'The Astronomical Work of Jeremiah Horrox', Univ. of London M.A. thesis, 1967.

Debus, A. G. *The English Paracelsians*, London, 1965.

  'Harvey and Fludd: the irrational factor in the rational science of the seventeenth century', *Journ. Hist. Biology*, III (1970), 81–105.

  Science and Education in the Seventeenth Century: The Webster–Ward Debate, London, 1970.

The Dictionary of Scientific Biography, 14 vols., New York, 1970–6.

Dijksterhuis, E. J. *The Mechanization of the World Picture*, trans. C. Dikshoorn, Oxford, 1961.

Dobbs, B. J. 'Studies in the natural philosophy of Sir Kenelm Digby, part II: Digby and alchemy', *Ambix*, XX (1973), 143–63.

Donahue, W. H. 'The Dissolution of the Celestial Spheres 1595–1650', Cambridge Univ. Ph.D. thesis, 1972.

  'A hitherto unreported pre-Keplerian oval orbit', *Journ. Hist. Astronomy*, IV (1973), 192–4.

Donnelly, J. P. 'Italian influences on the development of Calvinist scholasticism', *Sixteenth Century Journal*, VII (1976), 81–101.

Drake, S. 'Early science and the printed book: the spread of science beyond the universities', *Renaissance and Reformation*, VI (1970), 43–52.

Dunn, W. *Sir Thomas Browne: A Study in Religious Philosophy*, Minneapolis, 1950.

Edwards, G. M. *Sidney Sussex College*, London, 1899.

Elkana, Y. 'A programmatic attempt at an anthropology of knowledge', *Sciences and Cultures: Anthropological and Historical Studies of the Sciences*, ed. E. Mendelsohn and Y. Elkana, Dordrecht, Holland, 1981, pp. 1–76.

Elson, J. *John Hales of Eton*, New York, 1948.

Emden, A. B. *A Biographical Register of the University of Oxford A.D. 1501 to 1540*, Oxford, 1974.

  An Oxford Hall in Medieval Times, being the Early History of St Edmund Hall, Oxford, 1927.

Evans, R. J. W. *The Making of the Habsburg Monarchy 1550–1700*, Oxford, 1979.

  Rudolf II and his World, Oxford, 1973.

Feingold, M. *An Elizabethan Intellectual: John Rainolds, the Man and his Books*, Oxf. Bibl. Soc., occasional publications, forthcoming.

  'Jordan revisited: patterns of charitable giving in sixteenth- and seventeenth-century England', *History of Education* VIII (1979), 257–73.

  'The occult tradition in the English universities of the Renaissance: a reassessment', *Occult and Scientific Mentalities in the Renaissance*, ed. B. Vickers, Cambridge, in press.

  and Gouk, P. 'An early critique of Bacon's *Sylva Sylvarum*: Edmund Chilmead's treatise on sound', *Annals of Science*, XL (1983), 139–57.

Fletcher, H. F. *The Intellectual Development of John Milton*, 2 vols., Urbana, 1956–61.

Forster, J. *Sir John Eliot: A Biography*, 2 vols., London, 1864.

Foster, J. *Alumni Oxonienses, 1500–1714*, 4 vols., Oxford, 1891.

Foster, M. 'Thomas Allen (1540–1632), Gloucester Hall and the survival of Catholicism in Post-Reformation Oxford', *Oxoniensia*, XLVI (1981), 99–128.

Frank, R. G., Jr *Harvey and the Oxford Physiologists. A Study of Scientific Ideas*, Berkeley and Los Angeles, 1980.

'Science, medicine and the universities of early modern England: background and sources', *History of Science*, XI (1973), 194–216, 239–69.

French, P. J. *John Dee: The World of an Elizabethan Magus*, London, 1972.

Fuggles, J. F. 'A History of the Library of S. John's College, Oxford from the Foundation of the College to 1660', Oxford Univ. B.Litt. thesis, 1975.

Gabb, G. H. 'The astrological astrolabe of Queen Elizabeth', *Archaeologia*, LXXXVI (1936), 101–3.

Gabrieli, V. *Sir Kenelm Digby: un Inglese Italianto Nell'eta Della Controriforma*, Rome, 1957.

Garrod, H. W. *The Study of Good Letters*, ed. J. Jones, Oxford, 1963.

Gelbart, N. R. 'The intellectual development of Walter Charleton', *Ambix*, XVIII (1971), 149–68.

Gibson, S. 'Brian Twyne', *Oxoniensia*, v (1940), 94–114.

Gilbert, E. W. *British Pioneers in Geography*, Newton Abbot, 1972.

Gomori, G. 'New information of Janos Banfihunyadi's life', *Ambix*, XXIV (1977), 170–3.

Gough, J. W. *The Superlative Prodigall, a Life of Thomas Bushell*, Bristol, 1932.

Greaves, R. L. *The Puritan Revolution and Educational Thought: Background for Reform*, New Jersey, 1969.

Green, V. H. *The Commonwealth of Lincoln College 1427–1977*, Oxford, 1979.

Grendler, M. 'A Greek collection in Padua: the library of Gian Vincenzo Pinelli (1535–1601)', *Renaissance Quarterly*, XXXIII (1980), 386–416.

Gunther, R. T. 'The astrolabe of Queen Elizabeth', *Archaeologia*, LXXXVI (1936), 65–7.

Early Science in Oxford, 14 vols., Oxford, 1923–45.

'The great astrolabe and other scientific instruments of Humphrey Cole', *Archaeologia*, LXXVI (1926/27), 273–317.

Gysi, L. *Platonism and Cartesianism in the Philosophy of Ralph Cudworth*, Bern, 1962.

Hall, A. R. *The Scientific Revolution*, London, 1954.

and Hall, M. B. *Unpublished Scientific Papers of Isaac Newton*, Cambridge, 1962.

Hallowes, D. M. 'Henry Briggs, mathematician', *Transactions of the Halifax Antiquarian Society* (1962), 79–92.

Hardy, E. G. *Jesus College*, London, 1899.

Harris, L. E. *The Two Netherlanders, Humphrey Bradley and Cornelis Drebbel*, Cambridge, 1961.

Hepburn, R. W. 'George Hakewill: the virility of nature', *Journ. Hist. Ideas*, XVI (1955), 135–50.

Hesse, M. 'Hermeticism and historiography: an apology for the internal history of science', *Minnesota Studies in the Philosophy of Science*, ed. R. H. Stuewer, V (1970), 134–62.

H. G. S. 'Some correspondence of Brian Twyne', *Bodl. Lib. Rec.*, v (1926–8), 213–18, 240–6, 269–72.

Highfield, J. R. L. 'An autograph manuscript commonplace book of Sir Henry Savile', *Bodl. Lib. Rec.*, VII (1963), 73–83.

Hill, C. *Intellectual Origins of the English Revolution*, Oxford, 1965.
Milton and the English Revolution, London, 1977.

Houghton, W. E. 'The English virtuoso in the seventeenth century', *Journ. Hist. Ideas*, III (1942), 51–73, 190–219.

Huffman, W. H. and Seelinger, R. A. 'Robert Fludd's "Declaratio Brevis" to James I', *Ambix*, xxv (1978), 69–92.

Hunter, M. *John Aubrey and the Realm of Learning*, London, 1975.
Science and Society in Restoration England, Cambridge, 1981.

Huntley, F. L. *Sir Thomas Browne: A Biographical and Critical Study*, Ann Arbor, 1968.

Hutton, S. 'Thomas Jackson, Oxford Platonist, and William Twisse, Aristotelian', *Journ. Hist. Ideas*, xxxix (1978), 635–52.

Johnson, F. R. *Astronomical Thought in Renaissance England*, Baltimore, 1937.
'Gresham College: precursor of the Royal Society', *Journ. Hist. Ideas*, I (1940), 413–38.
'Thomas Hood's inaugural address as mathematical lecturer of the City of London (1588)', *Journ. Hist. Ideas*, III (1942), 94–106.

Jones, R. F. *Ancients and Moderns. A Study of the Rise of the Scientific Movement in Seventeenth-Century England*, 2nd edn, Berkeley and Los Angeles, 1965.

Jordan-Smith, P. *Burton's Anatomy of Melancholy and Burtoniana*, Oxford, 1959.

Josten, C. H. 'Robert Fludd's "Philosophical Key" and his alchemical experiment on wheat', *Ambix*, xi (1963), 1–23.

Kargon, R. H. *Atomism in England from Hariot to Newton*, Oxford, 1966.

Kearney, H. *Scholars and Gentlemen: Universities and Society in pre-Industrial Britain 1500–1700*, Ithaca, 1970.

Kelly, S. *The De Mundo of William Gilbert*, Amsterdam, 1965.

Kelly, T. *A History of Adult Education in Great Britain*, Liverpool, 1970.

Kemke, J. *Patricius Junius*, Leipzig, 1898.

King, H. C. and Millburn, J. R. *Geared to the Stars: The Evolution of Planetariums, Orreries, and Astronomical Clocks*, Toronto, 1978.

Kosman, L. A. 'The Aristotelian Backgrounds of Bacon's *Novum Organum*', Harvard Univ. Ph.D. thesis, 1964.

Larminie, V. M. 'The Life Style and Attitudes of the Seventeenth Century Gentleman, with special reference to the Newdigates of Arbury Hall, Warwickshire', Univ. of Birmingham Ph.D. thesis, 1980.

Larsen, R. E. 'The Aristotelianism of Bacon's *Novum Organum*', *Journ. Hist. Ideas*, XXIII (1962), 435–50.

Law, E. *The New Guide to the Royal Palace of Hampton Court*, London, 1882.

Lee, A. G. *The Son of Leicester: The Story of Sir Robert Dudley, Titular Earl of Warwick, Earl of Leicester, and Duke of Northumberland*, London, 1964.

Letts, M. 'Samuel Purchas, his friends and books', *Contemporary Review*, CXXXII (1932), 460–7.

Levack, B. P. *The Civil Lawyers in England, 1603–1641: a Political Study*, Oxford, 1973.

Levy. F. J. 'The making of Camden's *Britannia*', *Bibl. d'Hum. Ren.*, XXVI (1964), 70–97.

'William Camden as a Historian', Harvard Univ. Ph.D. thesis, 1959.

Looney, J. 'Undergraduate education at early Stuart Cambridge', *History of Education*, X (1981), 9–19.

Macray, W. D. *Annals of the Bodleian Library Oxford*, 2nd edn, Oxford, 1890.

A Register of the Members of St Mary Magdalen College Oxford, 8 vols., London, 1894–1915.

Madan, F. (ed.) 'Robert Burton and the Anatomy of Melancholy', *Oxf. Bibl. Soc.*, I (1925), 163–246.

Magyary-Kossa, J. von *Ungarische Medizinishce Erinnerungen*, Budapest, 1935.

Malcolm, N. 'Hobbes, Sandys, and the Virginia Company', *Hist. Journ.*, XXIV (1981), 297–321.

Mallet, C. E. *A History of the University of Oxford*, 3 vols., repr. New York, 1968.

Marsden, J. H. *College Life in the Time of James the First as Illustrated by an Unpublished Diary of Sir Symonds D'Ewes*, London, 1851.

McColley, G. 'The theory of a plurality of worlds as a factor in Milton's attitude toward the Copernican hypothesis', *Modern Language Notes*, XLVII (1932), 319–25.

McConica, J. 'Humanism and Aristotle in Tudor Oxford', *Eng. Hist. Rev.*, XCIV (1979), 291–317.

Merton, R. K. *Science, Technology & Society in Seventeenth-Century England*, 2nd edn, New York, 1970.

Micheletti, M. *Il Pensiero Religioso di John Smith Platonico di Cambridge*, Padua, 1976.

Miller, E. H. *The Professional Writer in Elizabethan England*, Cambridge, Mass., 1959.

Mintz, S. I. *The Hunting of Leviathan*, Cambridge, 1962.

Mollen, G. van der *Alberico Gentili and the Development of International Law*, Amsterdam, 1938.

Morgan, V. 'Approaches to the history of the English universities in the sixteenth and seventeenth centuries', *Bildung, Politik und Gesellschaft*, ed. G. Klingenstein, H. Lutz and G. Stourzh, Vienna, 1978.

Morison, S. E. *The Founding of Harvard College*, Cambridge, Mass., 1935.

Harvard College in the Seventeenth Century, 2 vols., Cambridge, Mass., 1936.

Mullinger, J. B. 'The relations of Francis Bacon, Lord Verulam, with the University of Cambridge', *Publ. Camb. Antiq. Soc.*, IX (1896–8), 227–36.

The University of Cambridge, 3 vols., Cambridge, 1873–1911.

Munby, A. N. L. *The History and Bibliography of Science in England: The First Phase, 1833–1845*, Los Angeles, 1968.

Munk, W. *The Roll of the Royal College of Physicians of London, comprising Biographical Sketches of all the Eminent Physicians*, 3 vols., 2nd edn, London, 1878.

Murdoch, J. E. and Sylla, E. D. (eds.) *The Cultural Context of Medieval Learning*, Dordrecht, Holland, 1975.

Nicolson, M. H. *Pepys' Diary and the New Science*, Charlottesville, 1965.

Norden, L. Van 'Peiresc and the English scholars', *Huntington Library Quarterly*, XII (1948–9), 369–89.

North, J. D. 'Nicholaus Kratzer – the King's astronomer', *Studia Copernicana*, XVI (1978), 205–34.

Orme, W. *Memoirs of the Life, Writings and Religious Connexions of John Owen, D.D.*, London, 1820.

Osborn, J. M. *Young Philip Sidney 1572–1577*, New Haven, 1972.

Ovenell, R. F. 'Brian Twyne's library', *Oxf. Bibl. Soc.*, New Ser., IV (1952), 3–42.

Pagel, W. *William Harvey's Biological Ideas: Selected Aspects and Historical Background*, Basel/New York, 1967.

Parker, W. R. *Milton, A Biography*, 2 vols., Oxford, 1968.

Parks, M. B. and Watson, A. C. (eds.) *Medieval Scribes, Manuscripts and Libraries: Essays presented to N. R. Ker*, London, 1978.

Parsons, E. J. S. and Morris, W. F. 'Edward Wright and his work', *Imago Mundi*, III (1939), 61–71.

Pasmore, S. 'Thomas Henshaw, F.R.S. (1618–1700)', *Notes and Records of The Royal Society*, XXXVI (1982), 177–88.

Passmore, J. A. *Ralph Cudworth, An Interpretation*, Cambridge, 1951.

Pattenden, P. 'Robert Hegge, an Oxford antiquary', *Oxoniensia*, XLV (1980), 284–99.

  Sundials at an Oxford College, Oxford, 1979.

Pattison, M. *Isaac Casaubon 1559–1614*, 2nd edn, London, 1892.

Payne, L. M. 'Sir Charles Scarburgh's Harveian Oration, 1662', *Journ. Hist. Medicine and Allied Sciences*, XII (1957), 158–64.

Pepper, J. V. 'A letter from Nathaniel Torporley to Thomas Harriot', *Brit. Journ. Hist. Science*, III (1967), 285–90.

Petersson, R. T. *Sir Kenelm Digby, The Ornament of England 1603–1655*, London, 1956.

Pitman, M. C. 'Studies in the Work of Henry Peacham', London Univ. Ph.D. thesis, 1933.

Porter, H. C. *Reformation and Reaction in Tudor Cambridge*, Cambridge, 1958.

Quinn, D. B. and Cheshire, N. M. *The New Found Land of Stephen Parmenius*, Toronto, 1972.

Rashdall, H. *The Universities of Europe in the Middle Ages*, ed. F. M. Powicke and A. Emden, 3 vols., new edn, Oxford, 1936.

  and Rait, R. S. *New College*, London, 1901.

Rattansi, P. M. 'Alchemy and Natural Magic in Raleigh's "History of the World"', *Ambix*, XIII (1966), 122–38.

Raven, C. E. *John Ray, Naturalist*, 2nd edn, Cambridge, 1950.

Read, C. *Mr Secretary Walsingham and the Policy of Queen Elizabeth*, 3 vols., Oxford, 1925.

Reif, P. 'The textbook tradition in natural philosophy, 1600–1650', *Journ. Hist. Ideas*, XXX (1969), 17–32.

Rigaud, S. P. (ed.) *Supplement to Dr Bradley's Miscellaneous Works with an Account of Harriot's Astronomical Papers*, Oxford, 1833.

Righini Bonelli, M. L. and Shea, W. R. (eds.) *Reason, Experiment and Mysticism in the Scientific Revolution*, London, 1975.

Roller, D. H. D. *The De Magnete of William Gilbert*, Amsterdam, 1959.

Rose, P. 'Erasmians and mathematicians at Cambridge in the early sixteenth century', *Sixteenth Century Journal*, VIII (supplement 1977), 47–59.

The *Italian Renaissance of Mathematics, Studies on Humanists and Mathematicians from Petrarch to Galileo*, Geneva, 1975.

Rouse Ball, W. W. *A History of the Study of Mathematics at Cambridge*, Cambridge, 1889.

Rowse, A. L. *Ralegh and the Throckmortons*, London, 1962.

Saveson, J. E. 'Descartes' influence on John Smith, Cambridge Platonist', *Journ. Hist. Ideas*, XX (1959), 258–63.

'The library of John Smith, the Cambridge Platonist', *Notes & Queries*, CCIII (1958), 215–16.

'Some Aspects of the Thought and Style of John Smith, the Cambridge Platonist', Cambridge Univ. Ph.D. thesis, 1955.

Sayle, C. 'The library of Thomas Lorkyn', *Annals of Medical History*, III (1921), 310–23.

Schmitt, C. B. *John Case*, forthcoming.

'Towards a reassessment of Renaissance Aristotelianism', *History of Science*, XI (1973), 159–93.

Schneider, H. *Joachim Morsius und sein kreis*, Lübeck, 1929.

Searle, W. G. *The History of the Queens' College of St Margaret and St Bernard in the University of Cambridge 1446–1662*, 2 vols., Camb. Antiq. Soc. Publ., vols. 9, 13, Cambridge, 1867, 1871.

Seaver, P. S. *The Puritan Lectureships*, Stanford, 1970.

Shapiro, B. J. *John Wilkins 1614–1672. An Intellectual Biography*, Berkeley and Los Angeles, 1969.

and Frank, R. G. *English Scientific Virtuosi in the 16th and 17th Centuries*, William Andrew Clark Memorial Library Seminar, Los Angeles, 1979.

Sharp, L. 'Walter Charleton's early life, 1620–1659, and relationship to natural philosophy in mid-seventeenth century England', *Annals of Science*, XXX (1973), 311–40.

Shirley, J. W. (ed.) *Thomas Harriot Renaissance Scientist*, Oxford, 1974.

Simon, J. *Education and Society in Tudor England*, Cambridge, 1966.

Slusser, M. 'Abraham Woodhead (1607–78): some research notes, chiefly about his writings', *Recusant History*, XV (1981), 406–22.

Smith, D. B. 'Jean de Villiers Hotman', *Scottish Historical Review*, XIV (1916–17), 147–66.

Smyth, W. H. 'Description of an astrological clock, belonging to the Society of Antiquaries of London', *Archaeologia*, XXXIII (1849), 8–35.

Sotheby Sale Catalogue, 22 June 1976.

Stern, V. F. *Gabriel Harvey, His Life, Marginalia and Library*, Oxford, 1979.

Sterry, W. *The Eton College Register 1551–1698*, Eton, 1943.

Stevens, H. *Thomas Hariot, The Mathematician, the Philosopher and the Scholar*, London, 1900.

Stone, L. *The Crisis of the Aristocracy 1558–1641*, Oxford, 1965.

Family and Fortune. Studies in Aristocratic Finance in the Sixteenth and Seventeenth Centuries, Oxford, 1973.

(ed.) *The University in Society*, 2 vols., Princeton, 1975.

Stubbs, M. 'John Beale, philosophical gardener of Herefordshire, part I. Prelude to the Royal Society (1608–1663)', *Annals of Science*, XXXIX (1982), 463–89.

Taylor, E. G. R. 'Hariot's instructions for Ralegh's voyage to Guiana, 1595', *Journal of the Institute of Navigation*, V (1952), 345–50.

Late Tudor and Early Stuart Geography 1583–1650, London, 1934.

The Mathematical Practitioners of Tudor and Stuart England, Cambridge, 1954.

Tudor Geography, London, 1930.

and Sadler, D. H. 'The doctrine of nauticall triangles compendious', *Journal of the Institute of Navigation*, VI (1953), 131–47.

Taylor, F. S. and Josten, C. H. 'Johannes Banfi Hunyades 1576–1650', *Ambix*, V (1953), 44–52.

Thomas, K. V. *Religion and the Decline of Magic*, London, 1971.

Tierrie, G. *Cornelis Drebbel*, Amsterdam, 1932.

Trentman, J. A. 'The authorship of "Directions for a Student in the Universities"', *Trans. Camb. Bibl. Soc.*, VII (1978), 170–83.

Trevelyan, G. 'Undergraduate life under the Protectorate', *The Cambridge Review*, LXIV (1943), 328–30.

Trevor-Roper, H. R. *Archbishop Laud*, 2nd edn, London, 1965.

Turnbull, G. H. *Hartlib, Dury and Comenius, Gleanings from the Hartlib Papers*, London, 1947.

Turner, A. J. 'Mathematical instruments and the education of gentlemen', *Annals of Science*, XXX (1973), 51–88.

Tyacke, N. 'Arminianism and English culture', *England and the Netherlands*, ed. A. C. Duck and C. A. Tamse, The Hague, 1981, vol. 7, pp. 94–117.

'Science and religion at Oxford before the Civil War', *Puritans and Revolutionaries, Essays in Seventeenth-Century History Presented to Christopher Hill*, ed. D. Pennington and K. Thomas, Oxford, 1979, pp. 73–93.

Venn, J. 'An astrological fellow', *The Caian*, VI (1897), 28–36.

Biographical History of Gonville and Caius College, 1349–1897, 4 vols., Cambridge, 1897–1912.

'Dr Gostlin', *The Caian*, III (1894), 86–92.

Early Collegiate Life, Cambridge, 1913.

and Venn, J. A. *Alumni Cantabrigienses, Part I. From the Earliest Times to 1751*, 4 vols., Cambridge, 1922–7.

Verney, F. P. *Memoirs of the Verney Family during the Civil War*, 2 vols., London, 1892.

Vines, S. H. and Druce, G. C. *An Account of the Morisonian Herbarium*, Oxford, 1914.

Wallace, M. W. *The Life of Sir Philip Sidney*, Cambridge, 1915.

Wallace, W. A. *Galileo's Early Notebooks: The Physical Questions*, Notre Dame, 1977.

Prelude to Galileo: Essays on Medieval and Sixteenth-Century Sources of Galileo's Thought, Dordrecht–Boston, 1981.

Wallis, H. M. 'The first English globe: a recent discovery', *Geographical Journal*, CXVII (1951), 275–90.

Ward, B. M. *The Seventeenth Earl of Oxford 1550–1604*, London, 1928, repr. 1979.

Waters, D. W. *The Art of Navigation in England in Elizabethan and Early Stuart Times*, 2nd edn, Greenwich, 1978.

Watson, F. *The Beginning of the Teaching of Modern Subjects in England*, London, 1909.

Webb, H. J. 'The mathematical and military works of Thomas Digges, with an account of his life', *Modern Language Quarterly*, VI (1945), 389–400.

Weber, K. *Lucius Cary, Second Viscount Falkland*, New York, 1940.

Webster, C. 'The curriculum of the grammar schools and universities, 1500–1660: a critical review of the literature', *History of Education*, IV (1975), 51–68.

The Great Instauration, London, 1975.

(ed.) *The Intellectual Revolution of the Seventeenth Century*, London, 1974.

Welsby, P. A. *George Abbot, The Unwanted Archbishop 1562–1633*, London, 1962.

Westfall, R. S. *The Construction of Modern Science: Mechanisms and Mechanics*, Cambridge, 1977.

Westman, R. S. 'The astronomer's role in the sixteenth century: a preliminary study', *History of Science*, XVIII (1980), 105–47.

'The Melanchton circle, Rheticus, and the Wittenberg interpretation of the Copernican theory', *Isis*, LXVI (1975), 165–93.

and McGuire, J. E. *Hermeticism and the Scientific Revolution*, William Andrew Clark Memorial Library Seminar, Los Angeles, 1977.

Whatton, A. B. *Horrocks' Transit of Venus across the Sun, with a Memoir of his Life and Labours*, London, 1859.

Wightman, W. P. D. *Science and the Renaissance*, 2 vols., Amsterdam, 1962.

Williamson, G. C. *George, Third Earl of Cumberland (1558–1605) His Life and his Voyages*, Cambridge, 1920.

Wilson, E. C. *Prince Henry and English Literature*, Ithaca, 1946.

Wilson, H. A. *Magdalen College*, London, 1899.

Wood, E. J. *Curiosities of Clocks and Watches from the Earliest Times*, London, 1886.

Wright, L. B. *Middle-Class Culture in Elizabethan England*, Chapel Hill, 1935.

Yates, F. A. *Giordano Bruno and the Hermetic Tradition*, London, 1964.

'Giordano Bruno's conflict with Oxford', *Journ. Warburg & Courtauld, Insts.*, II (1938–9), 227–42.

Shakespeare's Last Plays: A New Approach, London, 1975.

Theatre of the World, London, 1969.

Index

241

Pitiscus, Bartholomaeus, 100, 173
Plat, Sir Hugh, 211
Plato, Platonism, 12n, 13, 58–9, 114–16
Plotinus, 58
Pocock, Edward, 83
Pollard, Arthur, 105
Pope, Sir Thomas, 37
Pope, Thomas, 116–17
Pope, Walter, 88–9
della Porta, Giambattista, 58, 117
Potter, Francis, 70, 107, 187
Powell, Griffith, 44, 56
Powell, Thomas, 77
Poynet, John, 196
Praetorius, Johannes, 48, 58, 72, 127, 132
Preston, John, 61
Prichard, William, 107
Prideaux, John, 57–8, 75, 153, 158n
Proclus, 65n, 116–18, 120, 146
Ptolemy, 47–8, 100–1, 117, 142, 146,
   148, 150–1, 158
Purchas, Samuel, 57, 107

Radcliff, Thomas, 65n
Rainolds, John, 58–9
Ralegh, Sir Walter, 32, 72, 104, 106,
   136–7, 186, 196, 207
Ramsay, David, 199, 203, 208
Ramsey, John, 100
Ramus, Petrus, 14, 47–8, 50, 58, 66, 73,
   94n, 99, 116–18, 120
Randall, Thomas, 54
Rant, John, 52
Rawley, William, 52, 60
Rawlinson, Richard, 98
Ray, John, 81, 90
Recorde, Robert, 116, 117, 118, 168, 178,
   215
Reeves, Richard, 188
Regiomontanus, Johannes, 47–8, 117–19,
   147, 173
Regius, Henricus, 96n
Reif, P., 13
Reinhold, Erasmus, 47–8, 71, 118, 154,
   160
Restell, John, 49
Reuchlin, Johann, 58
rhetoric, 5, 16–17, 24–7, 29, 38, 46, 49,
   94
Ridley, Mark, 10, 51, 78, 110, 113, 118,
   187, 205
Ripley, George, 137n
Rishton, Edward, 106
Robarts, Richard, Lord Randor, 83
Roe, Sir Thomas, 145, 156n
Roffen, Nicholas, 26n
Rohault, Jacques, 96n
Rome, English College, 91–3
Rooke, Laurence, 184
Rous, John, 135, 149, 152
Rowley, William, 51n
Rowns, Nathaniel, 85
Royal Society, 9, 18, 87, 89, 114, 184,
   186, 188
Rudolph II (Emperor), 129, 198
Russell, Sir William, 1st Baron Russell of
   Thornhaugh, 197
Ryff, Walther Hermann, 97, 116

Sacrobosco, 67, 191, 201
Sadler, John, 88, 114

Sambuc, Johannes, 127
Sancroft, William, 64
Savile, Sir Henry, 4, 28, 31–2, 38, 47–8,
   55, 69, 72, 77, 80, 101, 103, 107, 109,
   124–31, 133–4, 137, 143–4, 147n,
   152, 153n, 156, 160n, 191
Savile, Samuel, 80
Savile, Thomas, 72, 83, 126, 128n, 130–3
Scaliger, Joseph Justus, 72, 130, 133–4,
   142, 145, 154
Scarburgh, Sir Charles, 33n, 67, 82, 88–9,
   115
Scheiner, Christophorus, 64n, 119
Shickard, Wilhelm, 144, 161
Schmitt, C. B., 14
Schoener, Johann, 60, 77
science, experimental, 15; historiography
   of, 2–3; new, 2, 7, 8, 21, 30, 86–90;
   professionalization of, 17–18, 96, 124;
   theoretical vs. practical, 177–9, 186–8,
   194–5, 211, 216; 'unenlightened', 7
Scotus, Marianus, 153
   Secol, Richard, 116
Sedley, Sir William, 32
Selden, John, 70, 73, 124, 143n, 146,
   149–50, 154n, 155–7, 187, 208
Sellar, William, 143
Seller, John, 188
Severin, Christian (Longomontanus), 66,
   105, 114, 142, 150
Sextus, Empiricus, 58
Sheldon, Gilbert, 75
Sherburne, Sir Edward, 109, 183
Sidney, Sir Henry, 125n
Sidney, Sir Philip, 82, 125–7, 129, 191,
   193
Sidney, Robert, Viscount Lisle and 1st Earl
   of Leicester, 125–7, 131, 133n, 191
Simpson, Nathaniel, 65
Singleton, Robert, 118
Sixsmith, Thomas, 66–7
Smith, Sir John, 91–2
Smith, John, 53, 88
Smith, Sir Thomas, 26, 39, 196n
Smith, Sir Thomas (mathematician), 138
Smith, Thomas, 142
Snell, Willebrord, 76n, 119, 144
Soame, Robert, 100
Spelman, Sir Henry, 33, 101, 148, 151–2
Spinoza, Benedictus, 52
Sprat, Thomas, 95n
Stadius, Johannes, 71, 101
Stafford, Robert, 58
Stähl, Peter, 183
Standish, Nicholas, 136, 144
Stay, John, 99
Stevin, Simon, 110
Stifelius, Michael, 100
Stone, L., 190
Strode, Thomas, 65
Swale, Richard, 52
Swan, John, 110
Sylvester, Edward, 156n

Tapp, John, 85, 176, 185
Tartaglia, Nicolo, 47, 118
Tatham, Thomas, 117
Taylor, E. G. R., 166, 171–3, 180, 186,
   188, 190
telescope, 66, 73–4, 113, 144, 188, 206
Telesio, Bernardino, 14, 58